www.wadsworth.com

wadsworth.com is the World Wide Web site for Wadsworth and is your direct source to dozens of online resources.

At *wadsworth.com* you can find out about supplements, demonstration software, and student resources. You can also send email to many of our authors and preview new publications and exciting new technologies.

wadsworth.com
Changing the way the world learns®

The Social Worker & Psychotropic Medication:

Toward Effective Collaboration with Mental Health Clients, Families, and Providers

Second Edition

KIA J. BENTLEY
JOSEPH WALSH
Virginia Commonwealth University

BROOKS/COLE
™
THOMSON LEARNING

Australia • Canada • Mexico • Singapore • Spain
United Kingdom • United States

BROOKS/COLE

THOMSON LEARNING ™

Social Work Editor: *Lisa Gebo*
Assistant Editor: *Susan Wilson, JoAnne von Zastow*
Marketing Manager: *Caroline Concilla*
Marketing Assistant: *Jessica McFadden*
Print Buyer: *April Reynolds*
Permissions Editor: *Joohee Lee*

Production Services: *Proof Positive/ Farrowlyne Associates, Inc.*
Cover Designer: *Bill Stanton*
Cover Printer: *Webcom Limited*
Compositor: *Black Dot Group*
Printer: *Webcom Limited*

 This book is printed on acid-free recycled paper.

Wadsworth/Thomson Learning
10 Davis Drive
Belmont, CA 94002-3098
USA

For more information about our products, contact us:
Thomson Learning Academic Resource Center
1-800-423-0563
http://www.wadsworth.com

International Headquarters
Thomson Learning
International Division
290 Harbor Drive, 2nd Floor
Stamford, CT 06902-7477
USA

UK/Europe/Middle East/South Africa
Thomson Learning
Berkshire House
168-173 High Holborn
London WC1V 7AA
United Kingdom

Asia
Thomson Learning
60 Albert Street #15-01
Albert Complex
Singapore 189969

Canada
Nelson/Thomson Learning
1120 Birchmount Road
Toronto, Ontario M1K 5G4
Canada

Library of Congress Cataloging-in-Publication Data
Bentley, Kia J.
   The social worker & psychotropic medication : toward effective collaboration with mental health clients, families, and providers / Kia J. Bentley, Joseph Walsh.—2nd ed.
     p. ; cm.
   Includes bibliographical references and index.
   ISBN 0-534-36542-6
   1. Psychiatric social work—United States. 2. Mental illness—Chemotherapy—United States. 3. Psychopharmacology—United States. I. Title: Social worker and psychotropic medication. II. Walsh, Joseph (Joseph F.) III. Title.
   [DNLM: 1. Psychotropic Drugs. 2. Mental Disorders—drug therapy. 3. Social Work, Psychaiatric.]
   HV689 .B46 2000
   362.2'0425--dc21   00-037875

✛

To Shela Silverman, M.S.W., of *our own Charlottesville,* my former student and supervisee and current colleague and role model extraordinaire: because she "gets" the whole partnership thing, and lives and breathes it every day with the folks at the drop-in center,

And to Pat Higgins, M.S.W., of *Western State Hospital,* Staunton, a deeply valued colleague and kindred spirit in (among other things) our fascination with psychopharmacology: because she loves being in the trenches, taking risks, and doing the right thing by her clients.

—Kia

More prominently, this time—
With love to my wife Margaret and our children,
Brian, Nathan, and Robyn.
—Joe

Contents

PART III KNOWLEDGE AND SKILLS FOR PSYCHOSOCIAL INTERVENTIONS

Preface
to the First Edition

We hope that *The Social Worker & Psychotropic Medication* will be a practical and useful resource for social work students and practitioners as they fulfill their daily roles in medication management in mental health settings. We also hope that the book will contribute to the conceptualization and clarification of the social worker's role in psychopharmacology. We are referring here not only to the expansion of the social worker's roles in this area but also to a shift toward a "partnership" model of practice. Ideally, the book will be recognized as one that begins to fill the acknowledged gap between current practice in mental health and current curriculum materials.

We have three specific goals for our readers. We hope that when they have finished the book, (1) they will be *aware* of the relevant facts and fictions about psychotropic medications, as well as the historical, political, and ethical context of their administration; (2) they will be *articulate* regarding the basics of psychopharmacology and the language of the field; and (3) using a range of techniques and strategies in collaboration with clients, families, and other providers, they will be *active* with regard to their clients' medication-related concerns. In essence, we hope that our book will help social workers be more responsive to the comprehensive needs of their clients.

The area of social work and medication management has piqued our interest because it seems to be a place where many interesting and even controversial issues are played out. Some of these issues include turf battles between psychiatrists and other providers, ethical issues between clients and their families, policy issues—from the state department to the local agencies—

and power issues between the client and the clinician. It is, however, also an area in which social workers have long been involved but have either not had the knowledge or skills necessary to act or been reluctant to use what they did know. We hope that our book will equip social workers with up-to-date knowledge and suggest values and skills they need to better fulfill their professional roles in mental health and related fields of practice.

We believe that the two most salient features of the book are that it is profession-specific to social work and is a practice-focused treatment of the topic. Despite the fact that social workers are the number one mental health professional providers in the country and the fact that treatment with psychotropic medication is at least part of the treatment of choice for most mental illnesses, no book has ever addressed the role of social workers in medication management. This book is intended to be primarily a major text for social work courses in psychopharmacology or a required supplemental text in clinical practice, human behavior, or mental health courses at either the B.S.W. or the M.S.W. level. No academic preparation or work experience is required to understand the book, although a basic course in biology or an introduction to social work practice might help.

The book is divided into four parts. Part One, "Social Work Roles in Medication Management," provides the context and foundation for the rest of the text. The first chapter, the "History and Overview of Social Work Roles in Medication Management," begins with four case scenarios in which the social worker is faced with the question of how to intervene appropriately in client situations that involve medication issues. We introduce our perspective on interdisciplinary collaboration, based on an appreciation of the stress/diathesis model of mental illness, then trace the history of the social work profession with regard to issues of medication use by clients. Then we review the social worker's six roles as they are—or should be—practiced today.

Chapter 2, "Defining Effective Collaboration," presents the three basic themes of partnership, balance, and integration, all of which provide a consistent foundation for the book. With regard to the *partnership* model of practice, we articulate the need to form relationships with clients and their families based on an appreciation of their strengths and viewpoints, on a view of the helping relationship as active and mutual, and on a perception of the social worker's role as an equal partner in problem solving. Another theme that pervades the book is that of *balance*. Social workers often must help their clients reach a balance between the costs and the benefits of using psychotropic medications. This process entails balancing the rights of individuals with those of society, as well as balancing the need to expand the social worker's role while understanding the legitimacy and uniqueness of the physicians' and nurses' roles. The theme of *integration* centers on the social worker's need to better integrate psychopharmacology issues and traditional psychosocial treatments. A combination of approaches is often the most powerful.

Part Two, "A Primer on Psychopharmacology," is the most technical part of the book. The intent here is to provide social workers with relevant information about the science of medication as they practice the six roles outlined in Chapter 1.

Chapter 3, "Basic Principles: Neurotransmission, Pharmacokinetics, and Pharmacodynamics," reviews the central nervous system, the brain, the properties of nerve cells, neurotransmitters, the way the body handles drugs, and the effects of drugs on the body. We also introduce the four classes of medication that are the focus of the book: antipsychotic, antidepressant, mood-stabilizing, and anti-anxiety drugs. Chapter 4, "Specific Medications for Specific Disorders," looks more closely at these four classes of medication. We discuss in some detail the side effects of the medications, with emphasis on adverse psychological, social, and physical effects. We then discuss the many types of drugs within each class and the symptoms and disorders they are intended to treat. We feature three case examples drawn from our own practice for each class of medication to illustrate how social workers become involved in medication issues. In Chapter 5, "Intervention Concerns with Special Populations," we go a step further to discuss how each class of medication may have different effects on different clients. We consider differences in effects with regard to gender, age, racial and ethnic background, and to persons who have a dual diagnosis of mental illness and substance abuse.

Part Three, "Knowledge and Skills for Psychosocial Interventions," includes chapters on psychoeducation, adherence, and monitoring. Chapter 6, "Medication Education for Clients and Families," discusses the rationale for providing medication education to clients and their families and reviews issues that are likely to arise in the implementation and evaluation of education programs. Chapter 7, "Medication Adherence and Refusal," addresses both the conceptual and the interventive knowledge needed to address these specific issues with clients and families. To that effect, we present a model for understanding adherence based on the client's characteristics, aspects of treatment, and the social environment, as well as illness itself. We address legal and ethical issues, with an emphasis on client self-determination. Finally, we provide an overview of interventions commonly used by social workers to increase adherence to the regimen of psychotropic medications. Chapter 8, "Medication Monitoring and Management," articulates specific psychosocial roles for social workers as they help clients manage their medication. This includes monitoring the effects of medications, dealing effectively with bothersome side effects, and approaching difficult decisions and problems productively, as well as negotiating with physicians and other health care providers. The chapter concludes with a definition of advocacy in psychopharmacology and with a discussion of clients' medication rights and steps in self-advocacy.

Part Four, "Future Directions," looks ahead to developments in psychopharmacology, including new drugs on the horizon, the movement by psychology and other health professions to obtain prescription privileges, and the increased public scrutiny that now surrounds psychotropic medications. For example, what will managed care mean for clients' access to medication? What do expanded roles for social workers imply with regard to their liability? The book closes with an easy-to-read glossary, which provides social work students and working professionals with demystifying definitions (and pro-nunciations) of the terms commonly used in this ever-expanding field.

A note about language. We have chosen to use the term *client* throughout the book, even though some recipients of mental health care prefer to be called *consumers, patients, psychiatric survivors, customers,* or other descriptive terms. Since our book's main focus is the social worker's interaction with ser-vice recipients, we believe that *client* is the most appropriate, nonstigmatizing term. Also, we use the term *physician* to refer to both psychiatrists and nonpsychiatrist M.D.s, because it is the most broadly descriptive of today's medication providers.

Our aim is to provide rich and relevant information. By "rich," we mean information that is sufficiently detailed yet simple enough to grasp and is rooted in a foundation of basic knowledge that leads to real understanding. By "relevant," we mean information that social workers need to know because of their own roles and responsibilities in mental health. Whether we achieved that goal is for the reader to decide.

ACKNOWLEDGMENTS

I am indebted and grateful to those who in some way shaped and stimulated my thinking about, and interest in, psychopharmacology and social work, especially the mental health consumers and families I have met through Alliance for the Mentally Ill activities in Louisiana and Virginia and during my tenure on the Virginia State Mental Health Planning Council. I am grate-ful especially to Marilyn Rosenson, Tib and Maizie Thibeaux, June Poe, Bob Trusdell, Mary Ann Beall, Luanne Holsinger, Linda Powell, and Shela Silver-man. I am also grateful to colleagues Ursula Gerhart and Harriette Johnson for their encouragement and groundbreaking writing on the topic and to col-leagues a little closer to home like Mary K and Stephen, who make VCU a great place to work and play. Major thanks, too, to my dean, Frank Baskind, for his continuing unambiguous support and to Elise Smithers for typing and managing all the references. And, of course, to Marti for thinking I am terrif-ic no matter how many copies this book sells.

My doctoral student John Bricout is largely responsible for compiling the glossary and deserves considerable kudos. He welcomed his assigned task with enviable eagerness and enthusiasm, and I am grateful. Perhaps the biggest thanks should go to my colleague, coauthor, and friend, Joe, who made the project a genuine pleasure and who every day finds a way to make me glad to be a social worker and teacher.

K. J. B.

Back in 1974 I had the good fortune to literally "stumble" into a career in the human services field at a key transition period in my life. I knew at the time that I had found my niche, and over the years have come to feel even more strongly that my career as a social worker is the most satisfying I could have hoped for. I have worked with many fine professionals from various disciplines who have contributed to my professional growth. Trying to name them all would make for an overly long list, and still I would inadvertently omit the names of some of my important influences. Instead, I would like to recognize the organizations for which I have had the pleasure of working. These include Harding Hospital in Worthington, Ohio; Columbus Area Community Mental Health Center, the Bridge Counseling Center, and North Community Counseling Centers in Columbus, Ohio; the Mental Health Association of Franklin County, Ohio; and the Daily Planet, Marshall Center, and Virginia Alliance for the Mentally Ill in Richmond, Virginia.

I would also like to thank a few individuals: First, my colleague and friend Kia Bentley for inviting me to work on this project and for always being so pleasant and helpful as I was adjusting to academic life. Second, Ellen Netting for her excellent role modeling and mentoring of my academic development. Finally I wish to dedicate this book to my wife, Margaret, and our children, Brian, Nathan, and Robyn, who remind me every day that one's commitment to family is the most important of all.

J. W.

We wish to express our gratitude to several people who have greatly contributed to this book in all its phases of development and production. Lisa Gebo, our editor at Brooks/Cole, has been a delight, and we appreciate her involvement in and care of our project. We also deeply appreciate the thoroughness and flair of manuscript editor Molly D. Roth, and the considerable efforts and production management skills of both Greg Hubit of Bookworks and Fiorella Ljunggren of Brooks/Cole. Special thanks go to the reviewers of the manuscript, who critiqued honestly and gently and thoroughly; the book is better because of them. They are William Berg, University of Wisconsin; Patricia B. Higgins, Western State Hospital; Harriette C. Johnson, University of Connecticut; Mary Fran Libassi, University of Connecticut; Jill Littrell, Georgia State University; Thomas F. McGovern, Texas Tech University Health Sciences Center; John Salamone, University of Connecticut; and Edward H. Taylor, University of North Carolina at Chapel Hill.

K. J. B. & J. W.

Preface
to the Second Edition

We are delighted to offer up to our students and colleagues the second edition of our book, *The Social Worker & Psychotropic Medication*. Because you responded so enthusiastically to the first edition, published four years ago, Brooks/Cole-Wadsworth Publishing (actually it was our fearless editor Lisa Gebo) asked us to simply update the text. We, of course, wanted to go beyond that. We wanted to add new content that we frankly can't believe we omitted last time and to expand content that was not really given sufficient attention. Importantly, we wanted to increase the critical perspective we brought to the topic and stress the social worker's role as a partner and a resource in the helping endeavor.

Specifically, we have

- completely updated information on all classes of medication and specific drugs;
- dramatically expanded the content on children and psychiatric medication across all topics;
- added comprehensive coverage of a fifth class of medication, the psychostimulants, and other drugs used to treat ADHD;
- added a large section on the use of herbs and vitamins and mental health treatment;
- expanded discussion of special populations and the use of medication;
- included content on measurement instruments that can be used to monitor the effects of medications;

- integrated more content on the implications of managed care for psychopharmacotherapy;

- added more human interest information on the history of drug development;

- included more data on effectiveness research associated with specific medications;

- given greater voice to a critical perspective about medication use in psychiatry;

- added an overall appendix of all currently available prescription medications and increased our use of tables and diagrams; and

- updated literature reviews and references to the research across all topics.

We hope you continue to value the book and find it useful in your work with clients. That remains the bottom line.

ACKNOWLEDGMENTS TO THE SECOND EDITION

It was fun to work on making the book better, although admittedly "visioning" and talking about our hopes and dreams was a bit more fun than putting ink on the page as the deadlines over the summer and fall bore relentlessly down on us. Perhaps the best part, though, was rekindling on a closer level the warm and satisfying collaboration with Joe. It is one of the most important of my career. I continue to be deeply grateful for the support of my colleagues here at VCU like Mary Katherine, Jaci, Ann, Ellen, David, Patrick, Anne, Sandy, Bob (and Bob), Michael, Amy, Jane, Bev, Joe, Randi, Humberto, Pam, and of course, Frank. A special word of appreciation to my mentor Dianne at FSU and Karen, my good buddy at UTK, for showering me with solid advice and unconditional positive regard over the years. Then there is Marti, who at the time of the first edition was very proud of me and didn't seem to care how many books sold. Interestingly, she seems to care a little more now. She is my refuge and my delight.

Kia J. Bentley
February 2000

I would like to thank Tracy Spahr, M.S.W., of Henrico County (VA) Public Schools, for her invaluable assistance in the development of the case examples in chapter four pertaining to psychostimulant medications. Randi Buerlein, M.S.W., from our own School of Social Work, was also helpful in this regard. Kathryn Meyersohn, M.S.W., a doctoral student in our School, participated in the updating and expansion of the glossary. Finally, I want to thank my co-author and colleague Kia, for being such a good friend.

Joseph Walsh

About the Authors

D r. Kia J. Bentley, a licensed clinical social worker, is an Associate Professor and Director of the Ph.D. Program in Social Work at Virginia Commonwealth University, where she has taught since 1989. Dr. Bentley has all three degrees in social work: a BSW from Auburn University (1978), an M.S.S.W. from the University of Tennessee, and a Ph.D. from Florida State (1987), where she received a "Distinguished Alumni Award" in 1997. Her current teaching focuses on mental health practice, mental and emotional disorders, psychopharmacotherapy and social work, theory and models of practice, and research. She has also developed and taught courses in mental health policy, law and ethics; and practice with persons with serious mental illness.

In addition to this text, Dr. Bentley is editor of an upcoming text by Brooks/Cole, *Social Work Practice in Mental Health: Contemporary Roles, Task and Techniques,* as well as numerous other publications on social work in mental health, including the social worker's role in medication management, the right to refuse medication, prescription writing privileges for social workers, and psychosocial interventions for people with schizophrenia. She has authored several articles on women's issues in mental health and in social work education as well as publication productivity in social work. Her current research investigates the meaning of medication for mental health consumers and role dilemmas in medication management for social workers.

Dr. Bentley served two terms on the Council on Social Work Education's Women's Commission and has been an active site visitor for their Commission on Accreditation for six years. In addition, she is a longtime member of the National Association of Social Workers and was a consulting editor of *Social Work* from 1994 to 1999. In Virginia, she is the former chair of the statewide Mental Health Planning Council and served for six years on the board of Virginia's chapter of the National Alliance for the Mentally Ill. She currently serves on Central State Hospital's Human Rights Committee. Dr. Bentley is a clinical supervisor and serves as a consultant and trainer to inpatient, outpatient, and consumer-run mental health programs.

Joseph Walsh, Ph.D., L.C.S.W., is an Associate Professor of Social Work at Virginia Commonwealth University. He received his academic degrees from the Ohio State University. Joe has been a direct services practitioner in the field of mental health since 1974, first in a psychiatric hospital and later in community mental health center settings. He comanaged the pharmacy at one community mental health center between 1983 and 1993. Joe has provided services to older adult and general outpatient populations, but he specializes in services to persons with serious mental illness and their families.

Joe has been at Virginia Commonwealth University since 1993 and currently teaches courses in generalist practice, clinical practice, research, and mental and emotional disorders. He continues to provide direct services to clients at the university counseling center and also at area shelters, clubhouses, and group homes. Joe was the 1998 recipient of the National Mental Health Association's George Goodman Brudney and Ruth P. Brudney Social Work Award, given annually to recognize significant contributions to the care and treatment of persons with mental illness. He is also the author of *Clinical Case Management with Persons Having Mental Illness: A Relationship-Based Perspective*, published in 1998 by Brooks/Cole-Wadsworth.

✛

PART I

Social Work Roles in Medication Management

Chapter 1

History and Overview of Social Work Roles
in Medication Management

Chapter 2

Defining Effective Collaboration

History and Overview of Social Work Roles in Medication Management

INTRODUCTION

Five Case Scenarios

Asocial worker employed at a Midwestern public mental health agency provides a range of psychosocial interventions for clients with mental illness. At the present time she is faced with the following dilemmas involving five clients on her caseload:

Mark is a 31-year-old white male diagnosed with schizophrenia; he lives with his parents and is primarily supported by public entitlements for mental disability. His active symptoms (delusions, hallucinations, and scattered thinking) are well controlled with antipsychotic medications, which he receives from the agency psychiatrist. However, the side effects of these medications are severe: Mark experiences persistent and uncontrollable spasms in his neck, arms, and back. He cannot sit still and continuously flails his arms and neck about. Because these spasms are both unsightly and disruptive to his physical coordination, he is reluctant to leave his house.

Puzzled by the severity of these side effects, his psychiatrist wonders if their origin is psychosomatic. Still, the paradox is clear: Mark can either maintain mental stability and experience physically disabling spasms or experience psychotic symptoms and feel more comfortable physically. Mark's parents, who can rarely reach the part-time agency psychiatrist by phone, frequently call the social worker to seek advice on resolving this apparently no-win situation. However, the social worker has no quick answers to the problem. Further, she cannot engage Mark in any rehabilitative activities because of his reluctance to be out in public, where his jerking motions in fact become worse.

Carla, age 33, has been diagnosed with schizo-affective disorder (including elements of thought and mood disorder), in which her paranoid delusions are the most prominent symptom. She lives alone and receives disability benefits but, unlike Mark, likes to be around people and even looks for jobs. She takes antipsychotic and mood-stabilizing medications willingly, which clarify her thoughts and calm her. However, the social worker has come to understand that Carla is by nature very forgetful. She often forgets to take her medications and even occasionally forgets her physician's appointments.

When Carla does not take her medications for a week or more, she becomes agitated and paranoid, tending to direct her distorted thoughts at people in her immediate environment. One day Carla calls her social worker in crisis. She is convinced that the downstairs neighbor is planning to murder her, and she is considering physical retaliation. Carla admits that she is out of medication, having misplaced her most recent supply. She asks if the social worker can get some medication to her immediately, because she fears losing control of herself. The physician, who works only ten hours per week at the agency, is not available, but the social worker knows Carla's type and dosage of medication and that it is available in the small stock supply of the agency's medication room.

John is a 34-year-old single unemployed white male, living with his sister and brother-in-law; he experiences dysthymia and demonstrates dependent personality traits. Though he is highly intelligent, cares about others, and has a notable self-deprecating wit, John shows extreme anxiety in all social situations and has a very poor self-image. For several months, the social worker has intervened to help John reach his goal of self-sufficiency as he sought better social skills, employment, and junior college enrollment. Making significant strides, John applies for jobs, attends interviews, and visits a regional college campus. However, with each initiative, he becomes almost incapacitated with anxiety and fear of failure. The social worker decides to refer him to an agency physician, who will evaluate medication that can help John deal with his depressed mood through this difficult time.

John impresses the physician as someone working hard to overcome his problems. The physician decides to prescribe a small dose of amitriptyline, a cyclic anti-depressant medication that may help John sleep better at night, stabilize his mood, and reduce his anxiety. The medication seems effective, and John's dose is gradually raised into an average therapeutic range. During their weekly sessions, the social worker helps John monitor the effects of his medication. Several months later, John begins working. He seems committed to make the experience a success, but the stress of his job responsibilities and his need to interact regularly with coworkers overwhelm him. One evening, John abruptly quits. In a panic, fearing that he has blown a rare opportunity to work, he takes a serious overdose of his medications. He survives but is hospitalized for one night for observation.

Learning of the overdose, the physician becomes angry and tells the social worker that he will no longer prescribe medications for John. He states that doing so would constitute irresponsible practice because the client is a suicidal risk. However, the social worker continues to see John, who seems truly remorseful about his action. He recovers from the crisis and states that he wants to continue focusing on the same goals. Further, because the medication has helped him move forward, John hopes that he can resume taking an antidepressant drug. The social worker feels placed in a difficult bind. She tends to agree with John, but the physician will not meet with him again. The social worker will violate agency policy and put her reputation as a team player in jeopardy if she arranges to transfer John's psychiatric care to another agency physician.

Darlene is a 22-year-old, single unemployed African-American female who lives with her older sister in an apartment. Though she has maintained a stable mood for one year, she has been hospitalized twice in the past three years for manic episodes. Symptoms of her bipolar disorder respond well to a combination of antipsychotic and mood-stabilizing medications. The social worker who provides Darlene with counseling has referred her to clubhouse and vocational training programs for additional service. Darlene, who comes from a highly successful and socially prominent family, at present depends on her parents for financial resources. Over the course of one week, Darlene calls her social worker daily, which is highly unusual, and complains of anxiety, inability to sleep, and a vague fearfulness that some harm may come to her from intruders. The social worker arranges for her to be seen on an emergency basis by the agency psychiatrist. During this appointment, which the social worker also attends, it is determined that Darlene is decompensating into a psychosis and requires hospitalization. The entire family, known by the social worker and involved in her treatment planning, becomes understandably upset but also furious with agency staff. Until now they have expressed satisfaction with the interventions. But now they wonder why the agency staff did not know that Darlene had consciously stopped taking her medication. While in the hospital, Darlene eventually confides to the social worker that she may have stopped taking her medication in order to prompt a decompensation because she was afraid to assume increased responsibility for herself. However, the family is so upset that before Darlene is discharged from the hospital, her parents convince her to transfer to another agency for follow-up care. The social worker understands from contacts with various family members that they are divided over this issue, but the wishes of the parents have prevailed.

Chandra is a 29-year-old university student who came to counseling because of stresses related to her demanding course load and failing marriage. She reported a history of sexual acting out and alcohol dependence and demonstrated present signs of compulsive behavior. Her social worker was suspicious about the basis of Chandra's presenting problems, but, in keeping with the client's wishes, focused on behavioral strategies to improve her academic adjustment. Soon after they began working together, Chandra's depression increased. The more personal the content that she disclosed to the worker, the more negative feelings surfaced within her. Chandra's memories became more clear, revealing that she was in fact a survivor of long-term sexual abuse by her father and brothers. She began to experience insomnia, nightmares, and an inability to concentrate, which made her academic work even more difficult. She also felt like drinking again. The social worker felt in a bind—she did not want to prompt feelings that overwhelmed the client, but neither did she want to ignore those feelings. Chandra, despite her fragile composure, wanted to explore her feelings as well. The social worker referred Chandra to the agency physician for a medication evaluation, and he prescribed desyrel for her worsening depression and sleep problems.

The counseling resulted in Chandra's greater awareness of her needs and conflicts, but it added to her everyday distress. She experienced anxiety attacks now and was hospitalized briefly for a loss of self-control and suicidal ideation. The physician added sertraline (for daytime depression) and lorazepam (for anxiety) to the medication regimen. The social worker was quite knowledgeable about medications and helped Chandra to understand the rationales for their use and to monitor her physical and emotional responses to them. Then the social worker became aware that the drugs alleviated some of the feelings that had helped Chandra understand her interpersonal needs. Further, as three medications from two drug classes were being prescribed, the worker was unsure of their interactive effects on Chandra's self-image. The situation became more complicated when, after a second suicidal threat, the physician discontinued the anti-anxiety medication and added a modest dose of perphenazine, an antipsychotic medication. It was intended to reduce Chandra's agitation and the transient delusional ideas she experienced when deeply depressed.

While it may be difficult for the reader to appreciate, Chandra's psychosocial growth was constant throughout this time. She was able to make better decisions about her life goals and relationships with family and friends. Even so, after one year of intensive intervention she experienced the recurrence of an adolescent eating disorder and, for the third time, needed to be hospitalized briefly, this time for dangerous purging behaviors. Her attending physician at the hospital, in consultation with the primary physician (but not the social worker), changed Chandra's medication regimen in consideration of the new diagnosis. She was prescribed the newer antipsychotic medication olanzapine (instead of perphenazine) and luvoxamine (instead of sertraline) because of its anticompulsive actions. The desyrel was continued for evening use. The social worker, still managing her counseling, became almost dizzy with this latest round of adjustments. At the hospital Chandra was diagnosed with major depression (recurrent, with psychotic features), post-traumatic stress disorder, bulimia, and borderline personality disorder. With such frequent changes, how could the social worker help this client sustain her courageous and difficult work in counseling and help her understand the purposes of all the medications?

These actual case scenarios exemplify the dilemmas a social worker may face in situations involving clients who take psychotropic medication. In the first example, the social worker seems to be in a no-win situation as she tries, with the client and family, to decide whether or not the client's use of psychotropic medication is appropriate. In the second example, the social worker needs to wrestle with the temptation to move out of her legal boundaries and dispense medication, especially because the act appears to be safe and in the client's (and possibly the neighbor's) best interest. In the third situation, the social worker has become entangled in a conflict between her client and a physician/colleague. The fourth scenario represents an instance of the social worker's mistaken assumptions about the extent to which collaborative treatment has been secured with her client's family. During a crisis she has found that there are trust issues that have not been fully addressed. In the fifth example the social worker becomes overwhelmed in her efforts to keep track of the various effects on one client of prescribed medications from three drug categories that are occasionally changed. She is also concerned about the effects of polypharmacy on the client's desire to confront her painful past. How can the worker effectively advocate for the client in any of these five circumstances? How much priority should she place on maintaining cooperative interdisciplinary roles? How can the social worker implement what seems to be best for the clients in light of complicating medication concerns?

THE CHANGING ROLES OF SOCIAL WORKERS

Professional practice in social work is largely based on biopsychosocial theories of assessment and intervention. In mental health treatment settings, both assessing mental status and monitoring medication should be included as a significant part of the person-in-environment assessment because these actions are so relevant to this client population's capacity for social functioning. Though medications affect functioning at a biochemical level, they equally impact the psychological and social concerns of clients and their significant others. In this chapter, we will attempt to outline the range of roles that social workers should be prepared to assume in working with clients who use or who consider using psychotropic medications. Traditionally, social workers have not emphasized a knowledge of medications as a key component of their professional training or continuing education; however, continued ignorance of this topic will only result in disservice to clients.

One model that attempts to explain the interplay between biological and environmental influences in mental health is the stress-diathesis (or stress vulnerability) model of mental illness (Mazure, 1995; Yank, Bentley, & Hargrove, 1993). This model asserts that though the cause of mental illness is apparently associated with genetic factors and abnormalities in brain chemistry and structure, the course of disorders is partly related to environmental factors. Liberman (1988, p. 9) writes that "vulnerability and stressors are moderated in their impact . . . by the presence of protective factors," such as skills in coping and competence, medication, and social support. If social workers can help build up protective factors, they can decrease the impairments and handicaps experienced by mental health clients and their families. Though the model was originally developed to explain the course of schizophrenia, social workers will find it useful because it clarifies how they can contribute to improved psychosocial functioning in clients and their families, particularly through medication management. This model suggests that though social workers most likely will not influence genes, chromosomes, or the size of frontal lobes, they surely can help build protective factors and, through psychosocial interventions, can help clients maximize the benefits of their psychotropic medication. While psychosocial interventions do have effects on neurotransmission, the nature of this impact is not yet known.

All social workers, particularly those in health and mental health service settings, work at least occasionally with clients who use medications as part of their overall intervention plans. However, social workers have only recently begun to elaborate a range of specific professional roles with regard to medication issues. Historically, they have functioned as physician's assistants, supporting client compliance with medications according to the physician's recommendations. Still, as indicated in our five case examples, the range of service delivery modalities for some client populations has expanded to a point where clients and families occasionally ask social workers, regardless of their level of competence in the area, to make difficult decisions about the use of psychotropic medication. Crisis situations, which demand immediate action by clients and their families, do not always allow social workers to postpone intervention in deference to the physician's expertise.

Social workers must possess a sound knowledge of medications and their consequences for clients' lives, but not merely to complement the physician's role. The social work profession brings a unique perspective to medication issues, based on its appreciation of client self-determination, its perspective that medication is only one part of comprehensive psychosocial intervention, and its view of the person-in-environment as the basis for assessment and intervention. Social work also promotes a partnership model of practice, which bases relationships with clients and families on an appreciation of their strengths and viewpoints and on the assumption that the helping relationship should be active and mutual, as described in chapter 2.

There are four reasons for these developments within the social work profession during the past 25 years. First, the presence of social workers in public mental health service settings of all types has increased in proportion to other professional disciplines (Manderscheid & Sonnenschein, 1994). The number of full-time equivalent social work staff in all mental health organizations in the United States rose from 17,687 in 1972 to 53,375 in 1990. Of the four main mental health professions (psychiatry, psychology, social work, and nursing), only nursing outnumbered social work in 1990. However, in outpatient mental health centers, social workers comprised 46% of client care staff (and

32.3% of total agency staff). Psychiatrists fell from 9.2% of all staff in 1972 to 4.8% in 1990. Likewise, nursing dropped from 3.3% to 2.2%. These statistics indicate that more social workers than before are providing services to clients, with fewer psychiatrists and nurses available for client care. In fact, the total number of employed social workers in this country increased by 18% between 1989 and 1998 (Handerscheid & Henderson, 1998).

Second, because national public policy emphasizes deinstitutionalization and community care, facilitated by the increased use of intensive case management and other psychosocial rehabilitation programs, psychiatric hospital use has decreased, while the number of persons in the community with mental illnesses has increased (Callicutt, 1997). Many people with mental illness have limited social functioning skills, frequently find themselves in crisis situations, and require continuous mental-status monitoring by social workers. Treatments that include psychosocial rehabilitation and case management, largely associated with the social work profession, have been found to be effective in helping persons with mental illness adjust to community living (Rapp, 1998). Thus, social workers are coming into broader contact with these client populations. Psychiatrists and nurses cannot assess clients under controlled conditions as regularly as when clients were more frequently hospitalized.

Berg and Wallace (1987) support the idea that the increased presence of people with mental illness in the community has complicated the role of the social worker in medication management. They found differences in knowledge and roles between inpatient and outpatient social workers. Inpatient social workers showed more knowledge about medications and subscribed more closely to the medical model than outpatient social workers. Outpatient social workers were more likely than inpatient social workers to consider issues about clients' rights, record clients' negative experiences with medications, and report their assessment of the physician's screening. They also tended to more actively encourage clients to take medications and work with families on related issues. Therefore, it appears from this study that outpatient social workers, perhaps because their interactions with other members of the treatment team are less controlled, develop greater autonomy in monitoring medication and have more influence on clients who depend on them for input about medications.

A third reason for the expanded demand for social workers involves the profession's increasing emphasis on collaborative approaches with consumers and family members (Bentley & Harrison, 1989; Walsh, 2000). Social workers are often the first point of contact for significant others who develop concerns about the mental status of their loved ones. The implications of this spirit of collaboration, which we call the partnership model of practice, are developed extensively in the next chapter.

Finally, new types of psychotropic medications (antipsychotic, antidepressant, mood-stabilizing, anti-anxiety, and psychostimulant drugs), introduced into the market since the 1980s, have proliferated. Accompanying this trend is a broad range of issues for consumers to consider: symptomatic indications for use, choices among drug types and classes, side effects, special precautions, the use of generic versus brand name drugs, and input into decisions of compliance and refusal of medications, to name just a few. The relative benefits and risks of using medication must always be weighed by all professional practitioners. Indeed, many states have required that professionals provide written information about medications to clients at the time of prescription in only the past 10 years (Ravid & Menon, 1993).

To understand the current challenges to the profession, social workers must also understand the historical forces that have fostered the current practice climate. They must look back at the evolution of medications as treatment resources and the development of social work as a subspecialty within the mental health field.

A HISTORICAL CONTEXT OF INTERVENTION FOR PEOPLE WITH MENTAL ILLNESS

The Treatment of People with Mental Illness Prior to 1950

Both psychiatric hospitals and general hospital wards serving persons with mental illness have existed in this country since its inception. Benjamin Franklin founded the Pennsylvania Hospital in Philadelphia in 1751, the nation's first to include services for the mentally ill, or, as Franklin wrote, "Those distempered in mind and deprived of their rational faculties" (Jones, 1976, p. 461). Still in operation, the first state-supported hospital devoted solely to the care of the mentally ill was founded in 1773 at Williamsburg, Virginia. During the next 65 years, 15 states established such hospitals, with the number of institutions growing to 123 by 1880.

This era of "moral treatment" emphasized active rehabilitation and structuring inpatients' lives to stabilize their uncontrolled thoughts and emotions. During the second half of the 19th century, however, as the population of the United States increased, these primarily public institutions became vastly overcrowded, so that moral treatment gave way to mere patient management that focused on control of unruly behavior. Though intervention came to include medications in the late 19th century, they were used to control aggressive behavior rather than to implement active treatment.

The concept of medication as restraint fostered suspicion in many social workers and other professionals through the 20th century. During the second half of the 19th century, bromides (sedative medications) were introduced. By the 1874 meeting of the Association of Medical Superintendents, the generic sedative chloral hydrate was established as the most popular drug used by hospital psychiatrists, despite its potentially dangerous side effect of respiratory system paralysis (Caplan, 1969).

Few advances were made in medication for hospitalized persons over the next 75 years. Through the 1940s the leading medical textbooks still listed nonspecific sedative drugs, such as barbiturates, bromides, and chloral hydrate, as well as rest, baths, and hydrotherapy, as primary treatments for psychotic persons. These treatments were assumed to provide no more than temporary relief (Valenstein, 1986). Various other somatic treatments, such as shock therapies and lobotomy, were developed in hospitals between 1900 and 1950, but these have been used to a much lesser degree since the antipsychotic medications were introduced. When these medications came into more widespread use in the 1950s, many social workers and other professionals perceived them as a negative alternative to counseling and rehabilitative interventions.

The Rise of Psychiatric Social Work

The now century-old tradition of psychiatric social work was one of several specializations (including medical social work and child welfare) that emerged during the first decade of the 20th century. This specialty emerged because hospital physicians and administrators needed to link their institutions with community treatment environments to ensure better, more responsive ongoing diagnosis and treatment for patients (Lubove, 1965). At that time, crowded institutions and population growth in major American cities caused pressure to discharge mental patients and insure their permanent adjustment to the community. Because medications were not used outside of hospitals at that time, social workers did not become involved in those issues.

Social psychiatry emerged in the work of America's preeminent psychiatrist of that time, Adolf Meyer, who emphasized a "multiple causation" perspective on treatment (Caplan, 1969). He emphasized the need for close contact with the patient's home and social environment, as well as the crucial role of social workers in facilitating suitable social environments for patients. Meyer emphasized the importance of seeing patients as social beings as well as physical organisms, defining insanity as a disease of social functioning as well as a manifestation of a disturbed mind. Mary Brooks Meyer, his wife, acted as a social worker in 1904 when he asked her to follow up on the progress of some discharged patients from Manhattan State Hospital.

When the New York State Charities Aid Association implemented a statewide aftercare program in 1904, they hired Edith Horton, a graduate of the New York School of Private Philanthropy, as an aftercare agent for two mental hospitals. As the first professional psychiatric social worker, Horton's duties included locating jobs, housing, and community resources for discharged patients. The need to focus on the life history and social environment of each client had in fact first been proposed by the Charities Aid Association in 1894. Interestingly, 100 years later, many states still struggle to develop service systems based on this same model of continuity of care, even though its driving idea is so old.

The principles of intervention in psychiatric social work were derived from the model of medical social work developed in 1905 by physician Richard Cabot and social worker Ida Cannon at Massachusetts General Hospital (Callicutt, 1983). With physician James Putnam, social worker Edith Burleigh adopted three roles for psychiatric social work: to provide an investigation of the client's social environment prior to discharge, to contribute to diagnostic assessment, and to complement the physician's treatment. In 1913, Mary Jarrett introduced the professional title "psychiatric social worker" and outlined the four practice functions: casework, clinic management, public education, and research (Southard & Jarrett, 1922). French (1940) later presented her own version of these four functions of the social worker in psychiatric settings as (1) analyzing social situations in light of the client's present difficulty, (2) interpreting problems and the psychiatrist's recommendations to the family, (3) helping the family and patient work out a plan for social adjustment, and (4) explaining the diagnosis and treatment plan to workers at other participating agencies. Although nowhere do they address medication as an issue, Southard and Jarrett also see the social worker's role as complementary to that of the psychiatrist, similar to that of the physician's assistant, still seen in many hospitals and clinics today.

While the field of psychiatric social work grew during the 1900s, few workers sought or found positions in the hospitals that used medications. French (1940) lists the following as reasons for negative professional attitudes: low pay, isolation from community contact, the need in some cases to live at the institutions, large caseloads, and the demands for nonprofessional duties within the institution. Her statistics support the lack of enthusiasm of members of the American Association for Psychiatric Social Work, founded in 1920, for mental hospital work. In 1920, 35% of association members worked in mental hospitals ($n = 6$), but by 1937, the percentage had dropped to 13.5% ($n = 55$). In her comprehensive volume about the field of psychiatric social work, French does not once mention medication.

The Introduction of Psychotropic Medications

By the 1960s, researchers had discovered drugs from the five major chemical groups, drugs that continue to be used in pharmacology today. These include the antipsychotics or major tranquilizers, the antidepressants, the mood stabilizers (lithium), the benzodiazepines (anti-anxiety agents), and the psychostimulants (Kaplan & Sadock, 1998). Thorazine, a brand name for the generic compound chlorpromazine, was introduced in the United States in 1954 and was followed by Haldol (haloperidol) in 1958. Remaining among the most frequently prescribed antipsychotic medications, both are used to clarify a client's thought processes through sedation and the reduction or elimination of hallucinations.

The first antidepressants introduced were the monoamine oxidase (MAO) inhibitors, which became available in the late 1950s. When the tricyclic antidepressant imipramine appeared in 1958, it became more widely prescribed because, unlike the MAO drugs, it did not require stringent dietary restrictions as a precaution against side effects. The mood stabilizer lithium, effective in treating persons with bipolar disorder, appeared in the United States in 1969, although it had been available in Europe since the 1950s. Librium, the first benzodiazepine, was marketed in 1957. Stimulants have been utilized in the treatment of attention/deficit hyperactivity disorder since 1936, at which time it was found that amphetamine drugs were effective in controlling the disorder. Methylphenidate, the most widely used and studied psychostimulant, was introduced in 1958 as a treatment for children with hyperactivity (Jacobvitz, 1990).

With these drugs, psychiatry had at its disposal five classes of medications; the 40 years since have been devoted to clinical studies and the development of related compounds. Four major additions since 1980 include the anticonvulsant drugs (carbamazepine and valproic acid), used as mood stabilizers and also as agents that increase the potency of other medications; the nonbenzodiazepine anti-anxiety agents, which do not present the same potential for physical addiction as benzodiazepines; new classes of antidepressant and anti-obsessive-compulsive drugs; and several new antipsychotic medications, of which clozapine and risperidone are among the best known. Though they serve the same clinical functions as the older drugs, these newer medications are derived from different chemical compounds, have somewhat different routes of action, and in some cases have fewer negative side effects (see chapter 4 for a full discussion of medication types).

Many physicians were reportedly reluctant to use the antipsychotic medication chlorpromazine when it was introduced (Johnson, 1990). While this may seem strange in today's age of biological psychiatry, resistance was due in part to the time-honored stance that medications work well for behavioral management but have limited curative potential. Physicians expressed concern that the medication would not actively treat the illness but serve only as a sedating agent, as previous medications did. They also feared that employing medication would steer professionals away from psychological treatment, be inferior to existing somatic therapies, and present too much uncertainty regarding side effects. A nationwide survey of state hospitals in 1956 revealed that only 19% of patients used chlorpromazine (or reserpine, a related sedative considered innovative at the time) because of professional resistance and the fact that state budgets did not yet include funding for the new medication.

One notable paradox arose: The new emphasis on biological psychiatry, through the increased use of drugs, compartmentalized the medical and social approaches to the treatment of mental illness. A sharper distinction evolved between psychiatry on the one hand and social work and related disciplines on the other. Contrary to the vision of Meyer and those who shared his psychosocial perspective, psychiatry would no longer be as concerned with rehabilitation or community support activities. This distinction eventually provided a rationale for social workers to assume more active roles, within a partnership model, in helping clients on psychotropic medication use a variety of interventions in their social adjustment.

SOCIAL WORK ROLE CATEGORIES

Physician's Assistant

In the role of physician's assistant, the social worker tends to accept unquestionably the physician's decisions about psychotropic drugs and, as such, is limited to helping clients take their medications according to the physician's recommendations. The worker is not expected to offer advice about any decisions involving the prescription and use of medication or any compliance strategy, although he or she does play a role in the assessment process. Psychiatric social workers were thought to function mainly as physicians' assistants through the 1970s.

For many years, the role of physician's assistant was the most common because of factors that included the relatively limited legal scope of the practice of social work, traditions of authority among the core helping professions, the focus of professional social work education on other areas, and social workers' negative attitudes about the relative appropriateness of medication as a primary means of intervention (Gerhart & Brooks, 1983). Psychiatrists and physicians have traditionally been, and still are, the primary providers of biological interventions for all types of emotional problems and mental disorders. However, over the past three decades deinstitutionalization and the new emphasis on community-based care has prompted social workers to broaden their psychosocial framework to include interventions using psychotropic medication. Though social workers are still limited to the role of physician's assistant in many settings, we see them moving away from this role for the many reasons discussed earlier in this chapter.

Consultant

In the past 25 years much of the professional literature concerning psychotropic medication discusses the roles that social workers play or ought to play regarding their clients' use of medications, thus augmenting the original physician's assistant role. In the late 1970s, McCollum, Margolin, and Lieb (1978) wrote that the social worker needs to be skilled in three areas. First, the worker must be able to assess clients for possible referral to physicians. This involves evaluating the client's current levels of functioning, the intensity of the observed suffering, and the client's capacity to manage his or her suffering. Second, the worker must prepare clients to actively participate in the process of assessment by the physician. To prepare the clients for referral, the worker's responsibilities include articulating the specific reasons for the referral, reviewing the client's attitude toward psychiatrists, discussing the client's expectations about medications, and closely monitoring the client's subjective experiences of effects after medications have been prescribed. Third, the worker must monitor clients; we will discuss this in a separate section below. Finally, we add another necessary worker skill: assessing the client's ability to pay for medication, the cost of which may be quite high.

Though McCollum et al. focus on the need for a consultative and collaborative relationship between the social worker and client, Miller, Wiedman, and Linn (1980) emphasize the need for the social worker to likewise conceptualize her or his relationship with the physician. Both social workers and physicians need to see themselves as consultants and collaborators with each other. Specifically, they need to work together to specify the range of the social worker's roles in medication management, interpret how important it is for clients to take their medication as instructed, devise systematic procedures to evaluate each medication's effectiveness, and use client files to record relevant data when monitoring a client's response. These authors further call on physicians to provide in-service training to other professionals on such issues as drug categories, adverse effects, and interviewing techniques. Social workers, in turn, can teach physicians about various aspects of psychosocial intervention. Of course, the activities discussed by Miller et al. imply that disagreements may arise among the physician, social worker, and client over many issues, with which they must openly deal to move toward constructive resolution.

Another part of the consultant role is validation, or working to empower clients to make decisions about the use of medication (Tobias, 1990). The validator "confirms, legitimates, substantiates, or verifies the feelings, ideas, values, or beliefs of the client as well-grounded, correct, or genuine within the client's system" (p. 357). Validation promotes active, effective client participation in rehabilitation planning and intervention. As a validator, the social worker seeks to uncover the client's perceptions and experiences, supporting as legitimate those components that can be channeled into action on the client's part. With regard to the use of medication, clearly the validator can assist the client to become a stronger consultant in interactions with all helping professionals.

Counselor

The term "counselor" is often used interchangeably with that of "therapist," but distinctions can be made between the two concepts. Counseling is generally concerned with helping people cope with normal problems and opportunities (Ivey & Ivey, 1999). It is sometimes defined as a type of psychotherapy, but one that is supportive or re-educative and that is applied to behavioral problems not strictly classifiable as mental illness (Campbell, 1996). Counseling is goal-oriented, while psychotherapy is person-oriented in terms of helping clients make adjustments in their general personality style. A counselor is more of a teacher and coach, while a therapist is more of a detective and analyst; the former stresses giving information and advice (Corsini &

Wedding, 1995). Counseling is thus a process of providing clients with information and advice, socialization skills, and practical help, as well as delineating alternatives, teaching problem solving, helping to articulate goals, and reality testing (Barker, 1998). It does not involve probing or attempting "depth" therapy.

In addition to the above characteristics, we add that the counselor always demonstrates empathy for the client, defined as the ability "to *perceive* accurately and sensitively inner feelings of the client and to *communicate* understanding of these feelings in language attuned to the client's experiencing of the moment" (italics added) (Hepworth, Rooney, and Larsen, 1997, p. 99). Research has consistently demonstrated that effective intervention depends on the client's sense of trust in the worker as a caring individual who understands his or her perspectives (Frank & Frank, 1993; Sexton & Whiston, 1994). In the role of counselor, then, the social worker helps the client problem solve and make decisions about practical matters related to medication use. This role overlaps at times with that of educator and advocate and may of course extend beyond medication management issues. The role of counselor is underscored, however, by the social worker's helping the client with problem solving related to medication issues, which are not necessarily related to issues of mental illness.

The process of problem solving has been articulated by Hepworth, Rooney, and Larsen (1997). The technique assumes that a client's inability to generate, implement, and evaluate problem-solving strategies contributes to the occurrence of maladaptive behavior. The goal of counseling is to help the client become a better problem solver through a process that increases both the number of effective response alternatives for resolving a problem and the probability that the most effective response will be selected from the alternatives.

Monitor

To monitor medication, the social worker must observe and help the client observe the positive and negative effects of medication and the appearance or persistence of symptoms in the client. The social worker may also help to check the client's use of medications as prescribed. He or she needs to help evaluate the client's responses to any discomfort, the importance of the physiologically adverse effects (i.e., dry mouth versus impotence), and any impairments in family or social functioning. Finally, the worker conveys information from the monitoring process back to the client, perhaps to the family, and to the physician. Through these activities, the social worker both helps the client monitor medication and serves as a resource to the physician.

Davidson and Jamison (1983) further define this role by delineating three types of adverse effects for the social worker to monitor: physical, psychological, and social. Through self-study (with current reference texts) and collaboration with medical personnel, the social worker can become educated about adverse physical effects. Adverse psychological effects involve any changes in the client's self-image and identity that emerge as a result of using medications. For example, clients may come to view themselves as "sick" people or may become overly dependent on medication as a solution to perceived emotional problems. They may also, as a result of the latter, avoid potentially healthy challenges in the social environment. Keen (1998) has also written about the adverse psychological effects of psychotropic medication, noting the paradox that while medicine may help the client think more clearly, clients can also interpret it as a message that they are crazy and cannot get well (see chapter 7 for a fuller discussion of this issue). Further, the side effects may make them appear even more disturbed to others, so that clients see themselves as marginal, different, and "ill."

Adverse social effects include any potentially negative consequences that go beyond the individual client to include the effect of medication use on one's standing with certain social institutions, such as hospitals, the Social Security Administration, or society at large. For example, people may overuse or physicians may overprescribe psychotropic medications to maintain qualifications for disability benefits or facilitate discharge from the hospital before the client's ego strength reaches a level that makes satisfactory community functioning likely. Further, medications initially used for symptom relief so that psychosocial treatments could be initiated can become the complete treatment. To their listing of adverse social effects, Davidson and Jamison might have added that if the client is dependent on the family, families have been given the difficult responsibility of monitoring both the client's response to medications and his or her development of additional self-care skills. This topic of extra-physical side effects, which we will fully develop in chapters 4, 7, and 8, merits particularly close attention by social workers because the health professions have largely neglected it.

Advocate

In their review of social work literature, Gerhart and Brooks (1983) state that social workers typically assumed either of the two roles of physician's assistant and consultant. While they agree that both roles are useful, Gerhart and Brooks found that social workers do not objectively weigh the benefits and risks of medication with regard to both physical and psychological adverse effects. They propose the implementation of a third role, that of the client advocate, based on their perception that medical expertise is not always the rule and that medication can have serious negative effects that might outweigh its benefits. Gerhart and Brooks define advocacy as the "representation of mentally ill individuals and groups by social work practitioners in an effort to present the client's expressed desires to those in the mental health system who have the power" to assess how medications are administered (p. 456).

The social work advocate ideally has a peer relationship with the physician and participates in all phases of decision making regarding the choices made for medication. Gerhart and Brooks claim that this role is more crucial now than ever because of the emphasis on community care, which makes the responsible monitoring of a client's medication needs and outcomes difficult for any single person to maintain, particularly for the physician. Gerhart and Brooks also claim that to function as an advocate, the worker must have a good working knowledge of mental illness, psychotropic medications, and laws and regulations about such issues as forced medications and the rights of persons with mental illness. Interestingly, Gerhart and Brooks admit that this role might best be filled by a specialist, such as a client-rights advocate, because he or she may have to oppose the physician and other professionals. However, we believe that social workers can competently carry out the advocacy role when they represent the client's position from a sound base of knowledge and professional values, although this can be difficult at times (see chapter 9).

Higgins (1995) goes beyond the types of advocacy we have just outlined. She suggests that social workers should function as political advocates for clients who cannot access medications they want to use. This situation developed quite dramatically with the introduction of clozapine in 1991. The medication had demonstrated benefits with some persons with schizophrenia who had not responded to more traditional antipsychotic medications. However, the cost of the medication, coupled with the need to monitor blood counts weekly, created a very expensive treatment regimen. Because some clients and families who could not afford the drug filed suits to gain access to it, adjustments were made in public insurance policies, helping to broaden its availability (Reid, Pham, & Rago, 1993). Because issues related to the cost of medication are serious and because restrictions on the availability of medication may arise, Higgins argues that social workers need to serve as advocates before not only physicians but also agencies, funding sources, and government regulators. Further, when funding caps limit a client's access to medication, social workers may need to become involved in decision making about which eligible clients should have access to medications such as clozapine. The relevance of Higgins' perspective is a reminder that medication issues should be considered in their broadest contexts. Bachur (1986) also stresses this point, arguing that considerations of drug use and misuse need to be studied not merely in the context of the individual and family but also more broadly, including informal helpers such as friends and neighbors, local community agencies, and government policy makers.

Cohen (1997) agrees that, of all professional helpers, social workers have the primary responsibility to serve clients as advocates. He restates the rationale that social workers are involved in all phases of psychiatric treatment and are the most highly represented profession in community mental health centers. Concerned about the negative effects of medication, Cohen is skeptical of psychiatry's willingness to address this issue adequately. He states that adherence to the medical model of treatment tends to result in some abuses in somatic intervention. He proposes that social workers as advocates undertake a greater amount of activity with clients in several areas, including knowledge of prior history of drug reactions; identification of negative physical, psychological, and social effects; and provision of oral and written drug information, perhaps independent of the physician.

Social workers need to be aware that empowerment and advocacy efforts with clients and families may lead them to decide to refuse medication or to negotiate extensively with physicians about the types and dosages of medication the client should take. These situations often give rise to value dilemmas for social workers. For example, Bentley (1993) holds that social workers need to support the right of refusal of medication or any other treatment for legal, empirical, and ethical reasons in light of the profession's mandate to respect each client's dignity, worth, and right to self-determination. A family advocate, Rosenson (1993) disagrees, stating that the professional's decision to proceed with appropriate medications even in the face of refusal is in some cases a prerequisite for the client to recover enough to participate in further decision making about treatment. Thus, social workers may find themselves in an ethical bind when clients or physicians choose strategies the social workers do not believe will work. Such issues are discussed in more detail in chapter 7.

Educator

The role of educator is crucial to the social work profession's maintenance of collaboration with clients and families. A major force contributing to the family advocacy movement was a perceived lack of efforts by mental health professionals to help clients and families understand the rationale behind decisions about medication and other interventions (Hatfield, 1981). The uses and actions of medication are complicated and confusing for many professionals as well as the general public, and there continues to be a great need for social workers to address the topic by directly providing educational materials and other information.

With the widespread development of client and family psychoeducational and medication education programs, this area has seen progress (Lefley, 1996; Leff, 1994). So that they can provide basic information about relevant medication issues during individual client interventions, social workers should strive to keep up with all ongoing developments in the field. Bentley and Reeves (1990) have outlined six educational units for social work students. These units can also apply to practicing professionals as areas of continuing education to be shared with clients and families. The topics include public and professional attitudes about psychotropic medication, changing social work roles in psychopharmacology, medication content in psychoeducation, ongoing medication-management techniques, ethical and legal issues in client refusal of medications, and current research and resources.

Further, Bentley, Rosenson, and Zito (1990) specify as educational four of their nine roles for social workers in helping clients adhere to appropriate medication schedules. These roles include educating clients and families about the purposes, actions, and effects of medication; teaching clients and families how to monitor positive and negative effects; teaching skills in problem solving regarding medication; and offering practical suggestions to help clients take medication appropriately. By emphasizing psychosocial themes of adjustment, the educator role complements the kinds of information generally provided to clients by physicians and nurses.

Researcher

A recurring theme in discussions of all role categories is the need for social workers to develop their own literature about issues of psychotropic medication to advance the profession's holistic and collaborative perspectives. For example, Davidson and Jamison (1983) recommend that social workers produce more literature on the potentially negative effects of medications, the impact of medicines on self-control and one's sense of personal responsibility for problem resolution, and the engagement of the hard-to-reach client in a comprehensive treatment program that includes medication. These three areas represent aspects of medication usage that other professions have not adequately addressed but that are consistent with social work's psychosocial theoretical framework. Cohen (1997, 1994) also calls for social workers to write more about specific case studies and to conduct research on the broad range of medication effects, both positive and negative.

Hogarty (1991), who has written extensively about the relationship of medication management to direct social work practice, identifies the potential for social workers to become more productive in research related to mental illness. He points out that there is now broad professional acceptance of the positive effects of the combined interventions of medication, counseling, and psychosocial rehabilitation for persons with serious mental illnesses. However, because researchers often cannot separate medication side effects from clients' outcomes, the optimal effects of various types of social work intervention have not yet been fully tested. Toward resolving this issue, Hogarty points to recent research indicating that low-maintenance dosages of psychotropic drugs sufficiently stabilize the mental status of many clients. That is, social workers are now in a position to conduct research to ascertain the main effects of drugs and psychosocial interventions as well as the interactions of these two types of treatment on clients' outcomes. Through these means they can evaluate the effectiveness of medication in ways that may support more treatment strategies involving low dosages of medication.

Social Worker Roles and Professional Values

The National Association of Social Workers' (1996) Code of Ethics provides guidelines for the professional conduct of all social workers. We believe that our roles for medication management and themes for practice are consistent with the code's six value principles of service: social justice, dignity and worth of the person, the importance of human relationships, integrity, and competence. In particular, our themes are echoed in four of the six ethical principles in the code. We will refer to these practice themes and related ethical principles throughout the book, but we introduce them here.

As the code asserts, in challenging social injustice, social workers "strive to ensure access to needed information, services, and resources (p. 5)." This principle relates to our responsibility to educate clients about available medication resources and to serve as advocates when necessary so that clients receive appropriate resources, even when issues of cost and access seem prohibitive. In respecting the dignity and worth of clients, social workers "seek to resolve conflicts between clients' interests and the broader society's interests in a socially responsible manner (p. 6)." One way this is accomplished is through our active participation with interdisciplinary teams, where we can integrate our medication roles and psychosocial interventions with the activities of physicians, nurses, psychologists, and others, sometimes with an advocacy stance but always in a spirit of collaboration, with a shared goal of constructing the client's best possible service milieu.

In recognizing the central importance of human relationships, social workers "engage people as partners in the helping process (p. 6)." Our notion of the partnership model of practice is a primary theme of this book; it is the subject of chapter 2 and is addressed in every chapter. We believe that collaboration with clients and families as well as with professionals underscores the principle of self-determination. This posture is a hallmark of our profession and a necessary stance with regard to the delicate, complex topic of psychotropic medications. Finally, as social workers practice within their areas of competence, they must "strive to increase their professional knowledge and skills (p. 6)." Because so many of our clients use medications and rely on us for some guidance with that process, we believe that at the absolute minimum social workers should be knowledgeable about the types, actions, purposes, and effects of the medications that their clients use. We also have a responsibility to keep abreast of changes in the field of pharmacology, including new types of medication.

SUMMARY

The purpose of this chapter has been to outline the range of roles that social workers have assumed in their work with clients who take psychotropic medication and to describe their development and contexts. In developing collaborative relationships with clients, families, and professionals, social workers are now involved in all areas of the client's life that impact social functioning. Here we restate the seven roles for social workers discussed in this chapter:

1. the physician's assistant, who echoes and supports the recommendations of the client's physician regarding issues of medication

2. the consultant (with the physician, family, and client), who performs preliminary screenings to determine clients' possible need for medication, makes referrals to physicians, monitors effects for the physician and client,

and regularly consults with physicians and clients on related issues while maintaining a nonadversarial position

3. the counselor, who demonstrates empathy for all concerns of the client and helps him or her make decisions, solve problems, and reach personal goals that are related to psychotropic medication concerns but may be unrelated to other issues of coping with mental illness

4. the advocate, who supports clients' expressed preferences and presents them to others in the mental health service system without necessarily maintaining a nonadversarial position. Advocates may assist clients and their family members with physicians and others to obtain services directly or with administrative or political bodies toward such ends as access to medication, access to funding for medication, or supplementary services related to the use of medication. By substantiating their ideas and feelings as legitimate, the advocate also validates the desires of clients or families to become more involved in their own advocacy efforts.

5. the monitor of medication effects (also one who helps the client cope with those effects), including both positive and negative physical, psychological, and social effects

6. the educator of clients, families, and perhaps other human service providers about broad issues relevant to medication, including actions, benefits, risks, and side effects, always from a social work perspective

7. the researcher, who uses case reports, single-case design methods, or more elaborate designs to document how medications impact the lives of clients and families, how they interact with other interventions, and how collaborative interprofessional relationships can be maintained to achieve coordination of intervention

Which of these roles are utilized and how they are implemented will depend on particular client circumstances as well as the intervention philosophy at the worker's agency. As a means of preparing for such interventions, the social worker should reflect on and be able to articulate responses to the following questions:

1. Why is medication being prescribed for my client?
2. Why is this particular medication being prescribed?
3. What are the specific desired effects of this medication?
4. What is the full range of its possible positive and negative effects?
5. Is there a long range plan regarding my client's use of medication? That is, how will it be determine when the medication will be adjusted or discontinued, whether it is effective or ineffective?
6. What is the client's attitude about taking these medications?
7. What is the client's belief system about how medications work?
8. Do I have a clear role or set of roles in the process of my client's use of the medication? Am I assuming these roles, or have they been articulated by others involved in the client's care?

9. How could my client's use of this medication impact, positively or negatively, on other interventions I am providing?
10. Do I have the opportunity to speak regularly with the physician and other health care providers about the medication?
11. Can the client or family afford this medication?

Barkley et al. (1991) have articulated additional questions for the social worker to consider, questions that are particularly relevant to the interests of both the client and family:

1. If the client is a child, is the medication designed to benefit the child or the child's caregivers?
2. Have the behavioral targets of the medication been clearly communicated to all persons concerned?
3. How will the effects of the medication be monitored? How frequently? By whom?
4. Will the physician be available to the client, family, and other caregivers?
5. Have the risks and benefits of the medication, as well as those of alternate interventions, been assessed and discussed with all relevant parties?
6. Within the family, should someone assume some responsibility for the client's adherence to the recommended dose and schedule?

It falls on social workers to make sure the voices of their clients are heard by all who interact with them. There may be occasions, of course, when social workers' competing values interpretations cause them to take different courses of action with clients, for example in strongly encouraging medication use as a means for clients to meet basic needs and preserving life. Though we will amplify these issues in the next chapter, we want to emphasize here that the social work roles we have discussed are ultimately defined as much by how they are implemented as by their substance.

2

Defining Effective Collaboration

Besides providing the historical context of social work roles in psychopharmacology, we suggest a philosophy of practice for social workers who seek to fulfill these roles successfully. We believe that the key component for achieving this success is effective collaboration—especially with clients and their families but also with other mental health care providers, such as psychiatrists, nurses, and psychologists. Specifically, we offer three key ideas that we believe undergird effective collaboration in mental health and related fields of practice. Social workers must (1) hold fast to a partnership model of practice, (2) maintain a balanced perspective in the face of complex issues related to rights and roles, and (3) work toward the successful integration of psychosocial services with psychopharmacotherapy. All the roles and practice strategies we suggest are built on this foundation.

PRINCIPLES OF A PARTNERSHIP MODEL OF PRACTICE

In a partnership model of practice, the social worker genuinely appreciates both the strengths and the limits of clients and their families, embraces a client-centered perspective, reconceptualizes the helping relationship and demystifies the helping process, redefines the social work role as a resource to clients, and appreciates the perspective of family members. Working toward partnership implies working toward a nonthreatening alliance of companions and a mutual sharing of expertise. Readers will notice that this approach echoes the principles often discussed in relationship to empowerment practice (Lee, 1994; Simon, 1994).

Appreciate Participants' Strengths and Limits

Clinical scholars and researchers at the University of Kansas have developed the "strengths perspective" for social work, a strategy that suggests a complete reorientation of practice toward the individual client's unique strengths and aspirations and away from pathology, symptoms, or weaknesses (Rapp, 1998). In its fullness the perspective goes beyond a minor shift in practice emphasis or a simple reframing of client problems into more positive terms. As Rapp suggests, work with clients should "reek of 'can do'" in every phase of helping because all clients, including those with mental illnesses, can learn, grow, and change.

While Weick, Rapp, Sullivan, and Kisthardt (1989) acknowledge that most social workers are intuitively comfortable with the strengths perspective, they also point to the difficulty many experience in adopting this perspective as their primary orientation. One such difficulty arises from the widespread reliance in the field of mental health on what some would call a pathology-based classification scheme, such as the DSM-IV, for decisions about treatment and reimbursement. Nevertheless, in this book we will openly struggle with how to reorient social work practice toward clients' strengths while still responding when the stated need of clients is to directly reduce problems or so-called deficits.

Appreciating clients' limits is as complex as appreciating their strengths. The key is to avoid automatically defining a client's mental illness, emotional disorder, or resulting handicaps as given limitations (in other words, avoid presuming incompetence or poor judgment). According to Deegan (1992), automatically viewing people with psychiatric problems as irrational, crazy, or unreasonable is fueled by "mentalism" (akin to sexism and racism). Deegan (p. 12) sees this attitude as a "spirit breaking central attitudinal barrier" that leads to a cycle of disempowerment and despair among people with mental illness. By *limits* we mean any existing barriers to progress, such as a lack of skills or inadequate resources. Social workers need to help clients realistically define their own situational limits and personal challenges (both of which may or may not be related to symptomatology), just as they would help identify their clients' unique strengths and assets. Ignoring or underplaying the sometimes severe limits that clients have in social functioning can result in exaggerated and harmful expectations on the part of the social worker. Similarly, ignoring or underplaying strengths can contribute to the depersonalization and demoralization that clients often feel in the mental health system.

Embrace a Client-Centered Practice

The client's perspective should be the "centerpiece" of work. While some see this as a given in social work, others will recognize it as a call to shift their focus away from the practitioner's or the agency's preconceived notions of where clients should be headed and truly "begin where the client is." It means that the agency agenda is *not* the centerpiece of practice and, therefore, dictating the nature and direction of the helping process; it also means the funding source of a program is not the centerpiece and, therefore, defining the goals of helping. Instead, social workers should assist in defining the client's goals in a way that truly emerges from the client's current life situation and desired outcomes, even if the result is some sort of reframing of the purpose of the whole helping endeavor. Knowing what the client really wants to work toward is the most important piece of information you can have. *It* defines the direction and pace of practice. A partnership model, however, does not mean that social workers are passive participants or quasi servants or that the agency context is totally irrelevant. It is not "If a client wants a donut, I will run out and get him a donut"; according to Rapp, "this is no more a partnership than when the professional dictates to the client" (1992, p. 56).

Self-determination is clearly a relevant issue. It has been described as perhaps "the most confounding concept in the intellectual underpinnings of social work" because of its "illusive" and "clouded" nature in real-world practice (Rothman, 1989, p. 598). Rothman describes self-determination as a moral imperative and a useful practice tool that fosters change and growth and reviews the potential limits to self-determination that all people experience, such as economic circumstances, resources, agency roles, values, mandates and pressures, and mental acuity and skill. The controversy then arises as to what extent a client's mental illness affects the clinical actualization of his or her self-determination.

For example, several years ago, Belcher and Ephross (1989) suggested that, at least for the homeless mentally ill, social workers may need to move away from "traditional practice models that view all clients as competent and able to make informed decisions" and instead move toward a more realistic view of the "needs, strengths, limitations, and diversity" of this population (pp. 423–424). On the other hand, Sullivan (1992) insists that mental health clients can know what's best and should be able to express their choice. Similarly, Runyan and Faria (1992) state that "treating clients as essentially normal, capable functioning human beings who happen to have a mental disorder" is the key to empowerment (pp. 40–41).

In fact, as far back as 1963, Soyer argued that the "self-determined aspirations" of the clients should be the focus of practice, even if those aspirations appear unrealistic (p. 77). Soyer offered two provocative reasons to justify the strong stance: (1) the client just might be right, and (2) perhaps only by living life can clients "try, test, and temper" their goals (p. 77). Kisthardt (1992) notes that making the client the "director" of the helping process "breathes new life into the time-honored maxim of self-determination in social work"

(p. 63); it also enhances the control clients have over their own lives (Moxley & Freddolino, 1990).

Rapp (1992) points out that the stated wants of clients do not differ from their needs (and for that matter, they do not seem different from most people's). He says people with mental illness want "a decent place to live and adequate income, friends and opportunities to recreate, an opportunity to contribute (work, family, helping others) and recognition for that contribution" (p. 48). The tendencies of social workers to avoid risks or their desire to save clients from failure, as Soyer (1963) states, too often "dampen rather than fire" the aspirations and desires of clients (p. 78). Mosher and Burti (1992) echo the persistent call for a helping process based on clients' needs as clients perceive them, but they also acknowledge that negotiation and compromise may help temper "completely unrealistic wishes" (p. 12). However, social workers still tend to let clients "self-determine" only when they happen to agree with their clients' decisions or direction. Too often they define their own professional perspective as "truth" and relegate clients' "interior knowledge" (Weick & Pope, 1988, p. 13) of self as unreliable or invalid. In later chapters, we will see how concerns about self-determination and clients' strengths and limitations affect medication management.

Reconceptualize the Client-Clinician Relationship

Many authors have called for a reconceptualization of the client-clinician relationship in psychiatric social work, specifically that clinicians try to reduce the social distance between them and their clients and families (Libassi, 1992), demystify the relationship and process (Rose, 1990), and reconsider power issues (DeChillo, 1993). Saleeby (1992) summarizes the needed reconceptualization as a give and take that begins with the demystification of the professional as expert, an operating sense of humility on the part of the helper, the establishment of an egalitarian transaction, the desire to engage clients on their own terms, and a willingness to disclose and share (p. 42).

With this reconceptualization, social workers seek to redistribute power among themselves, clients, and families and see them as equals in the helping arena. Although the social worker–client relationship clearly has some built-in power differentials arising from education and societal sanctions, Mosher and Burti (1992) suggest that by acknowledging such differentials through open and direct discussion, social workers can minimize them. However, like the models of feminist therapy in the 1970s, the partnership model of social work practice calls for clinicians to go beyond a mere acknowledgment of power issues to the actual redistribution of power. What does this mean in terms of the client's role or the family member's role? The answer is to be a full and active participant in the helping processes based on their own individualized expertise and experience. As long as providers, clients, and families are each seen as experts with rich experiences, unique perspectives, and specialized knowledge, achieving this ideal is realistic.

The social worker may teach the client or family member basic strategies shown over time to be useful in helping people reach their goals, whether this be problem solving, skills training, psychoeducation, cognitive-behavioral techniques, or other psychosocial and environmental interventions. But the client and family also share their own experiences, provide extensive input, generate and weigh options, and make decisions along the way. The social worker may serve to facilitate most of the "structure," while clients and families may provide most of the "content" of helping. Corrigan, Liberman, and Engel (1990) stress that both clinician and client should constantly share information, negotiate, and offer feedback. These activities are no different when addressing issues related to medication management.

The ideal, then, is to bring together the strengths and ideas of the client, the client's family, and the provider to produce the most powerful and productive overall partnership. The client shares her or his experiences and knowledge as an equal participant, offers a perspective that serves as important "data" to be incorporated into every step of the helping process. The role of the client is to make choices and to validate and legitimize the actions of the providers on her or his behalf. Freund (1993) also notes that the shifting roles help clients gain greater "interdependence." In this relationship the clinician helps clients learn through experience and may ask questions that may point to previously unrecognized issues; she or he also continuously highlights the choices available to clients. The social worker adjusts techniques or conditions in the treatment system to insure that it is client-driven.

Tobias notes that just as clients "must grapple with gaining power, social workers must grapple with the loss of power" (1990, p. 359). As Kisthardt (1992) points out, the mutual sharing of power in the client-clinician relationship "is both vexing and liberating" (p. 64). Although social workers may find themselves in the unfamiliar territory of defining roles and boundaries for practice, they will also be freed from the pressure to be something other than their genuine selves (such as the all-knowing, dispassionate expert). Because clients may not be familiar with such ideas about the helping relationship, social workers must model mutuality and partnership, especially in the engagement process. This calls for a dynamic working relationship between the social worker and clients and families that is characterized by mutuality, authenticity, and a sense of being "in process." Partners should constantly seek greater empathy and understanding of each other and work for clearer communication. Rapp (1998) emphasizes that warmth, acceptance, mutual respect, and trust can emerge through a natural evolution of honesty and kept promises.

Conceptualize the Role of the Social Worker as a Resource

The demystification of the helping process and redistribution of power have many implications for the role of the social worker. What is the role of the worker in such a reconceptualization? In the partnership model the essence of the social worker role is simply to be a resource for clients and families. Obviously, social workers are a resource on a number of levels (emotional, strategic, concrete/practical, informational) and in a number of capacities (educator, advocate, researcher, monitor, counselor, consultant). But the bottom line is that social workers are a source of whatever information, support, or "supplies" that are called for to achieve relief or recovery or to reach clients' specific "wants" and goals. The "supplies" we stress in this book are the assessment, planning, and intervention skills and techniques drawn from a problem-solving approach to social work, psychiatric rehabilitation, and clinical case management.

As a resource, the clinician focuses on assessing and clarifying issues to be addressed, teaching new skills, and emphasizing the use of environmental supports and resources. Describing the role of a case manager in mental health, Kisthardt (1992) says she or he should be an advisor, one who provides the "conditions, knowledge, and linkages" needed to address the concerns of the client. Less emphasis is put on the techniques of insight-oriented psychotherapy. Even so, purposeful conversation and reflective discussion are still major aspects of the helping process, not only as the means to establishing relationships, defining goals, and exploring potential strategies of intervention but also as the means to ventilating and sorting out feelings and receiving support and validation.

Interestingly, in terms of being a resource, not only can social workers share what they know, but they may go even further by sharing what they do not know (Everett & Nelson, 1992). That is, when gaps in their own knowledge base become apparent, social workers may share with clients their search for answers in the literature, lectures, or workshops. In this way their clients can see the clinical thought process right before their eyes, further demystifying the helping process.

Appreciate the Family Member's Perspective

Another significant dimension of the partnership model of practice is the clinician's own appreciation of the opinions, thoughts, and beliefs of the client's family members. Specifically, we suggest that the social worker view these as valid and valuable. Just as the client's perspective must be validated, so must that of the family, especially because they often provide expert observations of family interactions and of the client's behavior (Kassis, Boothroyd, & Ben-Dror, 1992). But on an even more basic level, we know that listening to the stories of family members—and we would add clients—even repeatedly, will deepen relationships among all participants. Thus, the partnership model involves the client's family in the helping process to the extent possible, given the client's desires.

DeChillo's study (1993) of collaboration among 14 social workers and families of 102 psychiatric clients in New York City found that the most significant variable related to the extent of social workers' collaboration was their attitudes toward family involvement in treatment and care. Similarly, in a recent study, Johnson found positive attitudes towards families of children with mental and emotional disabilities and the new expectation around open sharing and partnership. If social workers believed that medication was helpful, there was a positive correlation with a friendly perspective about families. Unfortunately, the authors noted that a substantial minority of social workers still held negative parent-blaming views of mental and emotional disorders in children (Johnson, Renaud, Schmidt & Stanek, 1998).

Spaniol, Zipple, and Fitzgerald (1984) suggest 15 ways professionals might share power with families, including many of the ideas already discussed in this chapter, such as clinicians' acknowledging their own limits and pointing to family strengths. The core notion is that families be viewed as "collaborative adjuncts" to the rehabilitation process (p. 80). Similarly, DeChillo (1993) offers six components of family collaboration that include recognizing the family as a key resource, involving the family in goal formulation, and providing education and practical advice about coping with mental illness.

However, in spite of a recent marked improvement in the clinician's view of families, the positive potential for family involvement is yet unrealized. Interestingly, in his study of collaboration between social workers and families of people with mental illness, DeChillo (1993) found that both the social workers and the family members surveyed rated the other group lower on perceived level of collaboration than either group rated themselves. One of two things seems to have occurred. Either both the social workers and the families exaggerated their own level of collaboration, or they both failed to recognize the actual level of collaboration in the other group. Other surveys have shown that families are dissatisfied with their level of participation in decision making and often feel their opinions are not valued (Cournoyer & Johnson, 1991). Interestingly, a follow-up satisfaction-with-services survey of 57 family members of people with mental illness showed that the amount of education about medication issues (or lack thereof) was one of the greatest areas of dissatisfaction (Solomon & Marcenko, 1992).

At the same time, the most recent research shows that families can successfully participate in the care of their relative in ways not thought of only a few years ago. For example, one study in the field of aging shows that family members can be trained to be case managers without increasing the amount of subjective burden they feel or changing the amount of contact with their relative (Seltzer, Litchfield, Kapust, & Mayer, 1992). Social workers in this project provided consultation and information to families to help them deal with inevitable obstacles in carrying out their tasks.

MAINTAINING A BALANCED PERSPECTIVE

A second strategy that undergirds effective collaboration with clients who take psychotropic medication, their families, and mental health providers is cultivating a balanced perspective in the face of complex issues related to clients' rights and professional roles. Specifically, social workers must maintain a proper balance among the rights of individual clients, their families, and society; between the costs and benefits of using psychotropic medication; and between the social worker's role in medication management and the legitimacy and uniqueness of other helping professions.

Rights of Individual, Family, and Society

The entire court system could be described as an attempt to establish an impartial mechanism to decide the distribution of rights between individuals and society. Determining the appropriate balance between these interests becomes more difficult when the individual has a mental illness or an emotional disorder. Although clients' rights issues gained attention in the 1970s with landmark court battles and passage of a client bill of rights, the struggle for balance is still seen in debates about such issues as involuntary commitment and the right to refuse treatment. Today's constriction of clients' rights seems to be related to many mental health providers' continued presumption that clients are incompetent and to the "bureaucratic paternalism" that too often characterizes the mental health system (Bentley, 1991; Winslade, 1981). That is, mental illness and involuntary hospitalization are often seen as synonymous with incompetence. Such attitudes can lead mental health professionals to make inappropriate decisions on behalf of clients and undermine their basic right to self-determination.

At the same time, while the enhanced involvement of families in recent years has been welcomed by all who embrace a partnership model, it has raised some important questions related to the appropriate role of families in clinical decision making. What does client confidentiality really mean in light of the care-giving family's "need to know"? What voice should family members have when it comes to clinical treatment decisions? As families have pointed out, their lives can be dramatically impacted by the choices clients make. Indeed, an entire body of literature exists about the family's burden of such caregiving. This literature speaks to the frustration, anger, grief, and pain that many families experience as they try to cope with mental illness in their loved ones. Trained to understand the systemic effects of individual choices, social workers must recognize the family's rights to pursue their ideas of what is their own and their loved one's "best interest."

However, the rights of clients, families, and society can and do clash, especially regarding medication management. Social workers can be caught between their desire to collaborate with families and their ethical and legal obligation to honor the decisions and confidence of their clients. Zipple et al. (Zipple, Langle, Spaniol, & Fisher, 1990) offer several helpful strategies for resolving such conflicts, such as sharing nonconfidential information with families, providing them with written information when appropriate, referring them to educational groups in the community, using release-of-information procedures, and, when necessary, using mediators. While it is true that in social work the client's rights hold the preeminent position, effective collaboration is achieved by trying to balance the rights of all who have a stake in the process. Establishing a partnership model of practice is an important factor. While social workers' obligation to hold the client's well-being in highest regard is clear, their obligations to themselves, their agency, and society are also recognized (National Association of Social Workers [NASW], 1997).

Costs Versus Benefits of Medications

Bentley and Reeves (1992) argue that "research on the efficacy of psychotropic medication as a therapeutic intervention . . . has affirmed their role as an important aspect of treatment" (p. 41). Bentley (1993) also argues that social workers should stand for balance and common sense. That is, while acknowledging the significant contribution that psychotropic drugs can make toward reducing symptoms and improving the quality of life for many people, social workers should not ignore the disturbing side effects of medications or the sociopolitical aspects of their use.

Relying on both scientific and historical analysis, Valenstein (1998) strongly advocates increased attention to the adverse effects of psychiatric drugs and makes a persuasive case that a more critical perspective is needed to fully grasp the social and psychological implications of the use of medications in mental health treatment. He exposes what he believes to be erroneous assumptions made about the causes of mental illnesses and the exaggerated claims regarding the effectiveness of drug treatments.

These arguments echo the earlier work of David Cohen in our own field of social work. In his seminal review of the history of social work and drug treatments, Cohen (1988) urges social workers to avoid repeating the failures of the past, when social workers either ignored or rationalized the negative effects of shock treatments on their clients. Therefore, Cohen asserts, social workers inappropriately aligned themselves with the psychiatric establishment rather than listening to their clients, and he warns that the same thing may happen today with psychotropic drug treatments.

For decades others in this field (Davidson & Jamison, 1983; McCollum et al., 1978) have suggested that social workers should pay more attention to not only the negative physical effects of these medications but also their negative psychological and social effects. These latter effects include the overuse of medications, their use for social control, and their potential to reinforce a negative sense of self. Gerhart and Brooks (1983) also urge social workers to be aware of the "seriously substandard" administration of antipsychotics in hospitals and community mental health centers (p. 454).

Responding specifically to Cohen's (1988) essay, Johnson (1989, p. 659) critiques what she believes is his overstatement of the risks of psychotropic medications, calling for a fuller evaluation of both the risks and benefits of drug treatment and the "wrenching dilemmas" that practitioners and clients face in this area. We also have some disagreement with Cohen (1988). For example, we do not believe that social workers should avoid encouraging psychotropic drugs merely because they have side effects or because they bring up issues of authority and coercion. As Jamison and Davidson (1983) state, psychotropic drugs are a "mixed blessing" (p. 140) and should be cautiously accepted as an ethical, humane alternative to deterioration. As Bentley (1993) states, "When medications are used properly, most clients are helped, families are relieved, and hospital stays are shortened" (p. 104). On the other hand, many authors (e.g., Brown, 1985; Cohen & McCubbin, 1990) caution that the renewed interest in psychiatric drugs is most likely related to the medical profession's desire to remain dominant in the field and for drug companies to reap healthy profits. Clearly such factors as the economic and sociopolitical aspects of prescription practices, drug-research budgets, managed care, and insurance reimbursements must be faced head on.

For example, we are just starting to learn more about influences on prescription-writing practices. It is no surprise to learn that informal contacts of physicians with their colleagues are a large influence, as are the image-building efforts of pharmaceutical companies regarding certain medications (Bond & Lader, 1996). In addition, a particular client's expectations and demands in a clinical encounter are very important, and her or his knowledge of the existence of alternative helping strategies (self-help, counseling) also influences prescription practices.

Expanded Roles with Regard to Related Professions

To maintain a balanced perspective of their role, social workers need to better understand the unique contributions that professionals in fields such as nursing, psychology, and psychiatry, and even nonprofessionals such as folk healers bring to client care. Social workers need to define what is unique about their own professional perspective, what is shared with related disciplines, and what falls outside their purview. As we will demonstrate later, this is a great historical challenge in and of itself. It is even more interesting in an area so closely identified with other professions—psychopharmacology.

The benefits of interdisciplinary collaboration are well articulated. For example, Sands (1989) notes that such collaboration "helps us arrive at a comprehensive understanding of the client [and] solve complex problems" (p. 1). Similarly, in their classic article Toseland, Zaneles-Palmer, and Chapman, (1986) note how teamwork improves services to the client as well as work satisfaction for professionals.

In mental health, social workers have tended to play key roles on interdisciplinary teams. In the Toseland et al. (1986) survey of 71 team members from 7 disciplines, social workers were reported as having a high degree of influence, second only to psychiatrists. Further, it showed that social workers tended to play a wide range of roles, including some that overlapped with other professions. Interestingly, there were strong differences of opinion among the team members in two areas: (1) whether or not team members ought to have equal power, and (2) whether there ought to be a clear differentiation of roles among the professions.

Claims of a unique perspective and expectations about roles may be inter-related. For example, social workers often refer to their unique "holistic perspective" as their profession's strength (Dane & Simon, 1991). However, nurses have also cited a "holistic perspective" as a key distinguishing aspect of their profession. One survey of physicians found that they perceived hospital social workers as having a limited understanding of clients' psychosocial problems and as performing only as discharge planners who arrange for concrete services (Pray, 1991). A large-scale survey of social workers, physicians, and nurses in a medical setting (Cowles & Lefcowitz, 1992) found disagreements among the three regarding professional roles. Unfortunately, other professionals did not think social workers had the ability to assess emotional problems. Overall, however, differences in the way roles were perceived related less to what social workers did than to what they did that was their exclusive domain.

Thus, though social workers see themselves as highly trained and knowledgeable clinicians, they constantly face having to explain and demonstrate who they are, often making a case for their indispensability, especially when in settings not dominated by social workers (Dane and Simon, 1992; Mailick & Jordan, 1977). Because often what they do is influenced by other professions who don't fully understand them, social workers have noted a discrepancy between what they can do, want to do, or were trained to do, and what they actually do (Harrison, Drolen, & Atherton, 1989). For example, Pray (1991) notes that the gatekeeping function of physicians and psychiatrists subtly defines what is deemed an appropriate role for social workers.

Dane and Simon (1991) relate this continued misunderstanding in part to the devaluing of women's work, because women constitute a large majority of social workers. They also note the divergent missions and training of other mental health professions, as well as the poorly defined and stressful roles that exist in many settings. In an analysis of the sources of strain between social workers and physicians, Mizrahi and Abramson (1985) provide insight into the social worker's long-standing struggle to be understood. Specifically, they note that physician training stresses hard science knowledge, puts little emphasis on the clinical relationship, and offers little opportunity for them to process their feelings. They also state that physicians are socialized to be the autonomous decision makers and authority figures. In stark contrast to social work training, which emphasizes values, relationship, and "process," the training and socialization of physicians leads to differing perspectives in a number of important areas, such as the role and rights of clients/families and the role and function of social work. Similarly, Mailick and Jordan (1977) note how differences among professional knowledge, values, and methods of communication influence collaboration.

Clearly, more training in interprofessional collaboration is needed. Weil (1982) suggests that social workers consider the barriers to collaborative relationships and openly address differences in socialization and status. Avoiding stereotypes is also crucial to prevent negative attitudes toward other professions. Greater interdisciplinary collaboration begins with mutual respect and mandates the bold confrontation of misperceptions and ignorance (Gibelman, 1993). Mailick and Ashley (1981) summarize this view:

> Of utmost importance in working with a collaborative group is the capacity to listen, to be respectful, to understand the implications of other professional opinions, to be willing to recognize and accept areas in which the expertise of colleagues is unique, and to defer to special knowledge when appropriate. (p. 135)

INTEGRATING PSYCHOSOCIAL INTERVENTIONS AND PSYCHOPHARMACOLOGY

A third strategy that undergirds effective collaboration with mental health clients, families, and providers is the successful integration of psychosocial interventions with psychopharmacotherapy. Social workers need not only to recognize the intrinsic power of combined treatments but also to appreciate the ideological and practical challenges that emerge, especially in managing parallel treatment (in which one professional provides psychosocial treatment at the same time that a physician provides medical treatment to the same client).

Gerard Hogarty, a social worker who has devoted much of his career to understanding the interactions between psychotropic drug use and psychosocial treatments among people with schizophrenia, concludes that the most powerful treatment is a combination of medication and psychosocial treatments and that the effects of each seem to contribute to the other's effectiveness—in other words, they are additive. For example, Hogarty and Ulrich (1998) noted that well-supported and conceptualized psychosocial treatment can reduce relapse rates by 50%. Many others have reached similar conclusions about the worth of psychosocial interventions. Beitman and Klerman (1991) show that either solid empirical research or decades of clinical experience support combining treatments in persons diagnosed with such mental illnesses as depression, panic, agoraphobia, obsessive-compulsive disorder, generalized anxiety disorder, anorexia, schizophrenia, and borderline personality disorder. Nonetheless, even though social workers know that it is productive to offer both kinds of treatments to clients, clients too often are not afforded the opportunity.

Competing Ideologies

One important barrier to combining treatments is the ideological conflict stemming from certain schools of thought. For example, those trained in psychoanalytic, interpersonal, or behavioral techniques may place less emphasis on medication than on psychosocial treatment. Those trained in biological psychiatry, on the other hand, place tremendous emphasis on pharmacology.

Thus, some professionals conclude that medication merely covers up symptoms and avoids the "real" issue, while others deride psychosocial interventions as "psychobabble" or "soft." Some assert that this split reflects the historical separation of body and mind (Bradley, 1990). Saleeby (1985) speculates that the lack of biological content in social work curriculums is related to professional suspicions about the medical model. He suggests that, rather than allowing biological content to narrow their perspective and contribute to reductionist thinking, social workers should see how knowledge about human biology and medication allows them to be more holistic. Others have called for a similar integration of biology and psychology in mental health. For example, in describing the treatment of people with bipolar disorder, Jamison and Akiskal (1983) write,

> Although biologic variables underlie the etiology of this disorder, its primary manifestations are behavioral and psychological, with profound changes in perceptions, attitudes, personality, mood and cognition. Psychological interventions can be of unique value to the client. (p. 185)

Similarly, Hoffman (1990) pleads with readers to reject the "two-track" model of treating depression, in which persons receive treatment as if they have two distinct disorders, biological depression (treated with medication) and psychological depression (treated with psychotherapy). He calls for a "unitary approach" that recognizes the complexities of treating disorders that have both biological and psychological components. "We have to take care to keep both the baby and the bath water in the same tub" (p. 371). Since social workers cannot prescribe medication or medically monitor its therapeutic effects, working toward an integrated approach means working toward open and productive partnerships with physicians and the effective management of parallel treatment.

Managing Parallel Treatment

A number of dynamics that deserve attention come up in the management of the relationships among client, prescriber, and social worker. These dynamics include referring a client to a prescribing physician, accepting client referrals from physicians, and managing the co-responsibility for the client's treatment.

Kanter (1989) has written extensively on the clinical case manager's role in collaborating with physicians, especially in maintaining effective medication regimens. A number of other authors have also commented on the increased frequency and need for so-called three-party treatment relationships. Pilette (1988), for example, attributes this rise to the expansion of the private practice marketplace and the increasing access of social workers and psychologists to insurance reimbursement, among other things. Historically, community mental health centers and HMOs have relied on nonmedical professionals to provide psychosocial treatment and on physicians to provide drug consultation. While the client may benefit from the respective strengths of each clinician, and the providers may benefit from covering all the clinical bases, the problems inherent to the arrangement raise many difficult questions.

For instance, who has the ultimate authority over and responsibility for the client's treatment? How will disagreements be handled? Who will decide about major changes in treatment? Questions about confidentiality (How much sharing is too much?) also arise. Bradley (1990) contends that the client's "entry route" is an important factor in answering those questions, that is, how the client came to the three-party relationship. Was she or he a client of a psychiatrist who referred the individual to a social worker, or vice versa?

Goldberg, Riba, and Tasman (1991) examine psychiatrists' attitudes toward prescribing medications for persons being treated by nonmedical psychotherapists. In this study, of the 60 respondents who prescribed such medication, 73% worked with master's-level social workers (MSWs). Three-fourths of the medication services were initiated by the nonmedical provider. Over two-thirds of the psychiatrists were satisfied with their current level of involvement in the cases; in fact, 25% said they wished they did less with clients, whereas 8% wished they did more. Interestingly, one of the concerns that psychiatrists raised most often was their need to know more clearly how they were to be available after hours or for emergencies.

Kelly (1992) advises pharmacotherapists (physicians, psychiatrists) to work only with people they know and trust and to make it clear they are not just a medication dispenser but a consultant. Kelly says the pharmacotherapist should consider the psychotherapist to be a responsible professional and a reliable informant but "not a medical colleague, supervisee or competitor" (p. 779). According to Kelly, the psychotherapist should also use a pharmacotherapist who appreciates the complexity of parallel treatment and considers herself or himself as a consultant, not a cotherapist or competitor.

Cathie Gray (1998), a social worker who has shared her own joys and struggles of collaborating with psychiatrists about medication, uses a line, a triangle, and a circle as symbols of her personal reflections. The line represents the hierarchies that exist in three-party arrangements, especially with respect to the "who's in charge" question. She jokingly confides that sometimes when things are going well, she is more than willing to see herself as responsible and "in charge," but when things are not, she figures it is easy to conclude it must be the medicating physician's responsibility! When thinking about the triangle, which represents the client, herself, and the physician, she says that she sometimes questions who is really the "third party," and frequently wonders about how to best manage information sharing. The circle is a metaphor for the interconnectedness of all the relationships among providers and the client and the recognition that when all the lines and triangles are removed, we are all are working toward the same goal in collaboration.

Also in collaborating with other providers, clinicians need to be aware of the potential influence that psychosocial treatment and medication can have on each other. For example, while psychosocial treatments may actually help a client adhere to a medication regimen, medication may in turn help clients become more cognitively or emotionally "ready" for psychosocial treatment.

Though medication may heighten the client's confidence in treatment on the one hand, it may also encourage magical thinking, increase the dependency on the clinician, decrease motivation for psychosocial treatment, or somehow derail progress (Bond & Laden, 1996).

In addition, both clinicians should be aware of transference and counter-transference issues that emerge in the three-party relationships. According to Bradley, these issues can emerge from the client, the psychotherapist, and the pharmacotherapist. Positive transference occurs with the client when she or he views medication as a nurturing act, a "gift-giving acknowledgment of pain" (Bradley, 1990, p. 314). It can symbolize for the client a form of feeding and serve as proof of both clinicians' empathy. On the other hand, the addition of a second therapist can be experienced as either "narcissistic injury" ("I must be sicker than I thought") or evidence of a lack of interest or competence on the part of the referring clinician.

Clinicians demonstrate countertransference when making referrals if they distance themselves from clients by devaluing their skills or investment in the client's case. Countertransference also occurs when clinicians interpret receiving a referral as an indication of their secondary status (Bradley, 1990). When making referrals to physicians, clinicians must face their own discomfort about exposing their work to another, while the physicians who get the referrals have to deal with sharing power and avoiding competition (Busch & Gould, 1993). Likewise, physicians must avoid being the "all-knowing doctor" or letting clients idealize them, thus devaluing the clients' psychosocial treatment. Interestingly, while stressing collaboration and frequent communication between the nonmedical provider and the physician, several authors warn against the collaboration becoming *too* close, making role distinctions unclear or skewing appropriate differences in approaches (Busch & Gould, 1993; Kelly, 1992).

Our suggested foundation of partnership, balance, and integration has implications for how and when social workers make referrals to physicians. For example, it seems reasonable to consider referral whenever a client experiences symptoms for which there are known useful drug treatments. This is particularly true when the client has only partially responded to psychosocial interventions. In deciding the timing of the referral, social workers must consider the severity of the client's symptoms and the extent to which the client's life is disrupted. New research, on the initiation of antipsychotic medication in particular, showed that a failure to start medication early on was associated with an overall poorer treatment response over the long haul (Haas, Garratt & Sweeney, 1998).

It is important to remember that any referral a social worker makes to a physician is really a referral for an evaluation of *possible* treatment with psychotropic medication. Therefore, any discussion with clients about such a referral should begin with an overview of what to expect in the evaluation process, including a review of the pros and cons of merely seeking an evaluation. However, clients will probably also want to discuss what they will do if either offered or denied a prescription. The social worker should therefore share basic knowledge about the costs and benefits of medication in keeping with their clients' particular concerns and circumstances, including any known potential interactive or additive effects with psychosocial treatments. Social workers should use all their clinical skills to help clients practically and emotionally manage decisions to seek a physician's evaluation and treatment, and to do so in a spirit of cautious optimism. After the medical evaluation, the client and social worker will continue to address client reactions and responses on a number of levels (see chapters 1, 7, and 8).

Because few studies exist about the referral process in social work and psychopharmacology, not much is known about it. Littrell and Ashford (1994) have examined the impact of treatment setting on the medication referral practices of social work field instructors and have found that in cases of major depression, the field of practice setting did not affect the sense of obligation to refer. On the other hand, with clients whose symptoms were less severe, those in mental health settings were more likely to make referrals than those in family service settings. How long clients had been in treatment had no effect on the obligation to refer. Perhaps one of the biggest contributions that Littrell and Ashford make is to raise this question: "Are social workers legally and ethically culpable should they fail to raise the possibility of medication referral?" (p. 123). We will revisit this question in the last chapter.

Research into the practices of managed care companies may give us more information about how parallel treatment is working or how referrals should work. This research may also intensify the turf battles that already are taking place. For example, one recent study showed that while social workers accounted for 20% of the claims in one managed care company (not counting psychosocial support services), 79% of clients saw only one provider. Psychiatrists tended to see more severely disabled clients (Sturm & Klap, 1999). This data, however, was presented as a way to allay fears that nonmedical providers are "taking over" behavioral health care. Another article acknowledged that when brief psychotherapy was called for, social workers did provide the least expensive care; however, the authors also argued that three-party arrangements represented "fragmented" services and implied that care by nonphysicians was poor (Dewan, 1999).

Bradley provides a fitting end to the discussion here:

> To reduce the potential for rivalry, fear, anxiety, idealization, devaluation and splitting, both clinicians must appreciate the power of interpersonal dynamics in any triadic relationship but also resolve themselves the ideological conflicts that have been inherent in the medication versus psychotherapy debate. (1990, p. 310)

SUMMARY

To summarize, we envision a collaborative helping process in which clients, families, social workers, and other providers are busy and involved, with their relationships characterized by honesty, genuineness, and warmth and their work clearly action-oriented. We envision social workers with a critical perspective on medication use in society but also with an appreciation of the power of integrated treatment to improve the quality of lives of people with mental illness and emotional distress. Finally, we recognize the special challenges inherent in the collaboration between a physician, who prescribes medication, and a social worker, who provides psychosocial interventions and supports. Collaborations characterized by equality, flexibility, decreased professional control, mutual understanding, and shared goals (Stewart, Banks, Crosson, & Poel, 1995) are likely to be at the heart of productive partnerships.

PART II

❖

A Primer on Psychopharmacology

Chapter 3

Basic Principles: Neurotransmission, Pharmacokinetics, and Pharmacodynamics

Chapter 4

Specific Medications for Specific Disorders

Chapter 5

Intervention Concerns with Special Populations

3

✛

Basic Principles: Neurotransmission, Pharmacokinetics, and Pharmacodynamics

S ocial workers often have limited interest in the details of psychopharmacology—indeed, it can make for esoteric reading. Still, a basic knowledge of the chemical processes associated with medications is essential for social workers whose clients use such drugs. Only with this knowledge can the social worker comprehend the nature and significance of changes in the client's physical and mental status and understand the physician's rationales for dosage and administration. When a client describes or demonstrates the effects of medications, positive or negative, these must be interpreted in terms of their pharmacology. This knowledge directly applies to the social worker/client relationship in four areas.

1. Understanding the effectiveness of medications in symptom reduction
2. Monitoring adverse effects, including the medication's physical, psychological, and social consequences
3. Educating clients and families about the course of physical and psychological adjustment to medications
4. Communicating with physicians, pharmacists, nurses, and others about the present and potential effects of medicine

The social worker's understanding of medication cannot be considered complete if he or she is aware only of its effects on thinking and mood. To promote a safe and effective drug regimen and to inform clients fully, social workers must also know the causes of the biological and psychological changes leading to symptom relief.

In this chapter, we introduce you to the central nervous system and the basic principles of *psychopharmacology* (defined as the study of drugs that affect a person's thinking, emotions, and behaviors). We describe the structure of the brain and nervous system; the properties of neurons and receptors; the processes by which the human body handles psychotropic drugs; and the effects of drugs on body chemistry. We also introduce some general information about the actions of antipsychotic, antidepressant, mood-stabilizing, anti-anxiety, and psychostimulant medications, although we discuss these more fully in chapter 4. We conclude with a careful review of the adverse effects that these medications can produce in consumers. So that the reader can grasp the rationale for medication treatment in a logical, holistic way, we have ordered chapter topics from the most general (nervous system) to the most specific (types of drugs).

The primary sources we used to research this material include Bernstein (1995), Julien (1998), Kaplan and Sadock (1998), Schatzberg and Nemeroff (1995), Skolnick (1997), and Stahl (1996).

THE CENTRAL NERVOUS SYSTEM

The social work profession's person-in-environment perspective promotes the worker's focus on transactions within and among systems at all levels (micro through macro). To maintain this perspective, the social worker must acquire and assess broad sources of information about social phenomena. Though no social system can begin to approximate the nervous system's elegance and mystery, a systems perspective will help you appreciate the complexity of the central nervous system's structure and processes. It is a massive and astoundingly intricate information-processing unit consisting of 100 billion nerve cells and even more connectors between these cells. Because psychotropic medications act on the nervous system, an awareness of its geography is an appropriate starting point for understanding how these drugs work. However, much remains to be discovered about the specific biological processes within the nervous system. Its complexity should remind the social worker that, in spite of great gains made each year in knowledge about the human body, scientists have just begun to grasp the nature of routine system processes and the impact of drugs on them.

THE BRAIN AND NERVOUS SYSTEM

The brain consists of nerve cells, glial cells, and blood vessels. Though *nerve cells*, also called *neurons*, carry out all the brain's functions, they make up only a fraction of its weight. *Glial cells*, which surround the neurons and outnumber them by a 10 to 1 ratio, have the sole function of providing an extensive supporting environment as their source of nourishment and a system for carrying away waste products. The brain is richly supplied with an intricate system of tiny *blood vessels*. Though it makes up only 2% of the body's weight, the brain receives 15% of its blood supply.

All human behaviors, including thoughts and emotions, are the result of neural activity, with changes in such behavior prompted by changes in brain chemistry. Chemical processes in the brain are influenced by a range of factors originating both inside and outside the body. For instance, the simple act of greeting a client in the agency's waiting room sets off a complex chain, or pathway, of cellular activities by which the social worker's nervous system interprets verbal and nonverbal messages from the client and initiates responses. A *pathway* is a series of interconnecting neurons working together for some coordinated purpose. Conversations with friends, practice interventions, or psychotropic medications are all prompts for chemical activities within and among neurons, activities that cause emotional or behavioral changes.

However, a strictly neurobiological perspective does not assume a purely materialist view of human functioning. Human behavior is always caused by transactions among biological, psychological, social, and even spiritual systems. In fact, biological science remains unclear about many basic processes in brain functioning. Why do people react with strong emotion to a beautiful sunset, work of art, or piece of music? What determines their methods of solving interpersonal problems? How do they come to develop their personal values or decide on ultimate life goals? While the nervous system is highly interactive with the environment, the means by which thoughts, feelings, and behaviors are mediated by the various sources of stimuli is unclear. Whatever your assumptions about identity, will, spirituality, or nature vs. nurture as the source of personality, we only wish to emphasize that all human experiences are accompanied by nervous system activities.

The basic function of the brain is to receive information from the outside world, use this information to decide on responsive courses of action, and implement these decisions with commands to various muscles and glands. Though the brain can be divided into sections to differentiate its many activities, its processes are highly interconnected. The brain is generally conceived of as having three sections: hindbrain, midbrain, and forebrain (see Figure 1).

The *hindbrain* consists of the brain stem (including the reticular formation), cerebellum, and pons. Located at the base of the brain, the *brain stem* links the brain with the spinal cord. It is the oldest area of the brain, appearing prior to the evolution of mammals. The brain stem is primarily occupied with the maintenance of involuntary life support functions. It consists of several subsections. At its base, the *medulla oblongata* regulates vital functions, including arousal, heartbeat, respiration, blood flow, muscle tone, and movement of the stomach and intestines. The *pons*, located just under the midbrain, links various areas of the brain with each other and the central nervous system. At the center of the brain stem and traveling its full length is a core of neural tissue known as the *reticular formation*. Nerve fibers from this system extend down the spinal cord and control the position and tension of muscles. The *cerebellum*, located behind the brain stem, receives information from

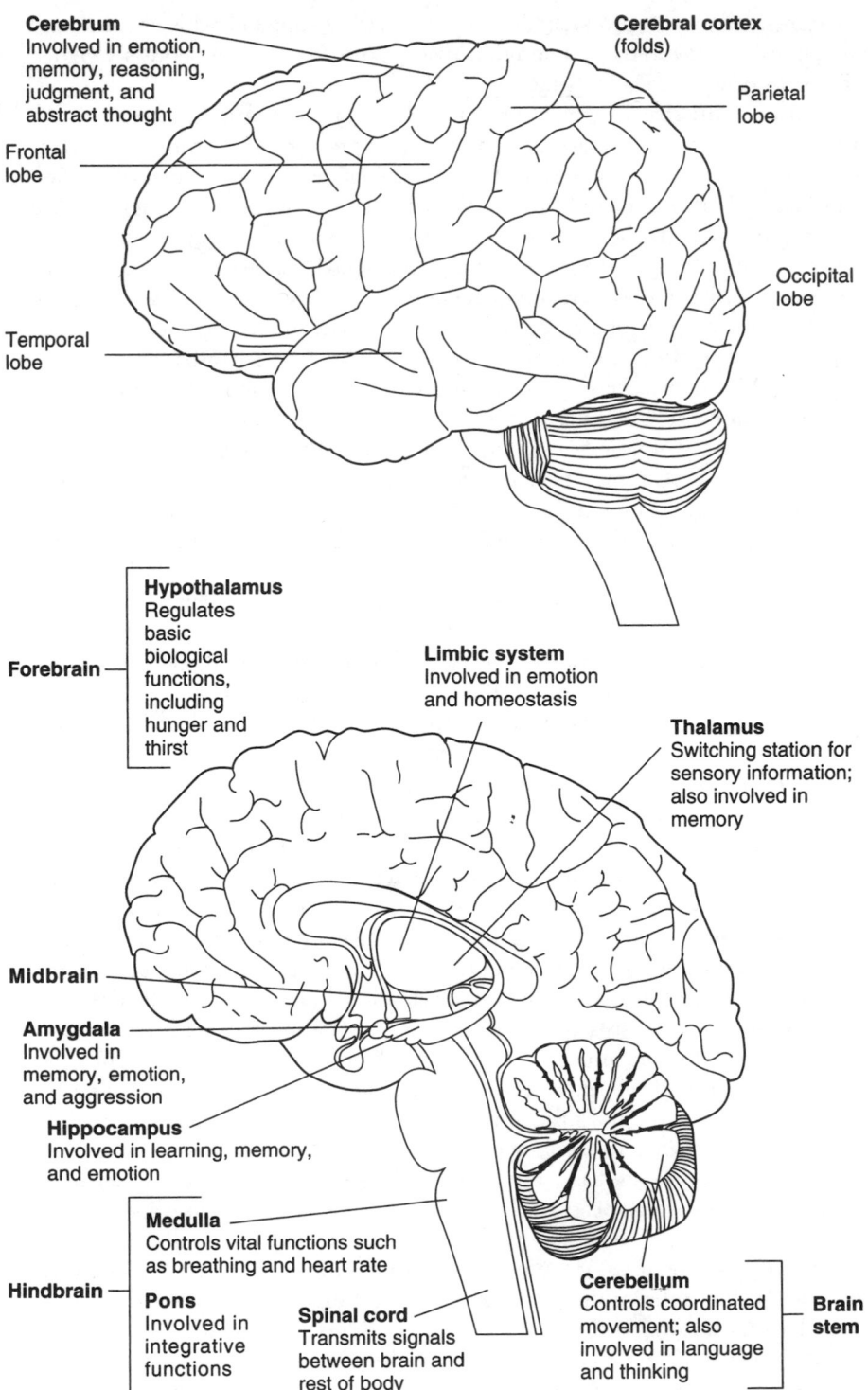

the muscles and joints, the organs of balance, the skin, and the eyes and ears. The cerebellum controls bodily functions operating below the level of consciousness, including posture, balance, and movement through space. Memory for certain kinds of simple learned responses may be stored there as well. Though the hindbrain does not include any targeted sites of action for psychotropic medications, some drugs do affect activities there, producing adverse effects.

The *midbrain* is located just above the brain stem. Though small, it represents a second level of brain evolution, more advanced than the hindbrain. The midbrain monitors and integrates various sensory functions and serves as a center of visual and auditory stimulation. On the upper surface of the midbrain, collections of cells relay specific information from sense organs to higher levels of the brain.

The *forebrain* is the largest section of the brain and consists of many specialized areas. Comprising a group of cell structures in the center of the brain, above the brain stem, the *limbic system* is a center of activities that create emotions. Thus, many psychotropic medications are targeted at neurons in this system. The limbic system also maintains the body's homeostasis, a concept from systems theory that should be familiar to social workers and that refers here to the constancy and stability of the body's physiological functioning. The limbic system permits people to adjust their internal states to maintain a constant climate in spite of external conditions, such as extreme heat and cold. It regulates such functions as body temperature, blood pressure, heart rate, and blood-sugar levels.

A major component of the limbic system, the *hypothalamus* is a relay station for internal regulatory systems, monitoring information coming from the autonomic nervous system and influencing the body's behavior through those pathways. The hypothalamus produces *neurohormones*, or chemicals manufactured in the brain, as one means of maintaining the body's homeostasis. Specialized neurons release neurohormones into surrounding capillaries, where the blood transports them into the pituitary gland. From this "master gland," or regulatory site, the neurohormones are eventually carried to target cells to regulate such things as temperature, balance, and appetite. Neurohormones also influence motivation, sexual arousal, eating and drinking, sleeping, waking, certain chemical balances, and emotions important to survival.

The limbic system includes other activity centers. The *thalamus*, a mass of gray matter located near the center of the forebrain, relays sensory information from the body to the brain. Because all sensory fibers extending into the cortex must first pass through it, the thalamus is a major integrating center. It helps initiate consciousness and makes preliminary classifications of external information. The *hippocampus*, an important center of learning, converts information from short-term to long-term memory. The *basal ganglia*, located on both sides of the limbic system, connect the cerebral cortex to other parts of the brain and help regulate skeletal muscle movements. Like the cerebellum, these nerve fibers are concerned with movement and control, particularly the initiation of movements. When the basal ganglia are unintentionally affected by certain psychotropic medications, adverse side effects result. This is the site at which dopamine is depleted in Parkinson's disease and one of the sites at which stimulant drugs act.

The *cerebrum is* the largest portion of the human brain and facilitates its highest intellectual functions. The center of emotion, memory, reasoning, abstract thought, and judgment, the cerebrum integrates highly diverse brain activities. It allows us to organize, remember, communicate, understand, appreciate, and create. The cerebrum is divided into two halves, each of which controls the opposite side of the body. On the surface of each hemisphere is an intricately folded layer of nerve cells known as the cerebral cortex. Characterized visually by its many folds, the cortex is an evolutionary product that enables humans to accommodate a much larger surface area than their skull size would otherwise allow.

The *cortex* is composed of four sets of lobes, each with distinct functions. The largest are the *frontal lobes*, which govern personality, emotion, reasoning and learning, and speech. The primary function of these lobes is motor (muscle) control, including fine motor control (coordinated small muscle movements, such as in the fingers), gross motor control (large muscles, such as those in the thigh), control of eye movements, motor aspects of speech, and motor learning and planning. The frontal lobes are also involved in decision making and purposeful behavior. The *temporal lobes* affect gross motor skills and the integration of sensory input. Their functions include hearing, perception, and the storage of memory. The *parietal lobes*, centers of long-term memory and information processing, receive sensory information from the body. Finally, the *occipital lobes* are entirely devoted to processing visual input.

The *spinal cord*, which runs from the brain stem to the base of the spine, is a part of the central nervous system but is also associated with two other systems. First, the *autonomic nervous system* (autonomic means, somewhat misleadingly, autonomous or independent) consists of neuron chains that extend from the medulla oblongata and spinal cord into the body's organs. These neurons regulate the unconscious and involuntary activities of the internal organs and blood vessels. The autonomic system includes two subsystems. The *sympathetic system* functions during the expenditure of energy, and the *parasympathetic system* is more prominent in the body's buildup of energy reserves. For example, the sympathetic system acts to speed up one's heart rate during exercise, and the parasympathetic system slows it down during rest. Because the autonomic nervous system's site of integration is the hypothalamus, this system is affected by some psychotropic medications.

Second, the *peripheral nervous system* consists of neurons that branch into the muscles from the spinal cord. It carries messages to and from the central nervous system to control voluntary muscle activity. Within this system, the *pyramidal nerve pathways* manage fine motor activities, while the *extrapyramidal pathways* govern integrated gross motor activities. The entire peripheral nervous system is composed of networks of these pathways, the cells of which are affected by some psychotropic medications to produce unwanted side effects. The center of integration of the peripheral system is the cerebellum; however, the cerebrum also includes pyramidal and extrapyramidal nerve tracts that connect the cortex to the spinal cord and muscles of the body.

The three sections of the brain represent different levels of the functioning of the nervous system. Much of the rear and base of the brain is specialized and committed to involuntary bodily functions such as the interpretation of incoming sensations, the control of movement, and the regulation of automatic life-support functions. The forebrain, particularly the frontal and temporal lobes, is less specific. Freed from the need to maintain basic bodily functions, its components interact in complex ways to produce thinking and the higher emotions. Psychotropic medications act not only on nerve pathways involved in thinking and feeling but also on other areas of the brain. To the extent that such drugs can reach their desired sites of action without negatively affecting other brain functions, they can serve as successful agents for intervention with clients.

PROPERTIES OF NERVE CELLS

As components in all systems do, neurons exist in the context of a local environment. The structure of that environment is maintained by the glial cells; neighboring organisms include adjacent neurons and cells, such as muscle or gland cells, which are affected along pathways. Each neuron receives input from the environment, then responds toward some externally directed activity. Our discussion will be limited to activities within and among nerve cells that impact human thought and emotion.

Neuron Structure

The *cell body*, or central area of the neuron, is the neuron's metabolic center (see Figure 2). Made up of lipid (fatty) material, the *cell membrane* separates the contents of the cell from the fluid enveloping it. Molecules or ions (groups of atoms with electrical charges) pass through this membrane to enter or leave the cell, but not at random. Special "channels" must be opened for such movement to occur, and opening these channels is governed by chemical activities within the cell. Each cell includes one single, long limb extension called an *axon*, through which the cell body sends signals to neighboring cells (see Figure 2). The cell also features numerous short extensions, called *dendrites*, which receive signals sent by other neurons. In the complex maze of the central nervous system, axon terminals are always found close to the dendrites of other cells. However, axons and dendrites do not actually touch each other. The minute amount of space separating them is known as the *synaptic cleft*. Each cell may have access to 1000 to 10,000 synapses (points of union). The synapse comprises the *presynaptic terminal*, the cleft, and the *postsynaptic membrane*. A presynaptic terminal is the ending of the axon of the nerve cell,

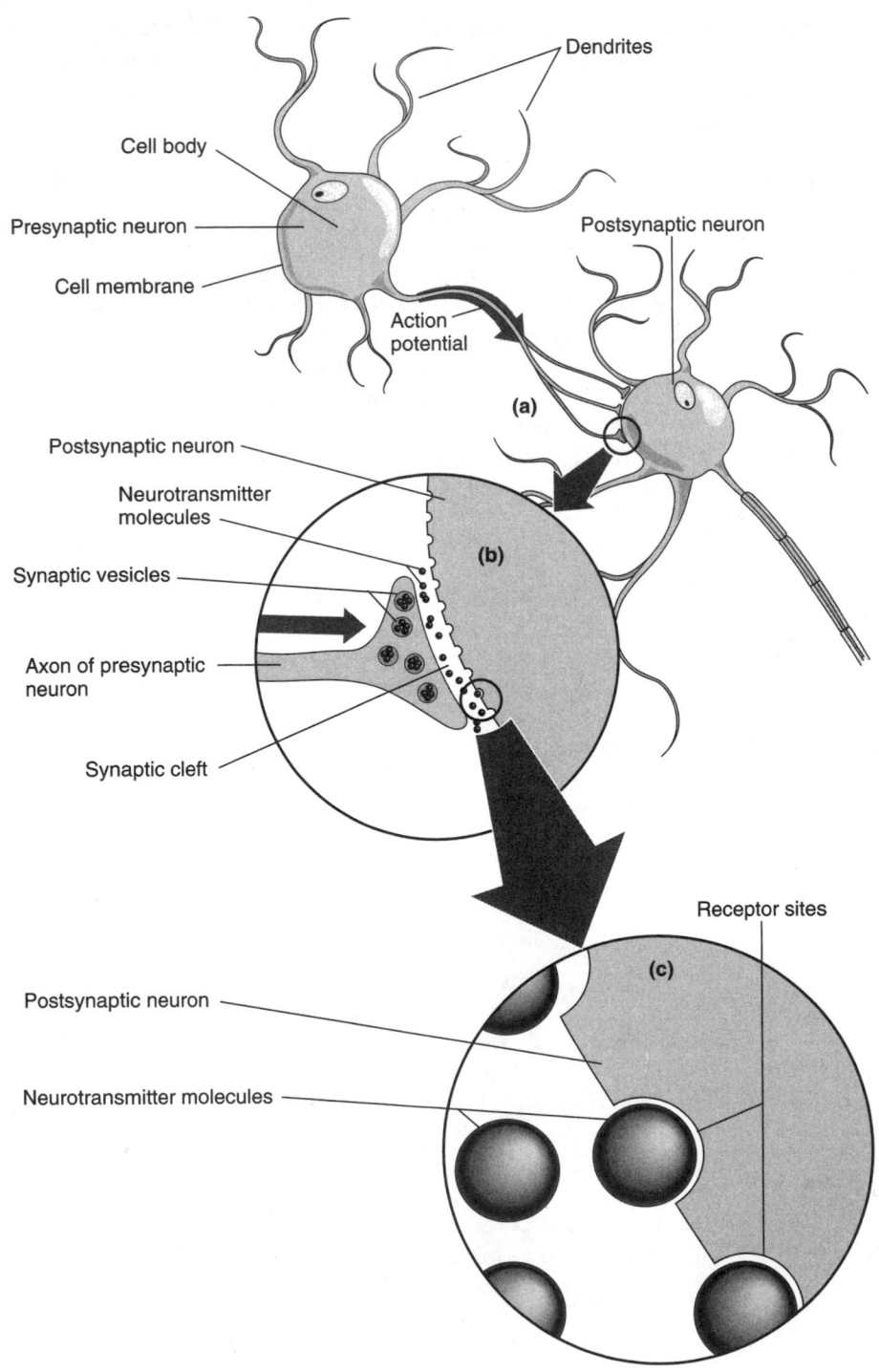

containing neurotransmitters that extend to the synapse; a postsynaptic membrane is a membrane of the cell body, or dendrite, on which neurotransmitter receptor sites are located.

Neuron Function

The transmission of signals through the nervous system involves all the structures of a neuron. The process begins when a cell generates a *nerve impulse*, or a momentary change in the electrical conductivity of the neural membrane. (At rest, neurons maintain a negative electrical charge; an impulse gives the neuron a temporary positive charge.) These impulses are generated at various speeds, sometimes as rapidly as 200 per second. The transmission of an impulse to a receiving cell is facilitated by a chemical neurotransmitter that is released by the axon into the synapse. The neurotransmitter attaches to special receiving areas, or *receptors*, in the dendrite of the neighboring cell. In turn, the receiving cell, having been acted upon, incorporates this impulse as environmental information and determines through its own chemical makeup how to respond. Generally, information is passed from cell to cell along a pathway. The process of signal transmission is no less complex when a social worker lifts a coffee cup than when she or he attends to a client during a lengthy assessment interview. The latter activity simply requires the use of more neuron pathways.

We offer now a more detailed description of these processes so you can understand their implications for psychotropic drug action. The axon terminals include small areas known as *synaptic vesicles*, which contain the molecules of a neurotransmitter produced in the cell body. Activities in the vesicles of the sending cell are *presynaptic* because they precede activities in the synapse. The receiving area of the synapse, on the dendrite of the nearby cell body, is called the *postsynaptic membrane*. Compared to the rest of the cell membrane, both pre- and postsynaptic membranes appear relatively thick and dark because they contain the proteins that are the building blocks of some neurotransmitters. The receptors on presynaptic neurons that regulate the release of neurotransmitters are called *autoreceptors*. Though each cell releases only one (sometimes two) type of neurotransmitter at its presynaptic axon terminal, each has receptors to match many different transmitters.

The release of a neurotransmitter into the synaptic cleft occurs when a rupture in the presynaptic axon membrane is followed by a temporary fusion of synaptic vesicles. The process by which a neurotransmitter crosses the synaptic cleft and attaches to a receptor in the postsynaptic membrane is called *binding*, which activates chemical changes in the postsynaptic membrane. These changes can either encourage (excite) or discourage (inhibit) the production of nerve impulses, depending on the chemical composition of the receiving cell. The neurotransmitter does not itself pass through the receiving cell; rather, it is the impulses that the neurotransmitter prompts that travel through the cell. After transmission is complete, the neurotransmitter either is discarded as waste by the glial cells or reenters the presynaptic terminal for storage and use at another time (this process is called *reuptake*).

At any given time, a nerve cell may receive a barrage of both excitatory and inhibiting impulses from many sources. Single cells continuously act on or respond to their environment. For instance, in reading this chapter, you have focused on the content before you, but perhaps you have also been listening to music, thinking about certain clients, shifting your posture every few minutes, or smelling the aroma of food cooking in the kitchen. These simple, effortless activities require the exchange of signals among millions of nerve cells along pathways, with each cell doing its part to sustain millions of pathways throughout the nervous system.

NEUROTRANSMITTERS

Drugs work by modifying natural events in the synapses along pathways in certain areas of the brain. Medication affects these events, and subsequently brain function, in the following ways.

1. Altering presynaptic activity to prompt neurotransmitter release

2. Altering postsynaptic activity to affect receptor binding

3. Interfering with normal reuptake processes

4. Altering the manufacture of receptors

An *agonist* is a substance that binds to a receptor and stimulates the same type of cellular activity as a neurotransmitter, thereby increasing its effect. An *antagonist* binds to a receptor but fails to stimulate its activity, thereby decreasing the effect of a neurotransmitter.

Although more than 40 chemical neurotransmitters have been discovered, and it is suspected that 100 or more of these substances exist, our knowledge of them is so limited that the intended benefits of psychotropic drugs are at present generally attributed to only six: acetylcholine, norepinephrine, dopamine, serotonin, gamma aminobutyric acid (GABA), and glutamate. All of these except GABA and glutamate are classified as *amines*, or organic substances that are the building blocks for amino acids. GABA and glutamate are complete amino acids. Other neurotransmitters are classified as *peptides* (strings of amino acids) and hormones.

All primary transmitters except glutamate are present in groups of neurons primarily located in the brain stem but also associated with more diffuse pathways in the central nervous system. Transmitters extend in pathways from the brain stem to other regions of the brain. Interestingly, acetylcholine, norepinephrine, dopamine, serotonin, and GABA together account for transmissions at less than half of the brain's synapses. GABA, the most prevalent of these substances, is found in 25% to 40% of the brain's synapses. Dopamine is used by only 15% of the nerve terminals in those areas where it is most highly concentrated. Acetylcholine is found in 5% to 10% of neuron terminals in the brain. Only 5% of neurons process norepinephrine where it is concentrated, and serotonin is found in less than 1% of central nervous system terminals.

However, all these substances are crucial in regions of the nervous system associated with emotional behavior.

The study of neurotransmitters and the effects of drugs on them represents a major field of neuroscience. Current knowledge about transmitter processes has been derived primarily from observations of activities within the peripheral nervous system. Establishing that similar mechanisms exist in the central nervous system is a far more difficult and somewhat speculative challenge. In fact, the specific actions of psychotropic drugs on neurotransmitter activity is in some cases still very uncertain.

Here are fuller descriptions of the major transmitters known or believed to be major agents in psychotropic drug treatment.

Acetylcholine

The first neurotransmitter to be identified, almost 70 years ago, acetylcholine is most highly concentrated in the brain stem but is also present elsewhere. It is released by all neurons that control the activities of the skeletal and smooth (involuntary) muscles, including the heart beat. It is also released by those autonomic nerve cells in the parasympathetic system that control some glandular functions. Acetylcholine is critical to the transmission of messages between the brain and spinal cord.

Norepinephrine

This transmitter, located in the sympathetic nerves of the peripheral and central nervous systems, is secreted by the adrenal glands in response to stress or arousal. Not widely distributed throughout the nervous system, it functions in two major *tracts*, or bundles of nerves that have the same origin, termination, and function. First, norepinephrine influences affective behavior by connecting the brain stem with axons in the hypothalamus and limbic system. The second tract, which extends from the brain stem to the cerebral cortex and hippocampus (the part of the temporal lobe essential in memory regulation), influences alertness. Norepinephrine tracts also extend toward the spinal cord, where they regulate anxiety and tension.

Dopamine

Dopamine is present in four nerve tracts that have different functions. One tract extends from the brain stem to portions of the limbic system, which influences emotional behavior, and a closely related tract extends to the cerebral cortex, which impacts cognition. Dopamine abnormalities in the limbic system are implicated in schizophrenia. A third dopamine pathway extends from the brain stem to the basal ganglia area of the forebrain, where motor activity is regulated. A lack of sufficient dopamine here causes physical tension, rigidity, and movement difficulties (i.e., the parkinsonian adverse effects of antipsychotic drugs). In its fourth tract, dopamine helps regulate the endocrine system, directing the hypothalamus to manufacture hormones that are eventually released into the bloodstream. There is growing research on the subtypes of dopamine (Bentley, 1999), as we will discuss later.

Serotonin

The tracts of this neurotransmitter originate in the midbrain and extend into all brain regions, particularly the hypothalamus. Serotonin is also present in blood cells and the lining of the digestive tract. This substance affects regions in the brain that facilitate sensory processes, muscular activity, and thinking. Strategically positioned in the midbrain, serotonin coordinates complex sensory and motor patterns during a variety of behavioral states. Serotonin, which, like dopamine, has recently been found to include several subtypes, is also a factor in regulating states of consciousness, mood, depression, and anxiety; it affects basic bodily functions such as appetite, sleep, and sexual behavior. Some hypothesize that this neurotransmitter contributes to affective disorders, states of high aggression, and schizophrenia.

Gamma Aminobutyric Acid (GABA)

GABA, an amino acid, is present throughout the central nervous system. Most neurons possess GABA receptors. There are two types of receptors, A and B; type A receptors have a role in anxiety and its modulation. This transmitter inhibits virtually all neurons; that is, it inhibits the firing of impulses from cells on which it acts and thus plays an essential role in controlling neuron excitability. Almost every cerebral function is likely to be influenced by drugs that act on GABA. These functions include the regulation of motor activity, cardiovascular reflexes, pituitary function, and anxiety. Certain antianxiety medications enhance GABA's effectiveness. Alcohol and sedatives such as barbiturates also act on GABA.

Glutamate (Glutamic Acid)

Glutamate has recently become a topic of major interest in psychopharmacology. It is a primary *excitatory* neurotransmitter in the brain, meaning that it stimulates nerve cell activity. Glutamate is also a chemical precursor of GABA. It is obtained from food and from metabolic processes (including those of the glial cells). Glutmate is stored in and released from nerve terminals, and its receptors (four types) are found on the surfaces of virtually *all* neurons. Glutamate activity has a major influence on cognitive functions via the cortex and hippocampus, motor functions in the pyramidal and extrapyramidal systems, and also impacts many cerebellar and sensory functions.

Researchers hypothesize that glutamate may influence the development of a variety of mental disorders, including schizophrenia and others (such as Alzheimer's disease), by a process of *excitotoxicity*. This term refers to a normal, temporary process of over-stimulating neurons for the purpose of restructuring them. In the nervous system, for reasons that are not known, glutamate may at times overexcite neurons to the point of permanently damaging or destroying them. Medications that diminish this out-of-control process may reduce the symptoms of the resulting disorders. It has also been hypothesized that an alteration (reduction) of GABA function in the prefrontal cortex, initiated by glutamate activity, may produce the symptoms of schizophrenia.

HOW A DRUG MOVES THROUGH THE BODY

The way in which the human body responds to the presence of a drug is called *pharmacokinetics*. Knowledge of pharmacokinetics can help social workers understand why some clients respond differently to the same medication than others and why, when a client stops taking medication, its effects can continue for a while. The four bodily processes important to understanding pharmacokinetics are absorption, distribution, metabolism, and excretion.

Absorption

Absorption is the process by which a drug enters the bloodstream, most commonly by the passive diffusion of the drug into the bowel wall. Factors relevant to efficient absorption include the chemical makeup of the drug and the other materials used in its production, as well as the activity of liver enzymes, which break down the drug. With oral medication, this efficiency depends on the drug's strength of concentration, its ability to dissolve into fatty tissue (of which intestinal cell membranes are composed), and the spontaneous movement of a consumer's intestines. Taking a drug on an empty stomach favors rapid absorption because the presence of other substances promotes competition for digestive enzymes and slows the absorption process.

Though most psychotropic drugs are prescribed orally, in tablets or capsules, some are administered intramuscularly. Medications injected into muscles enter the bloodstream more quickly than oral medications because they bypass the digestive process. Intravenous administration of drugs is the quickest, most direct route for absorption; however, it is rarely prescribed, because it is impractical and includes the highest risk of adverse effects. As of now, other routes of drug administration, such as the lungs and rectum, are not used to administer psychotropic drugs. The psychostimulant drug pemoline, however, can be administered through the skin with a 7-day patch.

Distribution

Distribution is the process by which a drug, having entered the bloodstream, travels to its desired site of action. Once in the bloodstream, the drug can take one of two routes. It can either dissolve in the blood plasma (the fluid part of the blood) for transport to the site of action or become attached, or bind, to plasma proteins. Binding is problematic because it prohibits the drug from advancing to its site in the brain. After binding, the drug breaks down or is metabolized, diminishing its intended effects. Though protein binding rates vary among drugs and even individuals, most psychotropic drugs are fairly high in protein binding capacity (up to 95% in some cases). Only the unbound portion of the drug can cross into the brain. Because average rates are already so high, small variations in the binding of a drug make a significant difference in its effectiveness.

The *blood-brain barrier* refers to characteristics of capillaries (blood vessels) in the brain, through which a drug must pass to enter neuron sites. Because these capillaries are tightly compressed, this barrier is relatively difficult for a substance to cross. Medications and other substances must be *lipid-soluble* to pass through brain capillaries because the cell membranes of these vessels are lipid, or fatty. In other areas of the body, capillaries are not so tightly bound, and water-soluble substances can leak through them into the surrounding tissue. Generally speaking, efficient absorption into the fatty intestinal wall implies that a drug will enter the brain efficiently.

A drug can enter the brain directly, through the circulatory system, or indirectly, through the cerebrospinal fluid after diffusing there from the bloodstream. Access of a drug to the brain depends in part on the blood flow at the intended site—a higher volume of blood increases the likelihood of entry. Access also depends on the drug's relative affinity for the receptors in that area of the brain. Distribution into the brain is facilitated by the large mass of blood vessels that feed it. Nevertheless, the amount of the drug that passes through the blood/brain barrier is usually small compared to the amount that remains in other areas of the body. Physicians take these facts into account when selecting drugs and dosages.

Metabolism

Metabolism is the process, generally carried out by enzymes in the liver, by which the body breaks down the chemical structure of a drug into derivatives that can be eliminated from the body. The drug's molecules are altered from lipid-soluble substances into water-soluble salts. High water-solubility prevents the drug from continuing to recirculate through the body. Instead, it can be efficiently absorbed into the body's water and excreted. First-pass metabolism refers to the extensive initial breakdown of the drug within the liver. This process significantly reduces the amount of drug that is available to proceed toward its site of action. *Bioavailability* refers to the amount of a drug that leaves the liver without being metabolized.

It is important to note that the products of metabolism, known as *metabolites*, may themselves be pharmacologically active and promote the primary drug's ongoing effect. That is, even though the metabolites represent a chemical breakdown of the drug, they may maintain a set of therapeutic effects on thought or mood similar to that of the original drug. The metabolites of most medications are well known, so their effects are taken into account by physicians making decisions about prescriptions. However, metabolism can be affected in a number of ways by physical disease processes in the body and by interactions among drugs. Also, the efficiency of metabolism, as well as kidney function, declines with age.

Excretion

Excretion is the process by which drugs are eliminated from the body, primarily by the kidneys. *Elimination* refers to all processes, including metabolism and excretion, that lower the concentration of a drug in the body. The speed of this process is proportional to the concentration of the drug in the body; that is, elimination proceeds more slowly as less medication remains within the consumer's system. The *blood level* refers to the measure of a drug's presence in the plasma at a given time; *steady state* refers to the point at which a consistent level of a medication is present in the bloodstream; and the *peak (plasma) level* of a drug refers to the time after ingestion at which it reaches its highest concentration in the bloodstream. This peak varies, depending on the type of drug and the amount ingested. Because elimination continues the entire time a drug is in the bloodstream, relative drug-elimination rates determine whether blood levels are increasing or decreasing. That is, the amount ingested and in circulation should correspond to the amount eliminated. *Clearance* is the amount of a drug excreted over a given amount of time. Excretion is carried out through the urine or bile, although sweat, feces, saliva, tears, and even milk in lactating women can also serve this function.

An important concept for understanding the frequency with which a client must take a prescribed medication is that of *half-life*, the time required for a drug to fall to 50% of its peak level. Half-life is determined by metabolism and excretion, after absorption and distribution are complete. To clarify a frequent point of confusion, a drug is not completely eliminated, as might be assumed, after two half-lives have passed. In fact, each successive half-life requires the same amount of time as the previous one but accounts for the elimination of only 50% of the remaining medication. For example, the antidepressant trazodone has a half-life of five hours; thus, 50% of the peak level of a single dose of trazodone is eliminated in 5 hours. However, only 75% is cleared in 10 hours, or two half-lives (50% of the remaining 50% equals 25%); 87.5% is eliminated in 15 hours, or three half-lives (50% of 25%, or 12.5%); 93.75% in 20 hours, or four half-lives; and approximately 97% in 25 hours, or five half-lives. Knowledge of a drug's half-life is essential to determine the dosage that must be taken to maintain a therapeutic level within the circulation. If a client takes a drug too frequently, his or her blood level will eventually rise to a point of toxicity, or poison. Similarly, taking a drug less frequently than is therapeutically advisable would limit or perhaps even eliminate its effectiveness.

In determining a psychotropic drug treatment, physicians try to insure that a steady concentration of medication in the consumer's bloodstream will be delivered to the site of action to produce the desired therapeutic effect.

When a drug's half-life is known, the prescribing physician can tell the consumer the frequency of dosage that will achieve a steady state; that is, the physician provides a schedule so that the amount entering the system will offset the amount leaving it. Logically, medications with longer half-lives should be taken less often than those with shorter ones. Of course, taking any medication more frequently than indicated by its half-life would be dangerous, leading to a buildup of the substance in the system and to toxic effects. Many antipsychotic medications and antidepressants can be taken once per day. Mood-stabilizing medications, on the other hand, are generally taken several times per day because of their shorter half-life. Most oral medications are taken at least once per day, but injectable medications can be consumed as seldom as once per month because they are stored and released slowly by muscle tissue.

THE EFFECTS OF A DRUG ON THE BODY

Pharmacodynamics is the study of the effects of a drug on the body. Social workers can use their knowledge of pharmacodynamics to respond to the client's and family's need to learn about medications, including understanding differential drug response and the reasons for all the drug's effects, both positive and negative. Pharmacodynamics offers several helpful concepts to the social worker, including the therapeutic index, dose response, lag time, and adverse effects. Because drugs interact with body tissues, individual consumer characteristics account for differences in what the drug can do. In general, drug action is influenced by a consumer's age (efficiency of metabolism), weight (rate of absorption), gender (hormonal differences), and any organ problems or diseases that interfere with the body's efficiency.

• The *therapeutic index* of a drug is the ratio of the lowest average concentration needed to produce a desired effect and the lowest average concentration that produces toxic effects. In *toxicity*, the amount of an active drug in the body exceeds the amount required for efficacy, putting the consumer at risk for serious adverse effects. A high therapeutic index implies that a drug is relatively safe, as opposed to a drug with a low therapeutic index. That is, a person will not likely overdose if he or she accidentally takes more than is prescribed.

• The *potency* of a drug is its relative strength, in grams, milligrams, or micrograms, required to achieve a desired effect. The *median effective dose* (sometimes signified as ED50) is the dose that causes a therapeutic effect in 50% of clients. However, a drug's effectiveness cannot be measured merely by its potency. Two different antipsychotic drugs, for example, may be administered in very different dosages. One milligram of haloperidol is the equivalent of ten milligrams of thiothixene, a similar drug. Though haloperidol is the more potent of the two, the effectiveness of both may be the same, and they may be equally safe when given in comparable therapeutic amounts. However, differences in potency do relate to certain types of adverse effects (see chapter 4).

- The *dose response* is the measure of a drug's therapeutic effect as a function of increasing dose. Many drugs demonstrate an enhanced therapeutic effect when given in greater amounts, but only up to a point. These drugs may become ineffective or harmful once that peak dosage level is passed. When plotted on a graph, dose responses of different medications can be compared with each other. Again, this information does not necessarily help the prescribing physician determine which medication is preferable, because two medicines may have different therapeutic and adverse effect profiles.

- *Lag time* is the time a medication takes to affect the targeted behavior. Lag time in part depends on the delay caused by the natural distribution of the drug, but in some cases it may reflect an adaptive response in the central nervous system. That is, the drug may reach the site of action, but the natural activity of neurons may change in reaction to it, temporarily thwarting the desired nerve cell activity. Some anti-anxiety medications demonstrate an almost immediate therapeutic effect after consumption, while antidepressants may take two to six weeks to produce a desired effect.

Although factors involved in lag time are not well understood, the time intervals are predictable. One theory holds that the presynaptic nerve fires more rapidly than usual in the presence of a neuroleptic drug. Eventually, though, the presynaptic neuron can no longer sustain the increased charge. When the neuron fatigues, the efficacy of the drug can be observed. This phenomenon has clinical implications; that is, it will do the physician no good to increase dosage to obtain a quicker response. To impact the symptoms of mental illness, one often has to wait.

- *Tolerance* refers to the body's reduced responsiveness to a drug because the sensitivity of receptors changes over time. Although tolerance may be observed most obviously with the benzodiazepines and can occasionally occur with cyclic antidepressants and some other medications, tolerance does not affect the therapeutic effects of most psychotropic drugs. However, some adverse effects of medications may diminish over time, making tolerance positive for many clients.

- *Adverse* or *side effects* refer to any effects of a drug that are unintentional and unrelated to its desired therapeutic effect. Though these effects are generally considered negative, the client may perceive some as either neutral or positive, such as the weight loss or increased energy that occurs with some of the newer antidepressant medications. Side effects generally occur because a drug acts on multiple sites in the nervous system, even though only one site is targeted for the positive effect. Negative side effects can have serious short- and long-term consequences for the consumer or relatively harmless but uncomfortable or inconvenient effects, such as sedation. Significant side effects may be themselves treated by the physician, sometimes with other medications. The social worker's important role in this process will be discussed in later chapters.

FIVE CLASSES OF PSYCHOTROPIC MEDICATION

In this discussion we are mainly concerned with psychotropic medications that belong to one of five categories: antipsychotic, antidepressant, mood-stabilizing, anti-anxiety, and psychostimulant drugs. Drugs in a particular category are primarily used to treat the same mental illnesses and psychiatric symptoms and, with important exceptions, tend to take similar actions. The following sections detail how each type of drug acts on the body and how the body handles each. We do want to emphasize, however, that drugs from each category are increasingly being found to have effectiveness with other types of disorders. As drugs initially developed for one condition or illness are sometimes used to treat other conditions, we must accept that there is no longer such a clear distinction between classes of medications.

Antipsychotic Medications

It is widely accepted that persons with schizophrenia have a relatively high concentration of the neurotransmitter dopamine or, in pathways extending into the cortex and limbic system, a high sensitivity at its receptor sites. Firm evidence exists that stimulating dopamine activity induces psychotic symptoms. Almost all the antipsychotic medications act by blocking postsynaptic dopamine receptors, binding to these receptors on all four of its pathways. Because of this mode of action, these medications are known as dopamine antagonists. The medications differ primarily in their potential adverse effects, their potency as indicated by the number of milligrams in equivalent doses, and their possible impact on other neurotransmitters.

It was once believed that there was only one type of dopamine receptor in the brain, but scientists have since identified five subtypes. These are grouped into two classes, one that produces therapeutic effects and one that produces adverse effects when affected by psychotropic drugs. The therapeutic actions of the antipsychotic medications result from their blocking one of these types of receptors. The reduction of dopamine activity in persons with schizophrenia is accompanied by a reduction in many of the *positive symptoms*, which feature an excess or bizarre distortion of normal functions (such as delusions and hallucinations). However, for reasons that are not clear, antipsychotic medications are not as effective in reducing delusional thinking or *negative symptoms*, which feature a loss or reduction of normal functions (withdrawal, poverty of speech and thought, lack of motivation). The negative symptoms may be related to the activity of other neurotransmitters and may be reduced by some of the newer medications.

Though the antipsychotic medications act on all dopamine sites in the brain, only one of these is the site of symptom-producing nerve cell activity. Other pathways extend from the midbrain to the basal ganglia and occupy areas of the brain that govern motor activity through the peripheral nervous system. A reduction in dopamine in these other areas causes negative side effects. Clients may experience muscle spasms, tremors, or stiffness because normal amounts of the transmitter are needed in these areas to facilitate muscle activity. The lack of dopamine in them gives rise to symptoms of parkinsonism and tardive dyskinesia.

Several new types of antipsychotic medication, all from the same chemical family, have been introduced into the American market and seem to act differently than previous drugs. These have become known as serotonin-dopamine antagonists, as they may block the activity of both neurotransmitters. In fact, clozapine, among the best known of these, is known to interact with nine neurotransmitter receptors (three subtypes of dopamine and three subtypes of serotonin receptors among them). It does not carry the risk of adverse effects for the muscular system. Although clozapine's action is still not completely understood, the drug may selectively act on only those dopamine receptors that produce psychotic symptoms. Its sites of action were once hypothesized as limited to the limbic forebrain and the frontal cortex, but recent evidence suggests otherwise. In blocking receptors for serotonin, clozapine and other new medications have demonstrated that this neurotransmitter affects psychotic symptoms in some people.

After oral administration, the peak effects of most antipsychotic medication are achieved within 2 to 4 hours. There is a significant first-pass effect in the liver, in which much of the chemical substance is metabolized before it enters the circulatory system. However, the metabolites also act as dopamine antagonists and thus have a therapeutic effect. The drugs are highly protein bound: Fully 85% to 90% remains in the bloodstream. The drugs have a high therapeutic index, making it difficult to overdose accidentally to the point of toxicity. Depending on the specific drug, there is a range in half-life from 10 to 40 hours. Because any point in this range is considered lengthy, antipsychotic drugs can be taken once per day to maintain a steady state.

Antidepressant Medications

There is uncertainty about how antidepressant medications specifically work. Until the early 1980s, it was believed that certain depressions resulted from a deficiency of norepinephrine or serotonin in the limbic area of the brain. The antidepressants developed in the 1950s and 1960s (and still used today) were thought to work by increasing the prevalence of norepinephrine and serotonin in the nervous system. However, newer antidepressants are known to act differently. Further, it is suspected that antidepressants have additional effects on presynaptic and postsynaptic receptors and perhaps other neurotransmitter systems. All of the antidepressant drugs have antianxiety effects as well, and some have become primary treatments for certain anxiety disorders.

Three types of antidepressants, each with different actions, are the monoamine oxidase (MAO) inhibitors, the "cyclics," and those drugs that are serotonin-specific. Despite uncertainties about their actions, some general characteristics of the drugs can be described. They must all be taken for several weeks before the client experiences beneficial effects, because their actions are initially resisted by cells at the sites of action. Many of the cyclic antidepressants have a low therapeutic index; that is, the amounts required for therapeutic effect and overdose do not differ greatly. This is a particular problem because these drugs are often prescribed for clients with self-destructive tendencies. Overdose can often be achieved with a 10-day supply of a cyclic drug.

The MAO inhibitors were among the first antidepressants. While still effective for some clients, they are not frequently prescribed because of rather extensive dietary restrictions needed to prevent serious side effects. These drugs act by inhibiting certain enzymes within cells that metabolize norepinephrine and serotonin, so that levels of those transmitters in the central nervous system increase. The MAO inhibitors are effective with some clients who do not respond to the other antidepressant medications. It has been found that there are two types of MAO in the nervous system—types A and B. Type A is the desired target of antidepressant action. At present new MAO inhibitors are in development that are selective for MAO-A and that are also reversible. That is, the drugs will have a therapeutic effect but will be eliminated from the consumer's system if any recognized toxic substances (certain cheeses, wines, and meats, as described in chapter 4) enter it. Thus new MAO inhibitors may become more commonly utilized in the future.

So named because of their chemical structure, the cyclic drugs (many of which have been called "tricyclics" and "heterocyclics") were the most commonly prescribed antidepressants through the 1980s. They are believed to work by blocking the reuptake of norepinephrine and serotonin and, to a lesser extent, dopamine. The metabolites of cyclic drugs are also active antidepressants. The drugs are highly effective, accounting for their long popularity. As a result of actions in other areas of the autonomic and central nervous systems, many cyclic drugs produce discomforting adverse effects. Fortunately, tolerance does develop to some of the adverse effects but not to the therapeutic effect. These medications are lipid-soluble and have a high rate of binding to plasma proteins. With a half-life of approximately 24 hours, they can be taken once per day.

The newer antidepressants, most of which are characterized by their actions on serotonin, add to the uncertainty about how antidepressant drugs act on relevant neurotransmitters. The selective serotonin reuptake inhibitor (SSRI) drugs block serotonin but in general do not interfere with norepinephrine's normal actions. The dual serotonin and norepinephrine reuptake inhibitors (SNRIs) do not affect other chemicals that are impacted by the cyclic antidepressants to cause adverse effects.

The drug bupropion is another type of drug, a norepinephrine and dopamine reuptake blocker, and it has a metabolite which is an even more effective reuptake blocker of these substances in key areas of the brain. Another emerging group of drugs, including trazodone and nefazodone, targets a subset of serotonin receptors as well as its reuptake. The actions of these new drugs may include stimulating certain other neurotransmitter building blocks in the cell body in ways that are not yet understood. More potent than the cyclics, these drugs also have long half-lives. One of their major attractions is that they have fewer adverse effects than the other types of antidepressants. They also offer less potential for overdose.

Mood-Stabilizing Drugs

Since its introduction in the United States as an antimanic drug in 1969, lithium carbonate has been the primary drug treatment for bipolar disorder. The lightest of the solid elements, lithium circulates through the body as a small ion that has a positive electrical charge. It is not clear how lithium achieves its therapeutic effect, but numerous theories have been considered. One hypothesis is based on lithium's high rate of passage through cell membrane ion channels, impeding the activity of the naturally occurring impulses that contribute to mania and consequently stabilizing electrolyte imbalances in the cell membrane. Another hypothesis differentiates the antidepressant and antimanic effects of the drug. The antidepressant effect of lithium may result from its reducing the sensitivity of postsynaptic receptors for serotonin, thus increasing the amount of that transmitter in the nervous system. Its antimanic effect may relate to reduced sensitivity in dopamine receptors and an inhibition of cellular enzymes that produce dopamine. Though highly effective, lithium does not take effect for several weeks after initiation. It is sometimes given, at least temporarily, with an antipsychotic drug to stabilize a manic individual.

- Lithium circulates freely through the body completely unbound to plasma proteins, unlike antipsychotic and antidepressant drugs. Distributed in the extracellular fluid, it enters body tissues at varying rates. Peak blood levels are reached in two hours (four hours for time-release forms), and there is complete absorption within eight hours of administration. The half-life of lithium is 24 hours on *maintenance doses*, defined as the minimum dosages required to maintain a steady therapeutic effect. The drug must be taken two or three times daily, except in its time-release form. Lithium is not metabolized in the liver into derivative compounds. The kidneys excrete 95% of the drug. At steady states, which occur in 5 to 8 days, an equilibrium is reached in that plasma lithium reflects lithium levels in the entire body; thus the drug can be efficiently monitored by measuring levels in the blood. Lithium is excreted by the kidneys in the first few hours after peak levels. Because lithium has a relatively low therapeutic index, adverse reactions (such as muscle tremor and kidney damage) can occur at blood levels only slightly higher than a client's therapeutic level.

- Certain antiseizure medications also act as effective mood stabilizers. Like lithium, their mechanisms of action are not clear. One theory holds that they control a "kindling" process in limbic system neuron tracts, a process that contributes to manic states. It is speculated that in mania a repetitive application of low-grade electrical or chemical stimuli is set in motion, eventually producing a manic episode. The drug carbamazepine, also a potent blocker of norepinephrine reuptake, inhibits such repetitive firing of sodium impulses, a highly active element. Such firing can potentiate a manic episode.

Carbamezepine binds to sodium when it is inactive. Carbamazepine may also inhibit those enzymes in the central nervous system that break down GABA. The GABA neurotransmitter may have antimanic properties and thus its increased prevalence in the nervous system may enhance mood stability. Valproic acid, another atypical antimanic medication, also has presynaptic and postsynaptic GABA receptor effects. By blocking the convulsive effects of GABA antagonists, it increases levels of GABA. While effective, all of these new medications may not be prescribed unless lithium is first ruled out; it has been used as a mood-stabilizer for a much longer time and has been more extensively tested. The anticonvulsant drugs may, however, be more effective in controlling certain types of mania.

Anti-Anxiety Medications

Though several types of anti-anxiety medication are currently available, the most frequently prescribed are the benzodiazepines. The name comes from their chemical structure, in which a benzene ring is fused to a diazepine ring. These drugs have frequently been referred to as "minor tranquilizers." Speculated to have evolved as fear regulators, natural benzodiazepine chemicals may exist in the brain, potentiated by the GABA neurotransmitter. (As described earlier, GABA is a major inhibitory neurotransmitter in the brain.) The benzodiazepine medications achieve their therapeutic effect by causing the GABA neurotransmitter to bind more completely with its receptor site. GABA receptors in various regions of the brain thus regulate the anti-anxiety (or anxiolytic) as well as the sedative and anticonvulsant effects of the benzodiazepines. While it is not clear how they specifically act as anti-anxiety agents, benzodiazepines act on the central nervous system by binding to specific sites near GABA receptors. That is, there are benzodiazepine receptors that enhance GABA activity and result in a blockage of stimulation in areas of the brain associated with emotion. The drugs also raise one's seizure threshold. The locations of both antiseizure and sedative activity are the cortex and limbic areas, where receptors are known to decrease anxiety. As a general rule, the benzodiazepines are anxiolytic in lower doses and sedating in higher doses.

Benzodiazepines are usually taken orally. Quickly absorbed in the gastrointestinal tract, they act rapidly—in many cases, within 30 minutes. Having a high therapeutic index, the benzodiazepines do not present a risk for overdose. The numerous company brands of these medications vary a great deal in their particular characteristics, but peak levels are generally reached in 1 to 3 hours, and most benzodiazepines form active metabolites. The drugs bind to plasma proteins, with the quality of distribution corresponding to their lipid solubility. Their half-lives vary widely (2 to 60 hours).

An important characteristic of the benzodiazepines is that with continuous use they are physically addictive at some dosages. Long-term use (perhaps no more than two weeks) can cause production of the body's natural benzodiazepine compounds to shut down. Thus, if the drug is abruptly withdrawn, no natural production of those substances will occur for some time. Clients must be taken off these medications gradually to prevent the effects of physical withdrawal, which can persist for several months, and in some cases up to one year. For these reasons, the benzodiazepines are generally designed for comparatively short-term use, even though physicians sometimes prescribe them for periods up to several years.

Several other, smaller classes of medications are also used to control anxiety. These include the beta-blockers, so named because they compete with norepinephrine at certain receptor sites in the brain and peripheral nervous system, sites that regulate cardiac and muscular functions. These medications effectively treat anticipatory anxiety; that is, they lower anxiety by reducing its symptoms of rapid heartbeat, muscle tension, and dry mouth. Because the client does not experience these physiological indicators, his or her subjective experience of anxiety is diminished.

Another type of anti-anxiety medication, buspirone, is a partial agonist of serotonin receptors. Although its impact on anxiety is not yet well understood, serotonin is believed to be anxiolytic in the hippocampus and limbic areas. To be effective, this medication must be taken regularly, like antidepressant and mood-stabilizing drugs but unlike the benzodiazepines. Buspirone also requires several weeks to take effect. It is quickly absorbed but has a short half-life. Because buspirone is not potentially addictive, clients who have taken benzodiazepines for an extended time will often be gradually changed over to buspirone.

Finally, the antihistamines are occasionally used as anti-anxiety agents. These drugs block histamine receptors associated with anxiety and agitation. Rapidly absorbed, antihistimines maintain a therapeutic effect for at least 24 hours. These drugs tend to sedate the consumer, however, and work effectively as anti-anxiety agents for only a few months. Though not addictive, they do not treat anxiety as effectively as the benzodiazepines.

Psychostimulants

Stimulants have been utilized in the treatment of attention-deficit/hyperactivity disorder (ADHD) since 1936, with the finding that amphetamine drugs were effective in controlling hyperactivity. Most (but not all) are currently classified as Schedule II drugs by the Drug Enforcement Agency because of their abuse potential. This is the most restrictive classification for medications, prohibiting both their prescription by phone and the writing of refills. The psychostimulants are approved for the treatment of ADHD, narcolepsy, and obesity.

As with many drugs, the precise mechanism of action of the psychostimulants in treating ADHD is not known. The drugs release dopamine (but also norepinephrine and serotonin) from presynaptic terminals in the frontal portion of the brain, where attention and impulsivity are regulated. They also inhibit norepinephrine and dopamine reuptake. Between 70% to 90% of children respond positively to the major psychostimulant drugs currently available, which include dextroamphetamine, methylphenidate, and pemoline. Moderate doses appear to improve attention, concentration, and cognitive functioning in adults as well. ADHD in adults remains a somewhat controversial and less thoroughly studied condition, but many adults with the disorder are regularly prescribed methylphenidate.

There are three primary medications prescribed from this class. Methylphenidate, the most widely used and studied psychostimulant, was introduced in 1958 as a treatment for children with hyperactivity. It has a half-life of only 2 to 3 hours which, while requiring that it be taken two to four times daily, is advantageous in that it does not impair sleep. Methylphenidate requires only 30 to 60 minutes to take effect but is associated with symptom aggravation 10 to 20 hours after a dose. A time-release form of the drug is available. Pemoline has a longer half-life (2 to 12 hours) and only needs to be taken once daily. Its lesser stimulant effect may also lessen its abuse potential. On the negative side, it has not been researched as extensively as methylphenidate and may require several weeks to demonstrate a therapeutic effect. Dextroamphetamine remains an alternative medication. It is fast-acting and needs only to be taken twice per day, with a 6 to 7 hour half-life. However, it has a high potential for abuse and diversion to the illicit drug market.

Children with ADHD can remain symptomatic through adolescence and early adulthood, but studies about drug effectiveness beyond puberty is not extensive. There is some evidence that treatment in childhood leads to better outcomes in adulthood.

ADVERSE EFFECTS OF
PSYCHOTROPIC MEDICATION

Social workers have firsthand involvement with the side effects of medication as monitors, client educators, and possibly the first line of intervention if clients develop concerns. As defined earlier, side effects are the physical, psychological, or social effects of a medication that are unintentional and unrelated to its desired therapeutic effect. We use the term "adverse effects" to refer to bothersome and potentially harmful side effects. Clients may experience some side effects as pleasant, such as the mildly sedative effect of some anti-anxiety drugs, but even these may present health and safety concerns. Because all medications act on areas of the nervous system, adverse effects are most readily recognized in their physical form. However, such effects may also be psychological, insofar as they affect the consumer's sense of self, and social, insofar as they impact how he or she is viewed by others. Still, the adverse physical effects are frequently of most immediate concern to the physician and social worker because of their potentially negative impact on physical well-being. All three types of adverse effects, however, are equally important to monitor.

Adverse Physical Effects: Definitions

Anticholinergic effects (ACE) Dry mouth, blurred vision, constipation, and urinary hesitancy. These side effects result from the suppressive action of some antipsychotic and antidepressant medications on the pyramidal nerve pathways (those parts of the peripheral nervous system that govern fine motor activities). Specifically, the drugs block cholinergic receptors, which is the source of the name of these effects.

Extrapyramidal symptoms (EPS) Akathisia, the dystonias, parkinsonian symptoms, and tardive dyskinesia. These effects are related to the actions of drugs on extrapyramidal nerve pathways via central basal ganglia pathways and occur most commonly with the antipsychotic medications. *Akathisia* is an internal state of restlessness, or the perceived need to be in constant motion, accompanied by muscle discomfort. *Dystonia* refers to the uncoordinated and involuntary twisting movements produced by sustained muscle spasms. *Parkinsonian effects* include the reduction in range of one's facial and arm movements, muscle rigidity and tremor, shuffling gait, drooling, and difficulty either starting or stopping movements.

In *tardive dyskinesia*, the word *tardive* is defined as "appearing late" (because these effects occur often, but not always, in some consumers who have taken a medication for many years), and *dyskinesia* refers to a distortion of voluntary movements. In contrast to dystonia, this condition refers to involuntary rhythmic movements in facial muscles, including spasms of the eyelids, repeated puckering of the mouth, licking or smacking movements, and lip tremors. The tongue may curl or push on the cheek. This disorder can also affect the body's extremities and trunk region.

Neuroleptic malignant syndrome Hyperthermia (high fever), muscle rigidity, fluctuating levels of consciousness, and instability in the autonomic nervous system. A rare (0.1% of consumers) but potentially fatal (15% to 25% of those afflicted) toxic complication of antipsychotic drug treatment, this syndrome generally occurs within two weeks after the initiation of treatment.

Orthostatic hypotension A sudden drop in blood pressure that occurs when rising from a lying or sitting position to a standing one, accompanied by dizziness, lightheadedness, weakness, and an unsteady gait. Though transient, this effect may cause one to fall and thus is of particular concern with physically frail persons, including older adults.

Sedation Drowsiness.

Sexual dysfunction Changes in sexual desire and capacity, including problems with erection, ejaculation, and impotence in men and orgasmic dysfunction in women. These symptoms relate to disruption in the normal functioning of the autonomic nervous system.

Tachycardia An increase in heart rate resulting from adverse effects of antidepressant medications acting on the autonomic nervous system. It is a serious concern for consumers with cardiac problems.

Adverse Physical Effects: Factors in Their Production

So far, in this chapter we have outlined the adverse physical effects of psychotropic medications. However, factors besides the chemical makeup of a drug also determine possible side effects. One factor, for example, is dosage. Generally speaking, the higher the dosage, the greater the likelihood of adverse reactions. The following five characteristics of clients also impact the occurrence of adverse effects (see chapter 5 for a more detailed discussion).

Age A person's rate of metabolism slows down during later life. For this reason, elderly consumers are particularly susceptible to such adverse effects as sedation, weight gain, and parkinsonian symptoms. Orthostatic hypotension (lowered blood pressure), though not more common among older adults, is potentially more serious because they are relatively frail and are prone to injury if they fall. However, young people are more at risk for dystonias (muscle spasms), indicating that there is not a simple correlation between age and all adverse effects.

Gender Women are at higher risk than men for tardive dyskinesia, parkinsonian symptoms, and akathisia. Women with bipolar disorder are also at higher risk for experiencing a manic reaction to antidepressant medication than are men. On the other hand, men are at higher risk for dystonia than women. These differences are apparently due to hormonal characteristics, but there is a need for more research to understand more fully how gender influences the positive and negative effects of medication (see chapter 5).

Diagnosis People with organic brain damage and affective disorders demonstrate a greater propensity for tardive dyskinesia and neuroleptic malignant syndrome than people with other diagnoses. Those with medical illnesses have an increased risk for neuroleptic malignant syndrome with antipsychotic medication and delirium with the antidepressants. Furthermore, depressed persons seem to be at a higher risk for orthostatic hypotension than other diagnostic groups, for reasons not yet clear.

Personality There is some indication that consumers who are action-oriented and have a high need to control their environment may react paradoxically to sedating medications, becoming agitated and confused rather than calmed.

Ethnicity As discussed in chapter 5, race and ethnicity are not frequently differentiated in research on drug effectiveness, but occasionally they are relevant factors in consumer response. Asian clients improve on lower doses of antipsychotic medications than Europeans or Americans do, but they also experience EPS at lower doses than comparison groups. Asian clients may also metabolize antianxiety medications at a slower rate and experience toxicity more often. Asian and Hispanic clients also respond more quickly to, and have more adverse effects from, cyclic antidepressant medications than other groups. African Americans seem to respond more rapidly than Caucasians to cyclic antidepressant medications.

Adverse Psychological Effects

Psychological side effects occur when the act of taking medication negatively affects the client's self-concept. No less important than adverse physical effects, psychological effects probably account for an equal number of cases in which clients discontinue medications (Sclar, 1991). We note these here briefly and discuss them in detail in chapter 7.

The ongoing use of any type of medication raises several concerns for clients regarding dependency. For instance, consumers must perceive at some level that, at least temporarily, they depend on a chemical agent to function at a desired level. Clients must also consider that their previous coping skills may have been insufficient to manage certain thought or mood problems. Though clients may be relieved to have a means to regain a higher level of stability, their sense of psychological efficacy may nevertheless be somewhat diminished.

Adverse Social Effects

Adverse social effects refer to the interpersonal and organizational barriers clients face daily as identified consumers of psychotropic medications. Auge and Herzlech (1998) have outlined aspects of the "sick role." In receiving the diagnosis of a mental disorder and accepting treatments for it, including medication, an individual acknowledges that he or she has a condition that requires the help of experts. Regarding social norms, the client may be temporarily excused from certain interpersonal and occupational responsibilities if he or she agrees to participate actively in treatment for the illness. Of course, a few clients may refuse to take medications, because they do not want to acknowledge a sickness or accept the stigma that accompany that role. As noted earlier, clients may not agree that they have a problem, may not agree with the details of its assessment, or may not believe that it is serious enough to require certain treatments, including medication. However, if clients with mental illness reject the sick role and also fail to maintain work, family, and other social responsibilities, they will be labeled as irresponsible. They may, for example, lose a job rather than be given temporary leave if they fail to manage ordinary work responsibilities.

Of course, acknowledging a mental illness does foster a social stigma. For example, many employers may be reluctant to hire persons with mental disorders if this becomes known or if they note medications and illnesses on job applications, despite the legal implications of the Americans with Disabilities Act (Bricout, 1999). Further, because of the chronic nature of some disorders, a person's genuine growth may go unacknowledged by those around him or her, assuming that serious problems will inevitably follow. The adverse social effects of taking medication are very serious and may be addressed by the social worker in the roles of advocate (in the case of job discrimination, for example), monitor, and educator.

SUMMARY

Psychotropic medications produce changes in a client's emotions, thoughts, and behaviors by altering existing processes in the central and peripheral nervous systems. They interfere with natural neurotransmitter processes—increasing or decreasing the levels of those chemical substances in nerve pathways—to produce change. Though the details of how these systems work still lie beyond the full comprehension of scientists, enough is known about the structure of the brain and its neurons that reasonable hypotheses exist to account for the actions of medications. Because drug actions are not specific enough—that is, because they affect sites in the brain beyond those which are targeted as the source of mental illness—adverse effects are common.

The social worker must be able to assess and monitor all medication effects as they impact the client's overall physical, mental, and emotional well-being. A physician may prescribe medications as a primary or secondary method of intervention, but in either case, drugs do not represent the entire problem-solving process in the treatment of mental illness. The social worker must be prepared to use other interventions to fully enhance a client's social functioning. A basic knowledge of pharmacokinetics and pharmocodynamics does, however, equip the social worker to understand the major positive and negative effects of drugs on clients, to explain such effects to clients and their families, and to make informed decisions about intervention from a biopsychosocial systems perspective.

4

Specific Medications for Specific Disorders

Having examined the structure of the body's nervous system, the characteristics of neurotransmitters, and the actions of psychotropic drugs within the body, we now turn more specifically to the range of drugs used in the treatment of mental disorders. In this chapter we outline the specific disorders that the five classes of medications are intended to treat and the symptoms they most significantly impact. We describe their adverse physical, psychological, and social effects as well; in chapter 8 we focus particular attention on the social worker's management of their adverse effects. We emphasize again that the social worker is in an ideal situation to mediate among the physician, the client, and his or her significant others to monitor both positive and negative effects of medications.

The primary sources we used to research this material include the American Psychiatric Association (1994), Bentley (1998), Bentley and Walsh (1998), Bernstein (1995), Campbell (1996), Julien (1998), Kaplan and Sadock (1998), Schatzberg and Nemeroff (1995), Skolnick (1997), Stahl (1996), and Walsh (1999, 1998). Additional sources are cited within the chapter.

ANTIPSYCHOTIC MEDICATIONS

Mental disorders that feature symptoms of psychosis, which the antipsychotic class of medication targets, are generally characterized by the client's being out of touch with reality. These disorders of thought greatly impair one's reality testing, or ability to evaluate the outside world objectively. The individual with psychosis is at least temporarily unable to evaluate the accuracy of his or her perceptions and thoughts, making many incorrect inferences about the outside world, even in the face of contrary evidence. With respect to the *Diagnostic and Statistical Manual of Mental Disorders (DSM-IV)*, disorders featuring psychosis include the schizophrenias, delusional disorders, other psychotic disorders, schizoaffective disorder, schizophreniform disorder, bipolar disorder, major depressions that include psychotic symptoms, and some organic mental disorders. People with schizotypal personality disorder, not technically a psychotic disorder, may also be treated with antipsychotic medications. Though other types of emotional trauma may include transient psychotic symptoms, such traumas are not classified as psychotic disorders if they are secondary to some other stress related to social functioning. Additionally, symptoms of high anxiety or agitation are sometimes treated with low doses of antipsychotic medications.

Symptoms of Psychotic Disorders

Though psychotic disorders are primarily disorders of thought, they can affect one's mood as well. Listed below are common symptoms of psychosis, all of which stem from the underlying thought disorder that the medications are intended to treat. Examples are in italics. Not all persons with psychosis exhibit all these symptoms, and some of these are not specific to psychotic disorders. Because the DSM-IV organizes diagnoses around clusters of symptoms, a diagnosis is rarely made on the basis of one psychotic symptom in the absence of other features.

1. **Delusion.** A false belief firmly maintained even though contradicted by social reality. Types of delusions include the following:
   a. **Persecutory delusion.** The belief that certain people or forces are attempting to bring one harm. *Spirits follow John to and from school each day to make sure that he is too distracted to perform his course work. John does not see the spirits but is certain that they are nearby.*
   b. **Thought broadcasting.** The belief that one's thoughts are overheard by others. *Sarah is anxious with her parents because she knows that they can hear her thinking about sex at the dinner table.*
   c. **Thought insertion.** The belief that others are putting thoughts into one's head. *Paul cannot sleep at night because corporate executives from a neighboring state are negotiating with him about adopting his business ideas. They relay information about their plans directly into his mind.*

  d. **Thought withdrawal.** The belief that others are taking thoughts out of one's head. *Paul also believes that other businessmen are stealing his ideas, which he does not write down but keeps in memory.*

  e. **Delusions of being controlled.** Experiencing thoughts, feelings, or actions as not being one's own but imposed by an external force. *Brenda feels that her deceased mother is controlling her actions and causing her to commit sinful acts, such as stealing money from her friends.*

  f. **Delusions of reference.** Experiencing actual events as having a special significance, usually negative. *Leon, who lives in a violent neighborhood, believes that every crime committed there is a manifestation of his evil nature.*

  g. **Somatic delusion.** A false belief in which the main content pertains to the functioning of one's body. *For three years Gail has continually believed that she is pregnant by a young man she admires in the neighborhood, even though they have never met.*

  h. **Grandiosity.** An exaggerated sense of one's power, knowledge, or identity. Grandiosity may be religious in nature. *Dave believes that it is his responsibility to mediate in the great war being waged here on earth between God and Satan.*

2. **Hallucinations.** The false sense perceptions of external objects that do not exist. Six common types are described below:

  a. **Auditory.** Hearing voices or sounds that are not in fact present. *Susan hears the voice of her father, who lives hundreds of miles away, asking for her support as he deals with his difficult job.*

  b. **Visual.** Seeing objects or images that are not present. *John is afraid to attend his socialization group because there is always an alien seated across the room from him, making him afraid.*

  c. **Tactile.** Feeling an object that is not present. *Robert feels a rubbing against his leg. He believes a woman who wants to become sexually involved with him is doing it. He also wakes up many nights with the sensation that someone is smothering him.*

  d. **Somatic.** Feeling an unreal experience within the body. *Kathy continually feels the sensation of blood streaming down the back of her throat.*

  e. **Olfactory.** A false sense of smell. *Mary reports that she constantly smells the aroma of rotting food.*

  f. **Hypersensitivity** (to sight, sound, and smell). This is not a true hallucination, but borders on such because the person's perceptual capacities are altered to a significant degree. *Holly, when becoming psychotic, reports that the colors of nature are blinding in their brightness and that objects are surrounded by misty, colorful halos.*

3. **Disturbances in the form of thought.** Loose associations, or thinking processes that become illogical, confused, and bizarre. Normal associations are the threads that guide logical thinking, but in psychosis these threads can lose their continuity. *Kevin cannot carry on any conversation for long, because his thoughts always get sidetracked onto tangents influenced by his*

preoccupation with colors. Thus, mention of a fire engine makes him think of and speak about roses, cherries, cardinals, etc.

4. **Disturbances in affect.** Disturbances in the experience and presentation of mood.

   a. **Flat affect.** Constriction of emotional expression or the feelings that accompany thoughts. Also, an incongruity between affect and thought; a shallowness in one's response to ideas and events. *Cynthia sits with her relatives at family gatherings and demonstrates no visible emotional reactions to their behaviors, giving the impression that she is lost in her own world. Regardless of the topic, she does not respond emotionally when old friends or neighbors talk with her.*

   b. **Inappropriate affect.** Inconsistent or exaggerated mood; a lack of ability to modulate mood in accordance with one's thoughts. *Cheryl tends to giggle uncontrollably when in groups of people, regardless of the nature of the interactions.*

5. **Weakened ego boundaries** (the boundary, or sense of distinctiveness, between the self and the external world). Losing the ability to distinguish between what comes from within and what comes from without. In boundary loss, perceptions take on an unfamiliar or unreal quality. *Laura believes that she is a psychological extension of her mother. She always reflects the same moods as her mother because, she believes, they are not distinct people.*

The following are nonpsychotic symptoms commonly seen in persons with psychotic disorders.

6. **Ambivalence.** The desire to do a certain thing accompanied by an equally strong desire not to do that same thing. Many persons with schizophrenia, for example, have great difficulty making or sustaining commitments to carry out any plans regarding life goals. *Scott cannot commit himself to attending his job-training program every day. He wants to work and has some confidence in his abilities, but at the same time he is overwhelmed with anxiety and self-doubt. As a result, he does not shown up at his training site several days per week.*

7. **Impaired volition.** Sustained deliberation giving way to whimsy in decision making, and goal-oriented behavior disintegrating into contradictory wishes and ill-sustained ideas. *Shirley cannot sustain a focus on personal goals. By turns, she wants to be a hairdresser, a housewife, a model, a foreign-language teacher, and an interior decorator. These goals change at least weekly, and she is unqualified for any of them.*

8. **Agitation.** A state of tension in which anxiety is manifested by hyperactivity and general perturbation. *Because of his chronic state of emotional discomfort, and because he feels threatened by what most people would consider ordinary demands of daily living, Howard tends to become easily upset. When frustrated at his inability to perform simple tasks or carry out normal conversations, he lashes out verbally at those around him, blaming them for his failures. Through this process, he is in fact venting his emotional distress.*

9. **Social isolation.** The disinclination or fear of making contact with other members of social groups, which may relate to the symptoms of psychosis.

Sandy has learned during the course of her schizophrenia that she experiences fewer hallucinations and feels calmer when alone, away from the stimulation she experiences in the presence of others. She now spends most of the day in her bedroom, reading novels. Her parents try hard to engage her in family and social activities, but Sandy resists, paradoxically to preserve a sense of well-being.

10. **Poverty of speech content.** Speech that contains little information because of vagueness or obscure word choices. *Brian speaks in short phrases and answers questions in one or two words. His friends are not always sure what he is saying, although as they spend more time with him they better understand the meanings of his odd words and terse phrasings. Surprisingly, Brian perceives himself as talkative. He is an example of a schizophrenic person whose mental life is active but who cannot communicate ideas adequately because of a poor social orientation. His odd choice of words is related to a detachment from social life and the commonly understood abstract terms that people use to convey ideas.*

11. **Mania.** A state in which one's mood is extremely elevated, unrestrained, or irritable. Though this will be discussed more fully in a later section of the chapter, we note it here because manic episodes can feature psychotic symptoms, most frequently delusions of grandiosity.

Besides these symptoms, people with chronic psychotic disorders sometimes neglect hygiene and personal appearance. When they exist, these behaviors generally indicate a preoccupation with mental processes at the expense of social and self-care concerns. By no means do all persons with serious mental disorders behave this way, but when they do, it indicates not a willful disregard for self-care but rather an impairment in their ability to focus their thoughts on the normal activities of daily living.

SPECIFIC MEDICATIONS

Origins

The field of psychopharmacology did not generate much interest among mental health professionals until after World War II. Drugs such as opium, morphine, bromide derivatives, chloral hydrate, and other barbiturate compounds were used only for the sedative control of the symptoms of mental illness in state hospital settings from the beginning of the 19th century. After the war, however, the great successes of the new antibiotic drugs led to a strong faith in the power of medications to treat diseases of all types. It was in this context that the first antipsychotic medications were introduced.

The story of the development of chlorpromazine is a fascinating example of how science and serendipity governed the early days of psychopharmacology (Sweazey, 1974). The drug's parent compound, phenothiazine, was synthesized in Germany in 1883 as the basis for a new synthetic blue dye. The field of organic chemistry was new and exciting at that time, and like other discoveries phenothizine was investigated for other possible uses. It was found to be ineffective as an insecticide and antimalarial agent, but in the latter experiments it demonstrated antihistaminic qualities.

By 1900 it had been discovered that in humans histamine substances caused shock (characterized by a rapid drop in blood pressure and a loss of fluid from the circulatory system), and research was initiated to develop antihistamines for treating shock in medical patients. From the beginning it was observed that these substances had a strong sedative quality, but this was considered to be an undesirable side effect. Synthetic antihistamine research was undertaken during the 1930s in Germany and France in response to the demands of treating World War II casualties, and it was discovered that the phenothiazine-derived compounds were most efficient for this purpose. They seemed to affect the central nervous system but not muscular functions.

Interestingly, as a side note, these drugs were used as early as the 1940s in some settings for the sedation of manic and other agitated psychotic persons. In the populous laboratories of the state hospitals, it had been observed that persons in acute psychotic states did not seem to suffer from allergic diseases; they seemed to have a decreased histamine sensitivity. Through a curious reverse logic, this led to the experimental use of antihistamines as a means of reducing the symptoms of schizophrenia.

In the early 1950s antihistamines such as chlorpromazine were utilized in medicine as presurgery anesthetics, pain medication, and treatment for shock. During its testing, alert researchers observed that chlorpromazine lowered the body temperatures of animals. Because cold water and cold packs had long been used as a means of sedating mental patients, it was hypothesized that the new drug might have the same effect. It failed to lower body temperatures but was effective in controlling agitated behavior. By 1952 a series of papers appeared in the medical literature, noting the positive impact of chlorpromazine on a range of mental disorders.

Between 1952 and 1954, chlorpromazine was formally tested as an antipsychotic drug with positive results. In the United States the Food and Drug Administration formally approved it in March, 1954, for the treatment of nausea and vomiting and in neuropsychiatry. The American drug company Smith, Kline, and French had difficulty with its marketing because of psychiatry's adherence to the psychodynamic model of treatment and the problem of public financing of the drug for state hospital use. Through aggressive lobbying, the company was able to persuade state legislatures to invest money in the drug, arguing that the resulting deinstitutionalization would lower the total cost of public mental health. Eventually chlorpromazine became widely used and, despite what we now know to be its extreme limitations, was rightly proclaimed as psychiatry's first wonder drug.

Current Medications

There are now many drugs available for treating psychotic disorders (see Table 4.1). Though all effectively reduce or eliminate the symptoms described earlier, not all are suitable in every case. Clients respond to them differently

Table 4.1 Antipsychotic Medications

Drug	Trade Name	Preparation*	Usual Daily Dosage
CONVENTIONAL ANTIPSYCHOTICS			
Acetophenazine	Tindal	T	60–120 mg
Chlorpromazine	Thorazine	T, C, S, I	300–800 mg
Chlorprothixene	Taractan	T, S, I	50–400 mg
Fluphenazine	Prolixin	T, I	1–20 mg
Haloperidol	Haldol	T, S, PI	6–20 mg
Loxapine	Loxitane	C, S, I	60–100 mg
Mesoridazine	Serentil	T, S, I	75–300 mg
Molindone	Moban	T, S	50–100 mg
Perphenazine	Trilafon	T, S, I	8–40 mg
Thioridazine	Mellaril	C, S, I	200–700 mg
Thiothixene	Navane	C, S, I	6–30 mg
Trifluoperazine	Stelazine	T	6–20 mg
Triflupromazine	Vesprin	I	100–150 mg
NEWER ANTIPSYCHOTICS			
Amperozide	Not yet available		5–20 mg
Clozapine	Clozaril	T	400–600 mg
Olanzapine	Zyprexa	T	10–20 mg
Quetiapene	Seroquel	T	150–800 mg
Risperidone	Risperdal	T	4–6 mg
Ziprasidone	Not yet available		

*T = Tablets, C = Capsules, S = Solutions, I = Injectable

because of variations in body chemistry, metabolism, and other personal characteristics. It is estimated that as few as 15% of persons with schizophrenia derive what might be called "optimal" benefit from antipsychotic drugs. Thus, as many as 30 to 50% of persons with chronic schizophrenia are really best described as "partial responders" (Lieberman, 1996). For reasons that are not clear, antipsychotic medications generally succeed more at treating hallucinations than delusions. Further, they tend to control the positive symptoms of psychosis (bizarre thinking and behavior) more so than the negative symptoms (apathy, withdrawal, and poverty of thought), although there is some evidence that the newer medications have an impact on negative symptoms. Most work by blocking dopamine receptors in the brain. The half-lives of all the antipsychotic drugs are relatively long (10 to 20 hours), so in many cases they can be taken once daily.

All these medications have adverse effects. Though some are more serious than others, all cause the client discomfort, so it is important to evaluate all effects throughout the treatment period. Table 4.2 summarizes the four categories of adverse effects of the antipsychotic medications. As defined earlier, sedation refers to the degree of drowsiness caused by the

Table 4.2 Adverse Effects of Antipsychotic Medications

Drug	Typical Adverse Effects
Chlorpromazine Chlorprothixene Clozapine Quietapine Thioridazine	Significant levels of sedation, blurred vision, constipation, urinary impairment, dry skin, weight gain, gastrointestinal discomfort, and lowering of blood pressure (lightheadedness)
Acetophenazine Haloperidol Perphenazine Thiothixene	Moderate levels of muscle spasms (in tongue, face, neck, and back); restlessness and anxiety
Fluphenazine Molindone Olanzapine Trifluoperazine	Moderate levels of sedation; greater possibility of spasms (in tongue, face, neck, and back); restlessness and anxiety
Loxapine Mesoridazine	Moderate levels of sedation, blurred vision, constipation, urinary impairment, dry skin, weight gain, gastrointestinal discomfort, and lowering of blood pressure (lightheadedness). Greater possibility of spasms (as described above), restlessness, and anxiety
Risperidone	Moderate levels of sedation, blurred vision, constipation, urinary impairment, dry skin, weight gain, and gastrointestinal discomfort
Triflupromazine	Significant levels of sedation; moderate levels of blurred vision, constipation, urinary impairment, dry skin, weight gain, and gastrointestinal discomfort; high possibility of lowered blood pressure; moderate levels of spasms, restlessness

drug. The anticholinergic effects (ACE) include dry mouth, constipation, blurred vision, and urinary retention. Hypotensive effects involve lowering of blood pressure. Extrapyramidal symptoms (EPS) include muscle spasms, stiffness, tremor, reduced movement in the facial muscles, and restlessness. These factors vary predictably between low- and high-potency medications. High-potency medications are those prescribed in lower milligram dosages (such as haloperidol), while low-potency drugs are given in high milligram amounts (such as chlorpromazine). Potency is unrelated, however, to effectiveness.

Two other types of potentially serious side effects of antipsychotic drugs include tardive dyskinesia and neuroleptic malignant syndrome. Defined earlier in this chapter, these are summarized in Table 4.3, along with other types of side effects and information about their treatment. Neuroleptic malignant syndrome, though rare, is the most severe because it represents an immediate life-threatening reaction to a medication. Symptoms evolve over a period of 1 to 3 days; the untreated course of the syndrome unfolds over two weeks. Clients with these symptoms must immediately stop taking the medication and receive emergency medical treatment.

Table 4.3 Types of Side Effects of Antipsychotic Medications

Reaction	Features	Treatment
Acute dystonia	Spasms of tongue, face, neck, back; mini-seizures	Antiparkinsonian drug
Akathisia	Restlessness with anxiety or agitation	Reduce dose, change drug, propranolol, benzodiazepines, antiparkinsonian drug
Anticholinergic effects	Blurred vision, confusion, constipation, dry skin, delayed urination, sweating, gastrointestinal discomfort, sexual dysfunction, weight gain	No medical treatment; specific symptoms may be alleviated with diet, exercise, use of fluids
Malignant syndrome	Catatonia, stupor, fever, unstable pulse and blood pressure	Stop medication
Parkinsonism	Motor slowing, retarded facila movement, rigidity, gait disturbance, resting tremor	Antiparkinsonian drug
Tardive dykinesia	Involuntary rhythmic movement in mouth and face; spastic movements in limbs	No treatment; gradual remission is possible

Tardive dyskinesia, also extremely serious, can be a long-term side effect of the neuroleptic medications. Though there is some controversy regarding its prevalence, its incidence increases by about 4% per year after 5 years of antipsychotic medication treatment (Jeste & Caligiuri, 1993). Tardive dyskinesia tends to occur later in treatment, and strike older adults and people with mood disorders. Its symptoms become more apparent when consumers take reduced doses of the responsible medication. The potential for permanent damage will continue with higher doses of medication, however, even though the observable symptoms may remit. The prognosis is variable, but anticholinergic drugs apparently worsen the condition. Finally, the more acute dystonias occur early on and strike younger people, males, and people with mood disorders. Anticholinergic (also known as antiparkinsonian) drugs may ameliorate the condition.

We will now describe the antipsychotic medications in more detail by separating them into two categories—the conventional and newer antipsychotic drugs.

Conventional Antipsychotics

The "conventional" antipsychotics, or those developed prior to the mid-1980s, are associated with symptom improvement for over two-thirds of people who use them. They are also available at a relatively low cost, and many are available in a variety of preparations (such as tablet, capsule, or injection). The well-known and bothersome adverse effects of the conventional antipsychotics are one of the disadvantages of their use. These effects have a notable impact on adherence and often contribute to a poorer quality of life for people with schizophrenia. In general, high potency drugs (such as haloperidol and navane) are associated with more EPS, whereas low-potency drugs (such as chlorpromazine and thioridazine) are associated with greater sedation and hypotension. Because EPS effects are often more easily managed, the high-potency medications are more frequently prescribed. They can also be administered intramuscularly where a peak blood concentration is reached in as little as a half hour (versus 2 to 3 hours when taken orally). In addition, finding the therapeutic dose occurs more quickly with high-potency drugs.

Most of the gains garnered from the drug treatment of schizophrenia occur in the acute phase of the illness, or the first 6 to 8 weeks following onset. More subtle gains may continue for up to 30 weeks. For the average consumer, there is general agreement that, on average, 300–750 mg of chlorpromazine or its equivalent dosage of another medication is needed to achieve a therapeutic effect. When a person first develops symptoms, a common medication strategy is to prescribe a high-potency short-acting benzodiazepine (a type of anti-anxiety drug) together with a low dose of high-potency medication. In this way the physician tries to quickly reduce psychotic symptoms while also reducing anxiety, with less worry about over-medication.

In the maintenance phase of treatment, exacerbation of symptoms occurs within a year in about 55% of clients receiving placebo versus 14 to 21% of those on conventional antipsychotic medications. While this decrease in the risk of relapse supports the use of antipsychotics in the later phases of treatment, there is more debate about appropriate dosing and medication management strategies in these phases. The minimally effective dose to protect 50% of persons with schizophrenia is typically between 50–150 chlorpromazine (CPZ) equivalents (the number of milligrams of chlorpromazine that are equivalent to the dose of the other drug). While higher doses may be needed by 25% of consumers, the final 25% can be maintained on even lower doses.

A maintenance strategy called "continued low-dose" may be gaining favor with stable persons with schizophrenia because of its demonstrated preventive effects on relapse and reduced side effects. This strategy is characterized by dose reductions below the standard (mean ratio of standard- to low-dose is 3.3 to 1). The APA (1997) recommends reducing dosages about 20% every six months during the maintenance phase until a minimum dose is established. "Targeted" or "intermittent" dose strategies, on the other hand, may be losing favor. This strategy calls for the administration of medication on some fixed schedule and making changes when the warning signs of relapse first appear. Subsequent relapse rates may be too high to justify widespread use of this strategy. A consensus also exists that oral medication is the first-choice route of administration for compliant consumers because of its ease of administration and respect for one's sense of autonomy. Nevertheless, injectible medications are always an option for reducing the risk of relapse, especially for consumers who have difficulty with adherence.

There are no substantial differences in efficacy among the conventional antipsychotics. As with all prescriptions, physicians prescribe a specific medication for a client based on factors including previous treatment response, the desired side-effect profile, the consumer's preference, and the phase of the illness. Psychiatrists often develop preferences for certain medications. Individualized titration is key in decisions regarding drug choice, dosage, and maintenance strategies. This is one of the most important points for social workers to understand as they collaborate with clients, families, and other providers around medication issues.

Adjunctive and Side-Effect Medications

A number of adjunctive medications are used for persons with schizophrenia to treat adverse effects and sometimes to enhance the efficacy of the primary antipsychotic medication or treat residual symptoms. These agents do not dramatically affect the consumers' functioning beyond what is experienced with the antipsychotics, but modest additive improvements or a reduction of side effects can improve the quality of life for some persons. Unfortunately, some of the adjunctive treatments also have adverse effects; thus decisions regarding their use takes place in a cost-benefit context. Depending on whether the physician is trying to reduce side effects or reduce residual symptoms, this might include reducing dosages, changing to a lower potency conventional drug, or moving to a newer antipsychotic. Table 4.4 provides a list of the generic names, brand names, classes of medication, and usual dosages of the common adjunctive and side-effect medications.

Under the category of *antiparkinsonian medications*, several types of agents are used to reduce the EPS experienced with antipsychotic medications. Trihexyphenidyl, a drug first used to treat Parkinson's disease, is a commonly used anticholinergic (an antagonist of acetylcholine) drug. Benztropine, another anticholinergic, is available in tablet and injectible forms and is effective in controlling tremor, spasms, and rigidity. Because of associated euphoria, anticholinergic drugs can be abused or combined with street drugs for enhanced effect. Diphenhydramine is the primary antihistamine used as an antiparkinsonian drug.

Other medications can also be used to treat EPS. Beta blockers, first used to treat hypertension and cardiovascular problems, have been found effective in treating akathisia. The anti-anxiety benzodiazepine drugs are sometimes used with antipsychotic medications to treat EPS, especially akathisia, though they are not yet formally approved for this use. In the absence of controlled research, controversy about the use of all antiparkinsonian drugs persists. Areas of uncertainty relate to the appropriateness of their prophylactic use, the appropriate length of treatment, and procedures for withdrawing the medications. Apart from treating EPS, benzodiazepines have also been tested for their ability to enhance the effects of antipsychotics or treat residual

**Table 4.4 Adjunctive and Side-Effect Medications
Used in Treating Schizophrenia**

Generic Name	Brand Name	Type of Medication	Usual Daily Dose
alprazolam	Xanax	benzodiazepine	0.5–4 mg
amantadine	Symmetrel	dopaminergic	100–300 mg
benztropine	Cogentin	anticholinergic	0.5–8 mg
biperiden	Akineton	antiparkinsonian	2–20 mg
carbamazepine	Tegretol	anticonvulsant	800–1200 mg
clonazepam	Klonipin	benzodiazepine	0.5–10 mg
clonidine	Catapres	antihypertensive	0.3 mg
diazepam	Valium	benzodiazepine	2–60 mg
diphenhydramine	Benadryl	antihistamine	25–200 mg
ethoprozapine	Parsidol	anticholinergic	50–600 mg
lithium carbonate	Eskalith	antimanic	900–2100 mg
lorazepam	Ativan	benzodiazepine	2–6 mg
metoprolol	Lopressor	antihypertensive	150–300 mg
orphenadrine	Norflex	antiparkinsonian	50–300 mg
procyclidine	Kemadrin	antiparkinsonian	5–20 mg
propranolol	Inderal	antihypertensive	60–120 mg
trihexiphenidyl	Artane	anticholinergic	2–20 mg
valproate	Depakote	anticonvulsant	1200–1500 mg

symptoms. Uncontrolled studies suggest that they may be a useful adjunct in acute situations for some consumers.

Some research supports the use of lithium as an adjunct to antipsychotic drugs with persons who also suffer from depression, tend to be aggressive or agitated, or have residual negative symptoms. Anticonvulsant medications such as carbamazepine and valproate have been found in some studies to have usefulness in clients with electroencephlogram (EEG) abnormalities or a coexisting seizure disorder and with hostile, agitated, or violent persons with schizophrenia.

The Newer Antipsychotics

The new antipsychotic medications were initially categorized as "atypical," although they have now been on the market for up to 10 years (see also Table 4.1). They do not seem to cause the same levels of EPS that are associated with conventional neuroleptics, although they do include adverse effects. While their precise mechanisms of action are not fully known, the newer medications tend to have broader action on neurotransmitters, impacting serotonin, acetylcholine, and norepinephrine, in addition to subtypes of dopamine receptors. While a major advantage of these medications is their improved side-effect profile for some clients, a clear disadvantage is their cost. Many can exceed $4000 a year. At 20 mg a day, the conventional medication haloperidol costs $10 a week compared to $106 a week for clozapine at 400 mg a day. It is also likely to be several years before the newer drugs are available in preparations other than tablet.

Clozapine was developed in the 1960s, but it has only been since the publication of an impressive study by Kane and associates (1988) that the drug has gained wide recognition and use in this country. They reported positive results for 30% of subjects in reducing both positive and negative symptoms in a relatively short time (two weeks) when compared to treatment with chlorpromazine. Given the fact that all of the subjects were those for whom a number of trials with conventional antipsychotics had failed, this was a major step forward. A number of well-controlled studies since then indicate that 40 to 60% of people with schizophrenia who are treated for at least four months with clozapine will have a positive response. One of the highly touted aspects of clozapine is its seemingly superior impact on negative symptoms, although this may be related to the fact that it does not bring on EPS, which often mimic negative symptoms.

The typical daily dosage of clozapine is between 300–600 mg, with a maximum allowable dose of 900 mg. Common side effects and the range of percentages of people who experience them include sedation (20 to 50%), hypersalivation (30%), weight gain (13 to 23%), tachycardia (12 to 25%), and seizures (in 6 to 8% of those on doses above 600 mg). Ironically, weight gain also correlates with a clinical response; those who gain the most weight also experience the greatest benefit. Agranulocytosis, a dangerous condition in which white blood cells become depleted, is said to occur in approximately 1% of cases; thus mandatory blood counts are still required. Because agranulocytosis is most likely to occur during the first six months of treatment (up to 80% in the first 18 weeks), consumers in the United States can reduce the frequency of blood tests from weekly to biweekly after six months. Other minor adverse effects include dizziness, constipation, nausea, orthostatic hypotension, and a transient fever during the first few weeks of treatment.

The development of risperidone, marketed in 1994, as a first-line resource—not just for those deemed "treatment resistant" like clozapine—is in part related to the concern about agranulocytosis. While numerous studies support risperidone's efficacy and possible usefulness in treating negative symptoms, existing data is limited, and there is a need for more controlled research. The most effective dose of risperidone for the typical consumer is 4–8 mg; larger doses are associated with the same EPS typically associated with conventional antipsychotics. One study noted the prevalence of side effects: weight gain (34%), sedation (33%), orthostatic hypotension (18%), and decreased sexual drive (10%) (Peuskens, 1995). Because risperidone elevates prolactin levels, disturbances in menstruation are possible. A few cases of neuroleptic malignant syndrome (NMS) have been reported, but the risk for consumers developing tardive dyskinesia is unknown.

Olanzapine was approved for use in the United States in 1996. It is similar to clozapine in chemical structure. The drug is believed to have a regionally selective effect on dopamine, affecting those neural pathways which go to the limbic system and frontal cortex. Olanzapine is effective in the acute phase of the illness when administered in daily doses of 10–20 mg. Research on the maintenance phase of schizophrenia or for those who are deemed treatment resistant is lacking. Weight gain, sedation, and a decrease in standing blood pressure are the most common side effects. It is said to produce about 50% fewer motor side effects than conventional medications. Its half life of just over 24 hours makes olanzapine amenable to a single daily dose.

Quetiapine, a strong serotonin blocker, is the newest antipsychotic, cleared for marketing by the FDA in 1997. It affects the dopamine pathways most associated with psychosis rather than those associated with EPS. Initial double-blind studies demonstrate its effectiveness in reducing positive and negative symptoms, although its impact on negative symptoms is less consistent. Quetiapine's short half-life of seven hours necessitates several doses over the course of a day.

Other antipsychotic medications are in various stages of development. In 1996 the FDA recommended that sertindole be approved for use in the United States, but it was withdrawn after minor changes were noted in consumer EEGs. Ziprasidone is a potent blocker of a number of serotonin, acetylcholine, and dopamine receptor subtypes, and it may be one of the only antipsychotic drugs to act presynaptically to moderate dopamine release and reuptake rather than changing post-synaptic binding mechanisms.

Researchers have predicted improved pharmacological treatments of schizophrenia in the near future. For example, on the horizon is research geared toward understanding the effects of antipsychotics on D3 and D4 receptors and of the possible role of the neurotransmitter glutamate in schizophrenia. At least two trends seem to have special relevance to social work: first, the increasing appreciation of the diversity of people with schizophrenia and second, improvements in the assessment of pharmacotherapy outcomes.

Table 4.5 outlines the effects of other drug interactions with antipsychotic medications. The impact and effectiveness of any medication, psychotropic or otherwise, depends on many factors, including the concomitant use of additional substances. The social worker's educator role is essential in making the client aware of these possible interactions. Though combining drugs is unavoidable in many circumstances, the client must be encouraged to discuss such combinations with the treatment team to evaluate potential risks fully.

Case Examples

Brad was a 30-year-old, single male, living alone, who had experienced schizophrenia since the age of 18. Highly delusional, he believed he was a central figure in a religious war taking place between God and Satan. He had frequent visual hallucinations, some of which represented real people in his life while others represented historical religious figures. Atypically, he had few auditory hallucinations. Despite the severity of his symptoms, Brad's level of social functioning was surprisingly strong, indicating some interpersonal skills. He managed his own apartment and finances and worked responsibly as a newspaper carrier, which required him to rise at 5:00 a.m. each day. He had

Table 4.5 Drug Interactions with Antipsychotic Medications

Drug	Possible Effect
Alcohol	Nervous system depression
Anesthetics	Hypotension
Antacids	Decreased absorption of antipsychotic drug
Anticholinergics	Decreased absorption of antipsychotic drug
Anticoagulants	Increased bleeding time
Antidepressants	Increased blood levels of both drugs
Antihypertensives	Hypotension
Barbiturates	Decreased blood level of antipsychotic drug, increased depressant effect
Beta blockers	Hypotension
Caffeine	Reduced antipsychotic drug effect
Carbamazepine	Decreased blood level of antipsychotic drug
Cigarette smoking	Decreased blood level of antipsychotic drug
Diuretics	Hypotension
Estrogen	Increased blood level of antipsychotic drug
Lithium	Possible additive toxic effect
Narcotics	Decreased ability to experience pain, increased respiratory depression
Sedatives/Hypnotics	Additive depressant effects

few relationships outside his family, but he did make occasional efforts to cultivate friends. Unfortunately, his bizarre ideas interfered with long-term friendships. His mother was his primary support.

Without medication, Brad was a social recluse, staying in his basement apartment for weeks at a time, staring into space and talking to himself. After entering treatment, his behavior did not improve because he refused to take his oral medications. He did not believe that he had any problems. The social worker could not initiate any psychosocial rehabilitation activities because Brad was unconcerned with most routine activities of daily life. However, the worker eventually engaged Brad in treatment through careful partnership building with Brad and his mother. Brad eventually saw the agency physician and agreed to take injectable fluphenazine, which the physician chose because of its effectiveness and the possibility that Brad, in his ambivalence, would not take oral medication.

Brad's symptoms improved dramatically. With the medication, his anxiety level decreased, his preoccupations with delusions abated (but did not disappear), and he more fully attended to his interpersonal needs. Eventually, at Brad's request, and after he seemed well engaged with his treatment team, his medication was changed to include the low-potency oral medication thioridazine, with trihexiphenidyl for control of side effects. The physician believed that thioridazine was both effective and relatively safe and that its sedating quality would help control Brad's anxiety and allow him to sleep. He began with a low dose, gradually increasing the dosage until it reached a point of perceived maximum effectiveness. The social worker continued educating Brad and his mother about the expected actions and side effects of these medications.

The drugs worked well until several years later, when Brad began complaining that sedation was interfering with his ability to manage his job and social activities. Reluctant to change an effective medication regimen, Brad's doctor agreed to place him on a high-potency medication, trifluoperazine, which would not be as sedating. This eliminated Brad's drowsiness but increased his extrapyramidal symptoms of hand tremor and general anxiety. In fact, he became hypomanic, indicating that the new medication was not as effective in controlling his symptoms as the former one. In the roles of consultant/collaborator and monitor, the social worker helped evaluate and reflect on these effects over time.

Brad reluctantly agreed to go back to thioridazine because the doctor felt that, all things considered, this would be the most effective plan. Though not happy, Brad came to accept that all medications have side effects, and the best he could do was make decisions about them based on the overall profile. Interestingly, Brad never agreed that he had a mental disorder, believing instead that the medication was prescribed merely to control his anxiety.

At age 23, *Valerie* had been extremely low-functioning since she was 16. She was completely dependent on her parents for support and material care. She was withdrawn, anxious, hostile, delusional, and continually hallucinating. Valerie tended to have grandiose thoughts, believing that she was more talented, better looking, more famous, wealthier, and more intelligent than other people. Through these fantasies and the auditory hallucinations consistent with them, she seemed to cope with her isolation.

Because Valerie had not responded to a series of psychotropic medications, the physician recommended treating her with clozapine when the drug became available in the late 1980s. A complicating factor in this plan was that she would need to be transported almost 20 miles to a pharmacy each week for the required blood tests, because home health care was unavailable for this service. Valerie, it must be emphasized, could tolerate the intrusions of very few people. It was a major accomplishment for the social worker to engage her in the intervention process and to help Valerie accept the safety of a weekly trip to the pharmacy and the drawing of her blood by yet another professional.

The social worker spent much time with Valerie's parents to cultivate their partnership and support in developing the relationship with Valerie. She visited Valerie frequently to demonstrate that she could be trusted and to teach Valerie how to use this medication. The social worker further acted as an advocate in arranging for the pharmacy to accept Valerie as a client. After 6 months, Valerie agreed to try the medication and travel to the pharmacy with the worker. Though not dramatically successful, the medication seemed to control the client's anxiety to a degree that she tolerated other facets of the treatment process without much reluctance. She eventually agreed to join clubhouse and job readiness programs.

Glenn was diagnosed with schizophrenia at age 22. He lived with his mother for the next 5 years, very socially withdrawn and without sufficient confidence or motivation to risk any interpersonal relationships. Though he had chronic schizophrenia, his thought processes were not thoroughly dominated by his auditory hallucinations and delusions. He did hear voices: One was the soothing voice of God, and the second was an unknown other who criticized and mocked Glenn, telling him that he would always be a failure. Furthermore, Glenn had rare tactile hallucinations, sensing someone rubbing his legs at times or smothering him while in bed. Despite this, Glenn was well attuned to the real world around him and had reasonable aspirations for job success and relationships. He also had friends, including an occasional girlfriend. Other people did not perceive him to have a mental disorder, although they did feel he was odd and rather withdrawn. Glenn had insight into his schizophrenia and worked to control his symptoms psychologically as well as through medication and rehabilitation programs.

Glenn's main problem with antipsychotic medication was that he was very sensitive to its side effects. His physician initiated five types of medicine at different points in time, none of which satisfied the client. Glenn tended to feel drowsy and experienced hypotension, significant muscle stiffness, and restricted coordination. Because Glenn experienced strong anticholinergic effects, the medications for treating EPS offered only limited assistance. He was particularly troubled by dry mouth and constipation. In addition to working on Glenn's overall rehabilitation, the social worker monitored his side effects and, in the role of consultant/collaborator, taught Glenn skills to be assertive with the physician about his reactions to the drugs. Eventually Glenn and the doctor settled on a small dose of thiothixene. Though a smaller dose than might effectively control his symptoms, it was potent enough to reduce Glenn's hallucinations and anxiety level so he could work with reasonable comfort in his rehabilitation program.

ANTIDEPRESSANT MEDICATIONS

A *mood* can be understood as a pervasive, sustained emotional state that colors an individual's perceptions of the world. There is no truly "normal" mood, and all people deal at times with feelings of depression. Furthermore, even a depression that occurs frequently and interferes to some degree with effectively managing daily tasks may not signify a problem requiring professional intervention. The line between a "normal," or manageable, depression and a situation requiring intervention is not clear and will be defined differently by laypersons and professionals alike. Clinical depression, or that type which suggests a mental illness, goes beyond mere feelings of sadness in relation to certain conditions of living. It consists of a lowered mood often accompanied by difficulties in thinking and psychomotor changes (either excessive physical activity from tension or slowed physical movements and reactions). Furthermore, depression can be masked by anxiety, agitation, and obsessive thinking. However manifested, clinical depression tends to persist and impair one's ability to deal with daily life and relationships.

The range of mood disorders that may be treated with antidepressant medications includes major depression (all types), dysthymia, some adjustment disorders (with depressed mood, anxiety, or mixed emotional features), bipolar disorder (depressed type), bipolar II disorder, and insomnia. Antidepressant drugs may also be used to treat some phobias and anxiety disorders including panic disorder, obsessive-compulsive disorder, and generalized anxiety disorder when they accompany or mask a primary depressive disorder. This broad listing of diagnostic categories indicates the lack of a neat correlation between diagnosis and appropriate medication intervention. All disorders are manifested by symptom clusters, which may overlap among various diagnostic categories.

Symptoms of Mood Disorders

A range of symptoms characterize how mood and associated disorders are classified. Furthermore, because the intensity and duration of the symptoms of depression vary, accurately describing symptoms is important in determining appropriate interventions, including medication. The primary diagnostic categories are described here, with examples of how their symptoms impact clients.

Major depression A severely depressed mood or loss of interest in almost all normal activities, which persists for at least two weeks and represents a significant change in the person's usual quality of functioning. Associated symptoms include weight gain or loss, sleep disturbance (insomnia or hypersomnia), psychomotor changes (physical agitation or retardation), decreased energy level, feelings of worthlessness, a general sense of guilt, concentration problems, and recurring thoughts of suicide or death.

Although not every person experiencing a major depression will experience all these symptoms, most will exhibit at least five of them. Episodes of major depression may occur only once or be recurrent. They may occasionally include brief psychotic features or occur as the depressive component of a bipolar disorder. However, before diagnosing depression, social workers must rule out organic causes. Eighty percent (80%) of persons with major depression will recover from the episode within a two-year period whether or not they use medications. The average duration of a depressive episode is six to eight months, although there is certainly much variability in this range.

Adrienne is a young adult who has recently left her family's home, where she was a victim of sexual abuse for many years. Because of her ongoing trauma, she feels extremely socially isolated after leaving home and experiences frequent episodes of depression. She is unable to sleep at night, feels worthless, feels guilty about what has been done to her, and cannot concentrate on most tasks, including her work. Contemplating suicide often, she has acted on these thoughts at times with serious attempts.

Dysthymia A chronic disturbance of low mood, once known as depressive neurosis, that persists most of the time for at least two years and is characterized by such symptoms as appetite disturbance, sleep disturbance, low energy levels, low self-esteem, concentration problems, and feelings of hopelessness. Though these same symptoms are found in major depression, dysthymia tends to last longer, with milder symptoms. Many people with dysthymia function with some degree of success and do not seek treatment because they have integrated the symptoms into their personality patterns and identities. When receiving professional intervention, people with this disorder may or may not be treated with medication. Sometimes dysthymia is identified as a secondary characteristic of another mental disorder, such as an anxiety or a substance-dependence disorder.

Judy has never felt that her life has any direction. She has failed in two marriages, works adequately but without any enthusiasm in a job for which she is overqualified, and spends time with friends without feeling much attachment to them. She thinks little of herself and does not expect her lot to change. Nevertheless, she attends to her daily responsibilities in a bland, routine manner with a persistently sad resignation.

Adjustment disorder A reaction to an identifiable environmental stressor that is maladaptive but persists for no more than six months. While the stressor is real, one's ability to work or maintain social relationships is more impaired than usual. This disorder is characterized by a depressed mood, tearfulness, and feelings of hopelessness (with depressed mood); nervousness, worry, and jitteriness (with anxious mood); or a combination of these symptoms (with mixed emotional features).

Peter's youngest son moved out of the family home four months ago to live on his own. Though he and his wife had planned this for months, Peter felt a severe loss once the move occurred. He could not sleep and had no appetite. Though their son keeps in touch regularly, Peter has realized that he was simply not prepared emotionally for this loss. He cannot seem to resume his own work and social routine because his son's absence is constantly on his mind. He has lost effectiveness at work and tends to isolate himself in the house. Peter wants to talk constantly about this loss to his wife and always breaks into tears when doing so.

SPECIFIC MEDICATIONS

Origins

The story of the development of antidepressant medications is unique from that of some other psychotropic drugs, in that the process was based on at least tentative pharmacological predictions (Kline, 1970). By the mid-1950s it was suspected that agitated and depressed mental states were accompanied or perhaps caused by changes in biogenic amine concentrations in the brain. Low levels of some of these amines appeared to be associated with depression. It was also understood that the inhibition of monoamine oxidase (MAO) in the nervous system enhanced amounts of biogenic amines and thus might stabilize some depressions.

Physicians and medical researchers observed that iproniazid, a drug introduced in 1951 to treat tuberculosis, seemed to have mood-elevating effects on those patients. Whether the mood change resulted directly from the drug's action or from general improvement in the patient's medical condition was not clear. Still, based on those findings, as well as the general inclination among researchers in the early days of psychopharmacology to test most new drugs for a variety of applications, the drug was studied for its potential in treating mental patients. Researchers in the United States first combined iproniazid with reserpine, an early antipsychotic drug, for their combined effects, and found that the former drug seemed to energize experimental animals and thus counter the bothersome sedative effects of the latter. It was eventually determined after further trials that the mood-energizing effect was specific to iproniazid. After its clinical successes, the drug was found to act as an MAO inhibitor, thus supporting the tentative biological theory of depression.

Already on the market as a treatment for tuberculosis, and with the pent-up demand for antidepressant medication, iproniazid was widely prescribed after its antidepressant efficacy was reported in 1957. Approximately 400,000 persons had been treated before iproniazid was quickly withdrawn from the market when reports of negative effects on liver function surfaced. This complication prompted the search for safer and more effective MAO inhibitors and led to the introduction of the next specific drug for depression, tranylcypromine, another drug with a different chemical composition but similar mechanism of action.

Imipramine, another new antidepressant drug introduced in 1957, was in fact not an MAO inhibitor. It was the first cyclic antidepressant (so called because of its chemical structure), and it quickly took over as the most widely used such drug in the world. Kuhn (1970) initially developed and tested imipramine in Switzerland as an antipsychotic medication; it was in fact synthesized as a phenothiazine derivative, similar to chlorpromazine in structure. Kuhn had previous research experience in sleep therapy, and it is a testament to his creative intellect that he also tested this new neuroleptic drug as a potential antidepressant. In its trials the drug demonstrated a strong antidepressant but weak antipsychotic effect. Its popularity was due to its effectiveness and also its lesser side-effect profile in comparison with the MAO inhibitors.

Current Medications

Today there are three general types of antidepressant medications: the *monoamine oxidase inhibitors, cyclic antidepressants,* and the *selective serotonin reuptake inhibitors.* The established medical practice with each is to begin by prescribing a low dose and then build to a level that seems optimally therapeutic, alleviating symptoms while limiting adverse effects. All of the medications require two to six weeks to produce their antidepressant effect.

Littrell's (1995) review of the literature provides some important guidelines for decision-making about the treatment of clients with depression. Appropriate drug treatment is likely to shorten the duration of a person's depression as well as its severity. Two-thirds of consumers respond to any of the three classes of medications, but up to one-third of consumers using placebos also demonstrate improvement. While this may seem to be an unimpressive evaluation of drug efficacy, almost half of nonresponders to one drug show positive response to an alternative drug (although it is possible that improvement could be related to a remission of the depression). Further, medication seems to impact the "vegetative" symptoms of depression (including insomnia and appetite loss) more dramatically than the person's level of social functioning. Persons with diagnoses of both dysthymia and major depression (in other words, those who demonstrate a chronic state of mild depression with periodic major depressive episodes; this is often called "double depression") are slightly less likely to benefit from medication (50%). They tend to recover from major depressive episodes more quickly than other clients but also tend to experience more frequent major depressive episodes.

Antidepressant Medications and Relapse Prevention

Most persons who experience an episode of major depression will experience a subsequent episode. The risk of recurrence, however, declines with the increasing duration of recovery. On the other hand, the depression-free period is thought to decrease with each subsequent episode. Approximately 20% of those who use cyclic antidepressants will experience a relapse within six months, even if they are taking medications. Over a five-year period 60% of consumers of antidepressant medication will experience a recurrence of depression, although these episodes may represent dysthymia (comparatively milder depression) as often as a major depression.

There have been few studies on the preventive potential for antidepressant medications in the recurrence of depressive episodes, so no statements can be made about this issue with any confidence. One reason that it is difficult to establish valid information about relapse prevention is that depression is a disorder that remits, sometimes permanently. It is difficult to differentiate the effects of medication in the context of "natural" remission, particularly because the medications require time to take effect. With an average duration of major depression of six to eight months and with much individual variation among depressed persons, one's improvement or decompensation with or without medication may be due to internal as well as drug-related factors. Most physicians will tend to lower doses of any of the antidepressants if a client has been stable for eight months or longer. A dose from the low end of the average therapeutic range may be continued as a preventive intervention.

Each of the first two classes of medications described below has a low therapeutic index, which means that there is not a great difference between

Table 4.6 Monoamine Oxidase Inhibitors

Drug	Trade Name	Usual Daily Dose
Isocarboxazid	Marplan	45–90 mg
Moclobemide	Aurorix	Not available in the United States
Phenylzine	Nardil	10–30 mg
Tranlaypromine	Parnate	10–30 mg

the amounts required for therapeutic effect and overdose. This is a particular problem for physicians because these drugs are often prescribed for clients who exhibit self-destructive tendencies and who may use the drugs in suicidal gestures.

The MAO Inhibitors

The MAO inhibitors (see Table 4.6) are effective medications, significantly relieving symptoms of depression in 52 to 70% of consumers (Frank, Karp, & Rush, 1993). At present the primary MAO medications marketed in the United States are phenelzine and tranylcypromine. Phenylzine has been studied more extensively. Structurally different from the antidepressant medications that have followed them, the monoamine oxidase drugs inhibit action on enzymes that metabolize norepinephrine and serotonin. The medications also have an inhibitory effect on dopamine. In addition to their antidepressant effects these drugs have utility in treating panic and other anxiety disorders, as well as "atypical" depressions, those that feature somatic and other anxiety symptoms. Tranylcypromine is structurally related to amphetamine and has a stimulant effect on some persons. The MAO inhibitors are often effective with some clients who do not respond to the other antidepressant medications and are sometimes the drug of choice for older adults, who tend to have an excess of MAO in their nervous systems.

Though they relieve some refractory depressions that do not respond to other drugs, the MAO inhibitors are not usually prescribed first because consumers must observe extensive dietary restrictions to avoid potentially serious adverse reactions. The MAO inhibitors react with foods rich in the amino acid derivative tyramine, prompting a hypertensive condition that can be fatal. Many popular foods including cheeses, wines, and some meats contain tyramine. Table 4.7 includes a list of their predictable side effects, and Table 4.8 presents many of the foods to be avoided when one takes MAO inhibitors. Because the consumer must exercise a significant amount of discipline to avoid all of these foods consistently, some people do not wish to take MAO inhibitors or are not good risks for taking them. The social worker should engage in problem-solving and explore the cost-benefit ratio with clients using these medications, reviewing dietary habits regularly, making sure the client keeps a written record of foods to be avoided, and quickly referring the client to a physician if the client, knowingly or by accident, consumes any prohibited foods.

Table 4.7 Side Effects of MAO Inhibitors

Common	Less Common
Constipation	Agitation
Dizziness	Blurred vision
Dry mouth	Headache
Hypotension	Hypertension
Insomnia	Hypomania
Nausea	Impaired muscle coordination
Sexual difficulties	Muscle cramps
Skin reaction	
Weakness	
Weight gain	

Table 4.8 Foods and Drugs to Be Avoided When Taking MAO Inhibitors

Foods	Drugs
Aged cheeses	Amphetamines and other stimulants
Banana skins	Cocaine
Beer	Decongestants
Broad-bean pods	Dental anesthetics containing epinephrine
Caffeinated beverages	Fluoxetine
Canned figs	L-Dopa
Chocolate	Meperidene
Non-fresh, fermented, or preserved fish, liver, and meats	
Pickled herring, sardines, and anchovies	
Red wine	
Yeast extracts	
Yogurt and sour cream	

In addition to dietary precautions, care must be taken in combining the MAO inhibitors with other drugs. Table 4.9 includes a list of the drugs most commonly taken with MAO inhibitors. In the role of educator, it may be important for the social worker to ensure that the consumer of MAO drugs has this information in writing.

During the 1980s it was discovered that there are two types of MAO inhibitors, type A (which breaks down norepinephrine and serotonin) and type B (which breaks down dopamine), and that medications that selectively impact type A will not produce the side effect of tyramine deamination. In development are several new selective MAO inhibitors that have less interaction with tyramine. One of these is moclobemide, available through much of the world but not yet in the United States. This medication has been found

Table 4.9 Drug Interactions with Atypical Antidepressants and MAO Inhibitors

Drug	Effect
Alcohol	Hypertensive crisis
Anti-asthmatic drugs	Hypertensive crisis
Antihistamines	Hypertensive crisis
Antihypertensive drugs	Hypertensive crisis
Antisthetics with epinephrine	Hypertensive crisis
Cyclic antidepressants	Nausea, confusion, anxiety, hyperthermia, hypotension
Diuretics	Hypertensive crisis
Fluoxetine	Nausea, confusion, anxiety, hyperthermia, hypotension
Sinus, cold, hay fever medications	Hypertensive crisis
Stimulants	Hypertensive crisis

equal in effectiveness to both the cyclic and SSRI antidepressant medications. Another drug currently in trials in selegiline, which is also promising in that it can be ingested as a small patch that adheres to the skin. While these new medications will not be completely free of dietary restrictions, they may become an attractive alternative to consumers due to their absence of anticholinergic effects.

Cyclic Antidepressants

The cyclic drugs, so named because of the number of "rings" in their chemical structures, were the most commonly prescribed antidepressants from the late 1950s through the 1980s. The first antidepressant of this class was imipramine. In 1992, Davis, Janicak, Wang, Gibbons, & Sharma summarized over 100 studies that support the effectiveness of cyclics for 60 to 70% of consumers.

As discussed in the previous chapter, the mechanism of action for these drugs is not clear, but they are believed to work by blocking the reuptake of norepinephrine and serotonin. Their metabolites also have antidepressant action. Unlike the antipsychotic medications, daily dosage does not vary much among these drugs and thus does not distinguish them. Only protriptyline is manufactured in a comparatively small dose, but it does not have different side effects than the others in its class. All the cyclic medications have relatively long half-lives, so they can be prescribed in once-daily doses. Most produce significant anticholinergic effects. These effects, described in the section on antipsychotic drugs, account for most of the unpleasant effects of the medications. Many consumers develop tolerance to certain of these adverse effects but not to the therapeutic effects. The drugs, described in Table 4.10, all of which have a demonstrated effectiveness, require two to six weeks to achieve therapeutic impact. The anticholinergic effects, unfortunately, begin

Table 4.10 Cyclic Antidepressants

Drug	Trade Name	Preparation*	Usual Daily Dosage	Adverse Effects: Sedation	ACE
Amitriptyline	Elavil, Endep	T, I	100–200 mg	High	Low
Amoxapine	Asendin	T	200–300 mg	Low	Low
Clomipramine	Anafranil	C	150–200 mg	High	High
Desipramine	Norpramin	T, C	100–200 mg	Low	Low
Doxepin	Adapin, Sinequan	C, I	100–200 mg	High	Moderate
Imipramine	Tofranil	T, C, I	100–200 mg	Medium	Moderate
Maprotilene	Ludiomil	C	100–150 mg	Medium	Low
Nortriptyline	Aventyl, Pamelor	C, I	75–150 mg	Low	Low
Protriptyline	Vivactil	T	15–40 mg	Low	High
Trimipramine	Surmontil	C	100–200 mg	High	Moderate

*T = Tablets, C = Capsules, I = Injectable

at the time of first administration. The drugs also have an immediate sedative effect which, while troubling to some consumers, may provide relief to a depressed person with insomnia.

The cyclic antidepressants are generally initiated for a consumer at dosage levels below those accepted as optimal. The dose is rather rapidly increased, however, for a period of one to two weeks until the usual therapeutic range is achieved. Because their optimal therapeutic effect will not occur for two to six weeks, a physician may ask the client to continue with a particular regimen for six weeks before either settling at that level or making another adjustment. Some clients may benefit from higher-than-usual dose levels, but it is also possible that another drug will be initiated as a replacement at that point.

Table 4.10 also summarizes the adverse effects of the cyclic antidepressants. Though these effects tend to be strongest in the first few hours after a person takes the medication, and some remit completely within a few weeks, many persist. The side-effect profiles of these medications vary. For example, amoxapine, desipramine, and nortriptyline are all comparatively low in both sedation and ACEs. One might assume, on this basis, that these drugs would be prescribed more frequently than the other medications. However, the medications are not equally effective in reducing symptoms in all consumers. Therefore, a medication with positive therapeutic benefit may be prescribed, even if it has a greater amount of adverse effects. Remember, too, that physicians tend to prescribe certain medications with which they have a history of success. If necessary, however, physicians will usually experiment with several medications until they find one with a high therapeutic benefit. Because the medications can be taken once daily, it is often desirable for clients to take

Table 4.11 Drug Interactions with Cyclic Antidepressants

Drug	Possible Effect
Alcohol	Sedation, decreased antidepressant blood level
Amphetamines	Increased antidepressant blood level
Antihistamines	Sedation, additive anticholinergic effects
Antiparkinsonians	Additive anticholinergic effects
Antipsychotics (all)	Sedation
Antipsychotics (low potency)	Hypotension, additive
Antispasmodics	Additive anticholinergic effects
Beta-blockers	Hypotension
Carbamazepine	Decreased antidepressant blood level
Cigarette smoking	Decreased antidepressant blood level
Dilantin	Decreased antidepressant blood level
Diuretics	Hypotension
Fluoxetine	Decreased antidepressant blood level
Oral contraceptives	Increased antidepressant blood level
Phenobarbitol	Decreased antidepressant blood level
Thyroid hormones	Increased antidepressant blood level
Sedatives	Increased sedation, decreased antidepressant blood level

the medication at night. Though they will be asleep when the side effects most prominently appear, the medication will remain in their systems the entire next day.

Decisions about discontinuing an antidepressant medication should be made by the client in consultation with the social worker and physician. In every case the drug should be tapered gradually, over a period of two to four weeks. An abrupt discontinuation may cause short-term but very distressing effects of anxiety, insomnia, and a rebound depression, particularly with the cyclic antidepressants. Other possible withdrawal symptoms include cardiac arrhythmias, nausea, anorexia, diarrhea, sweating, muscle soreness, headache, chills, fatigue, anxiety, and insomnia.

Table 4.11 lists possible adverse drug interactions in people taking cyclic antidepressant medications with other substances. All these effects are negative in that they either interfere with the targeted amount of medication that reaches clients' bloodstreams or else may cause clients to be unenthusiastic about taking their medications. Besides providing face-to-face education, the social worker should make sure that the client receives a written list of these interactions. The social worker might also help the client monitor certain routine practices, such as eating habits, that may interfere with the drug's effectiveness. For example, some clients experience stomach distress if they do not take their medication with meals.

Table 4.12 The SSRI Antidepressants and Bupropion

Drug (Tablets)	Trade Name	Usual Daily Dosage
Bupropion	Wellbutrin, Zyban	100–300 mg
Citaprolam	Celexa	20–60 mg
Fluoxetine	Prozac	20–40 mg
Mirtazapine	Remeron	15–30 mg
Nefazodone	Serzone	200–600 mg
Paroxetine	Paxil	20–50 mg
Sertraline	Zoloft	50–200 mg
Trazodone	Desyrel	150–300 mg
Venlafaxine	Effexor	150–375 mg

The Serotonin Reuptake Inhibitors
and Other New Drugs

A variety of drugs from a relatively new class, known broadly as *the selective serotonin reuptake inhibitors* (SSRIs), have been available in the United States since 1987 (see Table 4.12). Fluoxetine was the first of these. The fact that these drugs are selective for serotonin (although, as we noted in the last chapter, some of the newest medications from this class have additional effects) adds to the uncertainty about the relevant actions of antidepressant drugs on those neurotransmitters that correlate with depression. The actions of these new drugs may include the stimulation of certain neurotransmitter building blocks in the cell body in ways that are not yet understood. Bupropion, for example, is another newer antidepressant with actions believed to be very different than those of the SSRIs.

These medications are sometimes called "atypical" because they differ chemically from the cyclic antidepressants and the MAO inhibitors. Yet, as with the newer antipsychotic drugs, the new antidepressants have become standard medications within this drug category. The medications are more potent than the cyclic drugs and also have a long half-life. Two of their major attractions are their reduced overdose potential and the fact that they have fewer adverse effects than other antidepressant groups. Some are used to treat anxiety disorders. Fluvoxamine, for example, is a serotonin-reuptake inhibitor drug that is used almost exclusively to treat obsessive-compulsive disorder, generally with far fewer adverse effects than the cyclic drug clomipramine. Two new SSRI drugs currently in development for the treatment of both generalized anxiety disorder and depression are flesinoxan and sunepitron.

Several of the newer antidepressant drugs do not fit neatly into the SSRI classes including amoxapine, nefazodone, and bupropion. These drugs are atypical in their chemical structures. The first two drugs act on neurotransmitter systems in addition to serotonin, while bupropion is really in a class by itself. Its mechanism of action is not known, but it is believed to have impact

Table 4.13 Side Effects of Serotonin-Reuptake Inhibitors and Related Drugs

Common	Less Common
Anxiety and restlessness	Diarrhea
Constipation	Dizziness
Dry mouth	Excessive sweating
Headache	Memory impairment
Nausea and vomiting	Sexual dysfunction (impotence)
Sedation	Weight loss

on dopamine as well as other systems. These are equal to the older antidepressants in effectiveness (55 to 75%), and again tend to differ in side-effect profiles from each other and from other drugs (Frank et al., 1993; Janicak et al., 1993).

The SSRI medications demonstrate effectiveness rates of 60 to 70% across studies. Some of the serotonin-reuptake inhibitors differ chemically from each other as well as from bupropion. Much of their appeal comes from their side-effect profiles (see Table 4.13). Markedly less characterized by anticholinergic activity than other antidepressants, these atypical drugs are more agreeable to clients. Additionally, their overdose potential is much lower than that of other antidepressant drugs. Their potency varies somewhat, particularly that of fluoxetine and paroxetine, which are given in relatively low milligram doses. Unlike the MAO inhibitors and cyclic antidepressants, the SSRIs do not need to be gradually introduced to the consumer—they can be initiated at a therapeutic dose, although this may be adjusted upward or downward by the physician, depending on the client's response.

Table 4.13 outlines the adverse effects of the serotonin-reuptake inhibitors and other new drugs, and though the range of these effects overlap with the other antidepressant medications already discussed, the ACEs of the newer drugs are much less pronounced. Common side effects include anxiety, weight loss, headache, and gastrointestinal discomfort, but many consumers tolerate these without serious complaint. The most common side effects of bupropion are headaches, restlessness, and nausea. Though agitation and irritability may also occur, this medication is not associated with hypotension, weight gain, drowsiness, and ACEs. There is a possibility of seizures with very high doses. Table 4.14 includes a short list of drug interactions with the atypical antidepressants, demonstrating again that using drugs in combination tends to inhibit the effect that each drug might have by itself and may in fact produce additional unpleasant or even dangerous effects.

Recent Advances in the Drug Treatment of Depression

Among the advances made in the past few years with these medications include some indications about which of them work best with particular mood disorders. Additionally, it has been learned that some antidepressants are effective in treating anxiety disorders, panic disorder in particular. All anti-

Table 4.14 Drug Interactions with SSRI Drugs

Drug	Effect
Benzodiazepines	Increases effect
Buspirone	Decreases effect
Carbamazepine	Changes levels unpredictably
Cyclic antidepressants	Increases effect
Lithium	Changes levels unpredictably
L-Tryptophan	Toxic effect

depressant medications work with comparable effectiveness in treating major depression. There is some evidence, however, that atypical depressions, or those characterized by mood reactivity with transient remissions, may be particularly responsive to the MAO inhibitors. Delusional depression may require a combination of antipsychotic and antidepressant medication for successful treatment. For treatment refractory consumers, lithium may potentiate the antidepressant effect of a medication although it is not generally effective as a maintenance drug (41% relapse rates, compared to 23% for other antidepressant drugs) and for persons with bipolar disorder may initiate a manic episode (Stein & Bernadt, 1993).

Case Examples

Matt was a 35-year-old, single male who lived alone and worked part-time as a high-school communications system specialist. He suffered from a recurrent major depressive disorder that in its manifestations seemed due more to heredity rather than environmental factors. Since early adulthood, Matt had experienced occasional episodes of suicidal ideation, hopelessness, an inability to sleep or work, and social withdrawal. The disorder ran in his family. His father and two uncles had committed suicide. Matt had himself attempted suicide twice, both times seriously—these were not the ambivalent cries for help sometimes seen in depressed persons. After the second hospitalization, he was referred to the mental health agency for psychosocial and medication treatment.

With the introduction of a moderate dose of imipramine, Matt's depression was quickly stabilized. Though the drug did produce uncomfortable side effects, including dry mouth and constipation, Matt tolerated them without complaint. Challenges for the social worker included educating Matt about the ongoing role of the medication in controlling his depression, encouraging his adherence to it when Matt wondered, frequently, if it was necessary, and identifying the stressors that apparently put him at greater risk for a depressive episode. Because Matt's judgment seemed impaired when he was depressed, it was particularly important for the social worker to support continued medication use as well as provide supportive counseling. Fortunately, finding an effective medication was relatively easy in Matt's case. The client's negative subjective response to long-term medication represented the greatest initial concern to the social worker; however, over the course of several years, Matt accepted his need for regular medication. Responsive to the interventions, Matt continued to function well interpersonally and in his job.

Nora's circumstances were different. A 40-year-old working homemaker with a grade-school daughter and unemployed husband, Nora suffered from a depression that seemed to stem from the chronic stresses of overwhelming domestic responsibilities and a lack of personal support. She grew up in a culture that restricted women to the roles of mother and homemaker. Further, she accepted these roles even though she felt trapped and saw few options for resolving her family problems. Though getting an outside job was a partial solution for Nora, in that she enjoyed being away from home and with other people, it added to her range of daily pressures. Nora took two antidepressant medications, doxepin and protriptyline. Though her physician had experimented with various single drugs, Nora had not responded positively to any of them because her depression included a significant component of anxiety. Finally, a regimen was discovered that seemed to work for her.

The social worker's concern was that, even after experiencing even modest relief through medication, Nora showed no interest in psychosocial interventions. Because Nora decided not to address her personal and family problems in different ways, she ran the risk of staying depressed; that is, she was not changing at least one source of her depression, her environment. Instead, she was becoming medication reliant. Though Nora's medications were not physically addictive, the social worker did not want to promote such reliance indefinitely. Eventually the physician, client, and social worker had a series of meetings in which they agreed to a two-year plan for gradually decreasing, but not eliminating, Nora's medications. The social worker educated the client about the limitations of medication for ensuring a high quality of life over the long run. In the ensuing months, the social worker was able to work with Nora to identify problem-solving practices for coping with her family problems. These were further complicated by her husband's refusal to participate in treatment. The worker acted as a validator in helping Nora come to value her own aspirations for herself and the family, rather than subjugate herself so completely to her husband and child.

In contrast to Nora, *Patrick* had an extremely difficult time with antidepressant medication because of his sensitivity to their side effects. A strong obsessive-compulsive component to Patrick's personality contributed to his almost phobic reaction to the drugs. However, his physician felt that most of his adverse reactions were genuine, and so he worked at length with Patrick to find an appropriate type and dose. Patrick experienced some side effects common with cyclic antidepressants, such as dry mouth and blurred vision, but he also experienced urinary tract problems, impotence, and heightened anxiety. Patrick presented an unfortunate example of the wide range of discomforting side effects that medications can produce.

The role of the social worker in this process was to help Patrick monitor his response to the medications, communicate them to the physician, and in a collaborative mode evaluate the extent to which Patrick continued to experience significant symptoms of depression. Patrick and his physician finally settled on one of the newer antidepressants, sertraline. Not a perfect choice, because it made Patrick feel uncomfortably anxious, it allowed the social worker finally to move beyond the issue of medication and look with Patrick at how his low mood level related to his broader coping strategies.

MOOD-STABILIZING MEDICATIONS

Bipolar disorder is a disorder of mood in which, over time, a person experiences one or more manic episodes, usually accompanied by one or more major depressive episodes (American Psychiatric Association, 1994). The disorder is associated with chemical imbalances in the nervous system; thus mood-stabilizing medications are almost always utilized as a major (and sometimes only) means of intervention.

There are thought to be two types of bipolar disorder. Bipolar I disorder is characterized by one or more manic episodes, usually accompanied by a major depressive episode. Bipolar II disorder is characterized by one or more major depressive episodes accompanied by at least one hypomanic episode. That is, bipolar I disorder features manic episodes, while bipolar II disorder features depressive episodes. The latter disorder is distinct from the depressive disorders, with different etiology and course. There are six subtypes of bipolar I disorder, reflecting the nature of the most recent mood episode. The mood-stabilizing medications are intended to keep the individual's mood from swinging out of control in either direction. In its manic phase bipolar disorder is a condition in which poor insight is a prominent characteristic, which presents challenges for the physician and social worker who wish to ensure appropriate medication adherence.

The person with bipolar disorder does not necessarily swing from mania to depression with equal frequency. Fifty percent (50%) of persons with the disorder move through alternating manic and depressed cycles. A majority of persons (70 to 90%) return to a stable mood and level of social and occupational functioning between mood episodes. Approximately 10% experience "rapid cycling," which means that over a twelve-month period they will experience four or more manic or depressive cycles. Additionally, 40% have a "mixed" type of the disorder, in which a prolonged depressive episode features bursts of mania, as brief as a few hours in duration. This type is associated with a poorer prognosis.

Bipolar disorder has a lifetime prevalence of 1 to 2%. Bipolar I ranges from .04–1.6% in community prevalence studies, while bipolar II disorder has a prevalence of .05%. Bipolar II disorder is more frequently diagnosed in women. In Bipolar I disorder, the first mood episode is more often manic for men and depressed for women, but there is no gender difference in overall prevalence. The typical age of onset of a manic episode is the mid-20s, but bipolar disorder may begin at any time in childhood through midlife. Twenty to thirty percent (20 to 30%) of adults with bipolar disorder report that they experienced their first episode before age 20. In adolescence, mania is characterized by agitation, excitability, labile affect, aggression, and irritability. Approximately 30 to 35% of persons experience their first episode of the disorder between the ages of 20 and 30 and 25% report the first episode between ages 40 and 50 years.

Although the antidepressant medications work toward elevating a low mood into a normal range, and although this action seems synonymous with that of the "mood-stabilizing" medications, the actions of the latter are not the same. Mood-stabilizing medications are unique in that they also lower mood levels from a manic state.

The symptoms of major depression, described earlier in this chapter, characterize the depressive phase of bipolar disorder. What follows is a description of the symptoms of mania, as well as a description of how mood-stabilizing drugs can treat all aspects of bipolar disorder.

Symptoms of Mania

According to the DSM-IV, a manic episode is a distinct period in which a person's predominant mood is elevated, expansive, or irritable to a degree that seriously impairs relationships and occupational and social functioning. These episodes come on rapidly and may persist for a few days or several months. A diagnosis of mania requires that at least three of the following symptoms be present:

1. **Unrealistically inflated self-esteem.** *Jerry, a high-school science teacher, believes that he is the most intelligent scientist in the world and is on the verge of discovering a cure for all types of cancer.*

2. **Decreased need for sleep.** *Diane stays awake for 4 days during her latest manic phase, driving around town at night and trying to get her friends out of bed to organize parties with her.*

3. **Pressured speech.** The compulsion to talk both constantly and rapidly. *Debbie rambles on for hours, expressing anger at all who will not spend time with her. She quickly annoys and exhausts all who encounter her, so that they have to demand that she leave them alone. She has no idea that she alienates others with this behavior, not that such awareness would change it.*

4. **Flights of ideas.** Racing thoughts. *Claire cannot maintain a train of thought for more than a minute at a time. She talks about her pets, her dislike of work, her need for friends, her inability to tolerate certain neighbors, and her loneliness, all in rapid succession, guided only by her loose associations and without allowing others time to respond to her.*

5. **Distractibility.** Very short attention span and a tendency to be drawn to whatever is immediately perceived in one's environment. The attention of manic people shifts in response to extraneous stimuli that most people filter out. *Maude is sexually preoccupied with the male staff in the hospital, but they can distract her from making inappropriate comments by leading her into the kitchen. She immediately becomes preoccupied with the baking activities there.*

6. **Increased goal-directed activity.** The tendency to become extremely focused on whatever captures one's attention but rarely complete any complex task. This goal-directed activity is usually unrealistic. *Despite his lack of education and experience in business and his ignorance of how to even operate a computer, Bill decides to start a software company. He spends three days drawing up plans for such a venture, only to abandon them when he cannot enlist the interest of his friends in the project.*

7. **Involvement in pleasurable activities that offer potentially painful consequences.** For example, some manic persons go on buying sprees with credit cards. *Rod goes to the local mall and spends $800 on new shirts one night, feeling that he needs a wardrobe to fit his new image as a man of high society. Several days later, when his brother learns of the activity, he forces Rod to return the clothes.*

The medications discussed in this section are used to treat all three types of bipolar disorder and some types of major depression. Mood-stabilizing medications are sometimes prescribed along with antipsychotic medication for a manic type or antidepressants for a depressed type of bipolar disorder. Mood-stabilizers may also be prescribed for people with major depressive disorders who do not respond to antidepressants alone. With a related mood disorder, cyclothymia, an individual experiences mood swings that may be abnormally high and low but are not severe enough to indicate a bipolar disorder. Though cyclothymia may be a milder form of the disorder, it is not always clear whether this variety can or should be treated with mood-stabilizing medications.

SPECIFIC MEDICATIONS

Origins

Lithium is the oldest effective medication used to treat bipolar disorder (Johnson, 1984). Discovered as an element in Sweden in 1817, the substance was found to be highly soluble in uric acid. Its initial medical uses (beginning in 1859) were to treat bladder stones and gout (which is characterized by an excess of uric acid in the joints). Coincidentally, a "uric acid diathesis" theory of medical and emotional illness became widely accepted in the United States and Europe by the 1870s. A variety of ailments such as arthritis and rheumatism were treated with lithium and other alkaline waters because these were believed to clear one's system of harmful uric acid.

The first report of lithium being used to treat depression appeared in 1886. Hydropathic spas became popular as well, and at the turn of the century wealthy patrons traveled to resorts to bathe in mineral waters claimed to possess quantities of lithium. By 1900 a variety of lithium products (waters, salts, tablets, and even beer) were marketed for the treatment of various physical and nervous disorders. These products fell out of public favor by 1910, after the cardiac side effects of lithium were noted and the uric acid diathesis began to be discounted. Still, established ideas die hard, and in the 1920s a lithium bromide was developed as a sedative.

In the late 1940s an Australian physician named John Cade was investigating the organic causes of mental disorders. He was comparing the urine toxicity levels of persons with various disorders by injecting guinea pigs with the substance, and he discovered that the urine of manic-depressive persons was the most toxic. In order to refine his experiments (because the differences in toxicity were small), he searched for a substance that would make uric acid more soluble and chanced upon lithium. The guinea pigs injected with the solution containing lithium became markedly lethargic. Cade correctly hypothesized that lithium might thus be effective in stabilizing persons with mania, but initially for the wrong reason. (His guinea pigs had likely experienced toxic reactions to high lithium levels.) Still he conducted successful lithium trials with ten human subjects, and physicians in Europe began using lithium for treating bipolar disorder. It was not approved for use in the United States until 1970, partly because of the negative impact of the hypertension and deaths experienced by some persons who used a salt substitute containing lithium during the 1940s and 1950s. As American medical researchers argued for the safety of the controlled distribution of lithium, John Talbot in 1950 developed the important practice of monitoring lithium levels.

Current Medications

As described above, the primary medication used to stabilize the mood of a client with bipolar disorder is *lithium* (see Table 4.15), although several other medications, originally developed as *anticonvulsants*, have also proven effective. Carbamazepine or valproic acid may be prescribed for mania if the consumer does not respond to lithium or has a serious adverse reaction to it, or if the mood fluctuations are characterized by rapid cycling.

Lithium is relatively inexpensive because it occurs naturally. With a shorter half-life than the antipsychotic and antidepressant drugs, it must be taken more than once per day (unless in time-release form) to maintain a consistent blood level. Lithium takes two or more weeks to establish a therapeutic effect. Table 4.15 indicates the drug's availability in various preparations and dosage levels. After a consumer's manic episode recedes, lithium (or another mood-stabilizing medication) must still be taken as a prophylactic agent, to guard against recurrence. Frequently, consumers want to terminate a medication once they feel normal again. Stopping medication can put the individual with bipolar disorder at risk for the recurrence of a manic episode, however,

Table 4.15 Mood-Stabilizing Medications

Drug	Trade Name	Preparation*	Usual Daily Dosage
Lithium	Lithium carbonate	C, I	900–2100 mg
			8mEq (mg equivalents per 5 ml)
	Lithonate	C	900–2100 mg
	Eskalith	C, T (includes slow release)	900–2100 mg
	Lithobid	T (slow release)	900–2100 mg
	Lithotabs, Lithane	T	900–2100 mg
	Lithium citrate, Cibalith-S	I	8 mEq
Valproic acid	Depakene, Depakote	C	1200–1500 mg
Carbamazepine	Tegretol	T, I	400–1600 mg

*T = Tablets, C = Capsules, I= Injectable

because the mood swings are unpredictable and alternate with long periods of normal mood.

Pooled response rates from double–blind studies of lithium indicate significant improvement in 70% of clients. In these studies, improvement is defined as a sufficient remission of symptoms to permit the client's attending to activities of daily living. Lithium reduces manic symptoms by 50% in 50% of clients after three weeks of treatment; within two weeks, 20% of clients are completely free of symptoms. Lithium is more effective in treating classic mania than the mixed mania or rapid cycling types of bipolar disorder. When the full spectrum of bipolar disorders is considered, adequate response rates may be only 50% (Bowden, 1996).

Like other drugs, lithium is only effective as long as a steady blood level of the drug is maintained. Because the blood level equals that in the nervous system, lithium levels are more easily monitored than those of most other medications. People who take this drug must become accustomed to getting blood drawn regularly. The difference between therapeutic and toxic levels is not great, so monitoring lithium is particularly important. In the absence of adverse effects, routine monitoring of lithium levels can be performed monthly for 4 to 6 months. For the remainder of the first year, these measures can be obtained every 2 to 4 months, and every 6 months thereafter. A measurement of 1.0–1.5 mEg (milligram equivalents per liter of plasma fluid) is considered therapeutic. At lower levels, the medication has no effect, and the physician may increase the dosage. Levels higher than this amount indicate toxicity, requiring at least a temporary tapering of the medicine or a lowering of the prescribed dose.

Table 4.16 Side Effects of Lithium Carbonate

Common	Less Common	Potentially Serious (Toxic)
Confusion	Acne	Diarrhea (severe)
Diarrhea	Edema (swelling)	Dizziness
Fatigue/lethargy	Hair loss	Drowsiness (severe)
Hand tremor		Muscle weakness
Increased thirst		Nausea/vomiting (severe)
Increased urination		Slurred speech
Muscle weakness		Marked tremor/twitching
Nausea/vomiting		Spastic movements in limbs or face muscles
Weight gain		

When a client is asked to get a lithium blood level drawn, a physician's order is required, and the person should not take any lithium for 12 hours prior to the test. Taking it would cause a misleading elevation in the blood level at the time of the test. Physicians usually ask clients to have their blood drawn in the morning before taking that day's first dose. This way, clients will not be without a required dose for more than a few hours, and their schedule of usage will not be disrupted.

Most of the common side effects of lithium, listed in Table 4.16, are thought to be transient and benign. However, they need to be carefully monitored, particularly with the introduction of the medication or any dosage changes, because serious symptoms may develop. Thirst and weight gain are often experienced; other effects are less common. The potentially serious side effects listed in the table may result from the toxic effects of a buildup of lithium in the blood. Table 4.17 includes a listing of symptoms associated with mild, moderate, and severe toxicity. The social worker should assume that all side effects are serious and arrange for a client's evaluation by a physician. Severe toxicity can be deadly, implying that a dangerous overdose can also occur with lithium. When lithium toxicity is suspected, the social worker should advise the client to discontinue the medication immediately, contact a physician, and to begin ingesting large amounts of fluids to reduce the lithium blood level. The client should be taken to an emergency room. Medical staff will complete a physical examination, including a lithium level, and initiate hydration and electrolyte balancing interventions. Hemodialysis, or the extraction of lithium with an "artificial kidney," may be initiated and be repeated until lithium levels reach a stable range.

Table 4.18 lists drug interactions between lithium and other substances. It is a given that any effect that increases the lithium blood level is potentially serious because such an increase can produce a toxic effect. Note that antidepressants used with lithium may prompt a manic phase, which is why

Table 4.17 Signs of Lithium Toxicity

Mild/Moderate (1.5–2.0 mEq per L*)	Moderate/Severe (2.0–2.5 mEq per L)	Severe (Over 2.5 mEq per L)
GASTROINTESTINAL		
Abdominal pain (persistent/severe)	Anorexia	Coma
Dry mouth		Decreased urination
Nausea or vomiting (persistent)		Kidney failure
NEUROLOGICAL		
Dizziness (severe)	Blurred vision	
Drowsiness (severe)	Confusion (severe)	
Lethargy or excitement (severe)	Convulsions	
Marked tremor or twitching	Coordination impairment	
Muscle weakness (severe)	Delirium	
Slurred speech	EEG (electroencephal-ogram) changes	
	Fainting	
	Hyperactive muscle reflexes	
	Spastic movements in limbs, face	
	Stupor	
CIRCULATORY		
	Arrhythmia (irregular heartbeat)	
	Lowered blood pressure	

*Milligram equivalents per liter

antidepressants should not usually be taken with lithium. If the client has a primarily depressed type of bipolar disorder, lithium may be considered as a means of enhancing the effect of the antidepressant.

Medications from other classes may be used in conjunction with lithium, particularly to treat acute psychosis or agitation. Because clients with bipolar disorder frequently require immediate stabilization of manic mood, an antipsychotic medication may be used on a temporary basis until the lithium achieves a therapeutic effect.

After the remission of acute symptoms and a 6-to-12-week continuation stage, lithium treatment of acute mania may be gradually tapered. Physicians differ in their opinions about how long after recovery from a manic phase to prescribe lithium, but following a first or second episode it is generally done for at least one year beyond the point of stabilization. After a client

Table 4.18 Drug Interactions with Mood-Stabilizing Medications

Drug	Effect
LITHIUM	
Antibiotics	Increased toxicity
Antidepressants	Possible mania, tremor
Anti-inflammatory drugs	Increased toxicity
Antipsychotic drugs	Increased toxicity
Cardiovascular drugs	Possible toxicity
Diuretics	Increased excretion
Loop/distal-tube diuretics	Increased concentration
CARBAMAZEPINE	
Benzodiazepines	Decreased effect
Cyclic antidepressants	Decreased effect
Dilantin	Unpredictable
Valproic acid	Decreased effect
VALPROIC ACID	
Alcohol, other depressants	Increased effect
Antidepressants	Increased effect
Aspirin	Increased anticoagulance

experiences a third mood cycle, the physician may recommend permanent prophylactic use. Maintenance blood levels of lithium range from .6–1.2 mEq and can be maintained with doses of 300 mg three or four times daily.

Lithium for Relapse Prevention

Lithium is the best studied of the mood-stabilizing drugs with regard to maintenance therapy. It has better prophylactic effects on mania than depression. Still, its use does not preclude the possibility of a recurrence of mania. Clients experience 50% fewer recurrences of mania with the drug compared to placebo. Lithium has been shown more effective than placebo in preventing manic relapse (79% to 37%) in clients monitored for up to one year (Keck & McElroy, 1996). Longer term studies, however, indicate that a substantial number of clients do not adequately respond to lithium maintenance treatment. A five-year study of clients who had been symptom-free for two years indicated an 83% probability against relapse after one year, 52% after three years, and 37% after five years (Peselow, Fieve, Difiglia, & Sanfilipo, 1994). Two other major studies have determined a 36% recurrence of mania after five years (Maj, Pirozzi, & Kemali, 1990) and a 73% rate of relapse into mania or depression among clients followed for an average of 4.3 years (O'Connell, Mayo, Flatow, Cuthbertson, & O'Brien, 1991). Combination treatments of lithium and other medications (antidepressant, antipsychotic, and anticonvulsant drugs) produce an improved long-range outcome, but it is clear that bipolar disorder cannot be fully stabilized with lithium or any other drug.

The high likelihood that clients with bipolar disorder will eventually experience relapse reflects the nature of the disorder and the limitations of current medication regimens. Two-thirds of all bipolar clients experience multiple relapses. The social work roles of counselor, monitor, and educator are crucial in alerting clients to the possibility of relapse, even with long periods of normal functioning, and assessing any symptoms that may signal its recurrence. Clients should be informed that one of the most common reasons for relapse is discontinuing an effective medication regimen against medical advice. When a physician recommends discontinuing lithium, it is lowered gradually, usually by 300 milligrams per month. There is a possible rebound effect (rapid recurrence) of mania or depression with the rapid discontinuation of lithium.

Lithium should not be prescribed for women during pregnancy because it is associated with fetal heart problems. During the first trimester there is a potential for birth defects, and if used in the late stages of pregnancy, the infant may be born with lithium toxicity. Lithium is excreted in breast milk and thus should not be used by women while breast-feeding. Further, a pregnant woman's blood volume increases during pregnancy, making the monitoring of lithium levels difficult.

Lithium seems to have antiaggression effects on children and adolescents. It is not advised for children under age 8, as its effects on them have not been adequately studied. When used by older children and adolescents, who have naturally high clearance rates, a higher dose may be required to achieve a therapeutic effect. Adolescents appear to tolerate long-term lithium treatment well, but there are concerns about its accumulation in bone tissue and its effect on thyroid and kidney function.

Their decreased kidney clearance rates put older adults at a higher risk for toxic blood levels. Older adults are particularly susceptible to the side effects of any drug, particularly cardiac effects. They may be prescribed a smaller dose of lithium, because they metabolize it more slowly but also to guard against its side effect of lowering the heart rate.

The Anticonvulsant Medications

Two other medications, both anticonvulsants, are also effective drugs for the treatment of bipolar disorder. The antimanic effect of carbamazepine was discovered in the 1960s, when it was observed that the drug improved mood in many persons who used it for seizure control. However, it was approved for anticonvulsant use only by the Food and Drug Administration (FDA) in 1974. Carbamazepine, a potent blocker of norepinephrine reuptake, inhibits the repetitive firing of sodium channel impulses by binding to them. It may also function as an inhibitor of central nervous system enzymes that break down the neurotransmitter gama aminobutyric acid (GABA). The GABA neurotransmitter may have antimanic properties and thus its increased prevalence in the nervous system may enhance mood stability.

Valproate was FDA approved as an anticonvulsant medication in 1978, and in 1995 it received approval as a mood-stabilizing medication. Valproate also has pre- and post-synaptic GABA receptor effects. It increases levels of GABA by blocking the convulsive effects of GABA antagonists. Two other medications, gabapentin and lamotrigine, have recently been approved as anticonvulsants and are also being studied for their potential as mood-stabilizing agents.

Like lithium, the mechanisms of action of the anticonvulsant drugs in controlling mania are not clear. One theory holds that in limbic system neuron tracts they control a "kindling" process that contributes to the development of manic states (see chapter 3). Like lithium, these medications need to be taken more than once daily to maintain a therapeutic level. Their prescription does not require frequent blood tests, however, since they do not share lithium's characteristic of being evenly distributed throughout the circulatory and nervous systems. An advantage that these medications have over lithium is that, when effective, they begin to stabilize the consumer's mood in as few as two to five days.

There is a trend in psychiatry of prescribing the anticonvulsant drugs more frequently as an initial treatment strategy. Fenn et al. (1996) conducted a five-year study at a veteran's medical center and found that, while the use of valproate was negligible in 1989, the medication accounted for 25% of standard antimanic treatment for bipolar disorder in 1994, while there was a decline in the rate of lithium therapy from 84% to 43% of clients. Lithium and valproate may be used in combination for an additive antimanic effect, as neither interferes with the metabolism of the other. Lithium should not, however, be used with carbamazepine.

Table 4.15 includes the trade names, preparations, and average daily dosage requirements for the anticonvulsant medications. Carbamazepine is initially prescribed in doses of 200 mg twice daily, followed by escalations of 200 mg every few days, as a means of minimizing the experience of side effects. Therapeutic dosages range from 400 to 1600 mg daily. Therapeutic plasma concentrations, which should be acquired after five days on the drug, range between 8 to 12 micrograms per milliliter. A three-week trial is sufficient to determine its effect. Most clients can tolerate a 250 mg initial daily dose of valproate, perhaps at bedtime or with meals (to preclude reactions to early side effects), and increase this by 250 mg every few days. Therapeutic plasma concentration range between 50 to 125 micrograms per milliliter. Therapeutic levels range from 1200 to 1500 mg daily.

The common and generally transient side effects of carbamazepine include dizziness, sedation, short-term anorexia, constipation, diarrhea, and gastric distress resulting in nausea (see Table 4.19). Acute confusional states, double vision, and impaired muscle coordination may also occur but are less common. Extremely rare but serious adverse effects include anemia and agranulocytosis (lowered white blood cell count). Carbamazepine decreases

Table 4.19 Side Effects of Other Mood-Stabilizing Medications

Common	Less Common
CARBAMAZEPINE	
Confusion, memory disturbance	Anemia
Dizziness	Cardiac conduction
Lower white blood cell count (benign)	Double vision
Nausea	Dulling of vision
Sedation	Hepatitis
Skin rash	Impaired muscle coordination
Tremor	Lower white blood cell count
	Speech impediment
VALPROIC ACID	
Hair loss	Anxiety
Nausea/vomiting	Depression
Sedation	Hand tremor
	Headache
	Hepatitis
	Impaired muscle coordination
	Pancreatitis

the effect of benzodiazepine (anti-anxiety) medications and other anticonvulsant drugs when used in combination with them. No fatalities have been reported from overdoses of carbamazepine.

With valproate, common and short-term adverse effects include nausea, sedation, weight gain, tremor, and hair loss. Less common effects include anxiety, depression, hand tremor, headache, and impaired muscle coordination. Very rare but more serious side effects include damage to the pancreas and liver. When used in combination with antidepressant medications and alcohol, valporate increases their effects. It increases the effects of sedation and muscle stiffness when used with antipsychotic medications. Finally, valproate should not be used with another anticonvulsant medication because of the risk of significant additive side effects.

Overall response rates for the anticonvulsant drugs are similar to lithium, but a client who does not respond to one of these three medications may respond to another. Like lithium, valproate is more effective at controlling mania than depression. There is evidence that carbamazepine has a greater antidepressant effect, and it is occasionally used as an adjunct with traditional antidepressant drugs. Carbamazepine has been found equally effective to or slightly less effective than lithium in treating acute mania. Results across studies demonstrate that 60 to 70% of clients show significant recovery from a manic state with the medication. There is a summary response rate of 32% for depression and 52% for mania. Valproate is also comparable in effectiveness to lithium in treating acute mania, with 60 to 70% of consumers responding to its antimanic actions. Unlike carbamazepine, it has consistently been found more effective in treating rapid-cycling bipolar disorder.

Anticonvulsants for Relapse Prevention

In studies conducted during the 1980s, which focused on time periods ranging from one to three years post-manic episode, clients were consistently found to increase remission periods by 60% with the anticonvulsant drugs (Coxhead, Silverstone, & Cookson, 1992). Maintenance doses of carbamazepine range between 800–1200 mg. daily. Data from double-blind studies suggest that carbamazepine is similar to lithium in the maintenance treatment of bipolar disorder, but there is recent evidence that the former drug may have declining effectiveness after 3 to 4 years of use (Bowden et al., 1996; Post et al., 1996).

Carbamazepine maintenance effectiveness does seem to be greater in non-rapid cycling clients compared to rapid cyclers. A review of studies of the effectiveness of carbamazepine in the maintenance treatment of rapid-cycling bipolar clients indicates mixed results; summary response rates of 57% for depression and 59% for mania have been found (Calabrese et al., 1996). While there have been fewer studies of valproate, those which have been completed suggest a marked success rate in prophylactic management of mania (Keck & McElroy, 1996). Maintenance doses are similar to its acute phase doses, given its relatively narrow range of therapeutic effect. Thus valproate may be a better drug than carbamazepine in treating rapid cyclers, but more studies are needed to confirm this.

Both carbamazepine and valproate reduce the frequency of cycles with the same effectiveness as lithium. However, unlike lithium, these medications do not seem to potentiate a rebound mood episode with sudden discontinuation. Nonetheless, it is prudent to taper slowly in the absence of medical emergency, in keeping with standard pharmacological practice. Carbamazepine is tapered by approximately 200 mg per month, while valproate is tapered by 250 mg per month.

The same considerations about lithium in special populations apply to the anticonvulsant medications. However, carbamazepine is used with even more caution with children because it can precipitate aggression. It has also been associated with developmental and cranial defects in newborns and thus may represent a higher risk for pregnant women than valproate.

Medications Under Investigation

Drugs from several other classes appear to have potential as antimanic agents, by themselves or as adjuncts to the primary drugs. However, research on these agents is limited. Several *benzodiazepine* drugs, primarily used as anti-anxiety medications, have been tested for antimanic effect.

Clonazepam has received the most attention as an adjunctive drug for use with lithium, particularly in acute mania, because of its rapid onset, long duration of action, and anticonvulsant effects that may impede kindling. Lorazepam has similar characteristics but has not been tested as thoroughly. These drugs may eventually provide a viable alternative to the adjunctive use of antipsychotic drugs in stabilizing manic persons because the adverse effects of the latter drugs discourage some clients from adherence.

The *calcium channel blockers* (verapamil is the best known), used primarily in the treatment of cardiovascular disorders, are also under investigation as antimanic drugs. They have effects on intracellular calcium ion concentrations similar to those of lithium. Preliminary findings with nimodipine, one calcium channel blocker, have supported its utility as a mood stabilizer against both manic and depressive episodes (Post et al., 1996). If effective, the relatively mild side-effect profiles of these drugs, including safety during pregnancy, will make them attractive treatment alternatives.

Earlier we noted that a variety of antipsychotic medications are used with mood-stabilizing medications to control mania until the primary medications take effect. Among the newer antipsychotic medications, clozapine and risperidone have been tested as treatment adjuncts for bipolar disorder. It is hypothesized that due to their dopamine and serotonin antagonist activity, these drugs may impact on mania and depression as well as psychosis. One study indicated that risperidone was successful in decreasing agitation, psychosis, sleep disturbances, and rapid cycling among clients with bipolar disorder. The mild side-effect profile of the drug makes it a potentially attractive alternative to other antipsychotic medications. Clozapine has been found effective with clients who have schizoaffective disorder, and the overlap of symptoms suggests a possible role in bipolar disorder (Bowden, 1996).

Case Examples

Sharon was a single, 23-year-old college student referred for outpatient care following hospitalization for treatment of a manic episode. She had been psychotic during her mania, characterized by sleeplessness, hyperactivity, racing thoughts, hypersexuality, paranoid delusions, and alcohol abuse. Sharon, who had never lived away from her parents, was well stabilized on lithium and thiothixene at the time of her referral. An initial trial of haloperidol had to be discontinued because in combination with the lithium it had produced severe muscle stiffness, particularly in her arms and neck. Sharon was seen monthly, or more often as requested by the agency psychiatrist. The social worker always participated in these meetings to ensure collaborative continuity of care. Maintained with periodic adjustments throughout her agency involvement, the medications kept Sharon's mood stable. The thiothixene was gradually eliminated but had to be reintroduced in small doses on a few occasions when her anxiety level escalated because of environmental stress. Her bothersome side effects included weight gain and a mild tremor in one hand.

Sharon's mood disorder was exacerbated by environmental stresses, which required regular attention from the social worker. While outwardly successful, Sharon's father was alcoholic and physically abused his wife. Though most of the children had detached themselves from the family turmoil, Sharon remained materially and emotionally dependent on her parents. She became uncontrollably anxious whenever they left town, even for short weekend trips. With only two semesters remaining in her college curriculum, Sharon had begun to fail her classes; she later speculated that this was an effort to postpone the onset of adult responsibility.

The course of Sharon's bipolar disorder was connected to these issues. As a result, the social worker met with her weekly to help her develop strengths for coping with various age-appropriate responsibilities and to become less reliant on her parents. They worked on her fears, lack of confidence, poor self-image, and awkward interpersonal patterns, including her family and siblings in the process. To keep from driving the parents away, the worker did not confront them about certain family problems. Instead, the worker educated them about medications and the impact of mental illness on family systems. The worker invited the family to the agency's education and support group, which they did attend, although irregularly. The worker also validated Sharon's feelings of dependence, of which she was ashamed but which she needed to accept and work through. Because Sharon tended to be passive, the worker acted as an advocate for her regarding vocational training and clubhouse involvement.

Sharon made steady progress in her treatment, although it came slowly and she suffered some setbacks. She experienced two additional manic episodes over the next four years. The first occurred when she secretly stopped taking her medications, which prompted a regression, to avoid a planned but dreaded move into an apartment. The second episode took place one year later when Sharon was beginning a new job and her parents were out of town for several weeks. This time, she needed short-term hospitalization to get stabilized. Because the course of Sharon's bipolar disorder was closely related to her self-image, family situation, and management of stress, all these factors needed to be addressed in a holistic manner that included but was not limited to her medication treatment.

Mark, age 20, had already experienced three hospitalizations for manic episodes characterized by hyperactivity, delusions of power and importance, excessive spending, and ventures into high-risk investment projects that inevitably failed because of his poor judgment. His episodes of depression were relatively mild. During his most recent episode, Mark responded quickly to a combination of lithium and the antipsychotic drug trifluoperazine. The medications so effectively stabilized his mood that within three months he was taking a prophylactic dose of lithium. Though Mark did not report any side effects, his social worker and physician suspected that he was trying to present himself as positively as possible and might withhold negative reactions. Thus, because the client's history suggested that he might not present his mental status and use of medications accurately, the social worker's role of monitor was very important.

Negotiating appropriate social work interventions with Mark was problematic. He believed that his problem was purely a chemical imbalance beyond his control; therefore, exploring his style of functioning as a way to develop improved self-control was irrelevant. However, the social worker did initially help Mark secure an apartment and job-training assistance. Soon, however, Mark began to miss or cancel appointments with the social worker. He seemed to feel that his life was back on track and that he could manage adequately without help. Although the temptation often exists for clients with bipolar disorder to ignore psychosocial interventions when they are stable, the social worker was concerned about what he perceived as Mark's lack of insight into the seriousness of his disorder, which might ultimately result in another manic episode. Paradoxically, Mark tended to be most at risk for mania when his social, financial, and vocational problems stabilized. He did remain free of symptoms for a year on his small dose of lithium; however, his mania escalated again while he was absent from the treatment process. Through a partnership formed with Mark's father, the social worker learned that the client was developing symptoms of mania, but by this time Mark had given up his apartment and was traveling out of state.

Todd had a more subtle manic disorder. He never exhibited dramatic manic episodes; in fact, he had been diagnosed for several years with dysthymic depression and treated with a moderate dose of nortriptylene. He tended to mask his depression in an effort to conceal, perhaps even to himself, his situational problems. His social worker and physician were aware that Todd had experienced serious losses in the past few years, including the bankruptcy of his small business and the moving away of his adult son. They were also aware of his isolation from previous sources of support, including his church. Despite being articulate and superficially personable, Todd felt alone and unhappy.

One winter, Todd made a videotape for his son in which he described his reasons for wanting to die. After he sent the tape to his son, he drove halfway across the country to a mountain range and hiked aimlessly into the woods. Notified of possible trouble by the son, the police located Todd's car and found him asleep under a tree and unprotected from the cold weather. They transported him to a psychiatric hospital, where he was diagnosed for the first time as having a bipolar II disorder, which features depression. The manic episode, likely potentiated by Todd's biological predisposition, was prompted by his growing sense of helplessness. Because mood-stabilizing medications sometimes make antidepressant medications work better for depressed people, Todd's agency physician did not question the value of adding carbamazepine to his regimen and thus complied with the recommendations of the hospital staff. Todd responded positively and recovered quickly from his hypomanic state. Discharged within a week from the hospital, he resumed working with his agency social worker and physician, this time more productively. The social worker assumed the roles of consultant/collaborator and monitor in evaluating Todd's response to the new regimen with regard to his mood level.

ANTI-ANXIETY MEDICATIONS

Anxiety is an unpleasant but normal and functional affect that provides us with warning signs about perceived threats. It includes physiological and psychological symptoms that prepare us to confront or avoid a threat (Marks, 1987). The anticipated danger may be internal or external in origin. Anxiety is best understood from a biopsychosocial perspective. Our genetic endowment, psychosocial development, past experiences, and cognitive appraisal of internal and external events all influence its regulation. Four neurotransmitters, including noradrenaline, serotonin, dopamine, and gaba aminobutyric acid (GABA), are believed to be significant in regulating anxiety.

Anxiety begins as the body's physiological reaction to a threatening stimulus, but the emotions that follow our appraisal of that stimulus can be varied. The experience can be either positive or negative. An anxiety-producing situation may be perceived as a challenge when we appraise it as an opportunity for growth. Anxiety may be perceived negatively as a threat when we apprehend the possibility of harm. *Excessive* anxiety can be understood as the reaction to an event in that environmental or internal demands exceed our perceived ability to cope with the threat. Anxiety is problematic when it creates in us a sense of powerlessness, suggests a danger that is unrealistic, produces an exhausting state of alertness, produces a level of self-absorption that interferes with our problem solving, or creates doubt within us about the nature of reality.

Symptoms of Anxiety Disorders

Rather than describe all the specific symptoms of anxiety, as we did for the other major disorders, we will simply list and characterize the most distinguishable anxiety symptoms. These tend to occur together rather than in isolation.

1. **Motor tension.** Trembling, twitching, feeling shaky, muscle tensions, muscle aches and soreness, restlessness, easy fatiguability

2. **Autonomic nervous system hyperactivity.** Shortness of breath, the feeling of being smothered, accelerated heart rate, sweating or feeling cold, clammy hands, dry mouth, dizziness, lightheadedness, abdominal

distress (including nausea and diarrhea), hot flashes or chills, frequent urination, difficulty swallowing, the sensation of a lump in the throat

3. **Hypervigilance.** Feeling edgy or keyed up, an exaggerated startle
   response, difficulty concentrating or feeling that the mind is going blank,
   trouble falling asleep or staying asleep, irritability.

Anxiety disorders are common in all phases of life. They are the most
prevalent mental disorders in the United States, afflicting 28.7% of the population over the life span and 19.3% over a 12-month period (Kessler, Abelson,
& Zhao, 1998). The DSM-IV (American Psychiatric Association, 1994)
describes the 11 following anxiety disorders. In making a diagnosis it must be
determined that the symptoms are not primarily due to organic factors,
which might imply different or additional interventions.

Panic disorder with agoraphobia Recurrent and unpredictable anxiety
attacks, associated with certain situations and characterized by fears of losing
self-control. *Virtually housebound because of her fear of experiencing panic attacks
when outdoors, Geneva cannot go out to shop, drive anywhere in her car, or even take
short walks because when outside she feels certain she will die. Her heart races, her
limbs tremble, she cannot breathe, and she feels as if she is going to have a heart attack
or pass out. She has been subject to these terrifying experiences since living alone after
her husband's death. The only time she feels safe is in bed. She can go out in the company of others, but only because she feels that she will be assisted if any physical problems develop.*

Panic disorder without agoraphobia Recurrent and unpredictable anxiety attacks, not associated with particular situations but also characterized by
fears of losing self-control.

Agoraphobia without history of panic disorder Anxiety related to
exposure to feared situations where escape might be difficult. *Though Curt
does not want to go outside, this is only a problem during the daytime. He feels that
everyone is looking at him and perceiving him as an inadequate human being. Rather
than face this embarrassment day after day, Curt organizes his life around his fear of
being in open public places. He works a night shift, does all of his shopping at night
when few others are out, has no social life, and spends most weekends at the home of
his extended family, where he feels safe, in a city 40 miles away. Curt never feels
panic, but he is sufficiently distressed by anxiety that his life is ruled by fears of being
in public.*

Specific phobia Anxiety provoked by exposure to a specific object or situation. *Mark, a schoolteacher, is terrified of cats for reasons he cannot understand. Normally this does not interfere with his ability to function, but whenever he encounters a
stray cat on the playground, for example, he actually has to flee in terror. Though most
people find this amusing, it is genuinely distressing to Mark, who has to remove himself from social and other work situations whenever he sees a cat or suspects that one is
nearby.*

Social phobia Anxiety provoked by exposure to social situations in general. *A reasonably effective grade-school teacher, Heather cannot tolerate attending the weekly teacher meetings. Because she feels she has less talent than others on the staff, she fears that she will embarrass herself in these meetings, where all are expected to contribute to discussions about faculty policies. Heather has no similar anxieties elsewhere in her life. Still, the thought of these meetings fills her with intense fear and makes her restless, nauseous, irritable, unable to concentrate on her work, and unable to sleep during the nights before meetings. As she develops many excuses for missing the sessions, her performance evaluations suffer because the sessions are a required part of her job.*

Obsessive-compulsive disorder Obsessional thoughts cause marked anxiety; compulsive behaviors that serve to neutralize that anxiety. *Tracy attempts to control her persistent, free-floating anxiety with compulsive activity rituals. Each morning she performs a precise routine in getting dressed and groomed, including brushing her teeth and hair with the same number of strokes. She cleans her house in the same exacting way and becomes extremely upset if anything interferes with these routines, such as phone calls or unexpected guests. By noon of every day she has completed her schedule of rituals and can relax for the rest of the day.*

Posttraumatic stress disorder Anxiety associated with re-experiencing a traumatic event. *Six years ago Brian was in a car accident in which his father was killed. Brian was also seriously injured but recovered fully. Now, several years later, he has begun to feel increasingly anxious about traveling by car, particularly whenever he encounters an intersection resembling the one where his accident took place. Some days he feels so afraid that he will not take even short trips in the car. He has come to understand that he responds in near panic to cars resembling the one in his accident or to being in a place that resembles the scene of the accident.*

Acute stress disorder Any anxiety experience that occurs immediately after a traumatic event.

Generalized anxiety disorder Persistent, excessive worry that lasts for at least six months. *Having experienced much interpersonal and family trauma in her life, Roberta has developed a personality characterized by excessive worry about routine life events. She worries about her health, her family's health, her future, her finances, her personal safety when out in public, being alone, and some less routine matters, such as the condition of the ozone layer and her personal astrology. Not focused on any realistic issues that might generate anxiety, she instead projects her continuous free-floating anxiety on whatever happens to confront her at a particular time. Roberta can admit that her concerns are irrational but nevertheless cannot seem to change her outlook.*

Anxiety disorder due to a general medical condition Anxiety as a consequence of the condition.

Substance-induced anxiety disorder Anxiety as a consequence of a medication or toxin.

Other types of anxiety include adjustment disorders featuring anxiety, separation anxiety, and the sleep disorder of insomnia. Anxiety is a prominent symptom of many other mental disorders, and may be treated along with the other symptoms of those disorders. For example, the anxiety experienced by many clients with schizophrenia may be treated with an antipsychotic medication that contains anti-anxiety effects.

SPECIFIC MEDICATIONS

Origins

The anti-anxiety drugs, like others we have already described, were discovered serendipitously (Berger, 1970; Cohen, 1970). In the mid-1940s, drug researchers in London were investigating new antibacterial agents that might supplement or improve upon the actions of penicillin. Frank Berger examined the toxic potential of one such compound by injecting it into mice. He noticed that the substance produced an unusual short-term reversible paralysis of their muscles. The mice were sedate but maintained consciousness with no disturbances to their autonomic functions (respiration, heartbeat, etc.). Further, when the drug wore off the mice demonstrated a complete recovery. After clinical trials on humans, this substance, mephenesin, was introduced as a muscle relaxant. It had the drawbacks of weak action and too-rapid metabolism, however, and Berger soon undertook research for a similar but more effective compound. This resulted in the introduction of meprobamate, the first popular muscle relaxant and anti-anxiety agent, which had a duration of action eight times longer than the former drug.

By the mid-1950s, psychopharmacology drugs included meprobamate and chlorpromazine, but there was much demand among physicians for drugs of "intermediate" potency, ones not as strong as the antipsychotic drug but more tranquilizing than the new anti-anxiety agent. Leo Sternbach had done research on the chemical properties of "benzophenome" drugs during his postdoctoral studies in Poland in the 1930s. At that time his work was theoretical; he was not interested in developing active biological agents. In 1954, however, while working as a drug company chemist in New Jersey, Sternbach was inspired by developments in psychopharmacology to revisit those compounds for their potential as medicines. He synthesized new compounds from his original products but their effects as pharmacological agents was disappointing, so he abandoned the project. Ironically, he left one untested compound on his shelf. In 1957, during a routine cleanup of his laboratory, a chemist found this last compound and suggested that it be submitted for testing since its chemical analysis was complete. Two months later, its utility as a minor tranquilizer was established—the compound had hypnotic and sedative effects similar to meprobamate but was significantly more potent. The benzodiazepine substance became the focus of intense research by his drug company, and was introduced into medical practice as chlordiazepoxide in 1960. At

Table 4.20 Benzodiazepine Medications

Drug	Trade Name	Preparation*	Usual Daily Dosage
Alprazolam	Xanax	T	0.5–6 mg
Chlordiazepoxide	Librium	T, C, I	15–100 mg
Clonazepam	Klonopin	T	0.5–10 mg
Clorazepate	Tranxene	T, C	7.5–60 mg
Diazepam	Valium	T, C, S, I	2–60 mg
Estazolam	ProSom	T	1–2 mg
Flurazepam	Dalmane	T	15–30 mg
Halazepam	Paxipam	T	60–160 mg
Lorazepam	Ativan	T, I	2–6 mg
Midazolam	Versed	I	7.5–45 mg
Oxazepam	Serax	T, C	30–120 mg
Prazepam	Centrax	T, C	20–60 mg
Quazepam	Doral	T	7.5–30 mg
Temazepam	Restoril	T	15–30 mg
Triazolam	Halcion	T	0.125–0.25 mg

*T = Tablets, C = Capsules, S = Solution, I = Injectable

present three types of medication are primarily used to treat anxiety disorders: benzodiazepines, beta-blockers, and the atypical medication buspirone.

CURRENT MEDICATIONS

The Benzodiazepines

The benzodiazepines comprise the largest class of anti-anxiety medications and have been the most frequently prescribed since their introduction in the late 1950s. Compared to their barbiturate predecessors, the benzodiazepines (see Table 4.20) have a somewhat lower (but still real) potential for abuse, dependence, and tolerance, and a higher therapeutic index (the difference between therapeutic dose and overdose). The benzodiazepines are anxiety-reducing in lower doses and sedating in higher doses. As noted earlier, chlordiazepoxide was the first such drug; the second, diazepam, was for a time the most prescribed medication in the world. Six percent (6%) of the American population reported using benzodiazepines at least once in the late 1980s, but the percentage has dropped since then (Olfson & Pincus, 1994). More women use the drugs than men, probably due to gender differences in help-seeking and treatment traditions among physicians.

The benzodiazepine medications achieve their therapeutic effect by increasing the efficiency with which GABA binds with its receptor sites, thus blocking central nervous system stimulation in areas associated with emotion.

Table 4.21 Adverse Effects of Anti-Anxiety Medications

Substances	Common	Less Common
Benzodiazepines	Confusion	Allergic skin reaction
	Dizziness	Blurred vision
	Drowsiness	Depression
	Headache	Dry mouth
	Impaired muscle coordination	Nausea/vomiting
	Irritability/restlessness	Sexual impairment
	Memory impairment	Weakness
Beta-Blockers	Hypotension	Abdominal pain/diarrhea
	Sedation	Depression (mild)
	Slowed heart rate	Dizziness
		Insomnia
		Nausea/vomiting
		Sexual impairment
Buspirone	Dizziness	Insomnia
	Headache	Nervousness
	Nausea	Skin Rash
		Sweating

They are quickly absorbed in the gastrointestinal tract and have a rapid effect; usually within 30 minutes. There is variation in the dose range but most have relatively short half-lives. Unless taken on an as-needed basis, the medication must be taken two or three times per day to maintain a therapeutic effect.

The benzodiazepines comprise the largest class of anti-anxiety medications, and they are effective. As a treatment for most anxiety disorders, these drugs achieve a therapeutic effect within one week, and 75% of consumers demonstrate moderate to marked improvement. Their therapeutic benefit appears to peak after four to six weeks of use, but some consumers use the drugs for months or years without developing a tolerance. Longer-term use of the drugs is indicated in panic disorder, generalized anxiety disorder, and social phobia, because clients with these disorders experience ongoing anxiety rather than short bursts. Short-term use is indicated for clients with post-traumatic stress disorder (where psychotherapy usually plays a more significant role), older adults (who have lower rates of metabolism and a greater sensitivity to side effects), persons with insomnia (who can learn alternative means of resting), and those who abuse substances (during the withdrawal process).

Most adverse effects of the benzodiazepines are thought of as mild and transient (see Table 4.21). Dizziness, drowsiness, and impaired muscle coordination are most frequently reported. Sometimes consumers experience gastrointestinal distress. The medications may also produce a transient amnesia and a diminished quality of task performance, both of which remit after several weeks. These effects make the drugs less practical for persons whose jobs

Table 4.22 Benzodiazepine Withdrawal Symptoms

Transient	True Withdrawal
Agitation	Delirium
Anxiety	Depression
Blurred vision	Enhanced sensory perceptions
Diarrhea	Hypothermia
Dizziness	Nausea
Headache	Paranoia
Insomnia	Seizures
Muscle aches	Tinnitis
	Tremors

or lifestyles require fine muscle coordination. Less common adverse effects include vision impairment and decreased sexual drive. Depending on the duration of and level of discomfort with these adverse effects, the consumer may be advised to try another type of medication.

The benzodiazepines have a serious disadvantage in that they may become physically addicting over time. There is no clear rule about the time required for a person to become at risk of dependence, and many clients use the medication safely for years. It is estimated that only 6% of consumers abuse the medications, and only 15% of users take the drugs for longer than one year (Carter, Swift, & Turnbull, 1996). Still, addiction should always be considered a possibility. Clients who abruptly discontinue the benzodiazepine drugs may experience the withdrawal symptoms of nausea, loss of appetite, depression, depersonalization, irritability, insomnia, headache, trembling, sweating, dizziness, and impaired concentration (see Table 4.22). It is recommended that benzodiazepines be tapered weekly at a rate of 25% of the previous week's dose. Complete discontinuation for long-term users may require six to seven months.

The benzodiazepines interact with some substances to produce a differential response (see Table 4.23). The presence of any type of food decreases absorption time in the stomach and intestines. Some medications, including most antidepressants, increase blood levels of the benzodiazepine by slowing the client's metabolism. This enhances the drug's anti-anxiety action but also its adverse effects. Anticonvulsant drugs increase metabolism and thus decrease the blood level of the medicine. Alcohol use increases the effects of intoxication and sedation.

In the past twenty years, research has focused on the differential therapeutic indications for four subtypes of benzodiazepine drugs. The high-potency drugs, which may be short- or long-acting (alprazolam and clonazepam, among others) have the highest relative withdrawal potential but are well suited for the treatment of disabling anxiety states such as panic attacks. The low potency benzodiazepines, such as chlordiazepoxide and restoril, which also may be short- or long-acting, are indicated for the control of milder anxiety

Table 4.23 Drug Interactions with Benzodiazepines

Drug	Effect
Alcohol and other sedatives	Increased nervous system depression
Antacids	Decreased absorption efficiency
Antibiotics	Increased blood levels
Anticonvulsants	Decreased blood levels
Antihistamines	Increased nervous system depression
Barbiturates	Increased nervous system depression
Cimetidine	Increased blood levels
Cyclic antidepressants	Increased nervous system depression
Disulfram	Increased blood levels
Estrogen	Increased blood levels
Fluoxetine	Increased blood levels
Isoniazid	Increased blood levels
Tagamet	Increased blood levels

states and muscle relaxation. The short-acting drugs are appropriate for the short-term treatment of insomnia and anticipatory anxiety.

Buspirone

Several other classes of medication are used to control anxiety (see Table 4.24). Buspirone is a newer drug classified as an "azapirone," a term that refers to its chemical structure. It has impact on serotonin receptors, which are believed to be anxiolytic in the hippocampus and limbic areas. It balances serotonin levels, lowering them in persons who have too much (anxious persons) and raising levels in those who have too little (some persons with depression). Buspirone is quickly absorbed and must be taken regularly to achieve and maintain its effect. An average daily dose is 5 to 15 milligrams, three times per day, but this may be higher when the drug is used as a primary treatment for depression. Part of its attraction to physicians is that buspirone is not addictive. Frequently, clients who have taken benzodiazepines are changed over to buspirone. It does not have anticonvulsant effects or produce psychomotor impairment, withdrawal, or cardiac problems. It is thought to be suited for elderly clients, who are susceptible to the adverse effects of the benzodiazepines.

Buspirone seems particularly effective in treating generalized anxiety disorder and mixed anxiety and depression states. It requires two weeks or more to achieve full effect because, like the antidepressant drugs, it is initially resisted at its sites of action. Thus it is not useful for crisis intervention or the treatment of panic disorder. It is sometimes used as an adjunct to other antianxiety, antidepressant, and antipsychotic drugs. In one study (Rickels & Schweizer, 1990), consumers of buspirone and benzodiazepine drugs were functioning at the same level after 40 months, but while none of the buspirone users were still taking the drug, 65% of the benzodiazepine users were doing so.

Table 4.24 Other Anti-Anxiety Medications

Drug	Trade Name	Preparation*	Usual Daily Dose
BETA-BLOCKERS			
Atenolol	Tenormin	T, I	50–100 mg
Metoprolol	Lopressor	T, I	150–300 mg
Nadolol	Corgard	T	80–240 mg
Propranolol	Inderal	T, C, S, I	240–420 mg
AZAPIRONES			
Buspirone	Buspar	T	15–30 mg

*T = Tablets, C = Capsules, S = Solution, I = Injectable

Buspirone has recently been found to have additional therapeutic benefits. It reduces aggression and irritability in persons with brain injuries and organic disorders, such as dementia, and in children with developmental disabilities, mental retardation, and autism. It can be an effective adjunct to antidepressant drugs in treating obsessive-compulsive disorder. Buspirone appears useful in the treatment of alcohol abusers with anxiety because of its low abuse potential. It may also retard one's desire to return to alcohol consumption.

Buspirone does have limitations. Common adverse effects include dizziness or lightheadedness that occurs shortly after ingestion, but these rarely persist for more than 20 minutes. Less common adverse effects include headache, nausea, nervousness, and insomnia. Drug interactions have been reported with clients also taking the antipsychotic drug haloperidol, the MAO inhibitors, and antabuse. Adherence is an issue for some clients who prefer the sedation produced by the benzodiazepines. Buspirone's lack of sedative effect precludes its use in treating insomnia. Further, persons who have taken benzodiazepines seem to respond less well to buspirone than others. Cost must also be considered a limitation, as the drug is not yet available in generic form.

Other Anti-Anxiety Medications

The *beta-blockers* (see Table 4.24) inhibit norepinephrine receptor sites in the brain and peripheral nervous system. These drugs were originally developed to lower blood pressure in persons with hypertension but are also fast-acting and effective in treating anticipatory anxiety (specific situations in which unmanageable anxiety will be encountered). They lower anxiety by reducing the consumer's physical symptoms of rapid heartbeat, muscle tension, and dry mouth. The consumer's capacity to experience the physical symptoms of anxiety is thus diminished. This mechanism has shown that beta-blockers are effective in treating social phobia. The beta-blockers are not addicting but are prescribed less often than the benzodiazepines because they have a brief effect; only a few hours. Their adverse effects tend to be minimal and include sedation, hypotension, and dizziness. Beta-blockers are generally not pre-scribed for persons with cardiac problems or asthma.

The *antihistamines* (see Table 4.24) are still occasionally prescribed as anti-anxiety agents, particularly with children and adolescents. These drugs block histamine receptors in the nervous system which are associated with anxiety and agitation. Antihistamines are rapidly absorbed and maintain a therapeutic effect for approximately 24 hours. Antihistamines tend to be highly sedating, however, and are effective for only a few months before a tolerance develops. They are not addictive and are most frequently used as relatively safe sleep-inducing agents.

The newest anti-anxiety drug available in the United States is zolpidem (Brown & Lempa, 1997). It is an atypical drug, and impacts a smaller subset of GABA than the benzodiazepines. It is effective in the short-term treatment of insomnia. Another atypical drug, zopiclone, is not yet available in the United States.

Almost all of the medications initially developed as antidepressants are used at times for the primary or adjunctive treatment of anxiety disorders (Skolnick, 1997). In fact, these drugs tend to relieve anxiety prior to the onset of their antidepressant effect, which requires two to six weeks. There seems to be overlap between the biological causes of depression and some anxiety disorders, probably related to the serotonin neurotransmitter. The medications may also stimulate other neurotransmitters in ways that are not yet understood.

The MAO inhibitor phenylzine is useful in treating panic and other anxi-ety disorders, and tranylcypromine has a stimulant effect on some persons. The cyclic drug imipramine has been found effective in the treatment of panic disorder, although three to five weeks of use is required to achieve its effect. The selective serotonin reuptake inhibitors also have great utility for treating anxiety. Clomipramine was the first such drug (it is classified as a "cyclic" drug but has a strong serotonin affinity) and has been used since the 1980s to treat obsessive-compulsive disorder. Nine studies have demonstrated that it alleviates symptoms for 35 to 42% of persons with that disorder (Jenike, 1993). Fluvoxamine is used exclusively to treat obsessive-compulsive disorder, generally with far fewer adverse effects than clomipramine. The SSRI med-ications are also used for treating mixed anxiety and depression, panic disor-der, social phobias, and generalized anxiety disorder.

Special Concerns with Children and Adolescents

At present 8 to 9% of children and adolescents are thought to have diagnos-able anxiety disorders (Kearney & Silverman, 1998). In addition to those already described is separation anxiety disorder, characterized by excessive worry, reluctance to go to sleep, nightmares, or physical symptoms of anxiety when separated from a major attachment figure. Special physical characteris-tics of the young population include its higher rate of metabolism, smaller physical size, and greater tissue sensitivity.

Few controlled studies have been done on the effects of anti-anxiety medications on adolescents. Most have been done for obsessive-compulsive disorder, in which the SSRI drugs of clomipramine and fluvoxamine have been found beneficial. Separation anxiety disorder has been found responsive to imipramine and the benzodiazepines, and buspirone has been effective in treating generalized anxiety disorder. Still, less than half the drug studies on this population have focused on medications alone; most include counseling or behavior interventions (Kearney & Silverman, 1998). It must be concluded that the appropriateness of many drugs for this population has not been established. Use of the SSRI drugs may be preferable in adolescents because of their relatively well-tolerated side-effect profiles and their reduced potential for overdose. This is significant in that suicide is the second leading cause of death in the adolescent population. Antihistamine medications are commonly used to treat anxiety and insomnia in children as an alternative to the benzodiazepines.

Children and adolescents using anti-anxiety medications experience the same adverse reactions as adults. Some unique adverse effects for this age group include arrhythmia, the increased possibility of seizures, a stimulation of anger, and a loss of behavioral inhibitions. For these reasons the physician will usually aim for the lowest possible effective dose. Children may be more vulnerable than adults to adverse effects of abrupt withdrawal due to their higher elimination rates. Monitoring and laboratory follow-up may need to be more frequent.

Case Examples

Lynne was an unemployed 43-year-old divorced white female with two adult children and a history of labile moods and dependent relationships. Several months after divorcing her husband of 20 years, she entered counseling with a psychiatrist for help with anxiety and panic attacks. She was having great difficulty living on her own and coped with stress by withdrawing to her bedroom in states of high anxiety. Lynne was hospitalized for several weeks after becoming suicidal. Her doctor initiated treatment with both antidepressant and anti-anxiety medications, but soon after discharge she was tapered to a moderate dose of the benzodiazepine alprazolam. This became Lynne's standard medication regimen, which persisted through her transfer to a mental health facility.

Lynne received psychosocial intervention from a social worker and medication from a physician. After one year of intervention, during which she reached many of her psychosocial goals, including a successful employment experience, her physician and social worker became concerned that she was psychologically dependent on the medication. Though the drug served a therapeutic purpose, Lynne discounted the need to make further adjustments in her coping strategies and relationships with family, friends, and employers.

Fearing a return of anxiety attacks, Lynne initially resisted the suggestion to change medication but eventually agreed to a gradual one-year plan to transfer from the benzodiazepine to the non-addictive drug buspirone. The social worker, who met with Lynne much more frequently than the physician did, assumed a crucial monitoring and consultant role through this process. Every month or two, the physician decreased the alprazolam by 0.25 milligrams daily and increased the other drug. The social worker also increased her visits with the client. If Lynn experienced high anxiety, she could call her social worker between their biweekly visits. These instances usually came about because of Lynne's ambivalence about the change in medications rather than her primary psychiatric disorder. The social worker was careful to validate rather than discount Lynne's reactions to the change so that she would not feel a need to either hide or exaggerate them. The transition proceeded smoothly. Eighteen months later, the client was functioning well with a modest dose of buspirone. She did not report any bothersome side effects from the medication.

Don's treatment had a different outcome. Like Lynne, he had a history of extreme anxiety in all interpersonal situations. His symptoms were more debilitating, however, in that every situation in which he needed to be assertive made him panic. For example, he could not bring himself to approach his son's football coach about helping out during the team's practices. His marriage and job were both in jeopardy because he could not negotiate any conflicts with others. Clearly in need of medication to get through his daily life, Don took a high dose of diazepam. He also sought psychosocial support for developing personal strengths and assertiveness.

However, Don frequently took his entire daily dose of medication in the morning and extra medication later in the day, calling his social worker or doctor to request additional drugs toward the end of each month. Furthermore, he occasionally missed his appointments with the social worker. The social worker soon saw that Don was not acting as a full partner in the treatment program. Though appropriate to his care, the drugs were never intended to provide a long-term solution to his problems. The social worker and physician needed to address his fears of confronting his problems through psychosocial means. The social worker and physician carefully collaborated on the details of a strategy to set a limit with Don, asserting that he could not see the physician unless he kept his biweekly sessions with the social worker. Don tested these limits for several months by continuing to miss some sessions while requesting extra medication. Finally, when confronted again by the social worker, he decided to leave the agency. Regrettably, he did so passively, by ignoring his appointments and the social worker's calls. However, the agency staff did not deny Don his medication, but rather gave him a final month's supply to prevent withdrawal symptoms and give him ample time to seek services from another agency.

Vanessa, a divorced 35-year-old woman living with her sister, had milder, or less apparent, anxiety than these other clients did. Though she appeared cocky, confident, and assured, this outward demeanor masked a strong sense of inferiority and discomfort around others. She experienced chronic unemployment because, whenever she felt threatened by her employers, Vanessa acted out her anxiety with inappropriate, aggressive outbursts and later resigned in embarrassment. Assuming that she was more capable and functional than she really was, some mental health workers suspected that she was requesting medications unnecessarily. She received a moderate dose of the benzodiazepine clorazepate for several years; at the same time she was expected to work on her interpersonal problems with a social worker. However, because of her intense wariness of others, Vanessa did not develop a sense of trust in any professional helpers for many years, tending to alienate many social workers who suspected erroneously that she had a primary personality disorder. Her feelings of anxiety had to be validated so she would not feel so compelled to maintain her defenses. Once she found an accepting social worker and focused on her own distress rather than her aggressiveness, she could make strides in her personal growth and eventually be weaned off the medication. Vanessa is an example of the client who masks very real anxieties and requires a great deal of careful assessment and patience from a social worker who can tolerate an antagonistic defensive style. Clearly, one does not always demonstrate the classic outward signs of anxiety when experiencing serious symptoms.

PSYCHOSTIMULANTS

The psychostimulant medications (also known as *sympathomimetics* because they "mimic" the action of adrenaline) produce states of wakefulness, mood elevation, alertness, initiative, and enhanced competence. They are primarily used to treat persons with attention deficit hyperactivity disorder (ADHD). Ironically they do not produce a subjective effect of stimulation for those consumers, instead enhancing their ability to maintain concentration and self-control. The medications are controversial because they are controlled substances with abuse potential and are primarily used to treat a mental disorder that is itself ambiguous to many professionals. In the United States the number of children and adolescents diagnosed with ADHD has grown steadily since the 1970s and now totals 750,000 to one million persons (Lawrence, Lawrence, & Carlson, 1997). Since 1990 the number of children in the United States taking psychostimulants has grown two and one-half times (Hancock, 1996). The persistence of ADHD symptoms into adulthood for many persons has also been identified.

The social work profession is extensively involved with clients having ADHD in a variety of child care settings, particularly schools, where the condition tends to be diagnosed. Social workers participate as members of treatment teams with physicians, nurses, family members, psychologists, and teachers on behalf of their clients with ADHD.

Attention Deficit Hyperactivity Disorder

Attention-deficit/hyperactivity disorder (ADHD) is characterized by a persistent pattern (six months or more) of inattention and/or hyperactivity and impulsivity in behavior that is more frequent and severe than what is typically observed in others at a comparable developmental level (American Psychiatric Association, 1994). Approximately 3 to 6% of children under the age of 13 are estimated to have the disorder, and of those diagnosed nearly 90% are boys (Brown, 1998). Symptoms of ADHD are present by the age of seven years and continue in attenuated form into adulthood for 10 to 60% of persons with the disorder (Hallowell & Ratey, 1994).

In children, ADHD is characterized by a lack of self-control and ability to sustain direction. Children with ADHD are distractible, often do not finish what they start, and are irritable and impatient, often interrupting and pestering others. Their physical hyperactivity may be quite pronounced (boys with the disorder are more likely to be hyperactive than girls). Adults with the disorder are usually not hyperactive but are impatient, restless, and moody and have difficulty managing their time and setting priorities. The severity of the disorder is variable and likely to worsen in situations that demand sustained effort or high levels of structure. To receive the diagnosis the person must be impaired in at least two settings such as school, work, and home. The disorder may be predominantly hyperactive/impulsive, inattentive, or combined in nature.

There is controversy among professionals about the validity of the ADHD diagnosis. This is due to the purely observational criteria of DSM-IV, the inconsistency of symptoms (a child may function well in one setting but poorly in another), the belief that the condition is often designated by frustrated adults who cannot manage active children, and the lack of knowledge about a biological basis of ADHD (Goldman, Genel, Bezman, & Slanetz, 1998). A diagnosis of ADHD should be based on a medical examination (including tests of vision, speech, IQ, academic achievement, attention, and impulsiveness) and behavioral ratings and interviews with the client and significant others. The decision to medicate should be based on the conclusion of a physician and other involved professionals that the symptoms are severe enough to preclude age-appropriate social, academic, or occupational functioning.

Ethical Issues in the Drug Treatment of Children

We have noted throughout this chapter that medications from all five diagnostic categories may be prescribed for children and adolescents. However, we want to focus here on the ethical issues related to this practice because children are the primary recipients of psychostimulant medications. Concerns include the appropriateness of medication (rationale for use, alternatives, toxicity), the dangers of inadequate clinical management, the general problem of child and adolescent nonadherence in health care (fears of peer ridicule and a reluctance to accept being labeled as "ill"), the possibility of negative effects on physical development, and ethical issues in decision-making and the rights of minors (Petr, 1998).

There are also concerns related to *iatrogenic* effects, or what children may learn from the process of taking medications. Children and adolescents may learn to attribute adjustment problems to factors beyond their control and thus become less receptive to behavioral interventions. They may fail to acquire adaptive behaviors because their symptoms are suppressed and caregivers do not recognize the need to teach other coping strategies, may learn to take medication as a way of coping with a variety of adjustment difficulties, and may become more likely to abuse psychoactive substances (Gadow, 1992). These effects are possible within any age group, but children and adolescents have not yet had the opportunity to develop a range of healthy habits for coping with stress.

The social worker should view the absence of active parental or caregiver interest with the child using psychostimulant medications as a major treatment concern. With the developmental issues of this life stage, including beginning needs for separation from the family, drug management requires a strong social worker-family alliance to ensure that the young client's needs are addressed holistically.

As a consultant the social worker is likely to have a major role in the medication assessment process. It was noted earlier that the diagnosis of ADHD requires a thorough social history as well as medical examination of the client. The social worker may have primary responsibility for conducting the necessary interviews with family members, teachers, and significant others, and also providing the client and family with formal testing materials. In this process the social worker must also assess the attitudes of the client and family, including what they expect from medication and its possible impact on the consumer's self-esteem and sense of competence. This information will be important in the ultimate decision about whether or not to prescribe medication. The social worker's relationships with the client and family may increase the likelihood of compliance with whatever plan is adopted.

It is suggested that the social worker begin serving as an educator in describing the actions, benefits, and risks of the psychostimulants before they are prescribed. This may be the physician's primary responsibility, but the social worker should have sufficient knowledge to provide the client and family with verbal and written information. Of course, these activities may result in the client's decision not to take medication, and thus the process of education should be coordinated among members of the treatment team. The educator role will continue after the client begins using the medication because the social worker must put the client's unique responses into a context of what tends to occur for most clients who take the medication, as discussed earlier.

As a counselor and advocate the social worker can ensure that the needs and preferences of the client and family are made clear to all who participate in the intervention, both before and after medication is prescribed. This is particularly crucial in that the client may be a minor whose preferences are not given priority by adults involved in his or her care. The social worker often spends more time with the client and family than others on the treatment team; he or she may be best informed about their perspectives regarding medication and other interventions.

SPECIFIC MEDICATIONS

Origins

The first known stimulant, cocaine, was isolated in 1860 as a chemical salt, but it had been used for centuries by South American native cultures via the coca plant to fight off fatigue, lessen hunger, and increase endurance. The chemical extraction is more powerful than the plant and was used by soldiers in eastern Europe as early as 1884 to decrease fatigue.

The prototype of the current psychostimulant drugs is *amphetamine*, a substance of medical interest and controversy since it was synthesized in 1887. A California chemist named George Alles first developed this substance for clinical use in the 1930s while conducting drug experiments for the treatment of allergies (Leake, 1970). Specifically he was studying ephedrine, a chemically active agent derived from a plant long known to Chinese herbalists as an effective treatment for asthma. This substance is structurally similar to epinephrine, a natural substance which stimulates the peripheral nervous system. Because supplies of ephedrine for research were limited, Alles made successful efforts to develop synthetic compounds. He named two of these benzedrine and dexedrine. The first of these amphetamines was marketed to treat asthma orally and to raise low blood pressure. Because its side effect, central nervous system stimulation, was obvious, use of the drug was soon expanded to treat narcolepsy and obesity. It had also been noted in early trials of amphetamine that the drug had a paradoxical effect on some consumers; that is, it produced states of relaxation instead of alertness and excitation.

Amphetamines were used in the 1930s as bronchial dilators, respiratory stimulants, analeptics, and to treat parkinsonism. They were widely used by British, Japanese, and American soldiers during World War II. This was actually encouraged by American physicians, but was controversial because of concerns about the toxic effects of overuse. It was only after the war, however, that the amphetamines became well-known drugs of abuse. Japan had large stocks of the drugs which could be purchased without prescription. The drugs were later utilized for the treatment of various conditions including depression, until the development of the MAO inhibitors.

Amphetamines were first used with children in the 1920s by a Dr. Bradley, a Rhode Island physician, in a successful effort to help survivors of

Table 4.25 Psychostimulant Medications

Drug	Trade Name	Preparation	Usual Daily Dose
Amphetamine	Adderall	T	20–40 mg
Dextroamphetamine	Dexedrine	T, C*	20–40 mg
Methamphetamine	Desoxyn	T	20–40 mg
Methylphenidate	Ritalin	T*	20–40 mg
Pemoline	Cylert	T, patch	56.25–75 mg

*Available in time-release form

an influenza epidemic who developed neurological impairments become less agitated and more teachable. Stimulants have been used to treat ADHD since 1936, when it was found that the paradoxical effects of amphetamine drugs on some persons could be effective in controlling hyperactivity.

Current Medications

The primary psychostimulant drugs include methylphenidate, the amphetamines (including dextroamphetamine and methamphetamine, which are more potent substances), and pemoline. Except for pemoline, all are classified as Schedule II drugs by the Drug Enforcement Agency because of their abuse potential. This is the most restrictive classification for medications, prohibiting both their prescription by phone and the writing of refills. The psychostimulants are currently approved for the treatment of ADHD, narcolepsy, and obesity. At present they account for 95% of ADHD medication therapy in the United States (see Table 4.25). In this country 90% of children with ADHD take methylphenidate because it is effective, has been available the longest, and has been been tested most thoroughly. Five percent (5%) take dextroamphetamine and 2% take pemoline (Lawrence, Lawrence, & Carson, 1997).

While the entire mechanism of action of these drugs is not known, they release norepinephrine, dopamine, and serotonin from presynaptic terminals in the frontal portion of the brain where attention and impulsivity are regulated. They also inhibit norepinephrine and dopamine reuptake. Approximately 70% of consumers respond positively to any one of the drugs, and 20% of those who do not respond to one of the drugs will respond positively to another. Moderate doses appear to improve attention, concentration, and cognitive functioning in adults as well, although ADHD in adults has not been studied as thoroughly.

The common adverse effects of the stimulants are generally transient and include loss of appetite, weight loss, irritability, insomnia, and abdominal pain (see Table 4.26). Less common adverse effects include depression, increased blood pressure, tachycardia, nightmares, tics, skin rashes, toxic psychosis, and liver toxicity. All of the drugs except pemoline carry a "rebound" effect, meaning that the symptoms of ADHD tend to recur dramatically after the medication is eliminated from the consumer's body. They may stunt physical

Table 4.26 Side Effects of Psychostimulant Medications

Common	Less Common
Anxiety	Itching, skin rash
Insomnia	Fever
Loss of appetite	Dizziness
Gastrointestinal pain	Headache
Cardiac arrythmia	Blood pressure changes

growth among children and adolescents, but there is a rebound growth to normal height during drug holidays or after the drug is discontinued. Further research is needed on the impact of these medications on the physical growth and rebound growth of children.

In most cases several times a year consumers are given periodic drug holidays of at least two weeks as a means of assessing the status of their condition. These holidays are most practical when children are out of school and have fewer persistent demands on their attention. Studies of drug effectiveness beyond puberty is not extensive, but there is evidence that treatment in childhood leads to better outcomes in adulthood. Hechtman, Weiss, & Perlman (1984) found that children using psychostimulants for three years or longer had better outcomes relative to further psychiatric treatment, levels of education, independent living, and aggression. Because many children experience a natural reduction in the symptoms of ADHD as they grow through adolescence, physicians attempt to taper and eliminate the medication at intervals; generally every few years.

Methylphenidate, the most widely used and studied psychostimulant, was introduced as a treatment for children with hyperactivity in 1958 (Jacobvitz, 1990). It is approved by the Food and Drug Administration (FDA) for children six years and older. Methylphenidate releases stored dopamine, decreases dopamine reuptake, and inhibits monoamine oxidase activity. It is quickly absorbed into the bloodstream, requiring only 30 to 60 minutes to take effect and reaching peak blood levels within 2 hours. Its half-life is 2 to 3 hours, which necessitates that it be taken 2 to 4 times daily. It does not typically impair sleep. A time-release form of the drug is available, but there is some evidence that this preparation is less effective than the standard form (Fitzpatrick, Klorman, Brumaghim, & Borgstedt, 1992). Its slower absorption results in delayed onset and also increases sleep and appetite disturbances. One advantage of methylphenidate relative to other stimulants is its lesser appetite suppression effect.

Dextroamphetamine is approved for children three years and older. It is believed to work by increasing dopamine and norepinephrine transmission and inhibiting monoamine oxidase activity. Dextroamphetamine, the least expensive of the psychostimulants, is also fast-acting, and with a half-life of six hours the medication needs to be taken only twice daily. It does have disadvantages, including a potential for abuse and diversion to the illicit drug market. Its adverse effects, including a higher likelihood of anorexia, insomnia, and cardiovascular effects, are slightly more pronounced than those experienced with methylphenidate (Efron, Jarman, & Barker, 1997).

Adderall is an amphetamine; it is not a new medication but has recently been FDA approved as a treatment for persons with ADHD aged 3 years and older (Rodgers, 1996). It is composed of a unique mix of amphetamine isomers. Adderall has a rapid onset and with a 2-to-6-hour effect can be given once or twice daily in most cases. Because it is composed of different substances than the other amphetamines, Adderall may be useful for consumers who do not respond to them.

Methamphetamine is rarely prescribed for ADHD because it is a stronger amphetamine substance with greater abuse potential, but it can be effective as an alternative medication. It is also long acting, needing to be taken twice daily, and has fewer systemic side effects than dextroamphetamine. It is, however, more expensive.

Pemoline is structurally different from methylphenidate and the amphetamines. It seems to act through dopamine mechanisms in ways which are not well understood. Pemoline has a half-life of 12 hours (slightly longer for adults) and an 8-hour duration of action. It only needs to be taken once daily and is available in a chewable tablet; thus it may be easier for children (six years and older) and families to manage. The lesser stimulant effect of pemoline reduces its abuse potential and produces less anorexia and insomnia. Further, it is the only psychostimulant drug that apparently produces no rebound effect on discontinuation. As a Schedule IV controlled substance, it must be prescribed in writing but may include refills.

Pemoline does have drawbacks. It may require up to six weeks of use before demonstrating a therapeutic effect, and it is more expensive than the other stimulants. Most seriously, pemoline has not been researched as extensively as methylphenidate. There are reports in the literature of some deaths from liver toxicity, which has recently placed the drug out of favor with physicians.

Other Drugs Used to Treat ADHD

While the stimulants are the drugs of first choice in treating ADHD, alternatives are necessary. There is a high prevalence of ADHD and many clients will either not respond to the primary medications or experience intolerable adverse reactions. Evidence for the effectiveness of other medications for treating ADHD is emerging. These drugs have not been extensively evaluated with clients having the disorder but some clinical studies have demonstrated their promise.

Clonidine was originally developed to lower blood pressure but is also used to treat such conditions as opiate withdrawal, Tourette's syndrome, and smoking cessation. It has recently emerged as an alternative for treating ADHD. Clonidine decreases certain types of arousal by decreasing the activity of "alpha-2" receptors in the central nervous system (and thereby promoting the release of norepinephrine). The drug is quickly absorbed, reaches peak plasma levels in 1 to 3 hours and has a half-life of 6 to 20 hours. Clonidine has been effective with children who have severe problems with mood, activity level, cooperation, and frustration tolerance, but it is less effective at improving attention. It is sometimes prescribed along with a stimulant for a combined effect. One unique feature of this medication is that it can be dispensed with a 7-day patch. Common adverse effects include dry mouth and eyes, fatigue, irritability, sedation, dizziness, hypotension, and constipation. Less common adverse effects include insomnia, anxiety, and depression (Kaplan & Sadock, 1998).

The antidepressant drugs are differentially effective for persons with ADHD (Popper, 1997). The cyclic antidepressants, including imipramine, desipramine, and amitriptyline, have shown effectiveness with ADHD and are particularly useful for adult consumers who have a family history of depression or anxiety. Desipramine has been found effective in treating adults with ADHD in one randomized placebo-controlled study (White, 1996). The cyclic drugs should not be used with children, however, because their effectiveness has not been adequately demonstrated and they produce adverse effects of dry mouth, blurred vision, constipation, and sedation, all of which many children cannot tolerate. On the positive side, cyclic drugs have longer lasting effects, allow greater dose flexibility, and carry a lower risk of abuse. Bupropion is an antidepressant with a pharmacological profile somewhat similar to the stimulants but without abuse potential. Barrickman et al. (1995) in a double-blind study found that the drug was as effective as methylphenidate in treating ADHD, although there was a slightly greater improvement for subjects using the latter medication. The newer serotonin reuptake inhibitors have not yet been adequately tested as treatments for ADHD.

Case Examples

Tracy was referred to the elementary school's Child Study Committee by her fifth grade teacher. It was early in the school year, and the teacher had noted that the 12-year-old child (who had once been held back) was not motivated to do schoolwork, could not focus on classroom tasks, made inappropriate noises, was distracting to others, and had poor peer relationships. Tracy's mother attended the Committee meeting, which included a social worker, guidance counselor, psychologist, nurse, and the teacher, in addition to Tracy. This was a single parent who worked full-time to raise her family, which included a younger son as well as Tracy. The mother admitted that Tracy demonstrated the same problem behaviors at home and at the day care center that she attended after school. Her mother added that Tracy could not relax and go to sleep at night and may have been getting only five hours of sleep. All members of the Committee agreed that despite her behaviors Tracy was a warm child with an engaging sense of playfulness about her actions, problematic as they might be.

The social worker, noting that the child exhibited the same behavior control problems in a variety of life settings, recommended that the mother take Tracy to their physician to get an assessment and to get more information for later problem solving at the school. In the school setting all problems were framed as educational in nature. While Tracy's mother followed up on the referral, the social worker, teacher, and guidance counselor constructed a behavioral intervention for the classroom. This plan was based on the child's strengths of wanting to be helpful and having a particular desire to work with younger children at school as a mentor for their class projects. If Tracy would do her required work and not talk so much with her peers, she could be assigned to work with the younger children on a regular basis, deliver the teacher's notes to the office when needed, and be permitted to stay after school to help clean the room.

Tracy was assessed by her physician; she referred her to a pediatric psychiatrist who diagnosed the child with ADHD. A mid-range dosage of methylphenidate was prescribed for the child, and the mother agreed to support Tracy's regular use of the drug. Within four weeks significant positive changes were noted in the classroom, and the mother also reported positive changes at home and the day care center. It was not clear to what extent the school behavioral program, medications, and parent support (by the social worker) each contributed to the changes, but this ambiguity is often true of children with ADHD. The significance of the changes in all spheres led the social worker to conclude that the medications were a major contributor to Tracy's improvement. The social worker monitored Tracy's use of the medication through monthly phone conversations with her mother. The Child Study Committee reviewed the case every two months, in accordance with its policies. Six months into the intervention plan, Tracy was still functioning satisfactorily in the classroom and elsewhere and appeared to be a reasonably happy child. She was also getting along better with her classmates.

How long would Tracy take the medication? The social worker knew that she could not make specific recommendations on that issue but could only encourage her mother to keep in regular contact with their treating physician and to use the social worker as a consultant and counselor. The social worker knew that, in many cases, parents tend to stop focusing on the medications as long as the child is behaving well, and sometimes they stop making doctor's appointments. And what did Tracy think about taking medicine several times per day? She seemed to take it in stride. She complained of stomachaches for the first few weeks, but these stopped when she learned to take the medicine with food. "Mom didn't say too much about what the medicine was for," Tracy once said to the social worker. "She said it was just something I need, like glasses".

Patrick came to the attention of the school social worker at an earlier age than Tracy—he was only seven years old and in the second grade. A new student at the school, Patrick had already been diagnosed with ADHD and was taking a high dose of methylphenidate. His parents had sought help from the Child Study Committee because they had been frustrated for several years with Patrick's hyperactivity, poor attention span, and apparent lack of positive response to medical interventions.

Patrick was an adopted biracial (African American and Caucasian) child of this achievement-oriented professional couple. He had two brothers, aged eight and four, both of whom were also adopted. Of the three he was the only child who demonstrated behavior problems to his parents or the school. His parents reported to the Child Study Committee that Patrick had been diagnosed with ADHD at age three, after they became concerned about his general unruliness and lack of self-control. They believed that Patrick had been born drug-addicted and wondered what effect that might be having on his physical condition. His parents reported that Patrick could never focus on his homework and was not social. He seemed to prefer being by himself and loved computers, as many children do, for the colorful stimulation they provided.

During the family assessment, the social worker noticed that Patrick's parents were extremely anxious; almost frantic in their efforts to see that something more be done for their child. They had taken Patrick to several psychologists who specialized in the treatment of ADHD and were told that some of his behaviors were "just his personality." "He is an energetic child" was a comment from another. His parents' comments that "something is terribly wrong with Patrick," and "we want him to become a true member of our family" made the social worker concerned that Patrick might be feeling badly about himself. She was also concerned that the parents admitted to favoring high doses of methylphenidate, although it was apparently not working well. This could be contributing to his poor sleep quality. The Child Study Committee suggested that Patrick continue seeing a physician and perhaps have his medications reviewed. They also included the family in planning a classroom behavioral management program.

Patrick was soon evaluated by a physician who changed his medication to an amphetamine and also moderated the dose. His parents explained the ongoing need for medication to Patrick, saying "You have an illness that we have to treat. It's like having allergies." With the change in medication, there was some improvement in Patrick's behavior. It was more controlled, and he was sleeping marginally better, but he also become more irritable and defiant of authority figures. The social worker understood that this might be a manifestation of ADHD but could also be either Patrick's interpersonal style or due to the medication's side effect of anxiety.

The social worker, teacher, and guidance counselor implemented a behavioral program that addressed Patrick's low self-esteem by including much praise for his positive and social behaviors. His parents were encouraged to do the same. Still, Patrick continued to be a management challenge for the school and family. The social worker consulted regularly with Patrick, his parents, and his teacher. She tried to provide the parents with education about a comprehensive approach to helping a child with ADHD. She also focused on their own needs to relax and try to acquire some detachment from the Patrick's presenting problems, as doing so might benefit them as well as their son.

Robbie, age 27, came to the mental health agency for counseling because his five-year marriage and new career were falling apart. His wife Susan was threatening to leave him because he was sullen and irritable around the house, blaming his bad moods on work stress and paying little attention to her. She was also concerned that, while Robbie had always enjoyed drinking several beers every evening, he was increasing his alcohol intake. Susan had always been attracted to Robbie's physical energy and playful sense of adventure, but she was concerned now that he lacked any career focus. She wanted to start a family but felt that Robbie was not emotionally stable enough to do so.

The social worker spent several meetings assessing Robbie's present situation and background. Robbie had never experienced emotional problems in the past. He had been an energetic child and young adult who particularly loved outdoor activities such as camping and climbing. He had been a fair student but never a scholar; he was one of the average kids who tended to be bored in the classroom but produced satisfactory work. It was hard to get interested in reading, he said. He was more the athletic type. Robbie had attended community college (initially to prepare for a social work career) but did not finish. He had held several jobs as a recreations leader but was thrilled to be hired one year ago as the Youth Director of his Methodist Church. Robbie had always been a participating church member and loved working with kids. He particularly enjoyed planning and participating in their evening and weekend outings.

Robbie's current problems surfaced when he began this new job. He was great with the kids but was extremely disorganized in tending to the administrative demands of the job. Robbie could never focus on more than one office project at a time. Further, if he was interrupted from completing a task by a phone call or visitor, he could not remember later what he had been doing or where he left off. Robbie purchased a sophisticated "pocket organizer" and began sticking Post-It notes to his left hand and wrist, each one with his tasks for the day listed, so that he could remind himself of what he needed to accomplish. These efforts did not work. Robbie became increasingly frustrated and tense, which greatly affected his marriage. His pastor warned him, while being supportive of his talents, that he might need to leave the job if he could not manage the department better. Robbie started drinking more. He always liked to drink beer to relax himself at the end of a day, and now it was harder to relax.

The social worker suggested a medical evaluation, wondering if Robbie might have ADHD. She recognized that while he had never been diagnosed with the disorder as a youth, his classroom behaviors indicated that he may have have had a disorder of the inattention type, rather than the more noticeable impulsive/hyperactive type. This might also account for his present inability to manage the fairly basic administrative responsibilities of his job.

Robbie would not consider the evaluation at first—he called the physician only after his wife insisted he do so as a condition of their staying together. The doctor did make a diagnosis of ADHD, inattention type. He wanted to prescribe methylphenidate, but Robbie refused this because he was wary of all medications but also because he did not want to give up drinking. The social worker provided additional counseling and support to Robbie and his wife before the client could concede that he had in fact been medicating himself with alcohol. It had been his means of reducing his anxiety and tension for ten years but the prescribed medication might be a more effective substitute. Robbie agreed, with the support of his wife, to stop drinking and try the medication. He demonstrated a remarkably positive response, and this helped him keep both his job and his marriage. Robbie has been on the medication for one year. He hopes to be able to discontinue it, but he is careful to add that he would only do so if his physician supported the idea.

SUMMARY

This chapter has consisted of discussions of five major classes of medication, the symptoms they treat, the types of medication within those classes, and their effects, positive and negative, on clients who use them as part of their intervention strategies. In the next chapter we turn to special issues with psychotropic medication as they apply to specific populations of clients.

5

Intervention Concerns
with Special Populations

A major strength of the social work profession is its appreciation of human diversity—the understanding that all persons are unique and that members of different genders, age groups, and racial and ethnic populations tend to experience some biological as well as social differences. This appreciation of diversity impacts psychopharmacology as much as it impacts any other aspect of social work intervention.

In the previous two chapters, we outlined the actions and impact of psychotropic medications, as well as what they implied for the social worker's seven roles. However, besides those general actions, distinct reactions to some medications occur in some special populations. Because few other professions are as extensively educated about issues of diversity, social workers have a particularly important responsibility to understand these differences and communicate their implications to the client, physician, and others involved in client care. Keep in mind, however, there is not universal agreement about these specific effects; research in this area is new and much remains to be learned about how different populations react to psychotropic drugs. In this chapter, we will focus on the following groups: women, the elderly, children and adolescents, members of several racial and ethnic populations, and people diagnosed with both mental illness and substance abuse.

GENDER DIFFERENCES

General Considerations

More likely than men to take prescription medications, women consume 70% of all psychotropic drugs (Ettorre & Riska, 1995). When broken down into age groups, women also report greater psychotropic drug use between the ages of 45 and 64 (Robbins & Clayton, 1989). Still, women do not necessarily have a greater need for medications. Men tend not to accurately report their own medication use because of a cultural "psychological Calvinism," or a reluctance to admit use even when drugs are helpful. Casper, Belanoff, and Offer (1996) found in a sample of 497 students from three high schools that girls were significantly more likely to report emotional distress than boys on a standardized instrument. This may indicate a valid difference in distress levels but just as likely points to a greater proclivity among girls to be open about their emotional concerns.

The psychological and social factors of drug prescription and use, discussed in chapter 4, suggest an important area for study: why women are prescribed a disproportionate amount of drugs. One comparative study found that women were more frequently diagnosed with depressive disorders and received more drug prescriptions for their treatment (Rodin & Ickovics, 1990). As researchers, social workers might productively monitor their own caseloads for trends in medication use and response along gender lines.

While it is true women use psychotropic drugs extensively, ironically, they have been underrepresented in pharmacological research. Incredible as it may seem, it was not until 1993 that the Food and Drug Administration began to include women in the clinical evaluation of drugs; at the same time the FDA announced guidelines for the study and evaluation of gender differences in medication response. This lack of comparative data presents serious limitations in our ability to understand the effectiveness and risks of medication for women. Comparative gender research is essential because of known physiologic differences between men and women. Here we provide some information about what is known regarding gender differences.

Women have a lower ratio of lean body mass to body fat, differences in hormone levels through the life span (including changes during menstrual cycles, pregnancy, lactation, and menopause), and some differences in brain chemical composition (Yonkers & Ellison, 1996). Further, oral contraceptives can alter the metabolism of some amino acids that are significant to drug metabolism. These differences may affect a given drug's therapeutic efficacy, adverse effects, and interactions with other drugs. We will now review the implications of these differences in more detail.

Neurotransmitters

Several studies have reported neurotransmitter differences between the sexes. These differences include rates of serotonin-binding capacity, which is greater even in adolescent girls than in adolescent boys (Biegon & Gruener, 1992). Women develop more serotonin as they age, a process that may be mediated by hormonal changes (Kumar, Weiss, Fernandez, Cruess, & Eisdorfer, 1998). One study concludes that serotonin-response differences cause women to react to stress with greater physiological affect than men and to respond therapeutically to different doses of some anti-anxiety medications (Blanchard,

Yudko, Rodgers, & Blanchard, 1993). It is also speculated that serotonin levels play a role in the production of affective disorders related to the menstrual cycle (Veeninga, Westenberg, & Weusten, 1990). Though the practical effects of these differences are not great in most cases, they provide evidence of gender-specific medication effects that the social worker should note.

Absorption

Women empty stomach contents at a slower rate than men, which has impact on a drug's systemic absorption. This does not affect a drug's effectiveness, but it does affect the rate at which some drugs begin demonstrating a therapeutic effect. On the other hand, women have higher overall absorption rates for many medications, including the cyclic antidepressants, benzodiazepines, and antipsychotic phenothiazines (Pollock, 1997).

Distribution

A drug's concentration in a woman's body tissues is affected by her higher percentage of body fat (Xie, Piecoro, & Wermeling, 1997). Women maintain a higher volume of distribution for fat-soluble drugs; they have more body space available to contain such drugs. In the case of fat-soluble medications, a higher percentage of body fat also accounts for the relatively smaller blood plasma concentrations in proportion to dosage and a longer half-life. Conversely, water-soluble drugs have a lower volume of distribution in women, which increases plasma concentration and explains, for example, why women have less tolerance for alcohol than men. Increased body fat also affects drug elimination rates (in either direction, depending on the nature of the drug).

A lower binding capacity for numerous drugs including chlordiazepoxide, diazepam, and imipramine has been established in nonpregnant females vs. males (Jensfold, Halbreich, & Hamilton, 1996). More of these medications are thus available for action at receptor sites in the brain. A larger amount of a drug that is free from binding also increases its toxicity. Any medication of this type that has a low therapeutic index is more likely to become toxic, such as lithium and the antidepressant nortriptyline.

Metabolism

Women and men metabolize medications differently. Several variables have been found to influence liver metabolism and clearance, including hormones, pregnancy, race, food, and circadian rhythms (one's biological cycles). Hormonal fluctuations in the menstrual cycle result in a higher clearance of a drug during the mid-cycle. Oral contraceptives have been shown to inhibit the metabolism of several medications, including some benzodiazepines and the antidepressant imipramine (Fletcher, Acosta, & Strykowski, 1994). Other benzodiazepines, however, have an increased clearance rate in the presence of oral contraceptives.

Drug metabolism is related to the actions of certain enzymes, and one relevant set of enzymes (cytochrome) has been found to be more active in younger women than in older women or men. This results in shorter half-lives for several benzodiazepines and thus may increase their addictive potential (Pollock, 1997). Some women become dependent on these anti-anxiety medications and experience withdrawal upon their termination.

Classes of Medication

Some gender differences have been observed with regard to the symptoms of schizophrenia and the actions of antipsychotic medications. Women are more likely to experience late-onset schizophrenia than men, and even across age groups they tend to show more pronounced positive symptoms than negative symptoms (Lindamer, Lohr, Harris, McAdams, & Jeste, 1999). Their relatively fewer cognitive deficits account for the fewer negative symptoms (Goldstein et al., 1998). Women tend to show more positive responses to antipsychotic medications, which is good, but they also experience more severe side effects, including extrapyramidal symptoms and tardive dyskinesia. Even with similar dosing, age, and weight, females have higher plasma levels of antipsychotic medication than men (Yonkers, 1992). The hormone estrogen is said to be responsible for these differences, because it acts as a dopamine antagonist. Since most antipsychotic drugs act as dopamine receptor antagonists, the presence of estrogen may accentuate the effect of antipsychotic drugs. Women over age 67 were found in one study to have more severe forms of tardive dyskinesia, and this response was explained by the loss of estrogen as a protective factor in postmenopausal women.

Some gender differences also exist in the experience and treatment of affective disorders. Suhail and Cochrane (1995) found in a study of 992 admissions to a single British hospital that unlike men, women are more cyclical in their experience of affective disorders. They experience more wintertime depression and in bipolar disorder have higher rates of mania during the summers. A variety of studies have recommended guidelines for the drug treatment of women with affective disorders. Depressed women with panic attacks have been found to respond well to both MAO inhibitors and to cyclic antidepressants, while men with panic attacks responded well only to the cyclic drugs (Davidson & Pelton, 1986). Another study recommended that women be treated with lower doses of amitriptyline and imipramine, even lower doses of imipramine when taking oral contraceptives, and higher doses of cyclic antidepressants when experiencing a premenstrual exacerbation of depressive symptoms (Hamilton, Grant, & Jensvold, 1996). Premenstrual dysphoric disorder, a subtype of depressive disorder, has been successfully treated with all types of antidepressant medications. One study has found that plasma levels of sertraline were higher in young women than young men. Oral contraceptives can be related to the development of depression since evidence shows that their effect on amino acid metabolism results in a deficiency of serotonin in the brain (Mishell, 1989). The SSRIs may be the treatment of choice in these situations. In general, men have been found to respond more positively to antidepressant medications than women and also experience more adverse effects (Rodin & Ickovics, 1990).

PREGNANCY

Most research about the effects of medications on women focuses on pregnancy. This is because some psychotropic drugs are teratogenic, or potentially harmful to the fetus. The physician and social worker must consider four general issues when deciding which medications, of all types, to give a pregnant woman:

1. The risks and benefits of taking medication with regard to the mother's overall mental status
2. The effects of medication on the fetus
3. The long-term physical effects on the newborn (some of which may not become apparent for years)
4. The effects on the mother and newborn together if a current mental disorder is inadequately treated (Janicak, Davis, Preskorn, & Ayd, 1997)

In general, it is considered best to prescribe no medications for a pregnant woman, particularly during the first trimester, when the fetus faces its highest risk of damage. The blood-brain barrier, as well as the blood–placenta barrier, is the layer of fatty tissue that serves as a boundary between the circulatory system and those other organs; medication must penetrate these barriers to produce an effect within the enclosed structures. Medications cross the blood–placenta barrier as well as the blood-brain barrier, thus becoming part of the fetus's bloodstream. Additionally, physicians should avoid prescribing medications during breast-feeding, because most drugs pass through the milk, directly affecting the newborn. Professionals may also discourage breast-feeding in many cases. Though abstinence from drugs is always the physically safe strategy for the fetus or baby, it cannot always be implemented, because the physician, social worker, and client must carefully weigh all four of the above considerations in prescription and medication management. It is important to note that studies about the possible adverse effects of medication on fetuses are not extensive. Avoidance of medication is based largely on the possibility of adverse effects rather than their inevitability. Nevertheless, the social worker as educator can fully inform the expectant mother and her significant others about special risks in pregnancy.

By implication, it may be helpful to increase the intensity of interventions other than psychotropic medication during pregnancy to offset any precautionary drug measures taken by the physician. These interventions include supportive counseling, client and family education, assistance with mental status monitoring, and encouragement of client participation in psychosocial rehabilitation programs. They also allow the physician and social worker to monitor the client's physical and mental status more closely. The social worker may need to link her with community agencies that provide prenatal services.

Classes of Medication

When the risks of not taking medication, including unmanageable symptoms and self-care limitations, are more serious than those of using it, professionals must follow several principles. For psychotic disorders, it may be safer to use the high-potency medications (such as haloperidol and risperidone), which have fewer negative effects on the fetus than other medications, effects such as sedation, hypotension, gastrointestinal slowing, and tachycardia. The social worker can expect these medications to be discontinued several weeks before delivery so that the newborn will not experience problems related to withdrawal and other adverse effects. Unless the client has chosen to breast-feed, she should resume psychotropic medication immediately after delivery, particularly because there is always the possibility of postpartum psychosis. Furthermore, the physician may avoid or minimize antiparkinsonian drug treatment because this presents a further risk to the newborn. The nursing baby may experience infant extrapyramidal effects if his or her mother consumes these medications.

Antidepressant medications are also best avoided during pregnancy. Some antidepressants, such as nortriptyline and desipramine, have been studied in this regard more extensively than others. Because these drugs have not demonstrated adverse effects, they are considered relatively safe. Looking for alternatives to medications during pregnancy, the physician may consider electroconvulsive therapy, now used more frequently than in the recent past to treat depression in all populations.

Taking a newly pregnant mother off medications must be done gradually so as not to cause withdrawal in either the mother or the fetus. The social worker may need to increase his or her educational and family support roles through this process so that the client and her family understand the rationale for these changes and can actively help maintain a safe environment. Again, because postpartum depression may occur at any time up to 6 months after delivery, it may be necessary to begin antidepressant therapy at any time following delivery, at which point such therapy is safe.

Mood-stabilizing medications are more risky than those in other classes for the pregnant client. Lithium use may cause fetal heart problems, specifically the development of the large vessels of the heart. If lithium is used, the physician may prescribe lower doses than usual to avoid high peak levels. Carbamazepine has been associated with various developmental delays and cranial defects in newborns (supplemental folic acid is believed to reduce the risks of some of these). Valproate can also be teratogenic. Though the studies on which these findings are based are inconclusive, the possibility of serious negative effects makes the use of mood-stabilizing medications an extremely delicate problem. When they are used, the fetus needs to be monitored with sonography to detect any adverse changes. Thus, the social worker may need to assume some responsibility for planning and advocacy so that such procedures occur promptly and regularly. Furthermore, because a pregnant woman's blood volume increases and lithium levels become more unstable, the drug becomes more difficult to monitor during pregnancy. Here again, the social worker's roles need to expand to provide alternative services and to help the client monitor effects for the physician and treatment team.

The effects of anti-anxiety medications in pregnancy are also largely untested. Benzodiazepines have been reported to cause fetal abnormalities in the first trimester of pregnancy, even though other data disputes this evidence. There is evidence that lorazepam accumulates less in fetal tissue than some other similar medications (Janicak et al., 1997). A fetus can develop benzodiazepine dependence and experience withdrawal after birth. Diphenhydramine, on the other hand, should not be prescribed because it may cause withdrawal complications for the newborn. Because this medication is available without prescription, the social worker can help to ensure that the client is aware of pregnancy risks even with these types of drugs. For instance, "neonatal withdrawal syndrome" can occur with anti-anxiety medications.

It is worth noting that the newer medications from each class have not been tested with pregnant women as much as the older medications. Thus, even though the newer medications have fewer overall adverse effects for general populations, their effects on a fetus are less well known and thus they may not be prescribed during pregnancy.

OTHER GENDER-RELATED CONCERNS

Psychotropic medication may adversely affect the sexual functioning of both men and women. Symptoms may include a decrease in sex drive for both, an impaired ability to ejaculate or maintain erections for men, and an inhibition for orgasm for women. Because many clients are uncomfortable discussing these issues with professionals, part of the social worker's task in the partnership model of practice is to create an environment where these concerns, if present, can be shared. The social worker can also help determine if raising the possibility of these side effects, which are not inevitable, is worth the risk of increasing the client's anxiety. If the client is not sexually active while using medications, some of these effects may not be problematic; however, they will still impact a client's sense of self. Of course, adverse effects present a major problem to clients who wish to be sexually active. Physicians can make medication adjustments that may alleviate these side effects. In any case, the social worker can explore this area of the client's life as well as others to provide a relevant assessment in the event that psychotropic medications will be used.

OLDER ADULTS

General Considerations

Many of the normal physiological changes that come with aging are relevant to decisions about the prescribing of any medication. These include changes in the following areas:

1. **Rate of gastrointestinal activity.** With the aging population, the rate of gastrointestinal tract activity slows. This slows medication absorption and distribution, although ultimately these processes remain as thorough as in younger age groups. In most cases, medications will not, however, take effect as quickly.

2. **Body mass and weight.** Older adults have less total body water, less lean body mass, and more body fat (particularly women). As a result, the distribution efficiency of water-soluble drugs is reduced, while that of the fat-soluble drugs is increased. The plasma concentrations of water-soluble drugs such as lithium thus increase; conversely, concentrations of fat-soluble drugs decrease. A lower body weight implies that the physician may determine dosage levels on a "milligram by weight" basis rather than strict milligram dosages, though this occurs in some other cases as well, such as for people who weigh more than average.

3. **Reduction in serum protein levels.** It should be recalled from chapter 4 that a significant amount of many drugs is rendered inert in one's system because of binding with protein in the bloodstream and thus remaining unavailable to the desired site of action. In older adults, with a reduction in serum protein levels, there are higher levels of the free drug available for therapeutic action. As a result, a smaller dose of a given drug is required for an effect.

4. **Metabolism.** As people age there is a gradual decline in the quality and efficiency of liver and kidney function. Both therapeutic responses and side effects may occur at blood levels lower than expected. As the metabolism slows, the half-lives of all psychotropic medications increase, with the half-life of some medications doubling or tripling. Physicians will usually prescribe less medication for the same therapeutic effect. The social worker must also be aware that toxic amounts of medication may build more quickly in an older client's bloodstream. Toxicity (see chapter 4) also becomes problematic because of decreased rates of renal clearance (up to 50% less by age 70). Clearance is also less efficient in older men because prostate enlargement causes greater urinary retention.

5. **Cardiovascular efficiency.** The aging process impacts cardiovascular system functioning, as cardiac output and blood perfusion into other organs diminishes. Kidney function is therefore slowed and liver function compromised.

6. **Sensitivity of certain nervous system receptors.** Certain neurotransmitters in the brain become more sensitive in older people, another reason why the same amount of medication may have a greater effect. Studies have been done regarding age-related changes in serotonin availability (McEntee & Crook, 1991). A decrease in serotonin levels in older adults is associated with enhanced memory, and thus serotonin-antagonist medications may actually help some elderly people with memory problems. Older adults also experience a reduction in naturally occurring cholinergic neurons. As a result they are more sensitive to the anticholinergic effects of some antipsychotic and antidepressant medications.

In collaboration with other providers, social workers need to continuously try to assess the extent to which psychiatric symptoms in the elderly result from psychological problems, medical illnesses, using multiple medications, or all of these. Both the starting and maintenance doses of all psychotropic medications prescribed for the elderly are usually one-third to one-half the prescribed dose for young adults because of the changes noted above but also as a precaution against the dangers of polypharmacy, or the prescription of more than one medication to treat the same or other physical or mental disorders. These dangers include the frequently overlooked problems related to misuse of over-the-counter drugs by elderly persons, alcohol abuse among many older adults, and the impact of multiple drugs on their clearance from one's system (Schatzberg, Cole, & DeBattista, 1997). In the role of consultant, the social worker can continuously update the physician about the client's physical status and changes in usage of other medications.

Classes of Medication

Psychotic disorders among the elderly population, excluding organic disorders, are no more or less prevalent than at any point during life (Lader & Herrington, 1996). Members of this population, however, sometimes exhibit a serious problem with agitation, that is not related to a specific mental disorder but is responsive to low-dose antipsychotic medications. Drug treatment strategies for the elderly resemble those used for the general population, but physicians may implement them differently. Two significant concerns include the heightened sensitivity to anticholinergic effects and the risk of falls owing to hypotension. The high-potency medications (such as risperidone) have fewer anticholinergic effects but produce uncomfortable extrapyramidal effects and hypotention; the opposite is true for the low-potency drugs (such as clozapine). With their increased sensitivity to the anticholinergic effects of any drug, the elderly may experience "central anticholinergic syndrome," characterized by problems with short-term memory, confusion, and, occasionally, visual hallucinations. The effects of this syndrome resemble those of Alzheimer's disease. The newer antipsychotic olanzapine represents a promising alternative. A high-potency medication, it has been found in two recent international studies to have fewer adverse effects on body movements than haloperidol.

The elderly also experience an increased risk of tardive dyskinesia. Though the overall prevalence of tardive dyskinesia for persons using antipsychotic medication is about 24% (Jeste & Caligiuri, 1993), the risk increases with age. The onset of the disorder may be related to a cumulative effect of medications over time as well as their interactions with normal physiological changes in parts of the brain. With this movement disorder, older adults also demonstrate fewer instances of spontaneous remission. As with other risks, careful monitoring is essential; the social worker should report any evidence of tardive dyskinesia's onset to the physician and help determine appropriate interventions.

Because of their need to cope with medical disorders, physical pain, increased overall drug use, social isolation, and cumulative bereavement issues, elderly people are more predisposed to depression than younger individuals. Late-onset depression is frequently characterized by higher levels of cognitive impairment, insomnia, agitation, and mortality rates. Suicide rates are in fact highest among the older adult population (Janicak, Davis, Preskorn, & Ayd, 1997). Unfortunately, because of their multiple health concerns, these clients often receive too much, or sometimes too little, antidepressant medication. The social worker's challenge is to assess levels of depression and sort out the various physical and emotional issues contributing to it. It is a mistake to assume that it is normal for older adults to feel depressed or that they can tolerate it any better than younger people.

The typical side effects of the cyclic antidepressants are particularly troublesome for the older adult population. They include sedation, hypotension, anticholinergic effects, and cardiac effects. Physicians generally do not use them for persons with cardiac conditions or who are at risk of falling. The anticholinergic effects of constipation and urinary retention can go unrecognized until they cause significant problems for the elderly client. The MAO inhibitors, and phenelzine in particular, so difficult to manage in younger populations, present certain advantages for the elderly. They do not produce anticholinergic effects and, in fact, may counteract the production of natural but potentially harmful increases in monoamine oxidase in the aging brain. Of course, the risks of hypotension and dietary reactions remain. In short, the MAO drug class may be more suitable for the elderly than some younger populations.

The newer serotonin-reuptake inhibitors do not appear to pose any special risk for elderly clients. In fact, the absence of sedation, hypotension, and anticholinergic and cardiovascular effects make them particularly attractive. However, the side effects of nausea, nervousness, and insomnia trouble those persons already experiencing related problems. These drugs are also more expensive, which is often a concern for all consumers but sometimes more so with older adults who rely on public assistance or live on restricted incomes.

Trazodone and bupropion are two drugs that have been found effective with older consumers because of their low levels of anticholinergic and cardiac effects. Trazodone, however, is not problem-free. It has been associated with priapism, or persistent penile erection in men. A newer medication, nefasozone, has shown promise with this population. The newer compounds, however, have not been available for research as long as the older drugs; thus, all health care providers must take reports or observations of adverse effects very seriously.

Lithium is the only psychotropic medication that is water soluble, making age-related changes in response to lithium predictable. These changes are associated with alterations in the renal system and the increased sensitivity of some nervous system receptor sites. Decreased clearance rates put elderly consumers at risk for prolonged exposure to higher therapeutic and toxic blood levels. In recent years the anticonvulsant medications (carbamazepine and valproic acid) have been used more often as mood-stabilizing drugs of first choice.

Anxiety is highly prevalent among the elderly and may be manifested differently than in younger people. Phobic disorders and generalized anxiety disorder are the most common among older adults. Simple phobia is the only type that has been commonly found to have an initial onset after age sixty. Panic disorder is relatively rare, but sleep disturbances are extremely common, experienced by over 50% of older adults. The benzodiazepines, while effective medications, produce side effects of sedation, cognitive impairment, reduced psychomotor coordination, and falls due to hypotension, all of which are serious. Further, with a reduced clearance rate, older adults more quickly experience a toxic amount of these drugs. Many of these problems may be minimized by using benzodiazepines with shorter half-lives and less active metabolites. Generally, the short-acting, low-potency drugs such as lorazepam, oxazepam, and temazepam are well tolerated by the elderly population (Janicak et al., 1997). Unfortunately, these drugs can be abused, with the overprescription of benzodiazepines, particularly triazolam, a major problem in nursing homes (Butler et al., 1991). Physicians are becoming more reluctant to prescribe benzodiazepines at all, and more often use buspirone, which has been shown to be very helpful in the treatment of anxiety. The social worker may also use nondrug cognitive-behavioral interventions for anxiety, such as encouraging clients to sleep well, maintain good hygiene, avoid stimulants, reduce environmental agitation, and exercise regularly.

With the elderly population, physicians generally initiate treatment at low doses and gradually increase the dose over a period of days or weeks. Careful physicians will also prescribe as few drugs as necessary, because the elderly tend to take other medications to treat physical conditions. During this process, the social worker can help monitor the client for both therapeutic and adverse effects, enlist the client's cooperation in individualizing the drug routine (tailoring it to a client's characteristics and circumstances) as much as possible, and help to ensure adherence by offering medication education.

CHILDREN AND ADOLESCENTS

General Considerations

We have already addressed this issue in the previous chapter but will make some additional, more fundamental observations here. The use of psychotropic drugs in children and adolescents has often produced controversy. Most issues pertain to either the appropriateness of medication (rationale for use, alternatives, toxicity) or inadequacies in their clinical management (Greenhill & Setterberg, 1993; Sylvester, 1993). It must be emphasized that new drugs are rarely studied in children and adolescents before marketing. There is a consensus among physicians that the effects of all psychotropic medications except methylphenidate (used to treat ADHD) have not been adequately researched. The National Institute of Mental Health instituted a 5-year plan in 1991 for increased clinical research in this area, but stimulating widespread research has continued to be difficult. Fisher and Fisher (1997) assert in their literature review that there is no persuasive evidence that any psychotropic medications have positive effects on children and adolescents. While their perspective may be disputed, it is clear that there is a dearth of studies on the medication of children and adolescents and that any drug prescription must be done with extreme care and caution.

The symptoms for which psychotropic drugs are prescribed can be generally categorized as either behavioral inadequacies or behavioral excesses. Besides the disorders already discussed in this book, children and adolescents receive psychotropic medications for other disorders, including pervasive developmental disorders, Tourette's syndrome, sleep disorders, enuresis, and even conduct disorder. With this population, two special concerns arise: the child's often reluctant participation and the possibility that otherwise effective medications may harm physical development. Ranked from least to most troublesome with respect to side effects, the most commonly prescribed psychotropic drugs for children and adolescents are as follows: stimulants, cyclic antidepressants, and antipsychotic medications. Other drugs, such as beta-blockers, lithium, carbamazepine, and the atypical antidepressants, are more difficult to evaluate because of the relatively short time they have been available for research.

The psychopharmacological assessment and management of children and adolescents is more complicated than that of adults. This is due to (1) the need for comprehensive family involvement to ensure that the perspectives of all members are represented in decision making, (2) wide differences in physical development among children and adolescents, (3) the diagnostic ambiguity of emerging first episodes of mental illness, (4) ethical issues in decision making and the rights of minors, and (5) the impact of drug treatment on the child's self-concept.

Social workers should view the absence of active interest by parents or caregivers as a major treatment concern. When one adds psychosocial developmental issues (such as the adolescent's need to separate from the family) to the complications of prescribing medications, drug management requires a strong partnership between social worker and family to ensure collaboration. Because of fears of peer ridicule and a reluctance to participate in therapies that label clients as "ill," noncompliance with most interventions is a general problem in child and adolescent health care. The physician will usually start low, aiming for the lowest possible effective dose. Monitoring and laboratory follow-up may need to be more frequent than with other populations.

School-age children metabolize and clear psychotropic drugs rapidly, but paradoxically they are also more sensitive to their therapeutic effects, which complicates the issue of appropriate dosing. This is particularly true before puberty, after which sex hormones increase and compete with drugs for enzymes, slowing metabolism rates. Typically, children and adolescents can tolerate a higher ratio of milligrams to body weight. Young female clients seem to achieve higher blood levels than young male clients and experience more side effects from the same weight-adjusted dose. Children tend to have a greater level of fluid intake than adults, which produces a shorter half-life with water-soluble drugs such as lithium.

Classes of Medication

Antipsychotic medications can produce symptomatic improvement in members of this age group, although this is less marked in children under age 15. Both children and adolescents experience the adverse effect of sedation more often than adults do. They may complain less about these effects, so the physician and social worker can inquire about this effect regularly. Without consumer feedback, the social worker can also help to monitor indicators of "behavioral toxicity" including diminished activity, apathy, withdrawal, cognitive dulling, and sedation (Janicak, Davis, Preskorn, & Ayd, 1997). Long-term adverse effects of these drugs may include interference with the client's natural psychosocial stages, for example, stunted physical growth. An increased risk of tardive dyskinesia with ongoing use of medications also requires close monitoring. Some physicians assert that the risk of tardive dyskinesia may be greater due to the fact that the consumer's brain is still developing. The reduced risk of movement reactions (i.e., dystonia, akathisia, or parkinsonianism) among young persons using antipsychotic medications is offset by more pronounced anticholinergic effects. Extrapyramidal symptoms, including dystonic reactions and parkinsonianism, appear to be more prevalent among teenagers, especially males, than all other age groups. High-potency antipsychotic medications probably interfere less with learning than low-potency types, and the lower anticholinergic activity of the high-potency medications minimizes the risk of delirium, which can occur in young populations.

During the 1980s, an outpouring of research on mood disorders in children and adolescents resulted in the widespread use of antidepressants with this group. Besides uncomplicated depression, common syndromes these drugs are used to treat include hyperactivity (when stimulants are not effective), separation anxiety, refusal to attend school, and obsessive-compulsive behaviors. Several difficulties arise in the use of antidepressants with adolescents. First, hormonal changes make measuring effectiveness very difficult. High levels of sex hormones modulate the developing neurotransmitter systems in ways that diminish antidepressant efficacy. Second, nonpharmacological aspects of treatment are more difficult to control in this population than in others. Finally, as adolescents confront identity stressors, peer relationships, and independence issues, they may be tempted to misuse medication in an attempt to take control of their lives. Early enthusiasm about antidepressant medication treatment has waned somewhat. Amazingly, most studies indicate that antidepressant drug treatment is often no more effective than placebo; that is, there is no clear evidence of its effectiveness. In fact, the placebo effect in children is so profound in research on antidepressant drugs that the social worker and physician should always be cautious about attributing signs of clinical improvement to the biological effect of a medication. There is some evidence of the effectiveness of cyclic antidepressants.

Side effects common among younger people but uncommon among adults include cardiovascular toxicity (arrhythmia) and neurological symptoms (possibility of seizure). The cyclic antidepressants produce dry mouth, nausea, constipation, dizziness, blurred vision, drowsiness, appetite changes, headaches, fatigue, and sleep disturbances, including insomnia and nightmares. The adverse effects of the cyclic antidepressants are the same as those in older populations, except that the medications are more likely to increase blood pressure in younger people. Although a common cardiovascular effect is mild tachycardia, serious hypotension is rare.

Use of the serotonin-reuptake inhibitors with adolescents may be preferable because of their relatively well-tolerated side-effect profiles and their reduced potential for intentional overdose. The latter advantage is highly significant because suicide is the second leading cause of adolescent death. These atypical antidepressants appear relatively safe for children, although they may experience the same side effects as older persons. These side effects can sometimes be minimized by "halving" adult doses for children (splitting tablets in two and taking one of the halves as a full dose). Popper (1995) cautions, however, that the new antidepressants may be changing physician attitudes too quickly about prescribing such drugs; they are being used rather extensively without a background of research on which to base judgments about their benefits and risks. Finally, some evidence suggests that adolescents may have a higher risk of a manic episode while on cyclic or atypical antidepressant drugs. Abrupt withdrawal of antidepressants may cause children to develop gastrointestinal complaints and fatigue, which may be confused with continuing depression. Because of their higher elimination rates, children may be more vulnerable than adults to adverse effects of abrupt withdrawal.

Because children rapidly clear lithium, the physician may prescribe higher doses than those for adults to achieve therapeutic effect. Children may experience the same side effects that adults do, but they seem to tolerate long-term treatment well. However, carbamazepine must be used with special caution because it can precipitate agitation and manic symptoms in children. The most serious concerns in children and adolescents are the long-term consequences of lithium accumulation in bone tissue and lithium's effect on thyroid and renal function. Nonetheless, lithium appears to be somewhat better tolerated overall than the antipsychotic medications.

Relatively few studies of drug therapy for anxiety disorders in children and adolescents exist. Many physicians believe that anxiolytic drugs make hyperactive and psychotic children worse. Antihistamines are commonly used to treat anxiety and insomnia in children as an alternative to the benzodiazepines. A lowered seizure threshold, the potential for delirium, and worsening of tic disorders are serious but less common side effects of these anti-anxiety medications. Clomipramine has been established as the treatment of choice for children with obsessive-compulsive disorder (see chapter 4).

Tourette's disorder, an inherited biological disorder which is characterized by tics, noises, and coarse speech, does respond positively to medication. Haloperidol is the best-known and longest-used drug to treat this disorder, but others such as pimozide and clonidine are available as alternatives. Haloperidol has also been effective with persons having autistic disorder, although such children are at a high risk for tardive dyskinesia and other adverse effects. Alternative medications for autism include naltrexone, propranolol (for aggression and agitation), and fenfluramine (for hyperactivity).

With children, there is an additional concern related to iatrogenic effects, or new developmental problems the child acquires as a result of taking medications. Concerns have been raised in the literature (Gadow, 1991) that children may (1) attribute adjustment problems to factors beyond their control and become less responsive to behavioral interventions, (2) fail to acquire adaptive behaviors because their symptoms are suppressed and caregivers thus do not recognize the need to teach coping strategies, (3) come to regard medication as the primary or only effective way to cope with adjustment difficulties, and (4) become more likely to abuse psychoactive substances. Though these effects can occur within any age group, children and adolescents have not yet formed overall coping and adaptation styles.

RACIAL AND ETHNIC DIFFERENCES

Research is only beginning to focus on comparative issues in the area of racial variations in medication response. Some evidence exists that such differences do exist, but findings must be considered tentative. Perceived differences in mental disorders and treatment response among racial and ethnic groups may occur because of differences in treatment-seeking behavior, differential presentation of symptoms, and the accuracy of diagnosis (Adebimpe, 1994). Further, it is difficult to claim that any sample is representative of a racial or ethnic group, given the mixed lineage of participants and variable criteria used in self-identification. Cultural differences do exist in the ways individuals cope with stress, express emotion, and conceptualize and treat mental problems. Lantz (1987), for example, describes the work of an African-American "ghetto healer" in a large midwestern city who successfully treats neighborhood clients for "soul loss."

The range of biopsychosocial factors that influence psychotropic drug metabolism and response among ethnic groups include the following.

1. Diet and nutritional factors (influence on metabolic activity)

2. The actions of certain enzymes

3. Differences in consumption of cigarettes, caffeine, alcohol, herbs, and other psychoactive substances (influence on drug metabolism or response)

4. Sleep or activity and rest patterns (effect on other physiological events)

5. Environmental exposure to toxins or pollutants

6. Differences in exposure to psychological stress

7. Prescribing practices among physicians

8. Patterns of illness behavior among cultural groups

9. Cultural attitudes toward medication usage (Jacobsen, 1994; Turner & Cooley-Quille, 1996).

An important perspective that the social work profession can bring to ethnic understanding is what health and illness mean within a culture (Raffoul & Haney, 1989). In addition to a client's physical characteristics, a thorough physician will take into account the psychological and social factors noted above when he or she considers what medications to prescribe. The social worker's person-in-environment perspective places him or her in a sound position for helping to assess clients in this holistic manner, to evaluate the context of drug use by examining the social and cultural aspects of mental illness. Social workers can coordinate the necessary interdisciplinary approach in overall intervention, such as educating both clients and professionals, sharing expectations among clients and their significant others, organizing the activities of all participating professionals, and enforcing an affirming emotional tone between workers, clients, and families.

Some important work has been done in identifying enzymatic differences among the races, differences that influence the pharmacokinetics of medication. Lin, Poland, Wan, Smith, and Lesser (1996) conducted a worldwide study of a single set of enzymes (cytochrome P-450) in the human body. These enzymes are known to be significant in the metabolism of psychotropic drugs. It was found that, while present in all racial groups, these enzymes were most prominent in Caucasians, least prominent in East Asians, and somewhere along a continuum in other ethnic groups (more than ten were studied). This study is persuasive in suggesting that there will be differences in medication response among races and that medications should be prescribed differently as a result. Still, precisely how to adjust dosages is unclear to physicians because of the small amount of this type of research that has been done.

African Americans

With the above limitations in mind, we can note some of the specific differences in medication response that have been noted among racial and ethnic groups. Most of the existing research has been done with African Americans. First, it must be emphasized that many differences have been identified in how African Americans are diagnosed. Strakowski, Shelton, and Kolbrener (1993) found in a single-hospital study of 173 discharged clients that such persons are more likely to be diagnosed with schizophrenia than Caucasian persons and less likely to be diagnosed with affective disorder. The seeming over-diagnosis of schizophrenia may be related to a higher prevalence of positive vs. negative symptoms of mental disorder in members of this racial group. Cohen and Magai (1999) found that this trend held among 240 older adults with dementia, due to the fact that African Americans were more likely to present with symptoms of psychosis vs. depression. African Americans may not receive thorough assessments of mental status. Segal, Bola, and Watson (1996) found in a large-scale study in New York State (18,543 clients) that Caucasian emergency room physicians spent less time assessing African American persons than members of their own race. It has been noted that African Americans are less inclined to self-disclosure than Caucasians (Adebimpe, 1994).

Further, it has been consistently found that African Americans with mental illnesses are prescribed more medications, and at higher dosages, than Caucasians. African Americans are also significantly more likely to receive depot (injectable) medications than Caucasian persons (Citrome, Levine, & Allingham, 1996; Segal, Bola, & Watson, 1996; Strakowski, Shelton, & Kolbrener, 1993). African Americans are also less likely to receive lithium, anti-anxiety, and antidepressant medications. Ironically, or perhaps because of the above trends, African American families are less likely to seek professional help from mental health professionals for their children, and individuals of all ages are less likely to perceive themselves as having a mental illness (McMiller & Weiss, 1996). African American adolescents are less likely to be prescribed psychotropic medications than Caucasian adolescents (Zito, Safer, dosReis, & Riddle, 1997).

African Americans demonstrate a higher risk of depressive disorders resulting from medical illness, a higher prevalence of phobic disorders, higher rates of adjustment disorders with mixed emotional features, and episodes of delirium from drug interactions (Baker, 1994). The reasons for these differences are not known. In a comparative study of 263 cocaine addicts, Ziedonis, Rayford, Bryant, and Rounsaville (1994) found that Caucasian respondents had higher lifetime rates of major depression and suicide attempts. African Americans had lower lifetime rates of affective disorders, primarily due to differences in rates of dysthymia and major depression, but they also demonstrated "hyperthymia," or a state of overactivity not quite manic in severity. Ziedonis et al. have also found racial differences in rates of phobias and speculate that the impact of racism in society may increase the vulnerability of African Americans to phobias. The authors finally note that among the Caucasian cocaine addicts they studied, the rate of alcoholism was twice as high as in the African-American group, but that in both groups the men had five times as many alcohol disorders as the women did.

The apparent higher use of medications among adult African American persons is troubling in that they are at a higher risk for adverse effects with some medications. Glazer, Morgenstern, and Doucette (1994) found in a study of 398 outpatients at risk for tardive dyskinesia that the syndrome occurred 1.83 times more often in African Americans than in Caucasians. Strickland, Stein, Lin, Risby, and Fong's (1997) literature review indicates that these persons are "poor metabolizers" for antidepressant and anti-anxiety drugs. That is, they require lower doses with smaller increases than other races for the same effects. Lawson (1996) agrees, concluding from his literature review that they are over-diagnosed with mental disorders and are at a higher risk for adverse effects.

African American clients with either schizophrenia or depressive disorders respond better than Caucasian clients to phenothiazines and cyclic antidepressant medications, and they experience more anxiety reduction with antidepressant medications. This appears to be a consequence of African American clients having higher blood levels for a given dosage. Varner, Ruiz, and Small (1998) concluded that clients require lower doses of cyclic and SSRI antidepressant drugs for a therapeutic effect.

Persons of Hispanic Culture

There are far fewer studies of other racial and ethnic populations. However, the large and rapidly growing Hispanic population in the United States mandates the social worker's need to understand their orientation and response to medications. The reliance of this ethnic group on traditional social supports rather than professional intervention suggests that the social worker may have problems in maintaining contact with clients over time (Mendoza, Smith, Poland, Lin, & Strickland, 1991). More aggressive outreach activities, as is typical with case management practice, may be necessary to ensure a positive outcome with Hispanic clients.

Some evidence exists that Hispanic clients require less antidepressant medication and have more side effects at lower dosages, than Caucasians (Turner & Cooley-Quille, 1996). Hispanics also have certain enzyme differences that apparently affect metabolic processes, causing slower drug metabolism. People of Hispanic origin experience more side effects with antidepressants, and their particular liver enzymes make them more susceptible to alcohol toxicity as well (Kail, 1989). There are no reports of differences among members of this racial group with regard to lithium response. One study of 50 Hispanic persons with schizophrenia (Dassori et al., 1998) indicates that they may experience a higher level of negative symptoms than Caucasian or African American persons, more specifically, cognitive deficits. Still, like African Americans, these persons are reluctant (particularly younger persons) to participate in formal intervention programs (unless the professional is Hispanic), so little is known about their special characteristics regarding medications (Hosch et al., 1995; McMiller & Weiss, 1996).

Asian Americans

In working with Asian clients, it may be important for the social worker to elicit beliefs in traditional Asian medical practices and to involve family members in diagnosis and treatment planning, given the especially strong family orientation of these persons. Asian populations tend to expect Western medications to exert effects swiftly, to carry a high likelihood of severe adverse effects, and to be effective only for superficial manifestations of a problem (Lin & Shen, 1991). Flaskerud and Hu (1994) studied 273 low-income Asian

American clients with depression and found that the worker's ethnicity is a significant predictor of the client's attendance in session.

Ramirez (1996) has summarized that Asian persons demonstrate pronounced pharmacokinetic and pharmacodynamic differences from other races. Asians have a smaller body size than many other races; they also metabolize antipsychotic, antidepressant, and anti-anxiety medications more slowly. Thus lower dosages can be more effective but can still carry the potential for greater toxicity. There are mixed reports about lithium; some research indicates that it is cleared at a similar rate in Asian and Caucasian groups (Wing, Chan, Chan, Lee, & Shek, 1997), while others have found smaller doses necessary for Asian groups. Asian refugee groups show a high prevalence of posttraumatic stress disorder, for which MAO inhibitors have been demonstrated useful, as well as with depression and panic disorders. Asian persons, incidentally, are the only ethnic group to demonstrate seasonal differences in hospitalization for depression; occurring more often in the wintertime (Suhail & Cochrane, 1998).

PERSONS WITH A DUAL DIAGNOSIS
OF MENTAL ILLNESS AND SUBSTANCE ABUSE

In the past 10 years, attention has increasingly focused on the prevalence of substance abuse among people with mental illness and the difficulty in providing effective treatment for them. Substance abuse may occur in as much as 50% of relatively low-functioning people with long-term mental illnesses (Test, Wallisch, Allness, & Ripp, 1989). Substances most frequently cited as exacerbating psychotic or affective symptoms include alcohol, cocaine, marijuana, stimulants, and hallucinogenic drugs. Abuse is probably most common among those with depressive disorders (Ries, 1993). If inclined to take alcohol or other drugs, people with mental illness tend to use what is available in their environments rather than any particular substance.

Persons with dual diagnoses present social workers and other professionals with unique challenges. They tend to be younger, male, more often hostile and suicidal, at a higher risk of experiencing episodes of mental illness, and have a poorer long-term prognosis. When intoxicated they are more disinhibited and aggressive. Such persons with schizophrenia have a higher likelihood of tardive dyskinesia. When going through withdrawal from substance abuse, these clients, like all persons, may experience tremors, hallucinations, seizures, and delusions, complicating their existing symptom profile.

Recent research indicates that these clients are at a modest but significantly greater risk for violent behavior, most often involving family members (Arboleda, 1998; Swartz et al., 1998). They are also at greater risk of relapse, hospitalization, disruptive behavior, family problems, and residential instability (Drake & Brunette, 1998). Of most immediate concern to social workers is their tendency not to adhere to their medication and to mix prescription medications with alcohol or street drugs.

Negative interactions of these substances with psychotropic drugs is a major concern (see chapter 4). For instance, many substances can make the symptoms of schizophrenia more pronounced or promote a resurgence of psychotic symptoms. One of our clients, for example, liked to drink beer. Because he knew that it might interact with his antipsychotic medications to produce a high level of sedation, he decided not to take his prescription drugs on nights when he drank beer. The alcohol still interacted with his medications in a potentially dangerous way, and without a consistent blood level of the medication he was at a greater risk for decompensation.

With manic conditions, substance abuse can further impair a client's already poor impulse control. To help themselves relax, people with bipolar disorder and anxiety disorders often use self-medicating agents. Self-medication is also sometimes seen when clients try to reduce the side effects of some neuroleptic medications with such drugs as alcohol and marijuana. Stimulants may increase a client's affect and energy levels, which are diminished by some medications. Nicotine reduces some of the muscular side effects of neuroleptic drugs, but it also impairs the drugs' therapeutic potency (Arana & Hyman, 1991).

Some of the psychotropic drugs themselves can be abused (Ries, 1993). We have discussed the potential for abusing the benzodiazepines, which are used to treat anxiety. However, the anticholinergic drugs can also produce a "high" when taken in larger amounts than typically prescribed. Some preliminary studies, which require further substantiation, indicate that the serotonin-reuptake inhibitors may be abused presumably because they produce desirable side effects for some people, including weight loss and increased energy (Skolnick, 1997).

All helping professionals who treat clients with dual diagnoses face a major problem: substance abuse makes accurate diagnosis extremely difficult, therefore hampering the development of appropriate interventions. In one controlled study, among professionals using a structured interview format, the diagnosis of mental illness was significantly less reliable in the presence of substance abuse (Corty, Lehman, & Myers, 1993). Results from 47 diagnostic assessments of dual diagnosed clients by nine skilled interviewers, each client assessed separately by two interviewers, indicated the lowest frequency of agreement with regard to clients having either mood or schizophrenic disorders and slightly higher but still problematic with clients having anxiety disorders.

A further problem for treatment providers is the great difficulty in treating either of the two disorders (mental illness and substance abuse) when they coexist. Professionals in the mental health and substance abuse fields have tended to work apart over the years, holding different philosophies and areas of expertise. Social workers have complained at times that substance abuse counselors are too rigid, while the latter group has felt in turn that social workers do not confront clients and set firm enough limits about substance abuse. Lehman, Herron, Schwartz, & Myers (1993) randomly assigned 54 dual diagnosed clients to experimental and control treatment groups, with the former group receiving additional services for their substance abuse problem. No difference in outcome appeared after one year, leading the researchers to conclude that all clients were hard to engage in a treatment program, and that perhaps one year was not long enough to produce changes in social functioning with clients having dual disorders.

Fortunately, today there is increasing agreement that both approaches can be combined and well-coordinated in the best interest of the client. Collaborative interdisciplinary work can be fruitfully promoted in this area of intervention. Recent research indicates that clients do respond well to structured interventions; in fact, their gains in social functioning are comparable to those of non-dual diagnosed persons with mental illness (Blow et al., 1998; Dixon, McNary, & Lehman, 1998). For one example, a program in Maine has documented success in developing collaborative approaches to these clients through administrative linkages between the mental health and substance abuse systems that are still in place after several years of operation (Ridgely, Lambert, Goodman, Chichester, & Ralph, 1998).

When the client has both a substance abuse problem and a mental illness, the social worker needs to be aware of the complications that arise in providing effective psychosocial interventions, of which medication is an essential part. The bottom line is that both disorders need to be treated; the social worker should not assume that if one of the client's disorders is brought under control, then the other can be more easily addressed or perhaps will disappear by itself. Before assessing clients, the social worker first needs to understand whether they have two truly coexisting disorders, are medicating themselves with substances for the primary disorder, or have a drug-induced psychotic state that may abate with rapid intervention. Though drug-induced psychoses are transient, tending to resolve themselves in several hours or several days, they do require intensive interventions at times and perhaps a brief regimen of psychotropic medications. If the client is self-medicating, the social worker needs to understand why. Finally, however serious the adverse effects of prescribed medications are, clients should negotiate with the physician as the most appropriate means to alleviate discomfort.

Mental Illness and Alcohol Abuse

Polypharmacy, or combining different types of psychotropic drugs, is considered to be a risky practice in that drug interactions can have negative effects on the consumer. In treating clients with the dual diagnosis of mental illness and substance abuse toward the goal of abstinence from alcohol, however, there are indications at times for this practice. The adjunctive medications described below generally work by stabilizing the client's mood and anxiety levels, thus facilitating the physical and psychological processes of alcohol withdrawal. All of the findings below are based on a small number of studies (Janicak, Preskorn, Davis, & Ayd, 1997), so the social worker should be cautious in assuming their general validity.

For persons with schizophrenia, some evidence exists that while disulfram (Antabuse), a medication used to make alcohol physically distasteful to the consumer, may increase symptoms of psychosis, a similar drug known as naltrexone may help the client resist alcohol and also experience a decrease in hallucinations. For clients with depressive disorders, the cyclic antidepressant imipramine and the SSRIs have been shown in a few studies to reduce the client's craving for alcohol, but only during the first three weeks of use. For clients with bipolar disorder, lithium appears to have no utility as a deterrent to alcohol use, but the anticonvulsant drugs may have some beneficial effect. At the least, these drugs can help stabilize the physical condition of alcohol abusers who risk experiencing seizures during the process of withdrawal.

The anti-anxiety medications are well-established adjunctive drugs for clients with dual disorders. They are effective as a short-term treatment for 20 to 50% of persons who are going through withdrawal from alcohol dependence. These drugs, of which chlordiaxepoxide is the most widely used for this purpose, increase treatment adherence and days of abstinence, while decreasing anxiety and the risk of relapse. Finally, it is useful to encourage clients who abuse alcohol to take B and C vitamins, as alcohol depletes these substances in the body.

SUMMARY

Medical science, like other fields of science, is only beginning to appreciate the variability of effects that people demonstrate in response to all types of intervention. For years social workers have faced a major challenge in determining which treatments work for which clients under which circumstances. It has become clear that this same problem applies to drug treatments, which at one time were assumed to be more universal and predictable in their outcomes. Though not typically experts in chemistry, social workers offer an advanced perspective about individual and group differences in psychosocial functioning. With this professional strength and the partnership perspective, they can contribute important insights into the client's experience of taking medication in a social as well as physical sense.

✣

PART III

Knowledge and Skills for Psychosocial Interventions

Chapter 6

Medication Education for Clients and Families

Chapter 7

Medication Adherence and Refusal

Chapter 8

Medication Monitoring and Management

6

Medication Education
for Clients and Families

RATIONALE FOR MEDICATION EDUCATION

There are a number of excellent reasons, based on logic, common sense, and research, for providing mental health clients and their families with education about psychotropic medications. These include the human rights of clients, the increasing demands by clients and their families for up-to-date information, and the hope of increased compliance with medication. We will look briefly at these issues individually.

Many professionals have discussed medication education in the context of human rights of "patients" (Bisbee, 1988; Whiteside, Harris, & Whiteside, 1983). With growing legal pressures to provide all healthcare clients with full and accurate information about their diagnosis and treatment as a matter of right, a consensus has arisen that client safety and security is also a right. These rights closely relate to the notion of informed consent, the idea that to be able to make choices about treatment, clients need complete knowledge about the benefits and risks of all available treatment options, including medication.

Similarly, one can also see medication education in terms of supply and demand. That is, the increased emphasis on such education is surely related to the growing demands from clients and families for current knowledge. In addition to society's consumer orientation, this increased demand may be related in part to the renewed emphasis on biological factors in mental illness and their relationship to medication as a major treatment strategy (Goldwyn, 1988).

Data support the perception of such high demand for information. For example, a survey conducted in Philadelphia, of outpatients, their relatives, and close friends showed that acquiring knowledge about pertinent medications and side effects was of highest importance (Mueser, Bellack, Wade, Sayers, & Rosenthal, 1992). Out of 45 identified "educational needs," relatives of clients with either affective disorders or schizophrenia ranked knowledge of medication or its side effects as their number one educational need, clients diagnosed with affective disorders themselves ranked it second, and clients diagnosed with schizophrenia ranked it a still-high eighth. A more recent survey in St. Louis of 86 psychoeducation participants (family members, clients, and service providers) found that, while some differences emerged between the groups in terms of their rankings of problems and desired topics, issues around medication, compliance, and perceived "denial" emerged as most important (Pollio, North, & Foster, 1998). In two separate surveys of self-identified family caregivers, three-quarters identified medication benefits, compliance, and side effects as issues they wanted more information about (Gasque-Carter & Curlee, 1999; Ascher-Svanum, Lafuze, Barrickman, Van Dusen, & Fompa-Lay, 1997).

In another survey of psychiatric patients, Zind (1991) documented low levels of medication knowledge in her patients, including their mismanagement of missed doses. This survey of 116 men with schizophrenia showed that clients' knowledge about medications was very low, particularly concerning the interaction of drugs with alcohol and side effects. Interestingly, Zind also cited a low correlation between patients' actual knowledge and their perceived knowledge, suggesting that often clients think they know more than they actually do.

On a single day in one state hospital, Geller (1982) personally surveyed 281 inpatients and found that 54% showed no understanding at all of their medications. They could not state the name of their medication, how often they took it, or what the intended effect was. Only 22 participants interviewed (8.4%) could correctly name those three things. MacPherson, Double, Rowlands, and Harrison (1993) replicated Geller's study with a random sample of 100 long-term hospital patients on neuroleptics. Out of the 100 interviewed, only 8 named all their medications and only 23 named one. Many could describe the drug's color and shape, but by far most showed no understanding of therapeutic action. In fact, 73% did not know what tardive dyskinesia is. A different study of 253 inpatients on the day of discharge found that 37% of respondents said they did not know why they were taking their medication, even after receiving some individual and group instruction. While the good news is that 63% could name their medication, the bad news is that 47% did not know when to take it (Clary, Dever, & Schweitzer, 1992).

A related survey cited the attitudes of staff and family members toward both medication education and each other (Bernheim & Switalski, 1988). Whereas 91% of the staff thought that education about medication management would help families, only 19% of the families said they had received enough information from that same staff or facility. Less than 21% of families had been invited to a treatment or discharge planning conference. A nationally representative sample of mental health insurance claims shows very little family intervention activity in general, a mere 1% of claims (Dixon et al. 1999). A field test follow-up showed that only 8% of families attended any education or support groups, much less education specifically geared to medication-related issues. This research again points to the tremendous gap between what professionals know is needed ("best practices") and what they provide ("standard practices").

Perhaps the most often cited rationale for providing medication education is the hope that increased knowledge and support will increase the client's adherence to the prescribed drug regimen and thus will prevent relapse or rehospitalization. While strong evidence supports the connection between noncompliance and relapse (e.g., Hogarty et al., 1991), the evidence regarding the actual impact of medication education on compliance is less certain but still encouraging.

Professionals also hope that medication education helps clients and their families to participate more responsibly in the treatment process (see chapter 1). For example, many have noted that education provides a flexible and empowering means of engaging families in the treatment or rehabilitation process and that even if they forget the actual information, the educational efforts remain worthwhile. "Ultimately responsible," for managing mental illness, clients and families must build competence and "take charge of their illness" (Duchin & Brown, 1990, p. 255; Buckwalter & Kerfoot, 1982, p. 15). To do this, they need medication education to increase their knowledge and skill. It is not clear whether such an increase should be thought of as a desired "side effect" or as the main goal of medication education. In any case, medication education is seen as promoting cooperation, strengthening coping skills, enhancing clients' acceptance of their mental illness or emotional disorder, increasing hope for change, providing emotional support, reducing the family's burden, and helping clients and families acquire new skills. All are considered as protective factors in the stress–diathesis model (see chapter 1). As Goldman and Quinn (1983) state,

> We believe that education has multiple beneficial effects that could lead to reduced symptoms. It counteracts fears and defensiveness, contributes to patients' self-esteem and hope, suggests practical ways for patients to help themselves, encourages more effective communication with treatment personnel, and promotes healthy activities, including informed adherence to treatment recommendations. (p. 286)

It seems that the most important thing providers can do to help clients live in the community is to teach them necessary self-care. And for many, particularly those with a serious mental illness, medication may very well be the "cornerstone of community management" (McGill, Falloon, Boyd, & Wood-Siverio, 1983, p. 936); that is, clients may need knowledge of their medications to maintain independence in the community. Surprisingly, in many respects direct and full discussion of a client's own disorder and treatment is still a new idea, in spite of medication education efforts that go back several decades (Hayes & Gantt, 1992).

Studies that have evaluated medication education programs offer good reason to be cautiously optimistic about its potential impact on clients' understanding of medication, compliance, symptomatology, attitudes, fears, and ability to negotiate with clinicians. Indeed, in an uncontrolled evaluation of a pharmacist-facilitated medication group, Batey and Ledbetter (1982) noted that with education intervention came not only greater knowledge and increased compliance among consumers of medication but also more requests for information, greater client involvement in treatment, and even a higher level of staff comfort with clients.

Several controlled studies conducted in the 1980s also support this positive appraisal. For example, Whiteside et al. (1983) presented significant differences—in knowledge of personal medication regimens, side effects, and rationales for treatments—between the control group and those who participated in a structured patient education program that included written reinforcements for 28 medically ill psychiatric patients. Youssef (1984) randomly assigned 36 psychiatric patients a week from discharge to either a two-session group education program or no treatment. Those in the experimental group were significantly more compliant in terms of both their use of medication (using a pill count method) and their post-discharge appointment keeping. Robinson, Gilbertson, and Litwak (1986) examined the impact of different types of structured drug education strategies on 150 psychiatric patients ready for discharge. Results suggested that personal and individualized instruction paired with written materials was superior to the usual brief, general explanations given to clients about medication regimens.

In perhaps the largest and best known clinical evaluation of a medication education program, researchers evaluated the impact of their Medication Management Module in 28 field-test sites around the country involving 160 patients with schizophrenia (Eckman, Liberman, Phipps, & Blair, 1990; Eckman & Liberman, 1990). The Medication Management Module is a highly structured and comprehensive behaviorally oriented program that includes hands-on problem-solving and communication skills training (see chapter 8). The field-test sites included both public and private settings, inpatient and outpatient facilities. A range of professionals participated, including social workers, nurses, occupational therapists, psychologists, and psychiatrists. Results indicated the program effectively increased clients' knowledge of antipsychotic medications and their side effects, improved clients' skill in negotiating with health care providers about their medication-related concerns, and improved medication compliance as reported by both psychiatrists and caregivers. The effectiveness of this module was also field-tested with 8 inpatients on the verge of discharge in Japan with increased knowledge and skills in medication self-management as indicated by highly valid and reliable role-play test (Ikebuchi & Anzai, 1995).

Dow and associates compared a straight medication education program with a Medication-Related Communication Skills program adapted from Liberman's model. They both involved five 90-minute sessions over a 2 1/2 week period. While both groups in the comparison study increased their knowledge of medications, participants in the communication skills training groups showed an increase in the number of questions they asked MDs and an increase in the length of conversations. These participants were rated as more assertive, had better eye contact, and were deemed more likely to adhere to their medication (Dow, Verdi, & Sacco, 1991). A more recent study trying to assess what kind of education had the most effect on attitudes and knowledge was unable to document the superiority of either structured (instruction, discussion, and role-play, also adapted from Liberman) or unstructured (incidental) education (Kuipers, Bell, Davidhizar, Cosgray, & Fawley, 1994).

Another controlled, large-scale investigation examined both in-home visits with the family and clinical visits with patients for individualized education and training (Kelly, Scott, & Mamon, 1990). The study used 418 male VA patients with chronic psychotic disorders. Results indicated that those clients who received individualized education at the clinic were slightly more compliant than those with only the home visit (family consultation). The researchers noted, however, that for all their participants, compliance actually got worse over time, even if the experimental groups did less worse than the controls over time. Clearly, noncompliance remained a major concern for most participants in this study, in spite of impressive individualized interventions. However, all those who received treatment of any kind (clinic only, home visit only, combined) demonstrated significantly fewer symptoms and relapses than controls.

A number of more recent evaluations of medication education programs appear in the literature. For example, Rudnick (1997) evaluated a six-session group model in Israel consisting of one-hour meetings with a psychiatrist and a nurse involving both instruction and discussion. He reported both increased adherence and an increase in participant's sense of control. Using 39 matched and randomly assigned outpatients, Azrin & Teichner (1998) compared a single-session simple instructional meeting with a psychiatrist to a more comprehensive intervention involving a review of guidelines, pill-taking tasks, and reminders (with client alone and with another group in the presence of a family member). Adherence increased to 94% in both the latter groups, while it stayed at 73% for those receiving simple information. Not surprisingly, other large-scale comparative studies also speak to the importance of sharing specifics of the medication schedule (name, color, number, dose, times to administer, side effects) versus offering a simple fact sheet (Esposito, 1995).

In summary, medication education appears to rest on solid logical and ethical grounds, supported by encouraging empirical data. Nevertheless, a gap exists between what professionals, clients, and families all agree is needed and wanted and what is actually provided around the country. Before detailing the content of medication education programs, we will present some of the principles and structural issues underlying the implementation and evaluation of some of these programs for both adults and children.

ISSUES IN IMPLEMENTING AND
EVALUATING MEDICATION EDUCATION

Much of the medication education currently conducted is with adult mental health consumers. Let us begin our discussion there. Duchin and Brown (1990) state it is important to be aware of (and we add, capitalize on) two crucial characteristics of adult learners: (1) adults have life experiences, and (2) adults have a goal orientation.

Facilitators often make use of the first characteristic when they rely heavily on interaction among group members as a source for learning. That is, clients and families sharing their experiences with other group members is a major mechanism of learning. Even if a great deal of content is delivered didactically, the sharing approach is universally built into programs. Heyduk (1991) goes even further to suggest that programs must "involve patients in the teaching-learning process" and let participants guide the teacher in what they need to know (p. 32). Green (1998) notes that direct participation in the learning process adds to a sense of control around health issues. Because life experiences, both positive and negative, tend to lead to strong feelings and beliefs, social workers must provide an atmosphere that validates and encourages sharing but also allows for the presentation of accurate and balanced information. Open discussions can help participants examine their attitudes, clarify their feelings, and dispel myths about psychotropic medications and their use (Sclafani, 1977). Adults learn more effectively if past experiences are explicitly integrated into the process of learning (Green, 1998).

"Goal orientation" means that adult learners tend to apply what they learn, so medication education should address their individual hopes and dreams. The more quickly the information can be put to practical use, the better the retention (Green, 1998). In the health belief model, the extent to which people are motivated to reach their goals and to which they see these goals as related to some recommended behavior determines what course of action people will choose (Youssef, 1984). Thus, participating in medication education or adhering to medication regimens (or any number of other strategies; see chapters 7 and 8) will be most effective when successfully tied to clients' individual goals. This is true because clients are strongly motivated to achieve their goals. For people with mental illness, such dreams can include staying out of the hospital, getting or keeping a meaningful job, getting a place of their own, or feeling like a normal human being. This seems related to Swezy and Swezy's (1976) notion that medication education should be guided by the behavioral principle known as "the law of effect," which says that learning will be enhanced if learners understand how the knowledge relates to their own lives.

People with mental illnesses, however, may have special learning problems. For example, Halford and Hayes (1991), in trying to explain differences in treatment responses, concluded that mental health workers need to pay more attention to the client's level of cognitive functioning. Davidhizar and

McBridge (1985) list the learning problems of people with schizophrenia and note the potential challenge of impaired cognitive functioning among people with schizophrenia. Other potential learning problems they cite include difficulty with abstractions, handicapped intellectual functioning, denial of illness, feelings of dependency, the frequent need for medication adjustments, and family and financial issues. They also note that, at least for people with schizophrenia, an "unusual resistance to participation" in treatment (p. 137). For people with affective disorders, Daley, Bowler, & Cahalane (1992) identify at least two special issues in psychoeducation: the high recurrence rate of the illness (50%) and the high potential for successful suicide (15%).

Social workers should consider these facts not only when choosing content for medication education but when actually managing the dynamics of classroom interaction. At the same time, any psychoeducational effort should strive to debase myths, stereotypes, and misinformation about the limitations of the people who suffer from mental illness; it should reflect the social worker's sensitivity to real impairments of the population. The notion of targeting medication education at either professionals, clients, or families is one way of addressing the different needs of these groups. Although some argue that inclusive education is the most desirable because it draws people together and enhances the empathy and appreciation of these groups for each other (Cubine, Bentley, Poe, & McCafferty, 1999), the best way to respond to the specialized learning needs of each of the groups may lead to separate offerings or curriculums.

The principles of adult learning, as well as the special needs of mental health clients and their families, have led to much advice by the creators of medication education programs. For example, Harmon and Tratnack (1992) suggest a brief didactic method, using plain English, avoiding too much jargon and humor, providing frequent breaks, limiting class size to 12, and providing some incentive for participation such as a point system or a certificate. The latter strategy has been used at the Patient Learning Center at Bryce Hospital since 1977 (Bisbee, 1988). In addition, repeating information is helpful, especially when supplemented by written materials.

Though research tends to focus on adult drug education, many of the principles of and rationale for drug education apply to children and adolescents as well, even though they have unique needs. For example, families play a more critical role in the medication treatment of children and adolescents than they do in that of adults (see chapter 5). Knight, Wigden, Fortsch, and Polcari (1990) offer specific suggestions about how to tailor medication education for children. Perhaps most important is that children feel particularly out of control in terms of decision-making around treatment in general and medication in particular. Thus, drawing from the literature on diabetes education and on children's preoperative procedures, the authors suggest building on the principles of anxiety reduction in medication education programs. In addition, children do not retain information well. Depending on the developmental level of the targeted children, techniques that will help address both concerns (retention & anxiety) are called for. These might include puppet play (having the child pretend to be a nurse dispensing medications or to be himself or herself talking to a physician), art (having children draw a "before and after" medication picture), and frequent use of audiovisual aids. All the techniques should be used in the context of a supportive, reassuring environment. Adolescents, in particular, might benefit from the decreased isolation that a peer group may provide.

There is also a growing literature that speaks to the special medication education needs of the elderly. For example, in a gerontological nursing journal, Lewis and Crossland (1992) encourage medication education planners to emphasize brevity, repetition, the avoidance of technical terms, and sensitivity to sensory deficits. The Opdycke model described below is one that was developed by pharmacists for elderly patients, 40 to 50% of whom do not take their medication as prescribed (Opdycke, Ascione, Shimp, & Rosen, 1992).

However, the discussion of the special learning needs of children and the elderly seems to really speak to the whole area of relevance to all learners, and that's "learning readiness." Green (1998) stresses the leader's role in assessing barriers to learning either in the patient receiving education or the environment in which the education is going to occur. These could be language barriers, culture, psychomotor barriers, or a consumer's past experiences, denial, depression, symptoms, literacy, or even physical pain. Obviously after assessing barriers, part of the leader's role is then to address them and to help motivate patients so they are ready to fully appreciate the information on medication and actively participate in the educational process.

Duchin and Brown (1990) describe in detail four deficits of general patient education programs, which social workers may find helpful when analyzing or creating their own programs.

1. **Assessment error.** An erroneous assumption about the educational needs of the learners. In medication education, this might come up as underestimating clients' concerns about side effects or overestimating a family's need for information on brain biochemistry. One way to overcome this error is to read up on what mental health clients and their families want to know about their medication (a review of topics is covered in the next section). Another way to know what is needed and wanted is simply to ask and observe. For example, one researcher administered his own informal survey at his 9-week family education and support group. He thus gathered information about family members' knowledge of medications and other issues related to serious mental illness (Walsh, 1987).

2. **Analysis error.** An oversimplification of the behavioral goals of the educational effort. This might occur in medication education, for example, when medication compliance becomes the entire goal, even though studies point to other powerful outcomes, such as engaging clients in rehabilitation or making them feel validated and competent.

3. **Planning and implementation error.** Using inappropriate teaching strategies or relying on ineffective teachers. In medication education, this

error might include the use of long lectures and complicated homework assignments. Retaining unstimulating or condescending presenters would also be an obvious error in this category.

4. **Evaluation error.** An improper judgment about outcome. In medication education, this error would be evident in hasty conclusions about the effectiveness of education too soon after classes end or in conclusions based solely on whether the education was enjoyable to participants.

The delivery structures of drug education programs, like other such interventions, run a wide gamut. For example, interventions can be single session, two sessions, all day, or longer. They may meet from 2 hours a month to 3 times a week. When medication education is embedded in a larger psychoeducation program, which commonly occurs (e.g., Harmon & Tratnack, 1992; Hogarty et al., 1991; McGill et al., 1983), often the precise number, frequency, and/or duration of sessions devoted to medication is difficult to determine. Some clear themes do emerge, however. For instance, we have already mentioned the overwhelming preference for using a structured group process that relies on both didactic presentation and group interaction. Groups allow participants to give attention to the client-clinician relationship, to client involvement and client responsibility in self-care. They can help instill hope, highlight the universality of difficulties and fears about medications, contribute to other's learning, and provide a forum to model new skills and the processing of events. Clearly then the role of the leader is to establish structure and safety, to anticipate problems, to reinforce interaction, to model self-disclosure and call attention to the learning that is happening (Lewis & Crossland, 1992).

Professionals also tend to use written materials to accompany the sessions, such as trainer manuals, patient workbooks, and demonstration videos, available for purchase (Eckman et al., 1990). Ascher-Svanum and Krause (1991) used slides and worksheets built into a notebook. Youssef (1984) and a colleague put on a skit for their clients. Though most programs take place in an inpatient or outpatient setting, some call for the educator to work in the client's or the family's home (e.g., Spiegel & Wissler, 1987).

Excellent leadership is another key to a successful medication education program. Leaders in health education have traditionally been nurses (Harmon & Tratnack, 1992). Pharmacists have also frequently led medication education programs. However, social workers' training in group process and empowerment practice and their historical concern for aftercare and community management provides them with an excellent foundation for leadership as well. In one psychoeducational program, both a nurse and a social worker led the session on medication (Posner, Wilson, Kral, Lander, & McIlwraith, 1992). Indeed, the trend toward interdisciplinary collaboration is gaining momentum.

Interestingly, in a survey of 159 families using social work services, most thought of the psychiatrist as the most desired source of information, even though the social worker was reported to be the most available and therefore most used information source (Thompson & Weisberg, 1990). This same study stated that those family members with the most education received most of their information from psychiatrists, while those with the least education received most of their information from nurses. In terms of information exchange in psychiatric care, this seems to suggest a sort of class structure worthy of further research. A similar survey of non-NAMI members found that 72% preferred a psychiatrist to lead medication education programs, but social workers were still in the top three of professionals after psychologists (Ascher-Svanum, Lafuze, Barrickman, Van Dusen & Fompa-Loy, 1997).

One psychoeducational program, established at the Payne Whitney Clinic in New York, has the most clearly defined interdisciplinary roles we have seen (Greenberg, Fine, Cohen, & Larson, 1988). In this program, the psychiatrist serves as coordinator and consultant to the team. The nurses teach patients about their diagnoses and treatments, while the social workers meet with the patients' families for 4 to 10 sessions to help them develop the cognitive and behavioral skills they need. Occupational therapists follow a life skills curriculum that includes goal setting, social skills, and time management.

Nonetheless, professionals tend to have flexible roles. The leader's responsibilities, though few, are complex. The two key leadership roles are instructor and facilitator (Hayes & Gantt, 1992; Powell et al., 1977). Instructors find and choose curriculum materials, present them in an interesting way, and encourage discussion and questions. Facilitators provide support to participants and direct their interactions. In groups where clients and families are together, facilitators need to "modulate the level of affect" of families to protect clients and buffer them from "cognitive and information saturation" (O'Shea, Bicknell, & Whatley, 1991, p. 42).

The first task of facilitation, however, is recruitment. For inpatients, this may not be a problem; recruiting families, however, particularly minority families, may be a major challenge. One group of researchers found that 60 to 75% of families did not show up for their psychoeducational program, which suggested accumulated frustrations with or skepticism of the mental health system (O'Shea et al., 1991). Similarly, disinterest, a lack of resolve about the importance of the education, denial of the illness, family chaos, and the treatment setting may also contribute to such lack of involvement. However, family disinterest or a low priority of education has not been supported by the data reviewed earlier that suggests just the opposite.

Should leaders get special training to do medication education beyond their usual professional preparation and clinical experience? Of course, the leader should know much about medication and especially those topics usually included in medication education programs (see pp. 134 and 135). The leader should also embrace the partnership model of helping and feel very comfortable with empowerment practice. In any psychoeducational intervention, this includes believing that clients and families *can* learn and *can* live more productive lives. It also means being able to tolerate frequent repetition and a slow pace. In addition to these basic leadership requirements, Anderson et al. (1986) provide a detailed description of a model training program in their work on family psychoeducation, including extensive training goals, an outline of topics, and suggested teaching methods. They also provide advice to clinicians on how to control the sessions effectively, deal with impasses, and so forth.

Even so, leaders may not need additional specialized training, which can be expensive and time-consuming. One study compared the implementation of the Medication Management Module between professionals who participated in an on-site, two-day training program offered by their own staff with those who received only mail about their program and a brief telephone consultation (Eckman & Liberman, 1990). While those who participated in the on-site training were evaluated as most competent to use the model, those without training were also judged satisfactorily competent. Most important, the study cited no differences in client outcome between the compared groups. We include this study not to discourage participation in specialized training programs but to encourage the well-prepared but reluctant professional to forge ahead even in the absence of training. It has been noted that embarking on any educational effort in psychiatry "is not a light undertaking . . . however, well-trained mental health professionals generally have sufficient knowledge and experience . . . and psychologists, social workers and nurses have proved as effective as expert psychiatrists" (Falloon et al., 1984, pp. 205–206).

How do professionals evaluate the impact of their interventions? Key outcome measures include medication adherence, usually measured by pill counts, and reports of the client's family or psychiatrist. Some sophisticated studies have used blood levels. However, a specific measurement of medication adherence has yet to be satisfactorily tackled. For example, one researcher notes little correlation between pill counts and self-reports of compliance (Boczkowski, Zeichner, & DeSanto, 1985). Perhaps the most common outcome measure of medication education is actual knowledge of medications, usually judged by simply quizzing participants. Other outcome measures include satisfaction with health care providers, symptomatology, rehospitalization, and attitude toward treatment. Chapter 8 also summarizes several rapid assessment inventories used to monitor medications. The main point here is that researchers should assess the impact of medication education—and all interventions—using a number of measures. Agency-based single-subject designs offer a good option for practicing social workers to respond to the call, especially in managed care, for increased accountability and data-based decision-making. Program and practice evaluation efforts can be replicated, analyzed, revised, and replicated again.

CONTENT OF MEDICATION EDUCATION PROGRAMS

Several comprehensive medication education programs are widely used and adapted, or in some way deserve more detailed description here. The first was developed by Falloon and his colleagues, including a social worker, Christine McGill, as part of their behavioral family therapy project (Falloon et al.,

1984). In their comprehensive psychoeducational program, designed for people with schizophrenia and their families, family members and clients participate together in sessions that take place in the family home. Following a session on the nature of the illness (symptoms, cause, course), the second educational session is completely devoted to medication. In this session the leader uses a handout to guide the presentation and discussion. (This handout is available from the authors and reprinted in the appendix of Ascher-Svanum & Krause, 1991.)

After reviewing the previous session's main points and answering any questions the participants might have, the leader begins medication education by discussing the underlying rationale for medication. Using a stress–diathesis model of mental illness, medication is explained as a way of managing the chemical imbalance in the brain. A brief account of the introduction of antipsychotics into psychiatric care is given, followed by a review of the types of medications, their chemical and brand names, dosage issues, and their benefits. Using clear and simple graphs, the leaders highlight the reduced symptoms and relapse rates of those individuals who regularly take their prescribed medication. Throughout this presentation, they ask clients and families how this information relates to their own experience. For example, when presenting information on how individuals respond differently to various medications, the leader asks the client to describe her or his experience with such medications. When presenting information on relapse, the leader asks if the client has ever had a relapse related to cessation of medication.

The session continues with a list and discussion of common "warning signals," those symptoms that usually precede a relapse, such as increased tension or restlessness, poor concentration, and sleep difficulties. With input from both the family and the patient, the leader creates an individualized list (see chapter 8). Then, the leader reviews a "what to do next" set of options so that patients and families know how to respond if and when warning signals do appear. Because most clients taking medication experience side effects (a major complaint), the Falloon program devotes a good bit of attention to this topic. Side effects are defined as unwanted, often quite unpleasant effects of medication. In terms of the ultimate benefit to clients, however, some side effects may be a necessary evil; thus, successful side–effect management is a key to successful medication management. Common side effects, such as drowsiness, dry mouth, and muscle stiffness, are described along with brief advice on how to cope with them. The first overall strategy, for example, is to wait for a few days or even a week or two, because many side effects will wear off. Leaders give the client and the family opportunities to share how they have coped with side effects and to ask questions.

The Falloon program also includes a candid discussion of adherence issues. Reasons that people with mental illnesses stop taking their medication are outlined, including bothersome side effects, the medication serving as a reminder of the illness, and people searching for other cures (see chapter 7). Clients and families can then share times when clients have stopped taking their medication, exploring why they did it and what impact it had on each person. At this point, the group discusses alcohol and drugs. This program presents the idea that street drugs frequently make things worse and that very small amounts of alcohol may be acceptable, although neuroleptics may intensify its effects. Falloon, Boyd, and McGill (1984) conclude by pointing out that education is ongoing, that the professional keeps teaching and learning throughout the helping process.

Liberman and his associates have also developed an impressive medication education program, which has been in use for over a decade and more recently has undergone extensive field testing (see Eckman & Liberman, 1990; Eckman et al., 1990). Liberman's "stress-vulnerability-coping-competence" model of mental illness suggests that the use of psychotropic medication and psychosocial interventions to promote its use are protective factors that may forestall or prevent relapses in people with mental illness. His Medication Management Module (MMM) addresses four specific skills:

1. obtaining information on the benefits of antipsychotic medication,
2. knowing correct self-administration and evaluation of medication,
3. identifying side effects, and
4. negotiating medication issues with health care providers.

This module is one of 10 or so modules developed by Liberman and his associates, each targeting a specific social or independent-living skill. Money management, food preparation, grooming, dating and friendship, and conversational skills are examples of others. Though designed for use with groups of mental health clients in inpatient or outpatient settings, these modules are readily adaptable. The MMM begins with a general introduction to the goals and rationale of the module. Each of the four skill areas entails learning a number of requisite behaviors. Skill number 4, for example, includes learning to greet the physician pleasantly and being able to describe side effects clearly (see chapter 8). After viewing videotapes of people correctly demonstrating the specific skill, participants then do role-playing, receive feedback, and finally receive homework assignments.

The module also helps clients anticipate certain kinds of problems. Patients learn to handle their "resource management problems," which might include a lack of time to see the doctor or inadequate transportation to his or her office. "Outcome problems" are those disappointing or unexpected events that happen in the real world to upset even the best-laid plans. To address this problem, a leader might teach the client how to figure out what to do if the psychiatrist is called away for an emergency and thus unavailable as scheduled.

A pharmacist-directed model of medication education for the elderly might be adapted by social workers in collaboration with others. Opdycke, Ascione, Shimp, and Rosen (1992) describe their PRECEDE model, which stands for **P**redisposing, **R**einforcing, **E**nabling **C**auses in **E**ducational

Diagnosis and **E**valuation. Highly consistent with social work's "biopsychosocial model" of understanding behavior, the idea is to fully assess contextual factors that influence medication use.

Predisposing: client knowledge, values, perceptions of illness, causal attributions

Reinforcing: attitudes and behaviors of health care practitioners, peers, family, employer

Enabling causes: availability of resources, accessibility of services, patient skills

The PRECEDE model is a comprehensive package that begins with an assessment of learning needs via an in-depth medication history (previous use of all medications, effects, symptoms, home remedies) as well as a review of predisposing factors and past problems (nonadherence, inappropriate use, inadequate knowledge, inadequate communication with professionals). Content is then individualized (and provided individually) based on this assessment and patient feedback. The model, which relies heavily on the use of "patient education tools" such as medication information sheets, reminder packages and calendars, booklets, a wallet medication card, and a prepared list of physician questions, has reportedly been well received.

As discussed earlier in this chapter, Knight's model for medication education with children on an inpatient unit relies heavily on play and other creative techniques. It consists of four half-hour modules to be used with a peer group. Group membership is fixed for a cycle of four sessions, and then a new group is formed. Session 1 is titled "What does it feel like to take meds?" and includes data gathering and needs assessment, much like other models described. Session 2 is "Why do kids take meds?" and includes a discussion of symptoms and therapeutic effects. In Session 3, smaller groups within the larger group create posters on drug categories, specific medications, and side effects. Self-esteem and body image emerge as issues for the groups. The final session is focused on street drugs versus psychiatric medication and the whole issue of self-medication.

Other medication education programs may each emphasize different things or be more or less ambitious in their educational objectives. For example, unlike most other programs, the medication content in the "Survival Skills Workshop" includes substantial information on neurotransmission and brain function (Anderson et al., 1986). Most would agree with Azrin and Teichner (1998) that a "systems approach" is needed—that is, one that addresses/combines "multiple influences on successful performance" of a "complex behavioral sequence" (p. 850). What these authors are arguing is the need to pay attention to each "piece" of behavior in the chain of events that leads to taking medication, from making an appointment with a physician to ingesting the medication. For social workers, this might mean attending to everything from transportation, to assuring money is available to pay costs, to storing reminders, and of course, to social support.

It might be useful at this point to summarize common topics found in a comprehensive program. You can find more information on these topics throughout this book. Depending on the client's need, social workers can present the content broadly or make it specific to certain mental or emotional disorders or targeted to a particular medication.

- **Rationale for medication use.** All medication education programs should contain information on why medication is used in the treatment of mental illnesses and emotional disorders. The stress–diathesis model of mental illness provides a useful framework for presenting the rationale. Information on the effectiveness of medications in relation to psychosocial treatments might be useful as well. Many clients appreciate the analogy of the person with diabetes needing to use insulin regularly.

- **Benefits of medication.** Mental health clients and their families should receive accurate information about the benefits of medication, including its proven impact on certain symptoms and on relapse rates. Symptoms that tend to be less affected should also be reviewed.

- **Types of drugs.** Depending on the audience, the curriculum might include a thorough review of one type of medication (antidepressants or antipsychotics, for example) or might review all the categories of drugs.

- **Side effects.** Side effects: major and minor; physical, psychological, and social; common and not so common should be reviewed. Where relevant, discussion of tardive dyskinesia, neuroleptic malignant syndrome, and agranulocytosis should not be glossed over or diminished. Many programs spend a lot of time discussing creative or practical ways of coping with the range of side effects.

- **Dosage and equivalents.** Information on the differences in dosage among medications helps clients understand such things as changes in medication orders and the importance of taking correct doses.

- **Forms of drugs.** The pros and cons and general rationale for using various forms of drugs (such as tablets, injectibles, and patches) should be included.

- **Absorption and predicted response.** Discussion of the impact of individual metabolism on absorption rates helps clients understand better why individuals respond differently to psychotropic medication. Some programs present several theories of drug action and teach clients appropriate expectations about a medication's effects at different phases of the illness.

- **Interactions.** Common interactions, particularly those involving alcohol and drug use, should be taught to clients and families. However, information on complex interactions is best left to individual consultation with the physician, especially in light of increasing use of polypharmacy.

- **Addictiveness and withdrawal.** Sometimes the fears of clients and families are unfounded. Nevertheless, strong cautions are usually in order, especially with certain types of tranquilizers and sedatives. There is developing knowledge about drug withdrawal with some antidepressant medications, for example.

- **Self-administration principles.** Clients and families often need simple advice on how to take or store psychotropic medications, read labels, manage missed doses, or use reminders.

- **Adherence.** Frank discussion of why people stop taking their medication is crucial to compliance, including issues of identity and body image. Clarifying the attitudes and beliefs of both the client and the family is important, as is anticipating both short- and long-term barriers to medication use, such as fears of toxicity, high expectations of efficacy, or fears based on cultural or societal influences.

- **Communication/negotiation.** Though not enough programs include information on communication skills, many clients need help talking about medication to their social worker, case manager, therapist, or psychiatrist. Because clients often feel incompetent or frightened in this area, teaching such skills seems logical, perhaps necessary.

- **Emerging trends/research.** Clients and families are interested in and often heavily invested in the latest medication research: what scientists are testing and what new trends or philosophies of care have evolved.

SUMMARY

This chapter has provided a rationale for medication education, reviewed issues related to the implementation and evaluation of medication education programs, and discussed the content of such programs. Implicit in the chapter is a call for social workers to freely embrace the role of educator. Even in the face of understandable doubts about their competence to do so, social workers in all settings can and should start or contribute to such groups or programs, either alone or, ideally, in collaboration with other providers, clients, and families.

7

❖ *Compliance*

Medication Adherence
and Refusal

The regularity with which health care clients in general do not comply with, or at least do not completely adhere to, their prescribed medication regimen is widely discussed in relation to diabetes, epilepsy, hypertension, AIDS, and especially mental illness and emotional distress. Even people who are not taking psychotropic or other medications can appreciate nonadherence. Most can remember those antibiotics that they did not quite finish or the times they took extra painkillers because they believed that the dosages on the label weren't quite right for them. And for many, taking antibiotics or pain medications may not have the same underlying meaning, and certainly not the same side effects, as the psychotropic medications.

This chapter will discuss the social worker's need to address adherence and refusal holistically, including an awareness of related legal and ethical issues as well as the symbolic meaning of medications to clients and families. Much of this chapter is devoted to helping social workers understand the many theories and models used to explain adherence and nonadherence. We also present specific techniques, based on our own model of adherence, to help clients increase their adherence to medication regimens, including specific diets, such as those mandated for example by MAO inhibitors. We rely on the term *adherence* because the term *compliance* has lost favor in recent years because of a perceived negative connotation of passivity and obedience. Furthermore, noncompliance implies that the client has done something wrong or is deviant, which "does not often reflect reality from the client's perspective" (Morris & Schulz, 1993, p. 603). The promotion of medication adherence,

adherence vs compliance

or framework (e.g., DeGeest, Abraham, Gemoets, & Evers, 1994; Leventhal, Diefenbach, & Leventhal, 1992). Similarly, we will organize our discussion of these factors around four dimensions: characteristics of the client, aspects of the treatment, aspects of the social environment, and the actual mental illness or symptoms. Although more than 30 years of research into over 200 variables has not produced consistent information, the following review will still help social workers appreciate the complexity of adherence and thus, we hope, design multidimensional strategies and techniques to address it.

One of the most salient criticisms of the literature on adherence is that studies of clients' adherence are usually based on "an ideal image" of the client as a "passive, obedient and unquestioning recipient of medical instructions. Divergence . . . is seen as irrational in light of medical rationality" (Stimson, 1974, p. 97). Fenton, Blyler, and Heissen (1997), for example, noted that through the mid-1990s over 14,000 articles have appeared in the medical literature about medication adherence, but almost none were directed toward the subjective experience of consumers or their decision-making processes. There are a lot of reasons why people do or do not do what the physician says, some completely rational (whether appearing so or not) and some not so rational. We encourage social workers to understand adherence in light of the clients' views of their illnesses, treatments, experiences, interactions, and expectations. This more active view of clients will necessarily mean greater focus on the "social context in which illnesses are lived and treatments used" (Stimson, p. 97), an appropriate assignment for social workers. Other writers have echoed Stimson's call. For example, Conrad (1985) says social workers should reject the "doctor-centered perspective" of adherence and move toward a "patient perspective" that suggests greater emphasis on health beliefs, self-regulation, and the meaning of medication to clients.

CHARACTERISTICS OF THE CLIENT

As we mentioned in chapter 6, the health belief model states that people base health care decisions on (1) their understanding of some desired outcome, (2) their motivation to seek it, and (3) how they see that a recommended "treatment" (medication, behavior change) will help them realize the desired outcome (Youssef, 1984). Thus, people experiencing severe anxiety will more likely take their prescribed anti-anxiety medication if (1) they genuinely understand what a lack of anxiety would be like for them, (2) they are genuinely motivated to try to reduce their anxiety, and (3) they appreciate the connection between taking the medication and achieving or maintaining a reduced state of anxiety. Clearly, this model calls for medication education (see chapter 6). With some exceptions (e.g., Garavan et al., 1998), a number of studies of patients with serious mental illness have found a clear relationship between clients' insight into their illness or disorder (that is, a recognition that a problem exists and requires medical intervention) and the perceived benefits of medication and medication adherence (Nageotte, Sullivan, Duan, & Camp, 1997; Lin, Spiga, & Fortsch, 1979).

However, clients receiving medications may or may not place medical outcome or clinical efficacy at the top of their list. Instead they usually evaluate and balance a range of competing physical, economic, psychological, and social outcomes (Morris & Schulz, 1993). Thus, to truly understand the client's decisions about medication, clinicians must try to ascertain what outcomes an individual values most. A recent study shows that the desired outcomes of medication use reported by psychotic clients were mostly indirect; that is, the desired outcomes did not relate directly to symptom reduction but rather to keeping them out of the hospital or to helping them stay out of trouble (Adams & Howe, 1993). People with depression or anxiety may adhere to their medications because they simply want to "get back on track at work" or "be a better parent." On the other hand, clients may opt against using medications because the most compelling outcomes are to not be labeled "crazy," to remain sexually responsive, or to continue to enjoy fine red wine. These cost-benefit analyses are quite complex.

The self-regulation model suggests that "what appears to be noncompliance . . . may actually be a form of asserting control over one's disorder" (Conrad, 1985, p. 29). Self-regulation includes both the client's perception of the health threat and his or her management of coping devices and emotional processes (Leventhal et al., 1992). Not surprisingly, adherence has been found to be inversely related to perceived health (Aspler & Rothman, 1984). The healthier clients perceive themselves to be, the less likely they will adhere to a drug regimen. Conrad notes that people with epilepsy take their medication, often in spite of absolutely hating it, not just to control seizures, but to reduce their own worrying and to ensure a sense of normality. This again demonstrates why the use of analogies, such as diabetes or hypertension, can be useful.

Clients may regulate their own medication by increasing or decreasing doses or stopping medication altogether. Some authors claim that clients do this because they want to

1. test whether or not their illness or symptoms are still there, or just see what will happen;

2. control perceptions of dependence, because clients may see taking medications as a threat to self-reliance;

3. manage stigma, because the very act of taking medication relays certain information to other people and at some level acknowledges the client's differentness; or

4. practically manage their symptoms or side effects, or regulate the disruption of lifestyle.

Reducing the dose to decrease a bothersome side effect is said to be the most common example of self-regulation of medication. Increasing the dose during times of stress is also common (Morris & Schulz, 1993; Conrad, 1985).

Thus, the meaning that medication has for clients and their interpretation of being medicated is of utmost concern to the social worker trying to understand adherence issues and, indeed, clients' entire adaptations to their illnesses. Specifically, negative subjective experiences, such as the medication making the client "feel like a zombie," "useless," or "weak," have been associated with nonadherence. Not only the severity of symptoms or side effects, but also the client's interpretations and conclusions about the experience of taking medication play a key role in adherence (Awad, Voruganti, Heslegrave, & Hogan, 1996; Awad, 1992). It is encouraging that more and more research is focused on understanding client metaphors as windows into "meaning" and understanding the impact of taking medication on a consumer's identity and sense of self, including research planned by the senior author (e.g., Rogers, Day, Williams, Randall, Wood, Healy, & Bentall, 1998; Rhodes, 1984; Helman, 1981).

Almost all research of factors associated with adherence and nonadherence has tested demographic and other variables such as age, gender, socioeconomic status, level of education, type of disorder, and the length of time that symptoms have existed. A few studies have found significant relationships; for instance, Draine and Solomon (1994) have found that older patients with fewer symptoms and a greater array of daily activities have greater adherence. However, sensory or memory impairments, impaired dexterity, as well as complexity of drug regimens and cost concerns, may place elderly patients at risk for nonadherence. One study cites that living alone puts patients at greater risk of nonadherence (Seltzer et al., 1980), and another shows that patients with greater internal locus of control are more compliant with their lithium (Kucera-Bozarth, Beck, & Lyss, 1982). Researchers have begun to explore the role of visual memory and cognitive function as a factor in adherence to medication (Isaac, Tamblyn, & McGill-Calgary Drug Research Team, 1993). In addition, initial research has begun to uncover whether adherence is impacted by differential perceptions that stem from clients' diverse racial or ethnic backgrounds regarding drug toxicity and addictiveness. In general, however, no demographic variables seem consistently related to adherence or nonadherence (Frank, Perel, Mallinger, Thase, & Kupfer, 1992; Jamison & Akiskal, 1983).

ASPECTS OF TREATMENT

A number of factors related to the actual treatment itself are associated with adherence and nonadherence, including those that relate to the medication regimen, intended effects and side effects, the treatment system, and professional attitudes and behaviors. For one thing, long-term maintenance medications, the kind used by most mental health clients, are associated with greater nonadherence (Diamond, 1983). A study of male veterans in the general health care arena found that patient perceptions of being overmedicated were also associated with nonadherence. The authors further add that these perceptions turned out to reflect reality (Fincke, Miller, & Spiro, 1998).

Complex regimens are also associated with greater nonadherence. Thus, clients with more than one medication or with challenging dosing schedules (such as more than once a day) are at higher risk of nonadherence than others (Blackwell, 1979). Some have even speculated that physical aspects of the pill—the shape, size, color, and even taste—may contribute to adherence or nonadherence (Buckalew & Sallis, 1986). In addition, the cost of medication, perceptions of affordability, and general accessibility may each play a role. It seems obvious that if out-of-pocket costs for medication exceed the clients' budgets or if they cannot physically get the medications from a clinic or pharmacy, some nonadherence is likely. On the other hand, Morris and Schulz (1993) note that those who receive free medication are less compliant with medications, leading to the speculation that free medications are not as valued as those that require some personal sacrifice.

Not surprisingly, the quality and timing of drug effects also play a role in compliance. The delay between the time the client commences medications and the time when any significant therapeutic effect is discernible may frustrate the client and weaken the perceived link between the treatment and its benefit. Similarly, when medications leave the body's system slowly, depending on half-life, a client may become discouraged (see chapter 4). However, adherence improves when the actual effects of a drug most closely match the client's expectations for clinical improvement, which the prescribing physician may or may not share, and truly meaningful and reliable improvement in symptoms provides perhaps the greatest incentive for adherence. In an examination of imipramine adherence in a group of 53 patients with depression, over 80% of whom were described as compliant, researchers found that of all the variables studied, "effective prophylaxis," or prevention of depressive symptoms, was the one most associated with compliance (Frank et al., 1992).

On the other hand, nonadherence may be most heavily associated with negative physical side effects. While some providers and families argue that "illness-related" reasons figure most heavily in nonadherence, and especially refusal, clients themselves most often point to unwanted side effects as the most important factor. The most bothersome side effects for clients of a range of medications may not be the most frequent or the most severe side effects. For example, though thirst, excessive urination, weight gain, fatigue, dry mouth, and sleepiness are the most common side effects of lithium treatment (see chapter 4), clients rated weight gain, problems in concentration, mental confusion, and slowness as the most bothersome (Gitlin, Cochran, & Jamison, 1989). Clients rated mental slowness, weight gain, confusion, and memory problems as those side effects most likely to make them stop taking their medication. However, tremors and mental slowness are the side effects most associated with actual self-reported nonadherence. In this study, 80% of the respondents reported experiencing at least one side effect and 20% no side effects at all, but the average number of side effects experienced was 10.6, 3.4 of which occurred often.

For neuroleptics, akathisia (a subtle internal restlessness, agitation, and impatience) is most associated with nonadherence (VanPutten, 1974). A 1992 study examines the side-effect profiles of 185 California shelter residents who showed a range of diagnoses, symptoms, and medications. Mostly persons with schizophrenia and on neuroleptics, 63% of the residents reported a mild degree of at least one side effect and 36% reported between 3 and 13 different adverse effects (Segal, Cohen, & Marder, 1992). Dry mouth/throat, restlessness, weight gain or loss, diarrhea or constipation, depression, apathy, and dizziness were the most common. Severity ratings follow a similar order except that loss of sex drive and sensitivity to the sun were rated as severe, in spite of their low prevalence (below 6%).

Aspects of the larger treatment system itself may also contribute to nonadherence. For example, a system of services or a treatment plan that inadequately educates or prepares clients and families or one that structures an unfriendly aftercare environment may actually foster nonadherence. The attitudes and behaviors of the clinical staff, especially psychiatrists and social workers, play a crucial role in shaping medication adherence of clients. Marked ambivalence, antagonism toward medication itself, or an attitude of "oversell" on the part of providers is associated with nonadherence (Franson & Smith, 1998; Jamison & Akiskal, 1983; Weissman, 1972). Clients and families will immediately detect any pessimism about the client's capacity to change or a social worker's sense of hopelessness about prognosis. A study at the Affective Disorders Clinic at UCLA shows that physicians' attitudes toward medications, as reflected in their perceptions of how well the medications would work, are strongly related to adherence (Jamison, Gerner, & Goodwin, 1979).

In contrast, social workers' attitudes have received more speculation than systematic study (Bentley, Farmer, & Phillips, 1991). Interestingly, there has been a general assumption that social workers have historically opposed the use of psychotropic medication because such use focuses on physiological functioning or perceptions of misuse. Cohen's (1988) extensive literature review challenges this assumption. Other studies support his contention that social workers tend to see psychotropic medication use as a necessary and effective component of mental health treatment. For example, Berg and Wallace (1987) present 60 social workers in inpatient and outpatient mental health settings who said that use of medications with discharged clients is a positive step. Bentley et al. (1991) show that a group of social work students held quite positive views of medication, although they admit that their findings regarding social work attitudes are difficult to interpret. They see midrange attitude scores on a researcher-developed measure as possibly reflecting a "proper level" of medication acceptance, in that "both extremely negative or blindly positive attitudes may be inappropriate" (p. 287). On the other hand, midrange attitude scores may represent a high degree of ambivalence related to both positive and negative personal and professional experiences.

A lack of empathy toward medication-related dilemmas of clients and families is also problematic. Indeed, acknowledging medication issues as a serious concern and allowing clients and families to express and clarify their feelings about medication is a first step for social workers or any mental health care provider (see chapter 2). One program went even further. Morse, Simon, & Balson (1993) describe a program in which 20 physicians and nurses took placebos on the same pill schedule as their HIV patients to better understand and empathize with them. This meant taking three pills 5 times a day at 4-hour intervals and keeping a diary of reactions. Although this part of the study lasted only 1 week and involved no physiological changes or side effects, long-lasting changes occurred in provider attitude and empathy. The diaries revealed intense frustration with rigid schedules and stigma felt from the need to take pills in public.

The interpersonal interactions between clients and their social workers or physicians matter a great deal. Levy (1978) points out that "source attractiveness" may play a role in adherence. That is, a provider's focused attention on her or his client, as well as joking, laughing, and friendliness, may contribute to adherence. A study from the late 1960s, for example, uses observational ratings of psychiatrists to examine those characteristics of therapists that were associated with high versus low patient dropout from drug treatment. Low-dropout therapists, to no one's surprise, were more active and positive, delivering more personalized services (Howard et al., 1970).

The social worker's ability to communicate seems an obvious influence on adherence. Because clients must understand recommendations about medication in order to adhere to them, communication is essential to cooperation (Hays & DiMatteo, 1987). Indeed, many have noted that the responsiveness of providers and the perceived quality of the provider-client relationship play important roles in adherence (Weiden et al., 1994; Kane, 1983).

ASPECTS OF THE SOCIAL ENVIRONMENT

The societal and community culture of medications, the extent of family and social support, and general cues and contingencies in the environment all tend to influence adherence to psychotropic medications. Certainly, public attitudes about the use or acceptance of psychotropic medication relate to various ideas about the causes of mental illnesses and emotional distress. For example, a National Institute of Mental Health (NIMH) study conducted with members of the general public in the early 1970s found that those who believe that people with mental illness lack moral strength are twice as likely to view tranquilizer use as a sign of weakness (Manheimer et al., 1973).

Today, tremendous variability exists in society's acceptance, or lack of acceptance, of psychotropic medication use. First, people have many questions, such as, is the medication for "situational stress" or a truly long-standing "illness"? Is the medication addictive? It seems people more easily accept certain medications under certain circumstances with certain people and certain problems. To complicate matters further, the individuals whom the public will accept as users of medication is subject to change. People may fully support a coworker's daughter on risperidone for schizophrenia or a distant relative on lithium for bipolar disorder. People may completely accept a best friend on sertraline (Zoloft) for depression, but they do not want their spouses taking fluoxetine (Prozac) to increase productivity at work.

In popular culture, people often see psychotropic drugs portrayed in an intensely negative way, such as forced on people with mental illnesses. Movies such as *Mr. Jones, Nuts, The Dream Team,* and *Crazy People* are just a few examples. In addition, newspapers headline horror stories about acts allegedly committed by people because they use Prozac (fluoxetine), and best-selling books warn of continued psychiatric and psychopharmacological expansionism (e.g., Breggin, 1987; Szasz, 1994; see also chapter 9). However, countervailing influences also exist. Recent polls suggest a growing understanding of the biological basis of many mental illnesses and its treatment (Clements, 1993). Many contemporary dramas, such as *As Good As It Gets, Prince of Tides,* and *Awakenings,* suggest compassionate, reasoned, and appropriate use of psychotropic drugs. (See Wedding & Boyd, 1999, for a complete review of the portrayal of mental disorders and substance abuse in the movies.) In either case, "social myth can dominate the interpretive process" of mental health clients and families (Leventhal et al., 1992, p. 152.) Therefore, social workers must appreciate this larger societal context of psychotropic medication use, including their own vulnerability to popular culture's manipulation and influence.

Families can also exert positive or negative influences on medication adherence. If the family agrees with the prescribing physician, understands the rationale underlying medication use or somehow "believes" in it, and supports and perhaps even offers concrete help in achieving adherence or monitoring the effects of the medication, the family obviously has a positive influence. However, if the family presents undue pressure or competing beliefs, such as "All she needs to do is pull herself up by her bootstraps" or "If she would just turn it over to Jesus, everything would be OK," then the outcome is likely to be less positive. Interactions with friends, coworkers, and others can similarly affect decisions about medication use. Thale (1973) calls the effects of client, family, and societal attitudes toward psychotropic drugs— whether seen as "disgraceful weakness" or "intelligent use of science"—the "sociodynamics of medication" (p. 32).

ASPECTS OF THE ILLNESS OR SYMPTOMS

The last dimension in this framework for understanding adherence concerns factors related to the illness itself or its symptoms such as depression, anxiety, paranoia, grandiosity, hostility, and cognitive impairment. For example, if an individual does not take his or her medication because of a delusion that the drug is part of some germ warfare plot, this symptom will clearly influence nonadherence or even refusal. Perhaps a man in a manic phase simply believes he does not need his medication because he is king of the hill and can overcome his illness on his own. Or perhaps a woman is too depressed to get out of bed to go to the medicine cabinet or so depressed that she believes there's really no use, that treatment of her devastating illness is futile.

Everyone who has devised an explanatory model for adherence includes illness-related factors. Most psychiatrists—although not most clients—attribute medication refusal to these factors. Denial is usually discussed in this particular context. But denial is not seen as an understandable and rather typical human protective response to be addressed with compassion and patience; rather it is seen as an unacceptable symptom of illness that must be immediately exposed and obliterated. Importantly, if providers heavily emphasize client symptoms or "illness" as a cause of nonadherence, the logic of forcing medication against the client's will is set up, all in the name of her or his best interest.

A restatement may be useful here. To more holistically address various forms of nonadherence, as well as more effectively help with medication monitoring, social workers should draw from the wealth of knowledge that exists about factors that influence adherence, especially the complex physical, social, psychological, and emotional responses to medication. Table 7.1 summarizes a list of potential risks and protective factors for medication nonadherence as drawn from a range of resources cited previously or others (e.g., Duncan & Rogers, 1998; Hescue, Levin, & Merrick, 1998; Marder, 1998; Swartz, Swanson, Hiday, Borum, Wagner, & Burns, 1998; Dixon, Weiden, Torres, & Lehman, 1997; Budd, Hughes, Ian, & Smith, 1996; Agarwal, Sharma, Kishore-Kuman, & Lowe, 1998). The risks and protective factors are listed in order of the frequency of their discussion and their prominence in the literature.

LEGAL AND ETHICAL ISSUES IN ADHERENCE AND REFUSAL

Even though overt refusal of medication is said to be rare in more general mental health practice, a well-developed body of literature on the topic exists. Social workers should become familiar with this literature for at least two reasons. First, experience shows that social workers who work in either inpatient or outpatient mental health settings will likely encounter medication adherence and refusal issues regularly, depending on the number and characteristics of the clients in their caseloads and the agency environment. Second, the themes that emerge from the literature on refusal offer insight into the range of clients' rights issues in relation to medication monitoring and adherence.

As Lefley (1993) states, "The question of involuntary treatment embodies some of the most basic philosophical, clinical, and political issues in any society. . . . These issues are framed within the meaning of mental illness and any given time in history" (p. 7). Unfortunately, Lefley (1993) takes the position that most people who view mental illness as a strictly biological illness accept forced medication as a necessary evil, whereas those who see it mainly as a psychological phenomenon oppose forced medication. Following this logic, however, one could argue that those with cancer or Down's syndrome or

Table 7.1 Possible Risks and Protective Factors for Medication Nonadherence

Possible Risks

Bothersome or adverse side effects

History of substance abuse

Severe positive symptoms

Client ambivalence, anger, or grandiosity

Forgetfulness

Delay in achieving therapeutic effect

Poor client-clinician relationship

Unfriendly aftercare environment

Complex medication regimen

Episodic course of illness

Challenging dosing schedule

Multiple providers

Use of long-term maintenance medication

Young in age

Living alone

Unsupportive family

Free medication

Perception of being overmedicated

Possible Protective Factors

Belief that one has a mental illness

Adequate education and preparation of client and family

Use of depot medications

Positive subjective response to medication

Good client-clinician relationship

Provider and family empathy with client

Insurance coverage for medication

Respected client autonomy

Broad array of daily activities

Fewer symptoms

Client participation in assertive community treatment

Consistent outpatient care

Client strong internal locus of control

Positive perceptions of affordability

epilepsy should have restricted rights to make health care decisions simply because of the physiological and genetic natures of their illnesses. On the other hand, Lefley (1993) correctly identifies some of the important conflicts that emerge from this debate:

- the rights of the individual versus the rights of the group
- civil liberties versus survival needs of people

- the rights of the disabled versus the rights of caregivers
- the obligation of society to protect its citizens

The true portrait of a client's right to refuse may be best exemplified by what occurs in inpatient facilities for people with severe mental illness. A study in Virginia found that 45 of 348 admissions to a state hospital refused medication (12.9%), a slightly higher percentage than is normally found. However, because a clinician in Virginia can easily override a patient refusal, in this case 100% of those inpatients, almost all within four days, were administered medication anyway; 56% were treated involuntarily and 44% changed their mind and accepted the treatment (Kasper, Hoge, Feucht-Haviar, Cortina, & Cohen, 1997). Clearly these clients never had a true right to refuse. Their refusal simply kicked in the process designed to override their wishes. In Louisiana, out of 1969 patients admitted to a psychiatric unit in New Orleans, all 40 "refusers" were also subject to an administrative review. A total of 29 were later medicated: 22 involuntarily, 7 changed their minds and took medication, and 11 were not medicated and their initial wishes allowed to stand (Urrutia, 1994). Indeed, Winick concludes that abuse of psychotropic drugs is most common in institutions. Not only are patients often not truly allowed to refuse, but they also are rarely told the costs and benefits of medication, which is administered without proper supervision (Winick, 1997). Sadly, little effort is spent protecting the interests of those deemed mentally ill or incompetent (McCubbin & Weisstub, 1997).

Perhaps the two biggest questions that relate to the right-to-refuse issue are these:

1. What *is* in the "best interest" of the client?
2. Who decides?

Put simply, we believe that social workers should advocate the client's right to refuse medication (Bentley, 1993). The sole exception to this principle is a true emergency, such as when clients are physically harming themselves or others. Others have appropriately described a true emergency as (1) when the patient is "presently violent" and the state's interest is "grave and immediate" (Weiner, 1985, p. 346) or (2) when there is a "substantial likelihood of extreme violence, personal injury or self-destruction" (Judge Tauro, quoted in Ford, 1980, p. 337). One of the issues that social workers must confront is that some providers and family members define "emergency" much more broadly, even to the point that any refusal or even reluctance on the part of the client that conflicts with either the provider's or the family's judgment is grounds for forced medication. For example, Eisenberg, Hilliard, and Gutheil (1981) advocate including in the definition of emergency not only all potentially life-threatening behaviors but also any behavior that could be seen as "seriously health-threatening, either acutely or subacutely" (p. 98). Arguments to limit the client's right to refuse medication assume that people with mental illness, especially those who refuse medication, also have impaired judgment and that they need and truly want outside intervention (Rosenson, 1993). However, only one study seems to support this view. In it, 17 of 24 inpatients who refused medication report that overriding their refusal of medications might have been appropriate (Schwartz, Vingiano, & Perez, 1988).

A published debate between a social worker and a physician highlights the intensity of emotions around this topic. Remler, a physician, argues that restricting the right to refuse medication is a reasonably pragmatic approach for clients with such disorders as schizophrenia, brain damage, and mental retardation because they "simply can not be allowed to determine their behavior. . . . They do not want their behavior changed. . . . They must be coerced" (Remler & Cohen, 1992, p. 304). Cohen, a social worker, argues that Remler "transforms disturbed and disturbing men and women from moral agents into brain-disordered organisms" (p. 306). We also believe that automatically equating mental disability or, for that matter, involuntary hospitalization, with incompetence leads to a global indictment of the population that is destructive and stigmatizing (Bentley, 1991; Roth, Meisel, & Lidz, 1977). Presuming competence is an important check and balance in any due process procedure because doing so helps to establish the extent and direction of proof, much as presuming innocence does in criminal cases. Surprisingly, in a recent study, 20% of clinical social workers equated involuntary commitment with incompetence (Wilk, 1994).

Indeed, evidence simply does not support the argument that most people who refuse psychotropic medications are irrational, paranoid, assaultive, and dangerous (Zito, Routt, Mitchell, & Roering, 1985). Fears that refusals would result in significantly longer hospital stays, violence, and chaos have largely been proven invalid (Brooks, 1987; Cole, 1982). While some still argue that increased rights to refuse medication have resulted in greater costs, staff injuries, and client belligerence (Ciccone, Tokoli, Gift, & Clements, 1993), the actual evidence suggests that this is not the case. In examining the impact of a California Supreme Court case, Sheline and Beattie (1992) find that in their study over two-thirds of involuntarily committed patients still consent to treatment without incident. Those on no medication at all and the small percentage who did refuse were actually in the hospital the least amount of time. Nevertheless, two factors seem to keep the issue of violence and medication adherence in the forefront of provider's minds. First is very recent research noting higher rates of violence for a very specific subset of clients: young males who have both psychosis and substance abuse, who are receiving improper or insufficient treatment, and who have a history of conduct disorder (Fulfiler & Ruthazer, 1999; Arboleda-Florez, 1998). Second is the continued exposure to sensational high-profile media events in which violence and mental illness are linked.

The two preeminent value positions of the profession, self-determination and respecting the dignity and uniqueness of individuals, seem to call for a more client-centered response. An authority on social work ethics, Reamer (1987) says that "of course" clients who either refuse or withdraw consent to treatment should be considered legally and mentally capable. "The fact that clients may be taking psychotropic medication or may be disabled to some degree by mental illness does not in itself provide grounds for denying them the right to refuse or withdraw consent" (p. 427). Wilk's study (1994) of clinical social workers has found that although social workers generally support a range of client's rights issues, they show the least support for the right to refuse treatment. Only 30% supported a client's right to refuse medication, while 57% opposed it. Wilk concludes that her study has encouraging results except for this "disturbing minority who disagree with or appear to be indifferent to [clients'] hard earned rights" (p. 173). Interestingly, she notes that women in their 40s with 14 to 15 years of experience and who have received their MSW in the 1970s were the most supportive of client rights. Men in their 40s with 12 years of experience who had received their MSW in the early 1970s were the least supportive of client rights.

Cohen states that involuntary drugging is harmful to clients, saying that such action is "inhumane and unjustifiable" because it subverts the "ethical mandate" of social workers (Remler & Cohen, 1992, p. 307). Similarly, Bentley (1993) argues that if social workers are serious about respecting the dignity and uniqueness of individuals, they must also advocate strongly for the fair due-process procedures now required by law in the case of refusal. This advocacy recognizes that "forced drugging of a patient absent a determination that a person is not capable of rationally deciding what is good for himself" cannot exist (*Davis v. Hubbard,* 1980, p. 936). Social workers can also advocate for real procedural safeguards, ones that honor either what clients say they want or, in cases where substituted judgment is called for, ones that honor what the client would have articulated if she or he were competent. Thus, the expressed preference of the client should be the center of all deliberations. Otherwise, so-called procedural safeguards merely give the client the right to a second opinion (Stone, 1981). Unfortunately, this ideal is rarely achieved in the real world, where the perspective of the client is rarely recognized (McCubbin & Weisstub, 1998).

Note that this position differs from that in which the provider or family can ultimately determine "the best interest" of the client. As indicated earlier, deciding on the client's best interest is a complicated task, influenced by issues of power and paternalism. For example, should best interest be legally determined or clinically determined? Lawyers and psychiatrists have fought about that question for years. Should family caregivers decide? Brown (1985) points out that the more providers or others can portray themselves as acting in the client's best interest, the more they can expand their power base. Others argue that it is the families who "really care" about the patients and that civil libertarians and advocates are often overly concerned with autonomy issues (Rosenson & Kasten, 1991). Social workers, too, must avoid any professional arrogance that they really know what "best interest" is, given their historical commitment to client rights or their holistic perspective. This attitude flies in the face of the partnership model of practice with clients' families and other providers.

Social workers can look to the courts to provide a number of other "causes of action" that have provided a legal and ethical basis for allowing clients to refuse their medication. These include the right to privacy, prohibitions against battery, and freedom of religion. In any case, expanding clients' rights in treatment refusal has not led them to "rotting with their rights on" (Appelbaum & Gutheil, 1979) but instead helped reduce inappropriate administration of drugs and has reduced dosages (Brooks, 1987). Thus, as with all health care decisions, the bottom line is that respect for the autonomy of clients should be the basis of treatment and should only be "subverted," as Brabbins, Butler, and Bentall (1996) describe it, in the face of the strongest of arguments. They suggest clinicians use a three-prong proforma to record their efforts: (1) make note of the shared information on the reasons for prescribing, the costs and benefits of the medication, and alternative treatments, (2) make note of the client's capacity to consent and the steps taken to ensure the client was able to understand the treatment and weigh her or his options, (3) note the absence of duress, the advisement of the client's right to decline medications, and the consequences of that in real life.

Parish (1993) summarizes the arguments of clients, their families, the mental health system, and society regarding involuntary interventions, including medication. From the client's perspective, involuntary treatment may alleviate suffering, pain, and embarrassment; enhance recovery; or quicken "liberty." However, it may also cause a loss of self-determination, liberty, and an abridgment of civil rights. It often means living with uncomfortable side effects. From the family's perspective, forced medication may mean improved perceptions of family members' own personal safety, but it can also cause considerable dissension among them. From the perspective of the system and society, forced medication may be efficient and seemingly allows them to "do the right thing" but is clearly a form of social control, unlike any other permitted by society.

INTERVENTIONS TO ASSIST IN
MEDICATION ADHERENCE

Based on the model of adherence presented in this chapter, this section focuses on specific strategies and techniques the social worker can use to deal constructively with refusal and to help clients increase their adherence to their medication regimens. Wettstein (1999) has noted that refusal of medication and difficulties with adherence can be sporadic, time-limited, periodic, or continuous. Assuming mutual engagement in a working relationship, intervention begins with ascertaining the pattern of adherence and the client's individual reasons for nonadherence. Our model suggests, for example, assessment of the client's "health beliefs" and expectations about medication, including any ethnic or cultural influences. It suggests ascertaining the real desired outcomes for clients and their ability to make connections between taking medication and achieving those outcomes. Social workers can also assess whether the medication is accessible, affordable, and sufficiently simple to take, and if family and friends support its use or merely tolerate it. Finally, social workers can take stock of their own attitudes and behaviors, and the attitudes of those around them, to consider their influence on a client's adherence.

Thus, one of the most obvious and useful strategies for such intervention is reflective discussion with the clients and their families to clarify assumptions and build knowledge to help in other interventions. In chapter 8, we discuss many appropriate strategies, such as monitoring, coping with side effects, problem solving, decision making, negotiation, and advocacy. Medication education also serves as a major intervention for medication nonadherence (see chapter 6). In this chapter, we present a number of useful cognitive and behavioral techniques associated with increased adherence. Though the distinction between an "educational" strategy and a "cognitive" or "behavioral" one may not be clear, the latter two usually focus on precise behaviors that present either barriers or cues to adherence, as opposed to the former's more global effort to increase knowledge and change attitudes.

Behavioral strategies involve the systematic application of the principles of social learning and operant or respondent conditioning to problems with medication compliance. Positive reinforcement suggests that if taking medication is rewarded, it will likely increase in the future. To help clients and their families design such interventions, social workers can draw on many potential reinforcers, including consumables (food, drink, cigarettes), leisure activities (sports, gardening, hobbies), possessions (perfume, combs, books), activities (movies, special events, shopping), and manipulative rewards (money, tokens). Social reinforcement (that is, providing pats on the back, side hugs, congratulations, verbal praise, and smiles) is thought to be the most powerful action taken to increase adherence. With the permission of the client, families, peers, coworkers, roommates, or other people significant to clients can be trained to provide reinforcement for medication use.

Providing reminders, prompts, or cues is another useful and well-substantiated way to increase adherence if clients forget to take their medications. These prompts might include a note on the refrigerator door or on the bathroom mirror or a phone call from a family member or friend. Tailoring the medication means finding a way to fit the administration of the drug, or for that matter the prompt itself, to some idiosyncrasy or ritual of the client. Bentley et al. (1990) offers *Harry,* who learns to take his medication at 7:30 right before his favorite TV show, "Wheel of Fortune." A post-a-note reminder stuck to the remote control summarizes the main reasons he takes his medication (helps him to stay calm and to sleep). Engineers are now busy at work designing prototypes of medication containers that may revolutionize medication administration, and the monitoring of adherence, in the future (see chapter 9).

Contracting is a more formal and often written agreement that specifies the contingencies for both adherence and nonadherence. Though familiar to most social workers, contracting often occurs implicitly rather than explicitly in everyday practice. With specific "if-then" statements, delineation of participants' roles, and planned reinforcements, contracting is also extremely common to those who rely on behavioral techniques in other professions or areas of interventions. Bentley et al. (1990) presents *Tammy,* whose social worker helps to create a sophisticated contract in partnership with the family. Tammy takes her medication for a number of points each day (the points decrease the more she has to be reminded), which she can later exchange for backup reinforcers, such as talking to a friend on the phone and renting a video. At the same time, her parents are learning about giving simple, matter-of-fact prompts (as opposed to nagging or unhelpful ones), such as "If you take your medication now, you will get 8 points."

Though cognitive strategies are commonly used to increase medication adherence with people who have medical problems (DiMatteo & DiNicola, 1982; Turk, Salovey, & Litt, 1986), their use is not as well documented with mental health clients. The presumption is that such disturbed thinking or judgment contraindicates their use. Nevertheless, it seems reasonable that self-instruction, guided imagery, relaxation, reframing, and thought-stopping could help in a number of circumstances. For example, a social worker could lead the client in an exercise of guided imagery to help a former drug abuser on antidepressants imagine resisting offers of cocaine and reframing their thoughts of rejection and loneliness into stories of survival and hope. Clients could then learn how to recreate the imagery and practice the reframing at home.

A semistructured three-phase intervention that rests on cognitive theory and motivational interviewing techniques has recently been described in the literature as "compliance therapy" (Kemp, Kirov, Everitt, Hayward, & David, 1998). Here each client individually participates in 4 to 6 sessions lasting 20 to 60 minutes each (approximately $3\frac{1}{2}$ hours per client) over the course of 2 to 3 weeks. Phase 1 involves a review of the person's illness, her/his conceptualization of the illness, and the person's stance toward treatment. Negative experiences are acknowledged, as are the consequences of nonadherence. Phase 2 explores the client's ambivalence toward treatment and the meaning of illness and medication use, including around issues of identity. In phase 3 the clinician introduces analogies of mental illness and treatment with that of physical illness, describes famous sufferers of mental illness, and tries to reframe medication use as an "insurance policy." Data suggests that adherence is improved, as are attitudes toward medications and level of insight into illness. This model is particularly impressive because of its apparent focus on the client's lived experience.

Clearly, our suggested intervention in cases of refusal will also rest on the principles of partnership and self-determination. In certain cases of involuntary treatment, such as rare cases of unmanageable psychosis, the intervention should be "strictly time-limited, gentle, respectful and as non-intrusive as possible" (Parrish, 1993, p. 20). Although an apparent contradiction in terms, this nevertheless seems a goal worthy of pursuit. Fighting about medication is likely to be counterproductive; rather than forced treatment, social workers need an appreciation and empathy toward the client's choice and collaboration, negotiation, problem solving, and planning (Diamond, 1983). One psychiatrist writes, "I respected each patient's right to refuse while insistently keeping alive the possibility that they may decide to accept [it]" (Geller, 1982, p. 113). Problem solving and planning helps clients and families look at their options and prepare for possible crises. This process may involve increasing psychosocial supports, reviewing warning signs and planning for early intervention, or discussing advanced directives or other substituted judgment agreements. Bernheim and Lehman (1985) suggest that clients and families create a long-term timetable for ultimate compliance with treatment, of which medication adherence may only be a part. For example, clients and families could set yearly goals as follows: year 1 as achieving medication adherence, year 2 as self-administration and monitoring, year 3 as attending day treatment, year 4 as attending a support group, and so on. Carpenter and Heinricks (1983) specifically suggest that marked reduction of medication use should be part of any intervention program. Alternative strategies include "targeted" or "intermittent" use, in which clients receive medication only when faced with impending signs of relapse or a return of symptoms.

Social workers can also review their own service delivery and organizational structure for ways to create a climate conducive to accepting diversity in client choices and supporting adherence to a well-planned and supported treatment regimen. For instance, making appropriate training available to staff or revising policies and procedures can help create this climate. Though some note that social workers must sometimes accept that all of those efforts do not work, this is not permission to give up but a call for patience and persistence.

SUMMARY

This chapter has presented adherence as a major issue for clients, families, and mental health providers. Models of adherence give us insight into known risk and protective factors, and familiarity with legal and ethical issues provides even more insight into the complexity of addressing the issues related to adherence. Perhaps most important to remember is this: Health psychology research shows that when providers and family members support and reinforce choice and self-control, acknowledge the feelings of patients, and minimize external controls on behavior, then individuals develop self-regulation values and behavior and improve their adherence to treatment (Williams, Rodin, Ryan, Grolnick, & Deci, 1998). Thus, especially because nonadherence is multi-determined, achieving adherence and dealing productively with refusal over the long term calls for using a number of combined strategies such as self-monitoring, reinforcement, education, and cognitive, behavioral, and other psychosocial strategies in the context of a caring relationship.

8

Medication Monitoring and Management

onitoring both medication and the progress of treatment and general rehabilitation is crucial to reducing client symptoms and enhancing psychosocial functioning. This chapter specifically deals with how social workers can help clients and families monitor and manage their medication in everyday life. Monitoring and managing medications for social workers means helping clients, families, and providers keep track of the medication's therapeutic effects; cope with bothersome physical, psychological, and social side effects; solve any medication-related problems or dilemmas; make decisions about treatment; and negotiate with each other about medication-related issues. For the social worker, monitoring also means acting as an advocate on behalf of clients and their families. Of course, any discussion, with either clients or families, about the rationale, dosage, side effects, and impact of medications offers social workers an opportunity to clarify attitudes about any aspect of treatment and to address these concerns. Even with full medication adherence, clients and families still need education and support as they learn how to manage the illness or disorder.

As stressed in the chapter on medication adherence, "sophisticated and optimal treatment also entails careful attention to those psychosocial variables that may affect the ultimate outcome of the drug treatment regimen" (Docherty, 1986, p. 118). Docherty notes that monitoring drug response should also include monitoring the stress and activity levels of the client with an eye toward avoiding overstimulation. The social worker must first identify expected changes, then compare them to what actually occurs. Thus, as we have said, the role of the social worker in monitoring and managing medication is varied and complex and, like all roles in psychopharmacology, is meant to be carried out in the context of a partnership model of practice.

Luckily, there is now good evidence that mental health clients and their families can and do participate in monitoring and managing medications. For example, families usually understand the prodromal phase of their or their loved one's illnesses. McCandless-Glimcher et al. (1986) summarize the results of a number of studies showing that by far most psychiatric patients and their families can and do recall changes in thoughts, feelings, or behavior prior to the onset or recurrence of symptoms. In their study, 98% of the clients with psychosis knew when their symptoms were getting worse. In another study, 70% of clients diagnosed with schizophrenia knew when they were getting sick again, and 90% could tell when they were getting better (Herz, 1984). More than two-thirds of families and half of clients recognized signs of relapse over a week ahead of the actual relapse. This means that ample time often exists for social workers and others to help make decisions about what next steps can and should be taken. Furthermore, this ability to recognize an impending relapse has been associated with reduced hospitalizations among people with serious mental illness. For example, in a study of 38 clients with schizophrenia, only 8% of those judged to have "early insight" relapsed, versus 50% of those who could not recognize early symptoms (Heinrichs, Cohen, & Carpenter, 1985). Such early insight will most likely be as helpful to those with less serious mental illness or emotional distress and can help social workers design useful interventions for clients and families.

The legal and ethical issues in compliance and refusal will also arise in discussions about monitoring. That is, similar questions emerge in this arena, such as who makes decisions about treatment planning and implementation, what is the "best interest" of the client, and how can the rights of the individual on medication be balanced with the responsibility of families, providers, and society. Because ethical conflict is intrinsic to monitoring and all aspects of social work, translating the lofty values of the profession into strategies for action will always be a challenge.

One ethical issue that arises in monitoring medication is subtle coercion. If good evidence exists to encourage clients to use medication, where do social workers draw the line between coercion and encouragement? In spite of a partnership model of practice, which emphasizes equal power between social worker and client, vestiges of major power differentials persist. Because many agencies still strongly support these differentials, social workers and clients should watch for them, especially the ways that they influence the client's perceptions of decision-making freedom. For example, Cohen (1988) believes there can be no distinction between coercion and encouragement; therefore, social workers should simply not be in the business of recommending psychotropic drugs. However, we believe that even though the line is difficult to draw, social workers should not abandon the task of trying to find the right place to do so.

Ethical issues and conflicts also emerge in the daily management of interdisciplinary relationships (see chapters 2 and 9). For example, although we believe that social workers should actively assist in the medication-related dilemmas of clients and their families, we recognize that the prescribing physician holds the ultimate legal responsibility for choosing and adjusting the types of medication used, prescribing the actual dosages, and watching for precise therapeutic effects, physical side effects, and drug interactions. In addition, nurses and pharmacists each have a long and distinguished professional history related to distributing and explaining medications, a history that should be respected. For example, typically the administration and monitoring of medication is seen by nurses as their "occupational territory" and one of the most important things that distinguishes them from social workers (Jordan, Hardy, & Coleman, 1999). However, nurses apparently mean something a little different by "monitoring" than is described here. When nurses monitor, they look at weight, orthostatic hypotension, bowel movements, dental care, EEG data, heart rate, diet, and hydration and observe involuntary movements, tremors, and drowsiness. Nurses still admit that too often such monitoring of physical effects is not sufficiently comprehensive or systematic. These acknowledged complementary roles of other providers underscore the desirability of interdisciplinary collaboration.

CLIENT SELF-MONITORING OF MEDICATION

We uncovered one example of a fee-for-service medication monitoring service. It was operated by a pharmacist and was associated with impressive outcome data: increased adherence, social support, and independence of folks receiving the service (Gehres, 1986). For an unknown fee, the pharmacist would repackage a client's medications into a customized container; do weekly home visits to monitor adherence, efficacy, and toxicity; reinforce appropriate medication use; provide any needed counseling; and consult with the physician and family as needed. While an intriguing model, especially if it had been implemented in collaboration with a social worker, it doesn't appear to have "caught on." If we look to the literature in such areas as diabetes care or asthma, we see the beginning development of "self-management competencies," which may have relevance to understanding the full domain of needed skills and abilities of clients for facilitating their own recovery. Wilson (1993) characterizes five different areas of needed competency that seem to capture the areas of concern in this chapter. We discuss them as they relate to people taking psychiatric medication:

1. **Preventative medication behaviors.** Making sure clients understand how to use their medications as prescribed.
2. **Precipitant avoidance behaviors.** Making sure clients and families know what things to avoid, such as things that cause stress or overstimulation, or using substances that interact with medications.

3. **Symptom intervention.** Making sure clients and families recognize symptoms and have a plan for when they reoccur.

4. **Communication behaviors.** Making sure clients have the knowledge and skills to optimize their interactions with health care providers and even increase their capacity for self-management.

5. **Health promotion.** Working with clients to learn ways to prevent relapse or control symptoms and, in general, promote good mental and physical health (like diet and exercise).

We know that by far most clients will change their behavior or engage in some kind of self-treatment in response to recognized signs of relapse and side effects. Kabat-Zinn et al. (1992) present the self-regulation strategies of people diagnosed with anxiety disorders, including meditation, relaxation, and other techniques to reduce anxiety, often with good success. Booker et al. (1984) examine the "self-healing" or compensatory practices of 40 inpatients in response to their own depression, stimulus overload, or perceptual problems. Contrary to the myth that people with mental illness always withdraw in response to such symptoms, these researchers have found a high amount of problem-solving efforts.

Self-monitoring involves two things: the client noting the occurrence of some behavior and then systematically recording it (Kopp, 1988). Clients who monitor their own use of medication must track (1) the taking of medication, (2) symptoms, and (3) physical and psychological side effects. Admittedly, clients and social workers can find it challenging to distinguish between symptoms and physical side effects. Client self-monitoring not only helps social workers collect information on which to base daily treatment decisions but also helps clients develop some level of self-awareness and increases their involvement and sense of power in the treatment process (Kopp, 1988; Lukoff, Liberman, & Nuechterlein, 1986). Even clients who do not begin with much understanding of their illness or distress can develop it in the context of a caring therapeutic relationship (Heinricks et al., 1985). One program even used self-management as a major focus of an inpatient treatment effort. So they could become better prepared for self-medication after discharge, clients on a psychiatric unit obtained their own medication from the nurses' station (Coudreat-Quinn, Emmons, & McMorrow, 1992). The mandatory education program, like many of those discussed in chapter 6, included identifying and managing side effects and learning how to obtain more information on specific drugs.

Perhaps the most common concrete strategy for self-monitoring medications is using a checklist of symptoms, either an existing one or an idiosyncratic one developed from the known experiences of the client. Identifying the warning signs of relapse and common side effects is almost always part of comprehensive psychoeducational programs for mental health clients and their families (see chapter 6). Though an existing checklist may have dozens of items with rather general categories, such as "trouble sleeping," "avoiding activities," and "confusion" (see Table 8.1), social workers can help clients and families create measures that are more precise and individualized, and

Table 8.1 Symptom Checklist

_____ Nervousness, tenseness
_____ Trouble sleeping (too much, too little)
_____ More than usual fatigue, no energy
_____ Depression
_____ Difficulty thinking or concentrating
_____ Less active than usual
_____ Unable to get going (get up, go)
_____ Irritability
_____ Difficulty doing work
_____ Avoiding activities with others
_____ Moodiness
_____ Trouble eating (too much, too little)
_____ Confusion
_____ Hear voices
_____ Recurrent thoughts
_____ People are talking/laughing at you
_____ Others tell you that you are strange
_____ Get special messages (from the TV, radio)
_____ Lapses in memory
_____ Think someone is trying to hurt you
_____ Getting harassed by others
_____ Nightmares
_____ Religious concerns
_____ Headaches
_____ Think you have special powers
_____ Things look funny
_____ Think everyone can hear your thoughts
_____ Trouble talking so people can understand
_____ Feel like you are losing control of your thoughts
_____ Something is controlling or putting thoughts in your head
_____ Feel like hurting self
_____ Speech problems
_____ Sexual concerns
_____ You see things that others don't
_____ Heart pounding
_____ Feel like you are really not here
_____ Feel pressure in your head
_____ Feel something terrible or strange is happening to your body
_____ More active than usual
_____ Legal problems or trouble with the police
_____ Can't stop doing something over and over
_____ Having trouble getting along with other people
_____ Feel being controlled by a device (computer, electrodes)
_____ Feel like hurting others
_____ Everyone around you seems dead

Based on McCandless-Glimcher et al., 1986.

perhaps less overwhelming, such as "How many days last week did you wake up before 6:30 a.m.?" or "How much did you avoid contact with the members at Sunrise House today? a lot, a good bit, some, not much." Falloon et al. (1984) used the latter strategy in their 2-year, behavioral family management study in which participants identified two "warning signals" from the client's previous relapse. These then were rated monthly on a severity scale between 1 and 7.

Two more examples may help to demonstrate this approach. A social worker helps "Bob" create a graph to monitor the side effects of his antidepressant medication as well as his depressive symptoms. On it, Bob learns to keep track of his level of hopelessness, the number of hours he sleeps, dry mouth, and sexual dysfunction. The social worker also helps "Joan," a 62-year-old woman with a psychotic disorder and a history of numerous relapses and currently taking fluphenazine and benztropine, create a simple checklist of her unique "warning signals," on which she can write "yes" or "no," depending on whether or not she experiences the symptoms on a given day. Items include "Voices are using profanity," "Voices are getting louder," "Can sit through all of *Jeopardy.* " The sheet she fills out in the morning also has previously negotiated steps for her to take in case of problems. Obviously, as with any tool, clients and/or family members should be motivated and willing to use checklists that also are easy to use and are periodically checked for accuracy and relevancy.

In their comprehensive review of self-management interventions, Ivanoff and Stern (1992) report that individuals use a wide array of these techniques to address their physical and mental health concerns, including chronic pain, insomnia, depression, anger, anxiety, agoraphobia, and lack of assertiveness. Though self-monitoring "was the single component most often associated with positive outcome" (p. 37), they found not one study in the major social work journals that addresses the maintenance and generalization of self-monitoring skills. As such, social workers cannot assume that once clients have been taught to use self-monitoring techniques, they will do so indefinitely. The rationale for medication in general and medication monitoring in particular may need regular revisiting and reinforcement. Clients need to see that what they do impacts clinical decision making and the quality of their lives. Social workers can and should be a part of making those connections.

USING EXISTING MEASURES TO GUIDE MONITORING

In addition to the simple monitoring tools described above, social workers and clients could use one of the many existing rapid assessment inventories currently in use by clinicians and researchers with a range of disorders and symptoms (see also Bond & Lader, 1996; and the special issue of *Research on Social Work Practice:* Bentley, 1998; Dziegieliewski & Leon, 1998; Sundel & Sundel, 1998; Walsh, 1998). Here is a list of a few possibilities:

The *Psychiatric Symptom Assessment Scale* (PSAS), most often used for people with schizophrenia, includes 23 items, each rated from 1 to 7. The PSAS provides an overall score as well as scores for the domains of anxiety/depression, positive behavior symptoms, positive verbal symptoms, deficit symptoms, and paranoia (Bigelow & Berthot, 1989). The PSAS can be administered during the course of a 30-minute interview. All items and each point along the rating scale include assessment and rating guidelines.

The *Scale for the Assessment of Negative Symptoms* (SANS) and *Scale for the Assessment of Positive Symptoms* (SAPS) are complementary instruments (Andreasen, 1982; Andreasen & Olsen, 1982). The SANS includes 25 items rated along a 6-point scale with 5 subscales (affect, poverty of speech, apathy, anhedonia, and impairment of attention). The SAPS includes 35 items, 4 subscales (hallucinations, delusions, bizarreness, and positive thought disorder), and one global assessment of affect. Both are designed for use in conjunction with client interviews, clinical observations, family member observations, and reports from other providers.

The *Abnormal Involuntary Movement Scale* is a widely used and simple-to-use rating scale for dyskinesia. Clinicians rate the severity of movements in the face and mouth, extremities, and trunk on a 4-point scale based on their observations in response to certain simple requests (sticking the tongue out, sitting in various positions) (NIMH, 1985).

The *Barnes Akathisia Scale* measures the extent of movement disorder associated with use of antipsychotics. Clinician ratings are based on observations of at least two minutes of the person under two conditions, sitting and in conversation while standing (Barnes, 1989).

The *Simpson-Angus Neurological Rating Scale* involves clinician ratings on a 4-point scale of the severity of Parkinsonian side effects such as problematic gait, arm dropping, shoulder shaking, elbow or wrist rigidity, swinging of the legs, tremors, and salivation (Simpson & Angus, 1970).

The *Extrapyramidal Symptom Rating Scale* (Chouinard, Ross-Chouinard, Annable, & Jones, 1980) assesses the extent of parkinsonism, dystonias, and akathisia in consumers.

The newest scale noted here is the *Maryland Psychiatric Research Center Scale,* which is designed to more precisely measure dyskinesia induced by antipsychotic medications. It is a semistructured observational instrument that relies on a discrimination of anatomic areas and greater range of severity ratings (7-point scale) (Cassady, Thaker, Summerfelt, & Tamminga, 1997).

Hudson's *Generalized Contentment Scale* is a self-administered 25-item Likert scale developed by a social worker specifically to assess nonpsychotic depression over time (Hudson, 1992). It has excellent internal consistency, and the author provides clear guidelines regarding the meaning of scores along the continuum.

Brief Depression Rating Scale (BDRS) (Kellner, 1986) is another practical tool for the clinical social worker. The format of the BDRS is similar to a mania rating scale we describe later. Together the two scales can be used to assess clients with bipolar disorder as well as depression. The BDRS is an 8-item scale that measures depression by clinical observation. In this case, the social worker rates the following observations on a 9-point scale that ranges from "incapacitating" to "absent"; the areas included are depressive mood and feelings of despair; somatic symptoms; lack of interest, initiative, and activity; sleep disturbance; anxiety, worry, and tension; appearance; depressive beliefs; and suicidal thoughts or behavior. Individual items can be summed for a total score ranging from 8 (no depression) to 72 (high depression). The worker can monitor specific symptoms as well. The BDRS has demonstrated high interobserver reliability and concurrent validity.

The Mania Rating Scale (MRS) is an 11-item, clinician-administered instrument which can be completed by a clinician during a 15-to-30-minute interview (Young, Biggs, Ziegler, & Meyer, 1978). The scale items include mood, energy, sexual interest, sleep, irritability, speech rate and amount, language and thought disorder, speech content, disruptive and aggressive behavior, appearance, and insight. Scoring is based on both the client's report of his or her condition during the previous 48 hours *and* the social worker's observations during the interview (with an emphasis on the latter). Four scale items (irritability, speech rate and amount, speech content, and disruptive/aggressive behavior) are given greater weight to compensate for the anticipated poor reliability of manic clients. Each scale item includes 5 levels of severity, and a client receives an overall score of 0 to 60 from a summing of all item scores. The scale has demonstrated high inter-rater reliability, along with concurrent (compared with two other scales) and predictive (hospital days) validity.

The *Hamilton Anxiety Rating Scale* (HARS) (Hamilton, 1959) is a practical monitoring instrument and the most widely utilized pharmacological outcome rating scale for anxiety. The HARS, which is completed by the clinician, consists of 14 items scored along a 5-point Likert scale to yield total scores of 0 to 70. The scale includes two factors reflecting the psychological (anxious mood, tension, fearfulness, insomnia, intellectual and cognitive function, depressed mood, and behavior during the interview) and physical (muscular, sensory, cardiovascular, respiratory, intestinal, urinary, and autonomic functions) dimensions of anxiety.

Anxiety Rating for Children-Revised (Bernstein, Crosby, Perwien, & Borchardt, 1996) uses the HARS as its basis. It consists of 11 items scored on a Likert scale from 0 to 4 and includes the same two anxiety dimensions. With these instruments, both demonstrating satisfactory validity and reliability, the social worker has a useful means to monitor a client's anxiety over time, including response to medications.

Many instruments, most of which are behavior rating scales, are available for assessing and monitoring the symptoms of persons with ADHD. Because the symptoms of the disorder must be present in more than one social context, it should not be surprising that instruments have been developed for use by family members, teachers, and clients themselves, as well as for human service professionals.

One useful symptom measure for social workers is *ADHD Rating Scale-IV* (DuPaul, Power, Anastopoulos, & Reid, 1998). This instrument consists of 18 items taken directly from the DSM-IV list of symptoms for attention deficit/hyperactivity disorder. Some of the items have been reworded for clarity and brevity. Nine items are devoted to each of the two subtypes of the disorder (inattention and impulsivity/hyperactivity). Two versions of the scale have been developed; one for school and another for home settings, but both are very similar. The person completing the scale is instructed to read each item and consider to what extent it has been manifested in the client's behavior during the past 6 months. Each symptom is rated on a 4-point Likert scale (never/rarely, sometimes, often, and very often). The authors have developed scoring norms for assessing whether the disorder of ADHD exists, but the scale can also be used to monitor symptom fluctuation in persons already diagnosed and who may be taking medication. Social workers can adapt and complete either version of the instrument themselves; they can also provide family and school personnel with the form and review their responses. The *ADHD Rating Scale-IV* has demonstrated good internal consistency, test-retest reliability, and concurrent validity with client behaviors and other established instruments.

CONCRETE STEPS FOR COPING WITH SIDE EFFECTS

Clients cite bothersome side effects as a major reason for nonadherence. In addition, research has shown that the severity of such side effects is inversely related to the client's quality of life (Sullivan, Wells, & Leake, 1992). Thus, it is important that social workers respond to complaints and concerns about side effects in a way that supports the client's treatment goals, validates the client's experiences, and provides reasonable choices for action.

When complaints about side effects emerge, social workers should first make sure the medications are being correctly administered. However, because most physical side effects abate after a few days to a few weeks, physicians usually first recommend encouraging the client simply to wait a while. Social workers should recognize that this advice may sound simplistic and patronizing to clients asked to endure uncomfortable and meaning-laden physiological reactions.

The next piece of advice the prescribing physician usually gives is to reduce the dose, add another medication, or change the medication. Because management of dosages and schedules is largely an individual matter, relying on trial and error, minor or even major adjustments in medication are obviously extremely common. Direct observation by others and blood tests provide two possible sources of information about the effects of medication. However, because clients' descriptions of their experiences with the effects and side effects usually provide the most important information for these adjustments, later in this chapter we will discuss skills to help clients talk to and negotiate with their physicians and psychiatrists.

Client and family guides and manuals often provide the best sources of concrete and simple ways to live with some less serious physical side effects (e.g., Falloon et al., 1984; Mueser & Gingerich, 1994). For example, advice to deal with drowsiness centers on taking the medication at or near bedtime and scheduling short naps during the day. Clients may reduce akathisia or internal restlessness as well as muscle stiffness by stretching or other physical activity. Dry mouth can be helped by sucking on sugar-free candy or sipping water; constipation by drinking 8 to 10 glasses of water daily, eating fresh fruits and vegetables, and using stool softeners or Metamucil, if needed. With increased weight, clients may need to change medications or just get some commonsense advice about diet and regular exercise. Orthostatic hypotension, or dizziness upon standing, can be combated by helping the client practice getting up very slowly from a lying or seated position. Sensitivity to sunburn responds well to sunscreens and avoiding peak sun exposure. For some physical side effects, such as hormonal changes, tremors, and rashes, there are usually no quick solutions. Other side effects, such as agranulocytosis, aplastic anemia, acute dystonias, and neuroleptic malignant syndrome, demand immediate medical attention.

Tardive dyskinesia (TD) has created the most controversy to date about side effects, with the possible exception of concern over fluoxetine (see chapter 9). Critiques of psychiatry, for example, have speculated that "resistance and incomplete recognition" of TD has a long history and relates to issues of client subordinance, professional dominance, and the overreliance on drug treatments in general (Brown & Funk, 1986, p. 116). At the center of the controversy lie questions about true prevalence and the availability of effective treatment. Estimates of the prevalence of TD vary widely. Feltner and Hertzman (1993) estimate that about 20% of those who receive long-term treatment with neuroleptics will develop TD. Most cases will be "mild but persistent," but "some may be irreversible" (p. 25). Feltner and Hertzman also note that a 1992 report concludes that there are no safe and effective treatments for TD. Such treatments have included vitamin E, calcium channel blockers, dopamine agonists, lithium, and benzodiazepines. Apparently, the best advice offered by psychiatrists is still to discontinue the drug or reduce the dosage. Feltner and Hertzman report that 40% of the clients in their own studies who did this achieved a 50% reduction of TD symptoms. They also acknowledge that because reducing or stopping medication is quite difficult for some individuals with TD, social workers may need to make a careful assessment and review of risks and benefits. Clearly, social workers can and should participate in these important decision-making processes.

Besides monitoring physical side effects, both clients and social workers should monitor the psychological, emotional, and social side effects of taking medication. It is true that some people may need to take medication for the rest of their lives. Still, social workers might be insensitive to how this idea might affect the client's sense of identity as a self-determining human being. They are likely to need to help the client come to terms with the need to take medication, to gradually incorporate this idea into his or her sense of self. Clients may need support in adjusting to a new self-image and the ways that they believe others, friends, family, and "society," may view him or her. It may take months, even years before clients accept the reality of psychotropic medications in their lives; indeed, this may never happen. In the roles of consultant and educator, the social worker can work with clients, family members, and perhaps others in the client's social environment to help them understand anguish, anxiety, or even the normal ambivalence generated by this identity issue.

As discussed in chapter 2, a potential negative outcome of psychotropic medication use occurs when clients come to feel that *only* medication can help them function adequately, that they themselves and the providers in their lives are powerless to generate changes in other ways. Assuming a helplessness with providers and peers, clients may fail to fully invest in other interventions. Many of the case examples in this text reflect clients' complex reactions to learning that they need medications to function acceptably in their social worlds. As a validator, the social worker can help to ensure that these clients maintain an awareness of their strengths and other resources that will help promote healthy social functioning.

Some clients may also develop a dependence on the physician or other providers, including the social worker. Clients may become unassertive with caregivers—that is, not disclose the full details of medication effects and life events—if they fear that doing so may disrupt any predictable patterns of daily functioning established with people in their lives (Walsh, 2000). It is certainly undesirable for clients to withhold information about medication or any other intervention issues from professionals who need to understand their reactions to these strategies. If social workers develop a relationship of trust with clients in accordance with the partnership model of practice, this situation can be avoided.

Another very different adverse psychological effect is clients' anger at having to take medication. Their anger may center on the idea that they have been diagnosed with a disorder requiring medication, that they perceive providers to be promoting the notion that the clients are "ill," or that others in their environment, including family and friends, are stigmatizing them. These feelings may also represent a grief reaction. To accept that their situations can be dealt with constructively, clients may first need to be encouraged to experience and express these negative feelings, so that they can eventually work through them. On the other hand, clients may disagree that they have an illness, and never accept that there is a need to take medication. Again, the social worker can best address this issue through his or her relationship with the client, as well as through collateral work with the client's significant others. Appropriate roles include that of the consultant, who acknowledges the normalcy of the client's point of view. Medication education is another major component of this process.

In addition to regularly inquiring and helping clients articulate and reflect on these issues, depending on their level of functioning or interest, social workers might also encourage clients to keep a journal of their reactions or express their feelings in art. Although no art therapy program to date explicitly aims to help people monitor and cope with their own responses and side effects to medications, such therapy has helped people with such disorders as depression, bipolar disorder, and schizophrenia (e.g., Buchalter-Katz, 1985; Green, Wehing, & Talesk, 1987; Wadeson, 1987). In the field of social work, Potocky (1993) describes the use of an art therapy group in a residential facility to help residents increase their social skills through self-expression and social interaction. Admittedly, these approaches for encouraging expression, ventilation, and developing insight are intuitively appealing but in general untested and might best be thought of as potentially useful adjuncts to more traditional supportive techniques (Lisenbee, 1994).

However, it is hard to imagine techniques more relevant and useful to medication management than traditional social work strategies such as empathetic listening, support, reflective discussion, and interpretation. This is evident when helping clients manage the differences between their expectations of a drug's effect versus the actual effect. For example, clozapine has often been associated with dramatic improvements as shown in the movie *Awakenings*. Although some individuals who were formerly unable to complete logical sentences or participate fully in daily activities are now holding excellent jobs and are rediscovering the world, these success stories are by no means a universal or even typical response to clozapine. Without the same results, others using the same drug can experience overwhelming disappointment or despair. We suspect that this scenario is played out on a smaller scale in the lives of our clients all the time. Obviously, social workers can and should offer the warmth, empathy, support, and genuine concern that is needed in these situations, because both outcomes may require huge adjustments in emotional functioning, self-concept, and lifestyle.

Interestingly, there is evidence that persons with certain personality characteristics may be more responsive to both the positive and adverse effects of medications used to treat anxiety and depression. These findings are believed to be related to the expectations that persons have about the effects, both therapeutic and adverse, of medications; that is, the consumers may have a psychological orientation that influences their very real biological reactions to medications (Fisher & Greenberg, 1997; Frank & Frank, 1993). There is a trend for persons with high sociability to respond positively to medications compared to those who perceive themselves as more self-sufficient and inclined toward physical and emotional distance from others. For sociable persons the use of medications may represent a social encounter; the person is particularly tuned in to opportunities for bolstering the sense of self on the basis of interactions with others. In other studies, persons with the characteristic of acquiescence (stimulus accepting, uninhibited, and conforming) react more strongly to same-dose medications as non-acquiescers (those who are stimulus rejecting, inhibited, and independent). The rationale for this finding is that the acquiescer wants to interact with others, to evoke responsiveness from others, and to transmit a willingness to be part of a social structure. This is not an area of research that is being explored in depth today, but it is important to consider that the act of taking medications has different meanings for consumers, and some of these may facilitate or inhibit the response to some medications.

DECISION MAKING AND PROBLEM SOLVING IN MEDICATION MANAGEMENT

One could argue that problem solving is the heart of social work practice. As such, most texts on social work present various models of the problem-solving process and direct practitioners to work collaboratively through the steps with their clients as systematically as possible. Newer texts include substantial content on how to teach clients the problem-solving process and apply it to concerns and decisions that arise in everyday life (e.g., Hepworth, Rooney, & Larsen, 1997). Other helping professions also value such training for clients as an avenue for increased social competence. For example, D'zurilla (1986) looks at the effectiveness of problem-solving training across a wide variety of target groups, including people with alcohol dependency or psychiatric problems, depression, agoraphobia, stress, weight problems, marital and family problems, vocational indecision, and problems with academic achievement. He concludes that very promising support for using problem-solving training as a clinical intervention can help clinicians move away from defect models of psychopathology. Problem solving, then, becomes a portable self-management technique and coping strategy that serves as a buffer against future problems.

You can easily find specific examples of successful problem-solving training programs for people with mental illness and emotional distress. These are often presented as the backbone of family psychoeducation programs. Positive outcomes range from increased problem-solving knowledge and behaviors to more global measures of outcome such as increased social functioning and decreased depression. In examining the problem-solving sessions of their behavioral family management project, Falloon et al. (1984) show that "coping with illness" was the most frequent topic chosen, representing the content of 17% of all problem-solving sessions. Rather than being raised mostly at the beginning of their intervention project, as might be expected, the "coping with illness" concerns were evenly distributed throughout the two years, highlighting the need for social workers to continue to address and respond to medication, side effects, and symptoms over the long run.

Problem-solving training involves reviewing the six steps of the problem-solving process and then applying them to real decisions, problems, or questions. We have taken the following steps from Hepworth, Rooney, and Larsen

(1997), Falloon et al. (1984), and Mueser and Gingerich (1994) and have provided an example for each.

1. **Define the problem.** The first, most important, and most difficult step in problem solving involves determining what exactly the problem is. This is achieved through discussing the problem openly and sharing perspectives, either in a group or with a provider; clients may also define problems by themselves, using the learned steps outside clinical supervision. Mueser and Gingerich (1994) suggest providing a "Defining Problems Exercise" to help clients and families understand the challenges in defining problems. That is, they suggest offering a case vignette with which clients and families could "practice" every step of the process before working with their own problems.

2. **Generate possible solutions.** In this step, participants share their ideas for solutions to the agreed-upon problem in a nonevaluative environment. With such brainstorming, everyone should be encouraged to participate. Even outrageous ideas for solutions should be made welcome. Falloon et al. (1984) suggest that at least five or six solutions be identified and that great care be taken at this point to avoid evaluative comments, such as "That's a crazy idea" or "Yes, let's do that!"

3. **Evaluate the pros and cons of each solution.** This step involves evaluating the positive and negative aspects of each brainstormed idea. Mueser and Gingerich (1994) suggest moving through this step rather quickly by highlighting only main strengths and weaknesses. Falloon et al. (1984) also suggest avoiding lengthy debates but emphasizing that each idea has merits.

4. **Choose the "best" solution.** This step involves coming to consensus on a solution or some combination of solutions based on the evaluation. It calls for clear communication and a willingness to negotiate and compromise.

5. **Plan how to carry out the solution.** Even the best of solutions cannot be implemented without some plan of action. In this step, plans are broken down into manageable tasks; assigned to participants according to interest, time, resources, and ability; and included with a time frame for completion. Discussion that anticipates potential negative consequences may also help. Participants should practice steps that require some overt skill or activity. Mueser and Gingerich (1994) provide a suggested "Action Planning Worksheet," much like a typical social work contract. It should specify the task, the person assigned to carry it out, the target date for completion, and a column to be checkmarked upon completion of the task. Clients might want to place this worksheet on the refrigerator as a reminder. Falloon et al. (1984) suggest that someone in the family or group (when relevant) be elected as coordinator.

6. **Review implementation and praise *all* efforts.** At some future mutually agreed on time, the group will evaluate the progress of task completion in particular and problem solving in general. Social workers should lavishly praise all efforts. In cases in which individual clients use

the process on their own, they should be encouraged to reward all accomplishments. It may be necessary to return to other steps in the process, particularly if the tasks were completed but the problem remains. The cyclical nature of problem solving should be stressed. Partial success is a useful way to describe the most common outcomes of problem solving. Failure should be reserved for those rare occasions when no efforts are made to achieve progress.

It may help to consider how such problem-solving efforts might help in an actual case taken from chapter 1. Darlene is a 22-year-old, single woman, unemployed and currently living with her sister in an apartment but financially supported by her parents, who were very involved in her treatment planning and care. Darlene suffers from bipolar disorder, which has required a number of hospitalizations in the last 3 years. Though stable on a combination of antipsychotic and mood-stabilizing drugs, Darlene stopped taking them. Her parents became furious with the social worker and the agency when they found they did not know about it. Darlene finally revealed that she hadn't been honest about her adherence and was actually intentionally trying to prompt a regression out of her own fears of increasing responsibility. However, it was too late. The family decided to terminate care from this agency.

In this case, the client and family might have come together to solve a number of problems to prevent the impending relapse and the major disruption in service to Darlene. For example, they could have examined Darlene's worsening symptoms, her covert noncompliance, her fears of independence, the family's anger at the agency, or even continuous care for Darlene in the transition to a new provider. In discussing Darlene's worsening symptoms, joint problem solving would have afforded opportunities for the group to define the problem from each perspective, to express their feelings and disappointments, and to offer important reassurances. Darlene's nonadherence and her fears about becoming more independent would likely have surfaced. Brainstorming possible solutions might have yielded ideas such as increasing responsibility more slowly, adding psychosocial supports, arranging for additional counseling about her fears, learning more about medication, and adding tangible rewards for adherence. Each person in the group could help evaluate alternatives and select and monitor a solution or combination of solutions.

Hepworth, Rooney, and Larsen (1997) offer much guidance on how to prepare clients effectively for problem solving, how to introduce the process to them, and how to manage interaction during the sessions. These guidelines stress laying the groundwork for problem solving early in the intervention phase; maintaining a positive, collaborative stance; and being sure to praise and highlight connections between problem-solving efforts and goal attainment. As with skills training, problem-solving training begins with providing clients and families a rationale for the skill, which in this case is the use of a step-by-step process. Being specific when discussing problems and solutions, focusing on the present, breaking a problem into smaller parts (partialization), and listening actively are all keys to successful use of problem solving.

Because both teaching and problem solving work well in large audiences, many problem-solving training programs focus on families, groups of clients in clinics, support groups, clubhouses, or residential facilities as the targets of intervention. Nevertheless, social workers can readily teach problem solving skills to individuals. Though the content of training programs is remarkably similar, usually a review of the six steps just summarized, the suggested format often varies. For example, D'zurilla (1986) describes different methods of presentation for teaching problem solving, including didactic presentations, slides, video demonstrations and taped practice, specially created games, and group exercises. Role playing and homework are always crucial components of such programs.

Foxx and Bittle (1989) have developed a program that specifically addresses problem solving for medication issues. They present a curriculum for teaching people with mental illness what they call assertive problem solving, with similar curriculums for people with developmental disabilities, brain injuries, and adolescents. Curriculum materials include trainee score-recording forms, a facilitator's scoring guide, and evaluation forms to make precise tracking of progress possible. Participants are taught to use a problem-solving "cue card," which provides guiding questions for the participants to solve case scenarios. By applying the following questions to each problem situation, participants build problem-solving competence:

1. When will the problem be solved?
2. Where would you (or a friend) look for help?
3. Would you talk to him, her, or them?
4. What would you say?

Participants receive 48 problem-situation cards, with cases that deal with many topics such as obtaining professional help, stating one's rights, interpersonal issues, authority figures, community resources, and medication. Here are some examples of the problem situations that relate to medication, adapted from Foxx and Bittle (1989):

1. Every time you take your medication you become very fidgety and can't concentrate on one thing very long. What should you do?
2. A friend of yours has been taken off her medication for some time and doesn't understand why her doctor has placed her back on it. She is thinking of not filling the prescription and not letting her doctor know. How would you help?
3. You feel the treatment you've been receiving at the community mental health center is not helping. What should you do?

In example 1, the answers to the "cue card" questions might be

1. The problem will be solved when I am not fidgety and stop losing my concentration after taking my medication.

2. I could look up my doctor or pharmacy in the phone book.

3. I could talk to my pharmacist, doctor, or social worker.

4. I could say, "Whenever I take my medication, I get fidgety and can't concentrate. I am taking [name of medication]. What should I do?"

Social workers could easily adapt or expand not only the case scenarios but also the answers to the questions for use with other medication-related problems. These might include the ambiguity some clients feel about the rationale for medication use, the impact of medication on the client's sense of self, adherence issues, the client's concerns about his or her relationship with the prescribing physician, and any agency policy that precludes effective psychopharmacology practice.

NEGOTIATING MEDICATION ISSUES WITH HEALTH CARE PROVIDERS

Clients and families need certain communication skills and tools to discuss medication-related concerns with the client's providers. Similarly, as a foundation for a productive partnership, social workers must also have the knowledge and skills to negotiate with clients, families, and physicians and other health care providers. At the most basic level, providing clients and their families with a structured checklist of "agenda items" to be discussed with the prescribing physician might be extremely helpful. One approach (Chewning & Sleath, 1996) is for clients to be PREPARED for the meeting, that is, to discuss the

✔ **P** rescription

✔ **R** easons or indications for the prescription

✔ **E** xpectations or client-focused benefit

✔ **P** robability of benefits

✔ **A** lternative treatments available

✔ **R** isks of the medication

✔ **E** xpenses involved (both direct and indirect costs)

✔ **D** ecision

As presented in chapter 6, a few psychoeducation programs include how to negotiate with mental health providers. For example, both Collins-Colon (1990) and Dow, Verdi, and Sacco (1991) stress principles of negotiation in their respective successful medication-management protocols. They suggest teaching clients to remain calm during all communication, to learn how to accurately describe their current problems, to jot down individualized questions about their medications to bring to their appointments, to write down the answers and repeat them back to ensure clarity, to make sure all information is clearly understood before they leave, and to teach clients to be assertive, not aggressive.

In fact, assertiveness provides a solid base for the communication skills needed to effectively negotiate with health care providers. Galassi, Galassi, and Vedder (1981) review a number of definitions of assertiveness and conclude that it means being able to communicate one's desires and feelings directly. This includes being able to say no; to ask for favors or make requests of others; to express positive and negative feelings; to initiate, continue, and terminate conversations; to accept and give compliments; to express personal opinions; and to stand up for one's rights. Thus, assertiveness is a necessary precondition to effective negotiation. One can see how clients would need to be able to say "No, I don't want to discontinue medication until after I start my new job" or "Please change my medication to one that does not increase my appetite, because I already have a weight problem" or "Dr. Smith, I'd really like to clarify your availability after-hours" or even "I don't think the medication is helping."

Focused discussions with clients and families about assertiveness versus aggressiveness and nonassertiveness may serve as a helpful precursor to more specifically directed communication skills training. Clients can help articulate the differences in these three interactive styles and how their own and others' behaviors reflect them. Hepworth, Rooney, and Larsen (1997), for example, note that assertive communication is characterized by a relaxed posture and direct eye contact with appropriately varied eye contact and moderately expressive gestures. On the other hand, aggressive communication is characterized by a glaring stare, pursed lips, rigid posture, and loud and sarcastic speech. Nonassertive communication is characterized by evasive eye contact, nervousness, and soft, whiny, and hesitant speech.

Social workers can also help clients and families explore the feelings that each style elicits. How does it feel when someone points a finger and raises his or her voice? To understand how these differences relate to medication management, clients can generate examples (or social workers can create case scenarios based on their experience) of aggressive or passive behavior preventing some desired outcome, such as getting a timely appointment with the prescribing physician or getting the physician to agree to reduce dosage. Examples can also be shared of assertive behavior helping to reach a goal, such as getting a "drug holiday" or trying one of the newer generation of antidepressants.

Liberman, Kane, Vaccaro, & Wirshing (1987) detail how to teach clients the microskills of negotiating with their health care providers, one of the four skill areas in their Medication Management Module (see chapter 6). They provide 11 specific requisite behaviors under the heading "Negotiating with Health Care Providers," behaviors that look remarkably like those needed for assertiveness. Effective negotiation means that clients should be able to demonstrate the following skills (adapted from Eckman & Liberman, 1990; Eckman et al., 1990, 1992):

- pleasantly greet the provider
- describe their problem specifically
- tell the length of its occurrence
- describe the extent of their discomfort
- specifically request some action
- repeat or clarify the doctor's advice
- ask about the expected time frame of effect
- thank the provider for assistance
- establish and maintain good eye contact
- maintain good posture
- speak audibly and clearly

These skills can be taught using a structured skills-training process. We have summarized this process as six steps conducive to working with individuals, groups, or families.

1. **Discuss the rationale for the skill.** The first step involves engaging the clients in the training process by building together a motivating rationale for learning the skill and each behavior required to perform the skill. Clients need to see, for example, the connections among effectively asking questions of physicians, understanding the physician's dosage rationale, and acquiring a generally greater knowledge of and motivation for using the psychotropic medication.

2. **Identify the components of the skill.** Every skill can and should be broken down into manageable components or steps, which the client can help articulate. Thus, for example, clients who try to get clarification of medication orders should perform at least three steps: (1) looking at the physician/health care provider, (2) telling the provider what they heard her or him say about the medication orders, saying "I understood you to say. . . " or "Did you say that. . .," and (3) directly asking for feedback, such as "Is that right?" The extent to which components of any given skill are broken down depends on the functioning level of the client or family member.

3. **Model the skill.** In this step, the social worker actually demonstrates each of the components outlined in the previous step. The client or another group member can play the part of the physician. Given what is known about the power of observational learning, this step is crucial. It also reinforces a partnership model of practice. The social worker might begin by saying, "If I were to ask for clarification of the dosage levels, I would sit up straight, look at Dr. Jones, and say, 'I hear you saying you are

going to increase my dose because you want to see if it will lower my anxiety level faster so that I can get some better sleep, is that right?' Now, if you were the physician, you would say, 'Yes that's right, you haven't had any really bothersome side effects yet, so we'll try this and see how it goes.'"

4. **Role-play each component.** This is where the client walks through the components in a role-play exercise. Clients can help set the stage by providing examples from their own lives of situations where the skill might have been useful, obviously providing greater relevance.

5. **Evaluate the role play.** Next, the social worker offers much positive feedback that is behaviorally specific, then some corrective feedback. The social worker encourages the client to practice the role play again, incorporating the feedback received. Feedback should attend to both verbal and nonverbal behaviors, and participants should receive an opportunity to share their feelings about the role play.

6. **Apply the skill in real life.** Hepworth, Rooney, and Larsen (1997) call this step the "ultimate test of the skill training efforts" (p. 426). In this step, the client actually uses the skill in a real-life situation. Because this task usually entails some preparation, problem solving is almost always a useful and important adjunct to skills training. As in problem solving, social workers can help clients find the internal and external resources (that is, the courage, the time, the money, the telephone) to carry out the skill. Anticipating problems and disappointments is also important preparation. What will the client do if the physician ignores her requests for clarification? What if the physician belittles him? Debriefing and booster sessions can help consolidate learning and ensure proper credit. Praise is offered for successes, no matter how small.

Liberman's modules, as described in chapter 6, often rely on videotaped case scenarios as part of the modeling step of skills training. Videotape can also be used to provide effective feedback. These tools may become much more widely available in the future. In addition, more interactive and individualized computer-assisted instruction, video discs, and the like are being developed.

Liberman et al. (1987), in their guidelines for providers negotiating with clients and families about medication, echo the principles we have emphasized throughout the book, especially those discussed in relation to medication adherence and refusal. They suggest that all mental health providers

1. employ effective communication, including active listening, and acknowledge the client and family as "experts"; reinforce mutual collaboration; and encourage the expression of goals, needs, and wishes;

2. acknowledge the rights and responsibilities of clients and families concerned about and actively involved in medication-related dilemmas;

3. solicit their reactions and suggestions about medication management;

4. maintain a nonpunitive stance;

5. recognize and accept that not all treatment decisions will be accepted; and

6. be prepared for difficult negotiations.

Difficult situations may require compromise: restating your position while acknowledging the client's or family member's position; ignoring provocation, criticism, and threats; focusing on benefits; and, when all else fails, politely terminating the interaction. All suggested responses begin with listening empathetically to clients and their families and exploring their reactions to medication issues. Docherty (1986) reiterates, saying that "negotiation and collaborative decision-making" is an essential component of all client-provider relationships with "the rights and responsibilities of both made clear" (p. 124).

ADVOCACY IN MEDICATION MANAGEMENT

It has been said that "the history of the social work profession has in large measure been based on the premise of client advocacy," and yet "putting this rhetoric into practice techniques has been underutilized" (Lurie, 1982, p. 77). The underutilization of advocacy as an intervention technique in psychopharmacology is no doubt related to issues of status and power in interdisciplinary teams and to a lack of clear roles in medication management. Connaway (1975) and Mailick and Ashley (1981) were among the first to ask questions about how advocacy and interdisciplinary collaboration fit (or don't fit) together. For example, they both note that while collaboration calls up notions of cooperation and cohesion, advocacy implies subtle coercion and potential conflict. Thus, a healthy dose of political acumen can help a social worker make judgments about when and how to advocate.

In defining the social workers' role of advocacy, Gerhart writes that they "monitor the rights and entitlements of their clients" and "focus on influencing decision makers." Encouraging social workers not to equate routine brokering or linking services with advocacy, she describes true advocacy as simply making persistent demands to decision makers on behalf of clients and families in cases where services have been "refused, resisted or inadequately offered" (1990, pp. 271, 272; see also Gerhart & Brooks, 1983).

Here are some examples of situations that might call for either social worker advocacy or client self-advocacy:

- A clinician refuses to refer clients for medication screening.
- An agency structures all medication-review appointments during the daylight hours on weekdays.
- A psychiatrist seems to be overmedicating a client.
- A family physician will not adjust the medication in response to continuing concerns about side effects.

- A hospital administrator opts not to participate in a free clozapine trial program.
- A treatment team will not allow a trial program of intermittent medication.
- An agency discontinues its medication education program when a key staff person resigns.
- An agency will not allow use of a certain drug reported to be effective.
- An insurance company differentially reimburses cost of the drug depending on diagnosis.

As can be seen, advocacy is closely linked with client and family rights, particularly regarding access to quality treatment. In all mental health settings, clients' rights have long been a concern; certainly, regarding medication, these issues are even more pronounced (see chapter 7). A statement of our views of client rights, adapted from "Everyperson's Bill of Rights" (adapted from anonymous, undated), may be useful.

Mental Health Client's Medication Rights

1. The right to be treated as competent health care clients
2. The right to ask questions about the medication and its effects
3. The right to express one's own opinions about medication
4. The right to be listened to by the prescribing physician
5. The right to be educated about one's medication
6. The right to participate in psychopharmacological treatment planning and decision making
7. The right to make mistakes and to change one's mind
8. The right to choose not to assert oneself

Social workers perform two essential tasks that relate to medication management and their historic and ethical mandate to advocate for clients: (1) advocate directly for clients and families (see chapter 1) and (2) empower and facilitate clients to advocate for themselves. Willetts (1980) pointed out quite a while ago that clients themselves are often the most effective advocates because of their unique legitimacy and sensitivity to the issues. The rise of the mental health client and family movements over the past 15 years has proven that point. All advocates, whether social workers or clients and families, should have a general knowledge of psychopharmacology, mental illness, and mental health law, as well as an awareness of the interdisciplinary and sociopolitical challenges that emerge in the advocacy arena. Advocates must also have a foundation of good communication skills, some level of assertiveness, and a planned guide for action.

Shulman (1992) cautions that when helping a client advocate within a system, social workers often make a crucial error. Although social workers can apparently tolerate and forgive all sorts of behaviors on the part of the client and have little trouble finding strengths, they are often harsh on those with whom the client is trying to negotiate. Social workers can thus put clients at greater risk of being cut off by the system. To be an effective medium between the client and the mental health (or other) system, the social worker must first recognize and deal with his or her own feelings about other professionals until he or she can respond empathetically to them.

Gerhart (1990) outlines in detail the steps social workers should take on behalf of clients. We have adapted these guidelines for use by clients and families. Bentley has used them extensively at mental health client conferences and workshops.

Self-Advocacy Steps for Mental Health Clients

1. **Identify the complaint.** Think about your complaint: identify the facts and your feelings about them. Decide if this issue is worth fighting for. Forgive yourself if you decide it isn't. Psychologically prepare if you decide it is. Congratulate yourself no matter what you decide.

2. **Identify and minimize your risks.** Try to anticipate the consequences of your advocacy efforts without exaggerating or minimizing them. Look for allies in friends, organizations, and providers.

3. **Identify the appropriate decision maker.** In general, go to the first-line authority first. With medication management issues, most often the "decision makers" are physicians, treatment teams, medical directors, commissioners, or even legislative bodies. Who is the person who really made the decision, and who has the power to change it?

4. **Prepare your requests.** Write an outline of your anticipated presentation to the decision maker, including any available information and a consideration of objections they are likely to have.

5. **Practice your presentation.** Rehearse the presentation of your claim/request either in the mirror, with a friend, or with your social worker, paying close attention to your demeanor. Calmness, politeness, and strength of conviction will make you seem the most credible. Always try to request rather than demand.

6. **Present your request.** Make an appointment with the decision maker and present your claim as practiced. Use negotiation, compromise, expression of feelings, and other communication skills to achieve the best outcome possible. Advocates should be prepared to pursue decision makers persistently and assertively, in a manner that doesn't generate unnecessary hostility. They must "marshal data carefully," emphasizing their needs, desires, and values and their relationship to the specific requested changes (Gerhart & Brooks, 1983, p. 457).

This plan of action is particularly relevant for "case advocacy," or advocacy on behalf of an individual client or situation, such as approaching a psychiatrist about changing to an intermittent regimen of medication. It is also useful for "cause advocacy." Hepworth, Rooney, and Larsen (1997) provide a list of adjunct techniques needed for advocacy and social action at a more global level, to use either in conjunction with the direct approach or, when this approach fails, that includes the following: initiating legal action (e.g., suing for not referring for medication in the case of severe depression), forming interagency committees (e.g., for improving the quality of psychopharmacological care in a state hospital), providing expert testimony (e.g., on the psychosocial impact of long-term medication use), developing petitions (e.g., to request longer medication clinic hours), and contacting public officials (e.g., for ensuring that new effective medications will be covered by Medicaid).

SUMMARY

This chapter has presented social workers with a challenge to play a more active collaborative role with clients, families, and providers in helping clients manage and monitor their medication on a day-to-day basis. This means providing knowledge, skills, or insights to help keep track of client medication effects over time, to cope with side effects on a number of levels, to help make tough decisions about treatment, and to negotiate, communicate, and advocate with all concerned as the desires and dreams of the client dictate.

Table 8.2 Dimensions of Partnership in Medication Management

Dimension	Typical Models of Care	Partnership Model
Goals of medication	Reduce symptoms	Improve quality of life; emphasis on client priorities
Who selects medication regimen	M.D. provider	Client collaboration with providers to help define options
Education focus	Increasing compliance	Improving client's ability to understand and manage recovery
Monitoring and evaluating	M.D. evaluates impact on clinical status and levels of compliance	Client and providers evaluating range of outcomes and future options
Self-care by client	Largely ignored in mental health	Integrated into consultations with client and family
Control and status	Providers control processes and hold status positions	Emphasis on client control and their expertise/experiences acknowledged and valued
Refusal and reluctance	Seen as related to denial or paranoia	Seen as a right to be respected in all but emergency situations

An important question for this text has been, of course, if you embrace the partnership model, what does that mean in terms of medication management and the social work role? While we tried to answer that throughout this chapter and indeed the entire text, Table 8.2, adapted from the work of Chewning and Sleath (1996) distinguishes old ways of thinking about clients and medication and our partnership model, a more contemporary client-centered model.

Because we believe many of the medication-related needs and dilemmas of the clients we serve too often go unmet, in Part Three we have highlighted a range of psychosocial interventions and strategies to help social workers respond better to their clients' needs. It is about rolling up our sleeves and boldly using what we know.

PART IV

Future Directions

Chapter 9

Future Directions in Psychopharmacology: Implications for Social Workers

9

Future Directions in Psychopharmacology: Implications for Social Workers

Right now, a number of scientific, social, and political issues are emerging in psychopharmacology and psychopharmacotherapy that will likely affect the role of the social worker and the future of the profession at large. These include the rapid appearance of new drug treatments; creative new delivery routes or treatment philosophies; the explosion in popularity of herbs and vitamins to address mental health concerns; the growing debate about expanding prescription privileges among non-physician mental health care providers, such as psychologists, pharmacists, nurses, and social workers; and, finally, the increased public scrutiny and criticisms of psychotropic medications. Particularly loud is the call for more attention to the negative impact of these medications, as well as persistent questions about how drug companies, advertising agencies, and new models of health care financing such as managed care will influence drug availability and use. Because increased scrutiny has caused increasing concern among providers about liability and malpractice claims, we will discuss the implications of these developments for social workers.

NEW PHARMACEUTICAL TREATMENTS

As the 21st century begins, optimism pervades the pharmaceutical industry. In spite of the fact that advances in drug treatment often occur by serendipity, huge amounts of money are being invested in the discovery of new compounds, new derivatives, and new uses for existing drugs, as well as in using such complementary treatments as herbs and vitamins, either alone or in combination with other psychotropic medications. Advances in molecular biology, particularly continuing research into neurotransmission and central receptor subtypes, are hoped to lead to greater pharmacological specificity in the coming years (Langer, Arbilla, & Graham, 1991). For example, on the horizon is research geared toward understanding the effects of the atypical antipsychotics on D_3 and D_4 receptors (two subtypes of dopamine receptors), and examining the role of glutamate, an amino acid and common neurotransmitter, in schizophrenia. Thus research into new antipsychotics seeks a narrower or more precise spectrum of action in terms of targeting specific subtypes of receptors but a broader range of action in terms of the kinds of neurotransmitters that are targeted. Such not-yet or newly available drugs as amisulpiride (Solian), melperone, and flupenthixol all supposedly have fewer side effects than their counterparts because of these advances in research. The field, said simply, is moving toward discovering and refining drugs that affect some aspect of neurotransmission precisely where it is needed but not where it is not, ideally leading to drugs that produce desired therapeutic effects without unwanted side effects.

It seems almost weekly there is news about other new psychotropic drugs coming on the market. Current research with antidepressant medications, for example, is quite varied. It includes the development of new MAO inhibitors, such as moclobemide (Aurorix), which is different in chemical structure from currently available inhibitors and offers a lower risk of hypertensive crises related to tyramine consumption, thus requiring fewer dietary restrictions. A new generation of heterocyclics, such as mirtazapine (Remeron), is now on the market. Further development in the atypical antidepressants is seen in the continuing release of new selective serotonin reuptake inhibitors (SSRIs) like citalopram (Celexa) and even the development of completely new types of antidepressants, such as nefazodone hydrochloride (Serzone), which is pharmacologically distinct from the heterocyclics, the MAO inhibitors, and the SSRIs. The first new selective norepinephrine reuptake blocker is soon to be released in reboxetine (Edronax). Future refinements are likely to center on finding precise compounds that fit various individual symptom profiles, which also might include obsessive-compulsive symptoms, panic, and anxiety.

The mood stabilizer valproate, or divalproex sodium (Depakote), has emerged as an important alternative to lithium, particularly because approximately 30%, almost one third, of persons diagnosed with bipolar disorder do not respond to lithium. New research on anti-anxiety medications includes the testing of compounds similar in structure to buspirone (BuSpar), attempting again to find a drug that reduces anxiety without causing sedation and withdrawal.

We should note that currently the vast majority of clinical trials focus on the therapeutic effect of specific drugs in the first six weeks of treatment. Clearly more research is needed into effectiveness that extends beyond the acute phase of a disorder or symptoms and into the maintenance phase, which is shockingly under-examined. In addition, by far most clinical trials are conducted comparing one drug against a placebo, or at most, one standard first-line medication. Much more research needs to be conducted comparing numerous medications with each other, and in conjunction with psychosocial treatments. Our comments echo the increasing criticism and scrutiny of the clinical trials process. Suspicions are voiced about "deep biases" and "extensive ignorance of placebo effects" (David Cohen, personal communication, September 15, 1998) and the subtle influences of pharmaceutical company staff on the conduct of research (Mason, Bermanzohn, & Siris, 1998). Indeed, scholars are beginning to debate the ethics of allowing medication-free research or the use of placebos on one hand, and the need to not only use, but to standardize psychosocial interventions used in conjunction with drug trials (Carroll, 1997; Addington, Williams, Lapierre, & el-Geubaly, 1997; Carpenter, 1997).

In addition to new medications, innovations in the administration of psychotropic medications have been developed. A continuing development in drug treatment in recent years is the increasing prevalence and acceptance of polypharmacy, the use of numerous medications at the same time. As one group of authors put it, "polypharmacy is a clinical way of life" (Preskorn, Harvey & Stanga, 1998). Studies show that between 30% and 80% of people taking antidepressants are also taking two other kinds of medication. Physicians are aggressively trying to increase their client's therapeutic responses while decreasing adverse side effects by applying a more sophisticated understanding of pharmacodynamic and pharmacokinetic interactions among medications and foods. It is not yet clear if this trend toward polypharmacy will, or should, continue into the new millennium as new discoveries unfold regarding drugs themselves or their long-term effects.

In terms of routes of administration, new drugs may be made available that can be placed under the tongue, much like nitroglycerine in the treatment of angina, which seems an obvious breakthrough for people who suffer from panic (Yudofsky et al., 1991). In the 21st century, small external or internal pumps may inject drugs into the brain, or electrical devices may be transplanted into precise regions of the brain, all to stimulate specific chemical reactions. Dose sequencing and the intermittent administration of medications may come to respond to individual profiles and experiences even more quickly than implants. There is also reported to be a fast-acting (1 week) skin patch delivered MAO inhibitor (selegiline) undergoing clinical trials in the treatment of depression. The food interactions are not thought to be present when using the patch, so no dietary restrictions need be imposed.

Perhaps the next century will also usher in newer and more creative ways to incorporate health care reminders in the everyday life of mental health clients as it has for patients receiving primary health care services. For example, in diabetes care, some testing has shown that a voice messaging system is a useful adjunct for patients in monitoring their glucose levels, foot care, diet, and medication. These can improve both treatment adherence and patient satisfaction with care (Piette & Mah, 1997). Szeto and Giles (1997) write about the potential relevance of electronic aids such as microprocessors that connect to the tops of prescription bottles or the "MedMinder" container, a box that holds five prescription bottles and a sophisticated computer/ data management system for documenting medication use. This container has the capacity to provide both visual and auditory reminders.

Clearly, to most effectively fulfill their roles as educators, counselors, consultant/collaborators, and monitors, social workers need to stay abreast of these developments through reading, in-service training, conferences, and collaborative discussions with colleagues and clients. Professional social work organizations can help by sponsoring training and increasing the coverage of such topics in their workshops, journals, newsletters, and brochures. Schools of social work may have a special obligation and opportunity to respond to the need for more psychopharmacological content. In ever more settings, social workers can and should expand their roles as researchers by participating in the design and implementation of outcome studies. Social workers have a tremendous unfulfilled potential to increase knowledge about how combined medication and psychosocial treatments affect client functioning.

THE EMERGENCE OF HERBAL AND VITAMIN TREATMENTS

In the past five years there has been an upsurge of interest in this country among both the general public and health professionals about the potential for herbs and vitamins to serve as primary or supplemental treatments for mental disorders and emotional distress. Of course, people around the world have used substances other than FDA–approved, standardized psychotropic medications for centuries to treat what have been perceived to be emotional and psychological issues. Indeed, prior to the 20th century there was really no formal pharmaceutical industry in this country.

With highly controlled procedures for drug manufacture and testing and the power of universities and medical professions to shape cultural attitudes, ours has become a society that is skeptical of medicines that emerge from sources other than academic science. However, this is not so true in many other nations. A recent large-scale study in Australia found that the general public has a greater respect for "alternative" treatments such as vitamins, minerals, and special diets for treating depression and even schizophrenia than do providers (Jorn et al. 1997). A population study conducted in the United States during the years 1988–1994 found that 4.5% of respondents with depression were using alternative remedies, and only 6.5% used conventional antidepressants (Druss, Rohrbach, Kosten, Hoff, & Rosenheck, 1998).

"Alternative" is a term coined by health professionals that seems to emphasize the secondary status of herbal or nutritional methods. Others use the label "complementary" to refer to herbal and vitamin treatments to better highlight their potential as additive therapeutic agents when used along with standard medicines. (However, concerns about food and drug interactions should have equal import as with traditional psychopharmacotherapy). In this section we provide a brief overview of the status of herbs and vitamins as alternative treatments. *Herbs*, in general, are low-growing plants with soft, succulent tissues. Their stems are fleshy or juicy, at least when young, and most are perennials. They are most commonly used for food seasoning, fragrance, and also for medicinal purposes. *Vitamins* are organic substances that are essential in minute amounts for normal growth and activity of the body, because they help to convert foods into energy and tissues. There are 13 known vitamins, and although the human body produces three of these, all 13 must be obtained from plant and animal foods to ensure healthy development.

Herbs

One of the most fascinating developments in psychopharmacology during the past five years has been the increased interest in and use of herbal remedies for treating mental disorders. A major trigger of this development was the 1996 publication in the *British Journal of Psychiatry* (Linde, et al., 1996) of a meta-analysis of 23 European studies, conducted between 1979 and 1995 and involving 1,757 consumers, indicating significant improvement in persons who took St. John's wort for mild to moderate depression. Results indicated that the herb, a plant which blooms in early summer in Europe, West Asia, and North Africa (and the extract from which is known as hypericum), was as effective as several standard drugs including imipramine and amitriptyline. The authors concluded that subjects using the herb for 5 weeks to 2 months were three times as likely to experience significant mood improvement as subjects taking a placebo, with fewer side effects than standard drug therapies. It seemed to help about half its users; an effectiveness rate comparable to many studies of antidepressant drugs.

The reaction to these claims by the medical profession in this country has been one of skepticism and distrust (Schardt, 1998). Jacques Bradwejn, chief of psychiatry at the Royal Ottowa Hospital in Canada, expressed a typical view: the studies were reasonably well done but were not comparable in quality to the kinds of studies necessary to have an antidepressant drug approved by the FDA. There has been a consistent concern, too, that commercial herbs are not manufactured as carefully as drugs, and thus potency descriptors are not always reliable due to possible variation in the actual amount of therapeutic substance in any tablet.

Still, St. John's wort became the leading treatment for depression in Germany by the mid-1990s. It is said to reduce symptoms of depression with a dose of 300 mg of an extract containing .3% hypericum three times daily. Advocates point out that it does not interact with alcohol, is nonaddictive, includes no withdrawal symptoms, does not require a lengthy build-up period, enhances sleep and dreaming, and does not produce sedation. Its adverse effects, described as generally minor, include gastrointestinal discomfort, skin allergic reactions, itching, sensitivity to sunlight, and anxiety. Important in terms of accessibility, the herb represents a substantial cost savings to many consumers—an average monthly supply of hypericum costs only 10% as much as a standard SSRI drug. As with many psychotropic medications, the precise mechanism of action of hypericum is not known. It is speculated to have an inhibitory effect of serotonin and norepinephrine; another theory suggests MAO inhibition and inhibition of dopamine as well.

There are many other herbal remedies on the market which, while not receiving the same publicity as hypericum, have been used by some persons (but few physicians) for many years as treatments for various physical and emotional problems. These remedies have also been tested far less thoroughly than St. John's wort. These include kava (for anxiety), chamomile (for gastrointestinal ailments), echinacea (for influenza), saw palmetto (for urinary tract problems), ginkgo biloba (for depression and cognitive enhancement in older adults), valerian (for sleep and relaxation), cat's claw (to boost the immune system), wild yam (for hormone replacement), and feverfew (for headaches) (Tarlack, 1998).

Most researchers are cautious about advocating the use of herbs by themselves in the treatment of mental or emotional distress. They claim that there is insufficient evidence to support their efficacy, except for hypericum and, to a lesser extent, ginkgo, which has shown some effect in improving states of dementia (Wong, Smith, & Boon, 1998).

Vitamins

Nutritional deficiency models regarding the cause of mental illness have been in existence for several decades (Abou & Saleh, 1986). They do not receive much attention at present because they have been largely discounted. However, some researchers are producing evidence that vitamin deficiencies may be correlated with mental illness and that vitamins may play some role in treatment. The most commonly identified disorders, and the vitamin deficiencies associated with them, include alcoholism (thiamin), schizophrenia (niacin), depression (B6), and epilepsy (folate). Cobalam deficiency has been associated with psychosis (Hitto, 1997).

Organic psychoses are occasionally observed in persons with B12 deficiency. It is widely accepted that a subset of cognitive disorders in old age may result from vitamin deficiency and thus be treatable with vitamin replacement therapy (Schatzberg, Cole, & DeBattista, 1997). But this is an unusual phenomenon. While some vitamin deficiencies initially present with psychiatric symptoms, it is erroneous to assume that they are generally the primary causes of reversible conditions.

There is much evidence that the vitamin supplement folate may be significant in reducing depression. In several studies low folate concentrations in the bloodstream have been noted in 15 to 38% of clients with depression.

Low folate levels have also been associated with poor response to antidepressant treatment in two studies; one with 213 and the other with 99 outpatients (Fava et al., 1997; Wesson, Levitt, & Joffee, 1994). Folate has also shown in some studies to be associated with a positive response to lithium among persons with bipolar disorder. There is no cause-and-effect pathway suggested in discussing these findings, but a deficiency of this substance may be a contributing cause for mood disorders, since it is believed to be active in the process by which the body produces certain neurotransmitters. Folate deficiency may impede the processes of methylation and hydroxylation, which are important in the metabolism of neurotransmitters (Bender, 1984).

Regarding other disorders, some evidence exists for the utility of B6 and magnesium in supplementing the treatment of autistic children. The Feingold Food Program has been in existence in England since 1977 to treat children with attention-deficit hyperactivity disorder with a variety of vitamins and minerals. Some positive symptom outcomes have been reported from the experience (Colquoun, 1994). Several studies also indicate that persons with tardive dyskinesia have low vitamin E levels compared to controls (Brown et al., 1998). Efforts to treat the condition with vitamin E have not all been successful (Dorevitch, Kalian, Shalfman, & Lerner, 1997), but in one recent study of 33 clients with tardive dyskinesia treated with acetazolamide and thiamin there was a significant decrease in abnormal movements after two months (Cowen, Green, Bertollo, & Abbott, 1997). It is speculated that there may be numerous interacting causes of tardive dyskinesia, and that one of these may feature vitamin E deficiency.

What can social workers conclude from the emerging research on treating mental illnesses with herbs and vitamins? First of all, it makes common sense that if we truly recognize behavior and functioning as a biopsychosocial-spiritual phenomena, improving physical and nutritional health is likely to contribute to improving mental health. In one year-long controlled general population study, 129 healthy adults reported improved mood and anxiety when using high doses of vitamins and minerals (Benton, Haller, & Fordy, 1995). The researchers concluded that riboflavin and pyridoxine were particularly important. Still, while the symptoms of some mental disorders may be positively impacted by good physical health, including nutrition, other symptoms and disorders may not. Second, the evidence does seem to support the positive effects of hypericum in treating milder depressions, and folate deficiency may well contribute to depression and act as an inhibitor of antidepressant medication. Because so much of drug research has emerged from serendipitous findings over the years, it is also reasonable to speculate that alternative or complementary treatments will be effective for some persons. The best recourse for the social worker, it seems, is to be current with the literature in these areas and to encourage clients to talk to their physicians about the range of remedies they might consider and to maintain good physical health. These tasks clearly involve attention to the roles of consultant, counselor, advocate, educator, and researcher.

EXPANDING PRESCRIPTION-WRITING PRIVILEGES

Other professions have debated for years about who should and who should not be able to prescribe psychotropic medications. Gutierrez and Silk (1998) describe the evolution of increasing support of efforts to obtain prescription privileges for psychologists. They suggest that in spite of psychiatry's claim that this is a public health hazard, objective studies seem to support just the opposite. In fact, research in such service agencies as the Indian Health Service, Department of Defense, and the Department of Veteran Affairs, psychologists are already successfully writing prescriptions. The rationale for expansion is often tied to practicality and cost-effectiveness, specifically the under-availability of psychiatrists and the lack of psychopharmacological training of regular physicians, who write between 50% and 70% of psychotropic drug prescriptions in the United States (Olfson & Klerman, 1993; Wiggins, 1994). In 1990, the American Psychological Association convention voted, 118 to 2, to establish a task force to study this issue. While some psychologists describe their field as split over this issue, surveys in general show that psychologists strongly support the notion.

One of psychologists' biggest concerns is whether gaining prescription-writing privileges will somehow hurt the credibility of their profession and obscure their distinction from psychiatry (Boswell & Litwin, 1992). Nevertheless, as the debate continues, it will likely focus less on whether or not psychologists should seek this privilege and more on the conditions under which it should be allowed: Should privileges be completely unlimited or limited to certain settings, circumstances, or specific medications? Should psychologists be permitted to act independently or be required to have physician oversight and supervision?

Psychologists do not stand alone in their quest for prescription privileges. In fact, more than 40 states already allow nurse practitioners certain privileges and some pharmacists, especially Pharm.D.'s, are beginning to stir. One group of researchers, for example, describes a program in a San Diego veteran's hospital where three specially trained pharmacists acquired prescription-writing privileges in a clozapine program. The pharmacists had to extensively screen patients, enroll them in the tracking system, and actually initiate the medication treatment. The pharmacist then worked in close collaboration with a psychiatric resident in weekly evaluations, collaborated in other consultations as needed, and recommended any dose adjustments or side-effect medications. In the outpatient part of this program, pharmacists distributed the medication and were formally responsible for the monitoring (Dishman, Ellenor, Lacro, & Lohr, 1994).

While acknowledging the expertise of Pharm.D.'s in psychopharmacology, Sovner and Bailey (1993) argue that psychiatric nurse clinical-specialists also have sufficient training for prescription privileges. They note that nurses' training is more comprehensive than the Pharm.D.'s and includes content on the psychological aspects of prescribing, including the meaning of medication to the patient.

The early literature on social work and psychopharmacology (e.g., Brodsky, Fisher, & Weinstein, 1964; Hankoff & Galvin, 1968) rarely put forth the idea that social workers should seek training toward writing prescriptions. These articles mainly advanced the perspective that psychotropic medications represent a positive aspect of treatment for many people with mental illness and emotional distress and that social workers need to develop their ability to participate actively in the monitoring process as physicians' helpers. In the sole exception to this general position, Abroms and Greenfield (1973) suggested that social workers begin to work toward acquiring prescription privileges. They argued that this was a logical next step, given social workers' person-in-environment perspective, the new emphasis on medication in the field of mental health, and the increasing complexity of cases faced by social workers. Elliot and Kintzer (1973) responded by arguing against this recommendation with two still relevant concerns: (1) that adding content on pharmacology to the social work curriculum would broaden an already overly general educational experience and (2) that it actually might work against the maintenance of a psychosocial intervention framework. Interestingly, physicians call on many social workers to dispense medication or write prescriptions to be later signed by the physician (Miller et al., 1980).

DeLeon and Pies (1994) argue each side of this debate as it relates to nonphysician providers in general. DeLeon argues that adding prescription writing to any list of potential nonphysician activities among the helping professions would fill a desperate need for more holistic care, especially for those who have limited access to physicians. With improved curriculum and ongoing training and credentialing, this is a realistic goal. On the other hand, Pies disagrees, claiming that performance of a sound differential diagnosis with implications for treatment with psychotropic medication is a complex issue that goes well beyond the mere addition of course work in pharmacology.

Although we have made the case that expanding their knowledge base in psychopharmacology will help social workers respond well to their clients, we do not currently embrace prescription writing as either feasible or desirable. The 2-year MSW curriculum is simply too packed as it is, with subjects including basic practice theory and skills, advanced human behavior, cultural diversity, social policy and services, and single-case research. In addition, clients seem best served by productive interdisciplinary relationships, which stand the best chance of emerging when both parties genuinely respect and legitimize each other's expertise and acknowledge their own professional boundaries or limitations (Bentley, 1997). Even though social work has recognized biological issues as a crucial aspect of the biopsychosocial perspective, prescription writing would probably only serve to confuse and blur the providers' roles and responsibilities. The absence of any swell of support for prescription privileges among social workers supports this view. The minority voice says we should get over our fears and set up post-Master's institutes that would credential additionally trained, licensed social workers to prescribe medication (Dziegielewski, 1997).

It is clear that all professions, including social work, that consider expanding their professional domain need to consider accountability issues, including liability concerns. Even though we do not currently advocate seeking prescription privileges, we do support expanded knowledge and roles in medication management for social workers or, at the very least, significantly expanded application of existing skills to clients' concerns about psychotropic medication. But are social workers thus setting themselves up for increased liability risks? Will they be held liable for a failure to properly educate a client about missed doses, for example, or a failure to adequately monitor the side effects of medication, or coercing ambivalent clients into taking powerful medications with serious side effects? After all, even with the social worker's and the client's input, the physician is still clearly the one who makes the final decision about medications. In most cases, a nurse or pharmacist still distributes the medication. Interestingly, a few years ago, Littrell and Ashford (1995) boldly asked "is it proper for psychologists to discuss medication issues with clients?" The authors (both social workers) thoughtfully reviewed the ethics of nonmedical providers giving information about medications, including reviewing court cases that have emerged in pharmacy and nursing related to psychopharmacotherapy. Their conclusion is reassuring in terms of the thesis of this book, certainly. They say that prudent care not only finds these conversations permissible but may be required as a part of the obligation to provide coordinated care.

We have stressed our role as counselors, consultants, and collaborators with clients and other providers and have emphasized our role in helping clients to gain new knowledge and skills and to make informed decisions. Social workers are accountable for their own actions and ought to strive to achieve the highest standards of their own profession. For instance, one of the most difficult situations arises when social workers must decide what to do when faced with incompetence or inadequate care on the part of other providers. Though we discussed specific advocacy steps in chapter 8, we recognize they do not offer solutions for all real-world circumstances. Social workers every day have to weigh the consequences to themselves and others of "whistle blowing" against the consequences of remaining silent.

INCREASED PUBLIC SCRUTINY OF PSYCHOTROPIC MEDICATIONS

Keshavan and Kennedy (1992) devote an entire edited volume to dysfunction related to the use of psychotropic medications. Topics include overdosing, problematic interactions, drug-induced neuropsychiatric symptoms (dystonias, parkinsonism, TD, NMS, akathisia), abuse of and dependence on benzodiazepines and anticholinergics, and drug-induced systemic syndromes such as cardiovascular problems, sexual dysfunction, and immunological problems. However, the controversies surrounding the use of psychotropic medication have moved beyond scholarly journals, medical books, and college classrooms and toward newspapers and the popular press. Perhaps the best-known example of this is Prozac, the best-selling antidepressant. Tens of millions of people have received prescriptions for Prozac since its introduction in 1986. Some tout its wonders to treat depression, help reduce anxiety in people with panic, decrease the intrusive thoughts and rituals in people diagnosed with obsessive-compulsive symptoms, and treat bulimia. Others are amazed by its ability to improve concentration and productivity, even in asymptomatic persons. In his best-selling book, *Listening to Prozac*, Kramer (1993) enthusiastically endorses the medication, claiming that it carries more power to change people's behavior than long-term psychological treatments.

On the other hand, Barondes (1994) writes that he is disturbed by such support for Prozac and wonders if it is really just an expensive placebo, a question echoed by Ann Blake Tracy's title *Prozac: Panacea or Pandora* (1994). Both question just how long-lasting the changes are, how long someone has to take it, and at what cost. Others have tried to link Prozac to suicide or other acts of violence or aggression. Hundreds of suits have been filed against Eli Lilly, the makers of Prozac, with most being dismissed. The first case to go to trial involved a disgruntled worker who killed 8 and wounded 13 during a shooting spree in a Louisville printing plant after being on Prozac for about a month. After a 47-day hearing, the jury took five hours to rule in favor of the drug company, which then in turn claimed complete vindication. Mason and Pollack (1998) note that to date there has never been a successful suit against the company, and that such suits are decreasing in frequency. They discuss 28 appellate level cases in which Prozac was used most frequently to resolve custody or visitation conflicts and to try to explain criminal or irrational behavior.

Breggin (1987, 1991) and a number of other authors (Valenstein, 1998; Caplan, 1995; Walker, 1996; Hughes & Brewin, 1979) also harshly criticize psychiatry in general and the use of psychotropic medications in particular. They attack the over-reliance on chemical imbalances to explain commonplace human problems and urge their readers to see medications not as miracles but as chemical lobotomies. While strongly urging the use of psychosocial approaches, Breggin argues that "all of life is an alternative to drugs . . . The whole spectrum of secular and religious philosophy is better than biopsychiatry" (1991, p. 375).

This debate grows particularly active regarding the medication of children. The debate rages in the popular press with such popular books as *And they call it help* by Louise Armstrong (1993). It hits close to home in agency and facility philosophies and policies, as well as even among family members. New clinicians usually take little time to determine on which side of the falsely dichotomous "medication fence" a certain child mental health facility falls:

behavior management or medication? One concern arises that by medicating, clinicians may avoid proper focus on the "true" genesis (such as physical, sexual, or emotional abuse) of children's disorders. Widespread concern exists about overmedicating children, especially those diagnosed with attention deficit disorders or learning disabilities. In fact, public controversy surrounding Ritalin is probably second only to that of Prozac.

However, others worry more about an undermedicated society. What about all the adults and children who suffer from treatable illnesses but receive insufficient treatment or no treatment at all? What about those who receive inadequate dosages or an inadequate trial? What about people who receive some type of psychotherapy alone when a combination of medication and psychotherapy or psychosocial intervention would be best? For instance, Dr. Osheroff, a physician, sued Chestnut Lodge for failing to provide him with adequate treatment (medication) for his severe depression, instead providing long-term intensive insight-oriented psychotherapy on an inpatient basis. Over the course of many months, he deteriorated to such a poor physical and mental state that his family, worried about his survival, had him discharged and arranged for alternative treatment, which included medication. In a relatively short time, he was back working in his medical practice and resuming his life. Although the case was settled out of court and thus set no legal precedent, it spurred an important debate about the future of psychodynamic approaches for disorders and illnesses known to respond to medication (see Klerman, 1990; Stone, 1990).

As in the cases of Prozac and Dr. Osheroff, increased public attention on psychotropic medication and warnings about over-reliance or under-reliance have numerous legal and ethical implications. In fact, improper medication management is the most common legal claim against psychiatrists (Wettstein, 1992). Most complaints relate to negligence and lack of informed consent, such as failing to take an adequate history, prescribing an improper dose, prescribing a drug without proper indicators, failing to recognize or treat side effects and interactions, and failing to discuss the benefits, risks, and alternatives. Thus far, the courts have been unwilling to hold manufacturers liable for failing to warn consumers about the risks and side effects of prescription medication because of a "learned intermediary" rule. This says that since physicians decide which medication will be prescribed and how much, injury is best avoided by a direct warning from the physician (Walsh, 1993). Walsh, however, describes the case of a woman who sued Upjohn, claiming that Halcion (triazolam) was responsible for her severe anxiety, sleeplessness, decreased appetite, and suicidal ideation. In this case, the court looked not only at the warnings the physician had given his patient but also at the warning given by the pharmaceutical representative to the physician. The case record reports that a reasonable warning is one that not only conveys a fair indication of the nature of the dangers involved but also warns with a degree of intensity demanded by the nature of the risk. A warning may be found to be unreasonable in that it was unduly delayed, reluctant in tone, or lacking in a sense of urgency (Walsh, 1993, p. 68).

Because the costs of medication affect availability and use, they have clear ethical dimensions. For example, tremendous controversy centers on the availability of the new atypical antipsychotics in public settings. Even though research strongly supports the efficacy of these drugs with persons diagnosed with treatment-resistant schizophrenia, the drugs themselves and the required blood-monitoring system for some make the cost prohibitive for many community mental health centers and state hospitals. Although these drugs have been on the market for several years, those who might really benefit from it have very limited access to it (Reid et al., 1993). The great tragedy may be that even though the cost of the medications themselves is greater, the overall costs of care may not be dramatically increased because of lowered hospitalization costs of people on the newer medications (Nightengale, Crumly, Liao, Lawrence, & Jacobs, 1998). The National Alliance for the Mentally Ill (NAMI) has fought long and hard on moral grounds alone for making the new atypical antipsychotics and SSRIs more widely available. At one time NAMI actually began legal action against Sandoz, the maker of Clozaril (clozapine), claiming unreasonable price fixing, because the drug had been available in Europe for thousands of dollars less per year than in the United States.

Clearly, some of these issues have implications for the types of advocacy in which social workers become involved. Developing clearer ethical guidelines around psychopharmacology issues may also help clarify the advocacy role. For example, what should the relationship be between social workers' organizations and drug companies? Should drug companies be allowed or even encouraged to set up booths at social workers' national conferences, as they do at conferences sponsored by the American Psychiatric Association? Why or why not? Because the pharmaceutical industry invests up to 40% of its revenue on promotional activities, such as advertising, direct mail, and sales representatives, concerns have arisen about the relationships between this industry and practicing physicians (Caudill, Lurie, & Rich, 1992), as it has for the relationship between the industry and researchers. Neill notes that "a complex ideological and financial relationship exists between the drug industry and the prescribing psychiatrist, the vendor and the consumer, which has yet to be explored" (1989, p. 333). For example, after reviewing hundreds of drug advertisements in medical journals, Neill notes that even as drug companies exploit and manipulate physicians, drug advertisements minister to the psychological needs of physicians for prestige, identity, potency, and self-satisfaction. Although drug companies do not currently court social workers, if their role in medication management continues to expand, such subtle influences on autonomy may need to be confronted.

Unfortunately, drug advertisements apparently reinforce medical concepts of illness that tend to locate pathology in individuals, de-emphasizing the social context and competing psychosocial interventions. Additional remedies, such as psychosocial rehabilitation, improvements in housing, education, and jobs, are considered "totally beyond the pale" (Kleinman & Cohen, 1991, p. 868). Social workers are thus challenged to maintain their psychosocial emphasis and perspective even as they take on roles traditionally ascribed to the medical sphere.

Health care professionals are still a long way from understanding how new modes of financing health and mental health services, including managed care, will affect psychopharmacology practice. Should they worry that it may lead to even greater reliance on medications because of their sheer efficiency? Will people be "treated only from the neck up" (Flynn, 1994, p. 16)? Or should they be hopeful that the rhetoric of managed care, which supports empirically validated treatments such as combined psychotherapeutic or rehabilitative approaches, will finally be realized? Similarly, what will changes in Medicare and Medicaid coverage, which will most likely be reduced, do to psychopharmacology practices?

Poulson (1992) urges health care providers to consider not only increasing the number and types of providers who will either prescribe medications themselves or take leadership roles in medication management but also to look for other changes in health care delivery and managed care. These include the shift in decision-making authority from physicians to outside reviewers, the persistent demand for cost controls, the growing importance of the voice of the consumer, and increasing competition from drug companies.

FINAL WORDS

In this chapter, we have tried to summarize how social workers might respond to new treatments, expanded prescription privileges among related professions, the increased use of herbal medicines for mental and emotional health concerns, increased public scrutiny and criticism of psychotropic medications, and concerns about liability. In spite of many unanswered questions, we still envision social workers who hold fast to the principles of partnership, balance, and integration. We still see social workers who strive to fulfill their unique mission while working side by side with clients, families, and providers. Frankly, we see social workers who love their clients: who care deeply about their clients but whose concern is not contingent on the client doing what the social worker or agency thinks he or she should do or not do. Rather, social workers care because our clients are human beings just like they are, and social workers have something to offer. They love their clients by abandoning the "I told you so's" and being there over the long haul. Clients, in return, offer us the gift of daily work that has meaning and purpose. Social workers who succeed in achieving the partnership we describe and embrace the roles we put forth are working not only help to improve the quality of their own client's lives but we hope are also modeling the great promise of social work, a profession that is not afraid to pose difficult ethical questions, wrestle with the most complex cases, and confront its own future with vigor and pride.

References

Abroms, G., & Greenfield, N. (1973). Drug-prescribing and the nonmedical therapist. *Clinical Social Work Journal, 1*, 132–134.

Abou, S. M. T., & Coppen, A. (1986). The biology of folate in depression: Implications for nutritional hypothesis of the psychoses. *Journal of Psychiatric Research, 20*(2), 91–101.

Adams, S. G., & Howe, J. T. (1993). Predicting medication compliance in a psychotic population. *Journal of Nervous and Mental Disease, 181*, 558–560.

Addington, D., Williams, R., Lapierre, Y., & el-Guebaly, N. (1997). Placebos in clinical trials of psychotropic medication. *Canadian Journal of Psychiatry, 42*(3), 16–22.

Adebimpe, V. R. (1994). Race, racism, and epidemiological surveys. *Hospital & Community Psychiatry, 45*, 27–31.

Adelman, G. (Ed.). (1987). *Encyclopedia of neuroscience*. Boston: Birkhaeuser.

Agarwal, M. R., Sharma, V. K., Kishore-Kumar, K. V., & Lowe, D. (1998). Non-compliance with treatment in patients suffering from schizophrenia: A study to evaluate possible contributing factors. *International Journal of Social Psychiatry, 44*(2), 92–106.

Alpert, J. E., & Fava, M. (1997). Nutrition and depression: The role of folate. *Nutrition Reviews, 55*(5), 145–149.

American Psychiatric Association (1997). Practice guidelines for treatment of patients with schizophrenia. *American Journal of Psychiatry, 154*(4 Suppl), 1–63.

American Psychiatric Association. (1994). *Diagnostic and statistical manual of mental disorders* (4th ed.). Washington, DC: Author.

Anderson, C., Reiss, D., & Hogarty, G. (1986). *Schizophrenia and the family: A practitioner's guide to psychoeducation and management*. New York: Guilford Press.

Andreasen, N. C. (1982). Negative symptoms of schizophrenia: Definition and reliability. *Archives of General Psychiatry, 39*, 784–788.

Andreasen, N. C., & Olsen, S. (1982). Negative vs. positive schizophrenia: Definition and validation. *Archives of General Psychiatry, 39*, 789–794.

Anthony, W. A. (1993). Recovery from mental illness: The guiding vision of the mental health service system in the 1990s. *Psychosocial Rehabilitation Journal, 16*, 11–23.

Appelbaum, P., & Guteil, T. (1979). "Rotting with their rights on": Constitutional theory and clinical reality in drug refusal by psychiatric patients. *Bulletin of the American Academy of Psychiatry and the Law, 7*, 306–315.

Arana, G. W., & Hyman, S. E. (1991). *Handbook of psychiatric drug therapy* (2nd ed.). Boston: Little, Brown.

Arboleda-Florez, J. (1998). Mental illness and violence: An epidemiological appraisal of the evidence. *Canadian Journal of Psychiatry, 43*(10), 989–996.

Ascher-Svanum, H., Lafuze, J. E., Barrickman, P. J., Van Dusen, C., & Fompa-Loy, J. (1997). Educational needs of families of mentally ill adults. *Psychiatric Services, 48*, 1072–1074.

Ascher-Svanum, H. A., & Krause, A. A. (1991). *Psychoeducational groups for patients with schizophrenia: A guide for practitioners.* Gaithersburg, MD: Aspen.

Aspler, R., & Rothman, E. (1984). Correlates of compliance with psychoactive prescriptions. *Journal of Psychoactive Drugs, 16*, 193–199.

Auge, M., & Herzlech, C. (Eds.) (1998). *The meaning of illness: Anthropology, history, and sociology.* New York: Harwood.

Awad, A. G., Voruganti, L. N., Heslegrave, R. J., & Hogan, T. P. (1996). Assessment of patient's subjective experience in acute neuroleptic treatment: Implications for compliance and outcome. *International Clinical Psychopharmacology, 11* (Suppl. 2), 55–59.

Awad, A. G. (1992). Quality of life of schizophrenic patients on medications and implications for new drug trials. *Hospital & Community Psychiatry, 43*, 262–265.

Azrin, N. H., & Teichner, G. (1998). Evaluation of an instructional program for improving medication compliance for chronically mentally ill outpatients. *Behavior Research and Therapy, 36*, 849–861.

Bachur, J. A. (1986). A social work perspective. *The Gerontologist, 26*, 614–617.

Baker, F. M. (1994). Psychiatric treatment of older African Americans. *Hospital & Community Psychiatry, 45*, 32–37.

Barker, R. L. (1998). *The social work dictionary* (7th ed.) (p. 35). Silver Spring, MD: NASW.

Barkley, R. A., Conners, C. K., Barclay, A., Gadow, K., Gittleman, R., Sprague, R., & Swanson, J. (1991). *Task force report: The appropriate role of clinical child psychologists in the prescribing of psychoactive medication for children.* Washington, DC: American Psychological Association.

Barnes, T. R. E. (1989). A rating scale for drug-induced akathisia. *British Journal of Psychiatry, 154*, 672–676.

Barondes, S. H. (1994). Thinking about Prozac. *Science, 263*(5150), 1102–1103.

Barrickman, L. L., Perry, P. J., Allen, A. J., Kuperman, S., Arndt, S. V., Herrmann, K. J., & Schumacher, E. (1995). Bupropion versus methylphenidate in the treatment of attention-deficit hyperactivity disorder. *Journal of the American Academy of Child and Adolescent Psychiatry, 34*(5), 649–658.

Batey, S. R., & Ledbetter, J. E. (1982). Medication education for patients in a partial hospitalization program. *Journal of Psychosocial Nursing and Mental Health Services, 20*(7), 7–15.

Beitman, B. D., & Klerman, G. L. (Eds.). (1991). *Integrating pharmacotherapy and psychotherapy.* Washington, DC: American Psychiatric Press.

Belcher, J. R., & Ephross, P. H. (1989). Toward an effective practice model for the homeless mentally ill. *Social Casework, 70*, 421–427.

Bender, D. A. (1984). Review: B vitamins in the nervous system. *Neurochemistry International, 6*(3), 297–321.

Bentley, K. J. (1998). Psychopharmacological treatment of schizophrenia: What social workers need to know. *Research on Social Work Practice, 8,* 384–405.

Bentley, K. J.(1997). Should clinical social workers seek psychotropic medication privileges. No! In B. Thyer (Ed.) *Controversial issues in social work practice* (pp. 159–164). Boston: Allyn/Bacon.

Bentley, K. J. (1991). Voluntary recruitment of psychiatric patients for clinical research. *International Journal of Mental Health, 20,* 94–107.

Bentley, K. J. (1993). The right of psychiatric patients to refuse medications: Where should social workers stand? *Social Work, 38,* 101–106.

Bentley, K. J., Farmer, R. L., & Phillips, M. E. (1991). Student knowledge of and attitudes toward psychotropic drugs. *Journal of Social Work Education, 27,* 279–289.

Bentley, K. J., & Harrison, D. F. (1989). Behavioral, psychoeducational, and skills training approaches to family management of schizophrenia. In B. A. Thyer (Ed.), *Behavioral family therapy* (pp. 147–168). Springfield, IL: Charles C. Thomas.

Bentley, K. J., & Reeves, J. (1992). Integrating psychopharmacology into social work curriculum: Suggested content and resources. *Journal of Teaching in Social Work, 6,* 41–48.

Bentley, K. J., Rosenson, M., & Zito, J. (1990). Promoting medication compliance: Strategies for working with families of mentally ill people. *Social Work, 35,* 274–277.

Bentley, K. J., & Walsh, J. (1998). Advances in psychopharmacology and psychosocial aspects of medication management: A review for social workers. In J. B. W. Williams & K. Ell (Eds.), *Recent advances in mental health research: Implications for social workers* (pp. 309–342). Silver Spring, MD: National Association of Social Workers.

Benton, D., Haller, J., & Fordy, J. (1995). Vitamin supplementation for one year improves mood. *Neuropsychobiology, 32*(2), 98–105.

Berg, W. E., & Wallace, M. (1987). Effect of treatment setting on social workers' knowledge of psychotropic drugs. *Health and Social Work, 12,* 144–152.

Berger, F. M. (1970). Anxiety and the discovery of the tranquilizers. In F. J. Ayd & R. Blackwell (Eds.), *Discoveries in biological psychiatry* (pp. 115–129). Philadelphia: J. B. Lippincott.

Bernheim, K. F., & Lehman, A. (1985). *Working with families of the mentally ill.* New York: Norton.

Bernheim, K. F., & Switalski, T. (1988). Mental health staff and patients' relatives: How they view each other. *Hospital & Community Psychiatry, 39,* 63–68.

Bernstein, G. A., Crosby, R. D., Perwien, A. R., & Borchardt, C. M. (1996). Anxiety rating for children-revised: Reliability and validity. *Journal of Anxiety Disorders, 10*(2), 97–114.

Bernstein, J. G. (1995). *Handbook of drug therapy in psychiatry* (3rd ed.) St. Louis: Mosby.

Bigelow, L. B., & Berthot, B. D. (1989). The psychiatric symptom assessment scale (PSAS). *Psychopharmacology Bulletin, 25*(2), 168–179.

Bisbee, C. (1988, October). *Psychiatric patient education: Teaching patients about illness, treatment, and role.* Paper presented at the 40th Institute on Hospital and Community Psychiatry, New Orleans, LA.

Biegon, A., & Gruener, N. (1992). Age-related changes in serotonin $5HT_2$ receptors on human blood platelets. *Psychopharmacology, 108,* 210–212.

Blackwell, B. (1979). The drug regimen and treatment compliance. In R. B. Haynes, D. W. Taylor, & D. L. Sackett (Eds.), *Compliance in health care* (pp. 144–156). Baltimore: Johns Hopkins University Press.

Blanchard, R. J., Yudko, E. B., Rodgers, R. J., & Blanchard, D. C. (1993). Defense system psychopharmacology: An ethological approach to the pharmacology of fear and anxiety. *Behavioral Brain Research, 58,* 155–165.

Blow, F. C., Barry, K. L., BootsMiller, B. J., Copeland, L. A., McCormick, R., & Visnic, S. (1998). Longitudinal assessment of inpatient use and functioning of seriously mentally ill veterans with and without co-occurring substance use disorders. *Journal of Psychiatric Research, 32*(5), 311–319.

Boczknowski, J. A., Zeichner, A., & DeSanto, N. (1985). Neuroleptic compliance among chronic schizophrenic outpatients: An intervention outcome report. *Journal of Consulting & Clinical Psychology, 53,* 666–671.

Bond, A. L., & Lader, M. H. (1996). *Understanding drug treatment in mental health care.* West Sussex, England: John Wiley & Sons.

Booker, W., Brenner, H. D., Gerstner, G., Keller, F., Muller, J., & Spichtig, L. (1984). Self-healing strategies among schizophrenics: Attempts at compensation for basic disorders. *Acta Psychiatirica Scandinavia, 69,* 373–378.

Boswell, D. L., & Litwin, W. J. (1992). Limited prescription privileges for psychologists: A 1-year follow-up. *Professional Psychology, 23*(2), 108–113.

Bowden, C. L. (1996). Role of newer medications for bipolar disorder. *Journal of Clinical Psychopharmacology, 16*(2 Suppl. 1), 48–55.

Bowden, C. L., Brugger, A. M., Swann, A. C., Calabrese, J. R., Janicak, P. G., Petty, F., Dilsaver, S. C., Davis, J. M., Rush, A. J., & Small, J. G. (1994). Efficacy of divalproex vs. lithium and placebo in the treatment of mania. *Journal of the American Medical Association, 271,* 918–924.

Brabbins, C., Butleer, J., & Bentall, R. (1996). Consent to neuroleptic medication for schizoprenia: Clinical, ethical and legal issues. *British Journal of Psychiatry, 168,* 540–544.

Bradley, S. (1990). Non-physician psychotherapist—physician pharmacotherapist: A new model for concurrent treatment. *Psychiatric Clinics of North America, 13*(2), 307–322.

Breggin, P. R. (1987). *Psychiatric drugs: Hazards to the brain.* New York: Springer.

Breggin, P. R. (1991). *Toxic psychiatry.* New York: St. Martin's Press.

Bricout, J. C. (1998). *The relationship between employers' perceived organizational context and their impressions of the employability of job applicants with severe psychiatric and physical disabilities.* Unpublished doctoral dissertation, Virginia Commonwealth University, Richmond.

Brodsky, C., Fisher, A., & Weinstein, M. (1964). Modern treatment of psychosis: New tasks for social therapies. *Social Work, 9,* 71–78.

Brooks, A. (1987). The right to refuse medication: Law and policy. *Rutgers Law Review, 39,* 339–376.

Brown, A., & Lempa, M. (1997). New medications in development. *NARSAD Research Newsletter, 9*(3/4), 21–26.

Brown, K., Reid, A., White, T., Henderson, T., Hukin, S., Johnstone, C., & Glen, A. (1998). Vitamin E, lipids, and lipid peroxidation products in tardive dyskinesia. *Biological Psychiatry, 43*(12), 863–867.

Brown, P. (1985). *The transfer of care: Psychiatric deinstitutionalization and its aftermath.* Boston: Routledge & Kegan Paul.

Brown, P., & Funk, S. C. (1986). Tardive dyskinesia: Barriers to the professional recognition of an iatrogenic disease. *Journal of Health & Social Behavior, 27,* 116–132.

Buchalter-Katz, S. (1985). Observations concerning the art productions of depressed patients in a short-term psychiatric facility. *Arts in Psychotherapy, 12*(1), 35–38.

Buckalew, L., & Sallis, R. (1986). Patient compliance and medication perception. *Journal of Clinical Psychology, 42,* 49–53.

Buckwalter, K. C., & Kerfoot, K. M. (1982). Teaching patients self-care: A critical aspect of psychiatric discharge planning. *Journal of Psychosocial Nursing and Mental Health Services, 20*(4), 15–20.

Budd, R. J., Hughes, I. C. T., & Smith, J. A. (1996). Health beliefs and compliance with antipsychotic medication. *British Journal of Clinical Psychology, 35*(Part 3), 393–397.

Busch, F. N., & Gould, E. (1993). Treatment by a psychotherapist and a psychopharmacologist: Transference and countertransference issues. *Hospital & Community Psychiatry, 44,* 772–774.

Butler, R. N., Lewis, M. I., & Sunderland, T. (1991). *Aging and mental health: Positive psychosocial and biomedical approaches* (4th ed.). New York: MacMillan.

Calabrese, J. R., Fatemi, S. H., Kujawa, M., & Woyshville, M. J. (1996). Predictors of response to mood stabilizers. *Journal of Clinical Neuropsychiatry, 16*(2, Suppl.1), 24–29.

Callicutt, J. W. (1997) Overview of the field of mental health. In T. R. Watckins & J. W. Callicutt (Eds.), *Mental health policy and practice today* (pp. 3–16). Thousand Oaks, CA: Sage.

Callicutt, J. (1983). Contemporary settings and the rise of the profession in mental health. In J. Callicutt & P. Lecca (Eds.), *Social work and mental health* (pp. 30–41). New York: Free Press.

Campbell, R. J. (1996). *Psychiatric dictionary* (7th ed.). New York: Oxford.

Caplan, P. J. (1995). *They say you're crazy: How the world's most powerful psychiatrists decide who's normal.* Reading, MA: Addison-Wesley.

Caplan, R. B. (1969). *Psychiatry and the community in nineteenth century America.* New York: Basic Books.

Carpenter, W. T. (1997). The risk of medication-free research. *Schizophrenia Bulletin, 23,* 11–18.

Carpenter, W. T., & Heinrichs, D. W. (1983). Early intervention, time-limited, targeted pharmacotherapy of schizophrenia. *Schizophrenia Bulletin, 9,* 533–542.

Carrion, P. G., Swann, A., Kellert-Cecil, H., & Barber, M. (1993). Compliance with clinic attendance by outpatients with schizophrenia. *Hos-pital & Community Psychiatry, 44,* 764–767.

Carroll, K. M. (1997). Manual-guided psychosocial treatment: A new virtual requirement for pharmacotherapy trials. *Archives of General Psychiatry, 54,* 923–928.

Carter, C., Swift, R. M., & Turnbull, J. M. (1996). When are long-term anxiolytics warranted? *Patient Care, 30*(5), 165–176.

Casper, R. C., Belanoff, J., & Offer, D. (1996). Gender differences, but no racial differences, in self-reported psychiatric symptoms in adolescents. *Journal of the Academy of Child and Adolescent Psychiatry, 35*(4), 500–508.

Cassady, S. L, Thaker, G. K., Summerfelt, A., & Tamminga, C. A. (1997). The Maryland Psychiatric Research Center scale and the characterization of involuntary movements. *Psychiatry Research, 70,* 21–37

Caudill, T. S., Lurie, N., & Rich, E. (1992). The influence of pharmaceutical industry advertising on physician prescribing. *Journal of Drug Issues, 22*(2), 331–338.

Chewning, B., & Sleath, B. (1996). Medication decision-making and management. *Social Science & Medicine, 42,* 389–398.

Chouinard, G., Ross-Chouinard, A., Annable, L., Jones, B. D. (1980). Extrapyramidal Symptom Rating Scale. *Canadian Journal of Neurological Science, 7,* 233.

Ciccone, R., Tokoli, J. F., Gift, T. E., & Clements, C. D. (1993). Medication refusal and judicial activism: A reexamination of the effects of the Rivers decision. *Hospital & Community Psychiatry, 44,* 555–560.

Citrome, L., Levine, J., & Allingham, B. (1996). Utilization of depot medication in psychiatric inpatients. *Psychopharmacology Bulletin, 32*(3), 321–326.

Clary, C., Dever, A., & Schweizer, E. (1992). Psychiatric inpatients' knowledge of medication at hospital discharge. *Hospital & Community Psychiatry, 43,* 140–143.

Clements, M. (1993, October 31). What we say about mental illness. *Parade Magazine*, pp. 4–6.

Cohen, C. I., & Magai, C. (1999). Racial differences in neuropsychiatric symptoms among dementia outpatients. *American Journal of Geriatric Psychiatry*, 7(1), 57–63.

Cohen, D. (1997). A critique of the use of neuroleptic drugs in psychiatry. In S. Seymour & R. P. Greenberg (Eds.), *From placebo to panacea: Putting psychistric drugs to the test* (pp. 173–208). New York: John Wiley & Sons.

Cohen, D. (1994). Neuroleptic drug treatment of schizophrenia: The state of the confusion. *Journal of Mind and Behavior*, 15(1–2), 139–156.

Cohen, D. (1988). Social work and psychotropic drug treatments. *Social Service Review*, 62, 576–599.

Cohen, D., & McCubbin, M. (1990). The political economy of tardive dyskinesia: Asymmetries in power and responsibility. *The Journal of Mind and Behavior*, 11, 465–488.

Cohen, I. M. (1970). The benzodiazepines. In F. J. Ayd & R. Blackwell (Eds.), *Discoveries in biological psychiatry* (pp. 130–141). Philadelphia: J. B. Lippincott.

Cohen, N. L. (1993). Stigmatization and the "noncompliant" recidivist. *Hospital & Community Psychiatry*, 44, 1029.

Cole, R. (1982). Patient's rights vs. doctor's rights: Which should take precedence? In A. E. Doudera & J. P. Swazey (Eds.), *Refusing treatment in mental institutions: Values in conflicts* (pp. 56–71). Washington, DC: Association of University Programs in Health Administration.

Coleman, L. M., Fowler, L. L., & Williams, M. E. (1995). Use of unproven therapies by people with Alzheimer's disease. *Journal of the American Geriatrics Society*, 43(7), 747–750.

Collins-Colon, T. (1990). Do it yourself: Medication management for community-based clients. *Journal of Psychosocial Nursing and Mental Health Services*, 28(6), 25–29.

Colquoun, I. D. (1994). Attention deficit/hyperactive disorder: A dietary/nutritional approach. *Therapeutic Care and Education*, 3(2), 159–172.

Connaway, R. S. (1975). Teamwork and social worker advocacy: Conflicts and possibilities. *Community Mental Health Journal*, 11, 381–388.

Conrad, P. (1985). The meaning of medications: Another look at compliance. *Social Science and Medicine*, 20, 29–37.

Cordoba, O., Wilson, W., & Orten, J. (1983). Psychotropic medications for children. *Social Work*, 28, 448–453.

Corrigan, P. W., Liberman, R. P., & Engel, J. D. (1990). From noncompliance to collaboration in the treatment of schizophrenia. *Hospital & Community Psychiatry*, 41, 1203–1211.

Corsini, R. J., & Wedding, D. (1995). *Current psychotherapies* (5th ed.). Itasca, Ill: F. E. Peacock.

Corty, E., Lehman, A. F., & Myers, C. P. (1993). Influence of psychoactive substance use on reliability of psychiatric diagnosis. *Journal of Counseling and Clinical Psychology*, 61, 165–170.

Coudreaut-Quinn, E. A., Emmons, M. A., & McMorrow, M. J. (1992). Adherence and accuracy: Self-medication during inpatient psychiatric treatment. *Journal of Psychosocial Nursing and Mental Health Services*, 30(12), 32–36.

Cournoyer, D. E., & Johnson, H. C. (1991). Measuring parents' perception of mental health professionals. *Research on Social Work Practice*, 1, 399–415.

Cowen, M. A., Green, M., Bertollo, D. N., & Abbott, K. (1997). A treatment for tardive dyskinesia and some other extrapyramidal symptoms. *Journal of Clinical Psychopharmacology*, 17(3), 190–193.

Cowles, L. A., & Lefcowitz, M. (1992). Interdisciplinary expectations of the medical social worker in the hospital setting. *Health & Social Work*, 17(1), 57–65.

Coxhead, N., Silverstone, T., & Cookson, J. (1992). Carbamazepine versus lithium in the prophylaxis of bipolar affective disorder. *Acta Psychiatirica Scandinavia, 85*(2), 114–118.

Cramer, J. A., & Rosenheck, R. (1999). Enhancing medication compliance for people with serious mental illness. *Journal of Nervous and Mental Disease, 187,* 53–55.

Cubine, T., Bentley, K. J., Poe, J., & McCafferty, P. (in press). The MESA model of family-professional education: Virginia's experience in enhancing collaboration. Arete.

Daley, D. C., Bowler, K., Cahalane, H. (1992). Approaches to patient and family education with affective disorders. *Patient Education and Counseling, 19,* 163–174.

Dane, B. O., & Simon, B. L. (1991). Resident guests: Social workers in host settings. *Social Work, 36,* 208–213.

Dassori, A. M., Miller, A. L., Velligan, D., Slanda, D., Diamond, P., & Mahurin, R. (1998). Ethnicity and negative symptoms in patients with schizophrenia. *Cultural Diversity and Mental Health, 4*(1), 65–69.

Datz, F. L., Christian, P. E., & Moore, J. (1987). Gender-related differences in gastric emptying. *Nuclear Medicine, 28,* 1204–1207.

Davidhizar, R. E., & McBridge, A. B. (1985). Teaching the client with schizophrenia about medication. *Patient Education and Counseling, 7,* 137–145.

Davidson, J., & Pelton, S. (1986). Forms of atypical depression and their response to antidepressant drugs. *Psychiatry Research, 17,* 87–95.

Davidson, M., & Jamison, P. (1983). The clinical social worker and current psychiatric drugs: Some introductory principles. *Clinical Social Work Journal, 11,* 139–150.

Davis v. *Hubbard,* 506 F. Supp. 915 (1980).

DeChillo, N. (1993). Collaboration between social workers and the families of the mentally ill. *Families in Society,* 74, 104–115.

Deegan, P. E. (1992). The independent living movement and people with psychiatric disabilities: Taking back control over our own lives. *Psychosocial Rehabilitation Journal, 15*(3), 3–19.

DeGeest, S., Abraham, I., Gemoets, H., & Evers, G. (1994). Development of the long-term medication behavior self-efficacy scale: Qualitative study for item development. *Journal of Advanced Nursing, 19*(2), 233–238.

DeLeon, P. H., & Pies, R. W. (1994). Should non-physician mental health professionals be allowed to prescribe medicine? In S. A. Kirk & S. D. Einbinder (Eds.), *Controversial issues in mental health* (pp. 177–188). Boston: Allyn & Bacon.

Devane, C. L. (1990). *Fundamentals of monitoring psychoactive drug therapy.* Baltimore: Williams & Wilkins.

Dewan, M. J. (1999). Are psychiatrists cost-effective? An analysis of integrated versus split treatment. *American Journal of Psychiatry, 156,* 324–326.

Dewan, M. J., & Koss, M. (1989). The clinical impact of the side effects of psychotropic drugs. In S. Fisher & R. P. Greenberg (Eds.), *The limits of biological treatments for psychological distress* (pp. 189–234). Hillsdale, NJ: Lawrence Earlbaum Associates.

Diamond, R. (1983). Enhancing medication use in schizophrenic patients. *Journal of Clinical Psychiatry, 44*(6, no. 2), 7–14.

DiMatteo, M. R., & DiNicola, D. D. (1982). *Achieving patient compliance: The psychology of the medical practitioner's role.* New York: Pergamon Press.

Dishman, B. R., Ellenor, G. L., Lacro, J. P., & Lohr, J. B. (1994). Pharmacists' role in clozapine therapy at a Veterans Affairs Medical Center. *American Journal of Hospital Pharmacy, 51,* 899–901.

Dixon, L., Lyles, A., Scott, J., Lehman, A., Postrado, L., Goldman, H., & McGlynn, E. (1999). Services to families of adults with schizophrenia: From treatment recommendations to dissemination. *Psychiatric Services, 50,* 233–238.

Dixon, L., McNary, S., & Lehman, A. F. (1998). Remission of substance use disorder among psychiatric inpatients with mental illness. *American Journal of Psychiatry, 155*(2), 239–243.

Dixon, L., Weiden, P., Torres, M., & Lehman, A. (1997). Assertive community treatment and medication compliance in the homeless mentally ill. *American Journal of Pychiatry, 154,* 1302–1304.

Docherty, J. P. (1986). Psychopharmacology evaluation: Psychosocial issues. In D. C. Jimerson & J. P. Docherty (Eds.), *Psychopharmacology consultation* (pp. 118–129). Washington, DC: American Psychiatric Press.

Dorevitch, A., Kalian, M., Shalfman, M., & Lerner, V. (1997). Treatment of long-term tardive dyskinesia with vitamin E. *Biological Psychiatry, 41*(1), 114–116.

Dow, M. G., Verdi, M. B., & Sacco, W. P. (1991). Training psychiatric patients to discuss medication issues: Effects on patient communication and knowledge of medications. *Behavior Modification, 15*(1), 3–21.

Draine, J., & Solomon, P. (1994). Explaining attitudes toward medication compliance among a seriously mentally ill population. *Journal of Nervous and Mental Disease, 182,* 50–54.

Drake, R. E., & Brunette, M. F. (1998). Complications of severe mental illness related to alcohol and drug use disorders. *Recent Developments in Alcoholism, 14,* 285–299.

Druss, B. G., Rohrbach, R., Kosten, T., Hoff, R., & Rosenheck, R. A. (1998). Use of alternative medicines in major depression. *Psychiatric Services, 49*(11), 1397.

Duchin, S. P., & Brown, S. A. (1990). Patients should participate in designing diabetes educational content. *Patient Education and Counseling, 16,* 255–267.

Dulcan, M. K. (1992). Information for parents and youth on psychotropic medications. *Journal of Child and Adolescent Psychopharmacology, 2,* 81–101.

Duncan, J. C., & Rogers, R. (1998). Medication compliance in patients with chronic schizophrenia: Implications for the community management of mentally disordered offenders. *Journal of Forensic Sciences, 43,* 1133–1137.

DuPaul, G. J., Power, T. J., Anastopoulos, A. D., & Reid, R. (1998). *ADHD Rating Scale-IV: Checklists, norms, and clinical interpretations.* New York: Guilford Press.

Dziegielewski, S. F. & Leon, A. M. (1998). Psychopharmacological treatment of major depression. *Research on Social Work Practice, 8,* 475–490.

Dziegielewski, S. F. (1997). Should clinical social workers seek psychotropic medication privileges. Yes! In B. Thyer (Ed.) *Controversial issues in social work practice* (pp. 152–158, 164–165). Boston: Allyn/Bacon.

D'zurilla, T. J. (1986). *Problem-solving therapy: A social competence approach to clinical intervention.* New York: Springer.

Eckman, T. A., & Liberman, R. P. (1990). A large-scale field test of a medication management skills training program for people with schizophrenia. *Psychosocial Rehabilitation Journal, 13,* 31–35.

Eckman, T. A., Liberman, R. P., Phipps, C. C., & Blair, K. E. (1990). Teaching medication management skills to schizophrenic patients. *Journal of Clinical Psychopharmacology, 10*(1), 33–38.

Eckman, T. A., Wirshing, W. C., Marder, S. R., Liberman, R. P., Johnston-Cronk, K., Zimmerman, K., & Mintz, J. (1992). Technique for training schizophrenic patients in illness self-management: A controlled trial. *American Journal of Psychiatry, 149,* 1549–1555.

Efron, D., Jaman, F., & Barker, M. (1997). Side effects of methylphenidate and dexamphetamine in children with attention deficit hyperactivity disorder: A double-blind, crossover trial. *Pediatrics, 100*(4), 662–666.

Eisenberg, G., Hilliard, J., & Gutheil, T. (1981). The ethical aspects of the right to refuse medication: A clinicolegal dilemma for the psychiatrist and patient. *Psychiatric Quarterly, 53,* 93–99.

Elliot, C., & Kintzer, C. (1973). No prescription pads for social workers. *Clinical Social Work Journal, 1,* 134–136.

Esposito, L. (1995). The effects of medication education on adherence to medication regimens in an elderly population. *Journal of Advanced Nursing, 21,* 935–43.

Estroff, S. E. (1981). *Making it crazy: An ethnography of psychiatric clients in an American community.* Berkeley: University of California Press.

Ettorre, E., & Riska, E. (1995). *Gendered moods: Psychotropics and society.* London: Routledge.

Everett, B., & Nelson, A. (1992). We're not cases and you're not managers: An account of a client-professional partnership developed in response to the "borderline" diagnosis. *Psychosocial Rehabilitation Journal, 15*(4), 49–60.

Falloon, I., Boyd, J., & McGill, C. (1984). *Family care of schizophrenia: A problem-solving approach to the treatment of mental illness.* New York: Guilford Press.

Fava, M., Borus, J. S., Alpert, J. E., & Nierenberg, A. A. (1997). Folate, vitamin B-sub-1-sub-2, and homocysteine in major depressive disorder. *American Journal of Psychiatry, 154*(3), 426–428.

Feltner, D. E., & Hertzman, M. (1993). Progress in the treatment of tardive dyskinesia: Theory and practice. *Hospital & Community Psychiatry, 44,* 25–33.

Fenn, H. H., Robinson, D., Luby, V., Dangel, C., Buxton, E., Beattie, M., Kraemer, H., & Yesavage, J. A. (1996). Trends in pharmacotherapy of schizoaffective and bipolar affective disorders: A 5-year naturalistic study. *American Journal of Psychiatry, 153*(5), 711–713.

Fenton, W. S., Blyler, C. R., & Heinssen, R. K. (1997). Determinants of medication compliance in schizophrenia: Empirical and clinical findings. *Schizophrenia Bulletin, 23,* 637–651.

Fincke, B. G., Miller, D. R., & Spiro, A. (1998). The interaction of patient perception of overmedication with drug compliance and side effects. *Journal of General Internal Medicine, 13*(3), 182–185.

Fisher, R. L., & Fisher, S. (1997). Are we justified in treating children with psychotropic drugs? In S. Fisher and R. P. Greenberg (Eds.), *From placebo to panacea: Putting psychiatric drugs to the test* (pp. 307–322). New York: John Wiley & Sons.

Fisher, S., & Greenberg, R. P. (1997). The curse of the placebo: Fanciful pursuit of a pure biological therapy. In S. Fisher and R. P. Greenberg (Eds.), *From placebo to panacea: Putting psychiatric drugs to the test* (pp. 3–56). New York: John Wiley & Sons.

Fitzpatrick, P. A., Klorman, R., Brumaghim, J. T., & Borgstedt, A. D. (1992). Effects of sustained-release and standard preparations of methylphenidate on attention deficit disorder. *Journal of the American Academy of Child and Adolescent Psychiatry, 31,* 226–234.

Flaskerud, J. H., & Hu, L. (1994). Participation in and outcome of treatment for major depression among low income Asian Americans. *Psychiatry Research, 53*(3), 289–300.

Fletcher, C. V., Acosta, E. P., & Strykowski, J. M. (1994). Gender differences in human pharmacokinetics and pharmacodynamics. *Journal of Adolescent Health, 15,* 619–629.

Flynn, L. M. (1994). The impact of managed care. *Advocate* (newsletter of the National Alliance for the Mentally Ill), *16*(2), 1, 16, 23.

Ford, M. (1980). The psychiatrist's double bind: The right to refuse medication. *American Journal of Psychiatry, 137,* 332–339.

Forman, L. (1993). Medication: Reasons and interventions for noncompliance.

Journal of Psychosocial Nursing and Mental Health Services, 31(10), 23–25.

Foxx, R. M., & Bittle, R. G. (1989). *Thinking it through: Teaching a problem-solving strategy for community living—curriculum for individuals with chronic mental illness.* Champaign, IL: Research Press.

Frank, J. D., & Frank, J. B. (1993). *Persuasion and healing: A comparative study of psychotherapy* (3rd ed.). Baltimore: Johns Hopkins.

Frank, E., Perel, J. M., Mallinger, A. G., Thase, M. E., & Kupfer, D. J. (1992). Relationship of pharmacologic compliance to long-term prophylaxis in recurrent depression. *Psychopharmacology Bulletin, 28,* 231–235.

Frank, J. (1974). *Persuasion and healing* (Rev. ed.). New York: Shocken Books.

Franson, K. L., & Smith, S. L. (1998). Compliance: Problems and opportunities. *Clinics in Geriatric Medicine, 14*(1), 7–16.

French, L. M. (1940). *Psychiatric social work.* New York: Commonwealth Fund.

Freund, P. D. (1993). Professional role(s) in the empowerment process: "Working with" mental health consumers. *Psychosocial Rehabilitation Journal, 16*(3), 65–73.

Fulwiler, C., & Ruthazer, R. (1999). Premorbid risk factors for violence in adult mental illness. *Comprehensive Psychiatry, 40*(2), 96–100.

Gabe, J. (1990). Toward a sociology of tranquilizer prescribing. *British Journal of Addiction, 85*(1), 41–48.

Gadow, K. D. (1991). Clinical issues in child and adolescent psychopharmacology. *Journal of Counseling and Clinical Psychology, 59*(6), 842–852.

Galassi, J. P., Galassi, M. D., & Vedder, M. J. (1981). Perspectives on assertion as a social skills model. In J. D. Wine & M. D. Smye (Eds.), *Social competence* (pp. 287–345). New York: Guilford Press.

Garavan, J., Browne, S., Gervin, M., Lane, A., Larkin, C., & O'Callaghan, E. (1998). Compliance with neuroleptic medication in outpatients with schizophrenia: Relationship to subjective response to neuroleptics, attitudes to medication and insight. *Comprehensive Psychiatry, 39*(4), 215–219.

Garrity, T. F., & Lawson, E. J. (1989). Patient-physician communication as a determinant of medication misuse in older, minority women. *The Journal of Drug Issues, 19*(2), 245–249.

Gasque-Carter, K. O., & Curlee, M. B. (1999). The educational needs of families of mentally ill adults: The South Carolina experience. *Psychiatric Services, 50,* 520–524.

Gehres, R. W. (1986). A medication monitoring service for elderly patients offered by the pharmacist on a fee-for-service basis. *Journal of Geriatric Drug Therapy, 1,* 81–89.

Gelenberg, A. J., Bassuk, E. L., & Schoonover, S. C. (1990). *The practitioner's guide to psychoactive drugs* (3rd ed.). New York: Plenum Medical Books.

Geller, J. L. (1982). State hospital patients and their medication—Do they know what to take? *American Journal of Psychiatry, 139,* 112–113.

Gerhart, U., & Brooks, A. (1983). The social work practitioner and anti-psychotic medication. *Social Work, 28,* 454–459.

Gerhart, U. C. (1990). *Caring for the chronic mentally ill.* Itasca, IL: F. E. Peacock.

Gibelman, M. (1993). School social workers, counselors, and psychologists in collaboration: A shared agenda. *Social Work in Education, 15*(1), 45–51.

Gitlin, M. J., Cochran, S. D., & Jamison, K. R. (1989). Maintenance lithium treatment: Side effects and compliance. *Journal of Clinical Psychiatry, 50,* 127–131.

Glazer, W. M., Morgenstern, H., & Doucette, J. (1994). Race and tardive dyskinesia among outpatients at a CMHC. *Hospital & Community Psychiatry, 45*(1), 38–42.

Goldberg, A. I., Cohen, G., & Rubin, A. H. E. (1998). Physician assessments of patient compliance with medical treatment. *Social Science & Medicine, 47,* 1873–1876.

Goldberg, R. S., Riba, M., & Tasman, A. (1991). Psychiatrists' attitudes toward prescribing medication for patients treated by nonmedical psychotherapists. *Hospital & Community Psychiatry, 42,* 276–280.

Goldman, L. S., Genel, M., Bezman, R. J., & Slanetz, P. J. (1998). Diagnosis and treatment of attention-deficit/hyperactivity disorder in children and adolescents. *Journal of the American Medical Association, 279*(14), 1100–1107.

Goldstein, J. M., Seidman, L. J., Goodman, J. M., Koren, D., Lee, H., Weintraub, S., & Tsuang, M. T. (1998). Are there sex differences in neuropsychological functions among patients with schizophrenia? *American Journal of Psychiatry, 155*(10), 1358–1364.

Goldwyn, R. M. (1988). Educating the patient and family about depression. *Medical Clinics of North America, 72,* 887–896.

Grabowski, J., & VandenBos, G. R. (1992). *Psychopharmacology: Basic mechanisms and applied interventions.* Washington, DC: American Psychological Association.

Gray, C. (1998, October 3). The joys and struggles of the collegial relationship in the best interests of the client. Presentation at *Psychopharmacology for Clinical Social Workers and Other Mental Health Professionals,* sponsored by The Greater Washington Society for Clinical Social Work and the National Catholic School of Social Service, Washington, DC.

Green, B., Wehing, C., & Talesk, C. (1987). Group art therapy as an adjunct to treatment for chronic outpatients. *Hospital & Community Psychiatry, 38*(9), 988–994.

Green, K. (1998). *Home care survival guide.* Philadelphia: Lippincott.

Greenberg, L., Fine, S. B., Cohen, C., & Larson, K. (1988). An interdisciplinary psychoeducation program for schizophrenic patients and their families in an acute care setting. *Hospital & Community Psychiatry, 39,* 277–282.

Greenhill, L. L., & Setterberg, S. (1993). Pharmacotherapy of disorders of adolescents. *Psychiatric Clinics of North America, 16*(4), 793–810.

Greenwald, B. S., Kremen, N., & Aupperle, P. (1992). Tailoring of adult psychiatric practices to the field of geriatrics. *Psychiatric Quarterly, 63*(4), 343–364.

Grymonpre, R. E., Didur, C. D., Montgomery, P. R., & Sitar, D. S. (1998). Pill count, self-report, and pharmacy claims data to measure medication adherence in the elderly. *Annals of Pharmacotherapy, 32*(7–8), 749–754.

Gutierrez, P. M. & Silk, K. R. (1998). Prescription privileges for psychologists: A review of the psychological literature. *Professional Psychology, 29,* 213–222.

Haas, G. L., Garratt, L. S., & Sweeney, J. A. (1998). Delay to first antipsychotic medication in schizophrenia: Impact on symptomatology and clinical course of illness. *Journal of Psychiatric Research, 32*(3/4), 151–159.

Halford, W. K., & Hayes, R. (1991). Psychological rehabilitation of chronic schizophrenic patients: Recent findings on social skills training and family psychoeducation. *Clinical Psychology Review, 11,* 23–44.

Hallowell, E. M., & Ratey, J. J. (1994). *Driven to distraction: Recognizing and coping with attention deficit disorder from childhood through adulthood.* New York: Pantheon.

Hamilton, M., (1959). The assessment of anxiety states by rating. *British Journal of Medical Psychology, 32,* 50–55.

Hancock, L. (1996). Mother's little helper. *Newsweek, 127*(12), 51–56.

Hankoff, L., & Galvin, J. (1968). Psychopharmacological treatment and its implications for social work. *Social Work, 13,* 40–47.

Harmon, R. B., & Tratnack, S. A. (1992). Teaching hospitalized patients with serious, persistent mental illness. *Journal of Psychosocial Nursing and Mental Health Services, 30*(7), 33–36.

Harrison, W. D., Drolen, C. S., & Atherton, C. R. (1989). Role discrepancies in state hospital social work. *Social Casework, 70*, 622–626.

Hatfield, A. B. (1981). Self-help groups for families of the mentally ill. *Social Work, 26*, 408–413.

Hayes, R., & Gantt, A. (1992). Patient psychoeducation: The therapeutic use of knowledge for the mentally ill. *Social Work in Health Care, 17*(11), 53–67.

Hechtman, L., Weiss, G., & Perlman, T (1984). Young adult outcome of hyperactive children who received long-term stimulant treatment. *Journal of the Academy of Child Psychiatry, 23* (2), 261–269.

Heinrichs, D. W., Cohen, B. P., & Carpenter, W. T. (1985). Early insight and the management of schizophrenic decompensation. *Journal of Nervous and Mental Disease, 173*, 133–138.

Helman, C. G. (1981). "Tonic," "fuel," and "food": Social and symbolic aspects of the long-term use of psychotropic drugs. *Social Science & Medicine, 15B*, 521–533.

Hepworth, D. H., Rooney, R. H., & Larsen, J. A. (1997). *Direct social work practice: Theory and skills* (5th ed.). Pacific Grove, CA: Brooks/Cole Publishing.

Herz, M. I. (1984). Recognizing and preventing relapse in patients with schizophrenia. *Hospital & Community Psychiatry, 35*, 344–349.

Heszen-Klemens, I. (1987). Patients' noncompliance and how doctors manage this. *Social Science & Medicine, 24*, 409–416.

Heyduk, L. J. (1991). Medication education: Increasing patient compliance. *Journal of Psychosocial Nursing and Mental Health Services, 29*(12), 32–35.

Heyscue, B. E., Levin, G. M., & Merrick, J. P. (1998). Compliance with depot antipsychotic medication by patients attending outpatient clinics. *Psychiatric Services, 49*, 1232–1234.

Higgins, P. B. (1995). Clozapine and the treatment of schizophrenia: Implications for social work practice. *Health & Social Work, 20*, 124–132.

Hoffman, J. S. (1990). Integrating biologic and psychologic treatment: The need for a unitary model. *Psychiatric Clinics of North America, 13*(2), 369–372.

Hogarty, G. E. (1984). Depot neuroleptics: The relevance of psychosocial factors. *Journal of Clinical Psychiatry, 45*(Supp. 2), 36–42.

Hogarty, G. E. (1991). Social work practice research on severe mental illness: Charting a future. *Research on Social Work Practice, 1*(1), 5–31.

Hogarty, G. E., & Ulrich, R.F. (1998). The limitations of antipsychotic medication on schizophrenia relapse and adjustment and the contributions of psychosocial treatment. *Journal of Psychiatric Research, 32*, 243–250.

Hogarty, G. E., Anderson, C. M., Reiss, D. J., Kornblith, S. J., Greenwald, D. P., Ulrich, R. F., & Carter, M. (1991). Family psychoeducation, social skills training, and maintenance chemotherapy in the aftercare treatment of schizophrenia II. Two year effects of a controlled study on relapse and adjustment. *Archives of General Psychiatry, 48*, 340–347.

Hogarty, G. E., Goldberg, S., & Schooler, N. R. (1974). Drug and sociotherapy in the aftercare treatment of schizophrenia: II. Two year relapse rates. *Archives of General Psychiatry, 31*, 603–608.

Hosch, H. M., Barrientos, G. A., Fierro, C., & Ramirez, J. I. (1996). Predicting adherence to medications by Hispanics with schizophrenia. *Hispanic Journal of Behavioral Sciences, 17*(3), 320–333.

Howard, K., Rickels, K., Mock, J., Lipman, R., Covi, L., & Baumm, N. (1970). Therapeutic style and attrition rate from psychiatric drug treatment. *Journal of Nervous and Mental Disease, 150*, 102–110.

Hudson, W. W. (1992). *The WALMYR*

assessment scales scoring manual. Tempe, AZ: Walmyr.

Hughes, R., & Brewin, R. (1979). *The tranquilizing of America and the American way of life.* NY: Harcourt Brace Jovanovich.

Hutto, B. R. (1997). Folate and cobalamin in psychiatric illness. *Comprehensive Psychiatry, 38*(6), 305–314.

Ikebuchi, E., & Anzai, N. (1995). Effect of the medication management module evaluated using the role-play test. *Psychiatry and Clinical Neurosciences, 49*(3), 151–156.

Isaac, L. M., Tamblyn, R. M., & McGill-Calgary Drug Research Team. (1993). Compliance and cognitive function: A methodological approach to measuring unintentional errors in medication compliance in the elderly. *The Gerontologist, 33,* 772–781.

Ivanoff, A., & Stern, S. B. (1992). Self-management in health and mental health settings: Evidence of maintenance and generalization. *Social Work Research & Abstracts, 28*(4), 32–38.

Ivey, A. E., & Ivey, M. B. (1999). *Intentional interviewing and counseling: Facilitating client development in a multicultural society* (4th ed.). Pacific Grove: Brooks/Cole.

Jacobsen, F. M. (1994). Psychopharmacology. In L. C. Comez-Diaz & B. Greene (Eds.), *Women of color: Integrating ethnic and gender identities in psychotherapy* (pp. 319–336). New York: Guilford Press.

Jacobvitz, D. (1990). Treatment of attentional and hyperactivity problems in children with sympathomimetic drugs: A comprehensive review. *Journal of the American Academy of Child and Adolescent Psychiatry, 29,* 677–688.

Jamison, K., Gerner, R., & Goodwin, F. (1979). Patient and physician attitudes toward lithium. *Archives of General Psychiatry, 36,* 866–869.

Jamison, K. R., & Akiskal, H. S. (1983). Medication compliance in patients with bipolar disorder. *Psychiatric Clinic of North America, 6,* 175–192.

Janicak, P. G., Davis, J. M., Preskorn, S. H., & Ayd, F. J. (1993). *Principles and practice of psychopharmacotherapy.* Baltimore: Williams & Wilkins.

Jenicke, M. A. (1993). Obsessive-compulsive disorder: Efficacy of specific treatments as assessed by controlled trials. *Psychopharmacology Bulletin, 29,* 487–499.

Jensfold, M. F. (1996). Nonpregnant reproductive-age women, part 1: The menstrual cycle and psychopharmacology. In Jensfold, M. F., Halbreich, U., & Hamilton, J. A. (Eds), *Psychopharmacology and women* (pp. 139–161). Washington, DC: American Psychiatric Press.

Jensfold, M. F., Halbreich, U., & Hamilton, J. A. (1996). Gender-sensitive psychopharmacology: An overview. In M. F. Jensfold, U. Halbreich, & J. A. Hamilton (Eds.), *Psychopharmacology and women* (pp. 3–9). Washington, DC: American Psychiatric Press.

Jeste, D. V., & Caligiuri, M. P. (1993). Tardive dyskinesia. *Schizophrenia Bulletin, 19,* 303–312.

Jeste, D. V., Lindamer, L. A., Evans, J., & Lacro, J. P. (1996). Relationship of ethnicity and gender to schizophrenia and pharmacology of neuroleptics. *Psychopharmacology Bulletin, 32*(2), 243–251.

Johnson, A. B. (1990). *Out of bedlam: The truth about deinstitutionalization.* New York: Basic Books.

Johnson, H. C., Renaud, E. F., Schmidt, D. T., & Stanek, E. J. (1998). Social workers' views of parents of children with mental and emotional disabilities. *Families in Society, 79*(2), 173–187.

Johnson, H. C. (1989). Resisting the evil empire: Comments on "Social work and psychotropic drug treatments." *Social Service Review, 63,* 657–660.

Johnson, F. N. (1984). *The history of lithium therapy.* London: Macmillan.

Jones, R. E. (1976). Franklin and Rush: American psychiatry's two revolutionaries. *Hospital & Community Psychiatry,* 27(7), 461–463.

Jordan, S., Hardy, B., & Coleman, M. (1999). Medication management: An exploratory study into the role of community mental health nurses. *Journal of Advanced Nursing, 29,* 1068–1081.

Jorn, A. F., Korten, A. E., Jacomb, P. A., Rodgers, B., Pollit, P., Christensen, H., & Henderson, S. (1997). Helpfulness of interventions for mental disorders: Beliefs of health professionals compared with the general public. *British Journal of Psychiatry, 171,* 233–237.

Kabat-Zinn, J., Massion, A. O., Kristeller, J., Peterson, L. G., Fletcher, K. E., Phert, L., Lenderking, W. R., & Santorelli, S. F. (1992). Effectiveness of a meditation-based stress reduction program in the treatment of anxiety disorders. *American Journal of Psychiatry, 149,* 936–943.

Kail, B. L. (1989). Drugs, gender, and ethnicity: Is the older minority woman at risk? *The Journal of Drug Issues, 19*(2), 171–189.

Kane, J. M. (1983). Problems of compliance in the outpatient treatment of schizophrenia. *Journal of Clinical Psychiatry, 44*(6), 3–6.

Kane, J., Honigfeld, G., Singer, J., & Meltzer, H. (1988). Clozapine for the treatment-resistant schizophrenic: A double-blind comparison with chlorpromazine. *Archives of General Psychiatry, 45,* 789–796.

Kanter, J. (1989). Clinical case management: Definition, principles, components. *Hospital & Community Psychiatry, 40,* 361–368.

Kaplan, H. I. & Sadock, B. J. (1998). *Synopsis of psychiatry* (8th ed.). Baltimore, MD: Williams & Wilkins.

Kasper, J., Hoge, S., Feucht-Haviar, T., Cortina, J., & Cohen, B. (1997). Prospective study of patients' refusal of antipsychotic medication under a physician discretion review procedure. *Archives of General Psychiatry, 154,* 483–489.

Kassis, J. P., Boothroyd, P., & Ben-Dror, R. (1992). The family support group: Families and professionals in partnership. *Psychosocial Rehabilitation Journal, 15,* 91–96.

Kearney, C. A., & Silverman, W. K. (1998). A critical review of pharmacotherapy for youth with anxiety disorders: Things are not as they seem. *Journal of Anxiety Disorders, 12*(2), 83–102.

Keck, P. E., & McElroy, S. L. (1996). Outcome in the pharmacologic treatment of bipolar disorder. *Journal of Clinical Psychopharmacology, 16*(2, Suppl.1), 15S–22S.

Keen, E. (1998). Are pharmacology and constructivist psychotherapy mutually exclusive? *Journal of Constructivist Psychology, 11*(1), 31–47.

Kelly, G. R., Scott, J. E., and Mamon, J. (1990). Medication compliance and health education among outpatients with chronic mental disorders. *Medical Care, 28*(12), 1181–1197.

Kelly, K. V. (1992). Parallel treatment: Therapy with one clinician and medication with another. *Hospital & Community Psychiatry, 43,* 778–780.

Kellner, R. (1986). The brief depression rating scale. In N. Sartorius and T. A. Bans (Eds.), *Assessment of depression* (179–183). New York: Springer-Verlag.

Kemp, R., Kirov, G., Everitt, B., Hayward, P., & David, A. (1998). A randomized controlled trial of compliance therapy: 18 month follow-up. *British Journal of Psychiatry, 172,* 413–419.

Keshavan, M. S., & Kennedy, J. S. (1992). *Drug-induced dysfunction in psychiatry.* New York: Hemisphere Publishing.

Kessler, R. C., Abelson, J. M., & Zhao, S. (1998). The epidemiology of mental disorders. In J. B. W. Williams & K. Ell (Eds.), *Recent advances in mental health research: Implications for social workers* (pp. 3–24). Silver Spring, MD: National Association of Social Workers.

Kisthardt, W. E. (1992). A strengths model of case management: The principles and functions of a helping partnership with persons with persistent mental illness. In D. Saleeby (Ed.), *The strengths perspective in social work* (p. 59–83). New York: Longman.

Kleinman, D. L., & Cohen, L. J. (1991). The decontextualization of mental illness: The portrayal of work in psychiatric drug advertisements. *Social Science & Medicine, 32*(8), 867–874.

Klerman, G. L. (1990). The psychiatric patient's right to effective treatment: Implications of Osheroff v. Chestnut Lodge. *American Journal of Psychiatry, 147*, 409–418.

Kleijnen, J., & Knipschild, P. (1991). Niacin and vitamin B6 in mental functioning: A review of controlled trials in humans. *Biological Psychiatry, 29*(9), 931–941.

Kline, N. S. (1970). Monoamine oxidase inhibitors: An unfinished picaresque tale. In F. J. Ayd & R. Blackwell (Eds.), *Discoveries in biological psychiatry* (pp. 194–204). Philadelphia: J. B. Lippincott.

Knight, M. M., Wigder, K. S., Fortsch, M. M. & Polcari, A. (1990). Medication education for children. Is it worthwhile? *Journal of Child and Adolescent Psychiatric and Mental Health Nursing, 3*(1), 25–28.

Kopp, J. (1988). Self-monitoring: A literature review of research and practice. *Social Work Research & Abstracts, 4*(4), 8–20.

Kramer, P. D. (1993). *Listening to Prozac: A psychiatrist explores antidepressant drugs and the remaking of self.* New York: Viking.

Kucera-Bozarth, K., Beck, N. C., & Lyss, L. (1982). Compliance with lithium regimens. *Journal of Psychosocial Nursing and Mental Health Services, 20*(7), 11–15.

Kuhn, R. (1970). The imipramine story. In F. J. Ayd & R. Blackwell (Eds.), *Discoveries in biological psychiatry* (pp. 205–217). Philadelphia: J. B. Lippincott.

Kuipers, J. Bell, C. Davidhizar, R. E., Cosgray, R., & Fawley, R. (1994). Knowledge and attitudes of chronic mentally ill patients before and after medication education. *Journal of Advanced Nursing, 20*(3), 450–456.

Kumar, A. M., Weiss, S., Fernandez, J. B., Cruess, D., & Eisdorfer, C. (1998). Peripheral serotonin levels of women: Role in aging and ethnicity. *Gerontology, 44*(4), 211–216.

Langer, S. Z., Arbilla, S., & Graham, D. (1991). Current developments in preclinical neuropharmacology which will impact on pharmacotherapy of major mental illness. In H. Y. Meltzer & D. Nerozzi (Eds.), *Current practices and future developments in the pharmacotherapy of mental disorders* (pp. 3–10). Amsterdam: Excerpta Medica.

Lantz, J. (1987). Guilt and restitution: A ghetto healer's approach. *Voices, 23*, 42–45.

Lawrence, J. D., Lawrence, D. B., & Carson, D. S. (1997). Optimizing ADHD therapy with sustained-release methylphenidate. *American Family Physician, 55*(5), 1705–1712.

Lawson, G., & Cooperrider, C. (1988). *Clinical psychopharmacology: A practical reference for the non-medical psychotherapist.* Rockville, MD: Aspen.

Lawson, W. B. (1996). Clinical issues in the pharmacotherapy of African-Americans. *Psychopharmacology Bulletin, 32*(2), 275–281.

Lawson, W. B. (1986). Chronic mental illness and the black family. *American Journal of Social Psychiatry, 37*, 50–54.

Leake, C. D. (1970). The long road for a drug from idea to use: The amphetamines. In F. J. Ayd & R. Blackwell (Eds.), *Discoveries in biological psychiatry* (pp. 69–84). Philadelphia: J. B. Lippincott.

Lee, J. A. B. (1994). *The empowerment approach to social work practice.* New York: Columbia University Press.

Lee, S., Chow, C. C., Shek, C. C., & Wing, Y. K. (1992). Folate concentrations in Chinese psychiatric outpatients on long-term lithium treatment. *Journal of Affective Disorders, 24*(4), 265–270.

Leff, J. (1996). Working with families of schizophrenic patients: Effects on clinical and social outcomes. In M. Massimo, A. Rupp, & N. Sartorius (Eds.), *Handbook of mental health economics and health policy, Volume 1: Schizophrenia* (pp. 261–270). Chichester, England: Wiley.

Lefley, H. P. (1994). An overview of family-professional relationships. In D. T. Marsh (Ed.), *New directions in the psychological treatment of serious mental illness* (186–198). Westport, CT: Praeger.

Lefley, H. P. (1993). Involuntary treatment: Concerns of consumers, families and society. *Innovations and Research, 2,* 7–9.

Lehman, A. F., Herron, J. D., Schwartz, R. P., & Myers, C. P. (1993). Rehabilitation for adults with severe mental illness and substance use disorders: A clinical trial. *Journal of Nervous and Mental Disease, 181,* 86–91.

Leventhal, H., Diefenbach, M., & Leventhal, E. A. (1992). Illness cognition: Using common sense to understand treatment adherence and affect cognition interactions. *Cognitive Therapy and Research, 16,* 143–163.

Levy, R. (1978). Facilitating patient compliance and medical programs: An area for social work research and intervention. In N. Bracht (Ed.), *Social work in health care: A guide to professional practice* (pp. 281–292). New York: Haworth Press.

Lewis, R. E., & Crossland, M. M. (1992). Organization of a medication group for older pateints with mental illness. *Geriatric Nursing, 13*(4), 187–191.

Libassi, M. F. (1992). The chronically mentally ill: A practice approach. In S. M. Rose (Ed.), *Case management and social work practice* (pp. 77–90). New York: Longman.

Liberman, R., Kane, J., Vaccaro, J., & Wirshing, W. (1987, October). *Negotiating medication issues with schizophrenic patients.* Workshop conducted at the Institute on Hospital & Community Psychiatry, Boston, MA.

Liberman, R. P. (1988). Coping with chronic mental disorders: A framework for hope. In R. P. Liberman (Ed.), *Psychiatric rehabilitation of chronic mental patients* (pp. 1–28). Washington, DC: American Psychiatric Press.

Lieberman, J. A. (1996). Pharmacotherapy for patients with first-episode, acute, and refractory schizophrenia. *Psychiatric Annals, 26*(8), 515–518.

Lin, K. M., Poland, R. E., Wan, Y. J., Smith, M. W., & Lesser, I. M. (1996). The evolving science of pharmacogenetics: Clinical and ethnic perspectives. *Psychopharmacology Bulletin, 32*(2), 205–217.

Lin, I. F., Spiga, R., & Fortsch, W. (1979). Insight and adherence to medication in chronic schizophrenics. *Journal of Clinical Psychiatry, 40,* 430–432.

Lin, K., Poland, R. E., Smith, M. W., Strickland, T. L., & Mendoza, R. (1991). Pharmacokinetic and other related factors affecting psychotropic responses in Asians. *Psychopharmacology Bulletin, 27*(4), 427–436.

Lin, K., & Shen, W. W. (1991). Pharmacology for southeast Asian psychiatric patients. *The Journal of Nervous and Mental Disease, 179*(6), 346–350.

Lindamer, L. A., Lohr, J. B., Harris, M. J., McAdams, L. A., & Jeste, D. V. (1999). Gender related clinical differences in older patients with schizophrenia. *Journal of Clinical Psychiatry, 60*(1), 61–67.

Linde, K., Ramirez, G., Mulrow, C. D., Pauls, A., Weidenhamer, W., & Melchart, D. (1996). St. John's Wort for depression—an overview and meta-analysis of randomized clinical trials. *British Medical Journal, 313*(7052), 253.

Lisenbee, K. (1994). *Art therapy: An effective treatment for consumers diagnosed with a long-term mental illness?* Unpublished manuscript, School of Social Work, Virginia Commonwealth University, Richmond.

Littrell, J. (1995). Clinical practice guidelines for depression in primary care:

What social workers need to know. *Research on Social Work Practice, 5*(2), 131–151.

Littrell, J., & Ashford, J. B. (1995). Is it proper for psychologists to discuss medications with clients? *Professional Psychology, 26,* 238–244.

Littrell, J., & Ashford, J. B. (1994). The duty of social workers to refer for medications: A study of field instructors. *Social Work Research, 18*(2), 123–128.

Lloyd, A., Horan, W., Borgaro, S. R., Stokes, J. M., & Harvey, P. D. (1998). Predictors of medication compliance after hospital discharge in adolescent psychiatric patients. *Journal of Child & Adolescent Psychopharmacology, 8*(2), 133–141.

Lloyd, K., & Moodley, P. (1992). Psychotropic medication and ethnicity: An inpatient survey. *Social Psychiatry and Psychiatric Epidemiology, 27*(2), 95–101.

Lubove, R. (1965). *The professional altruist: The emergence of social work as a career 1880–1930.* Cambridge, MA: Harvard University Press.

Lukoff, D., Liberman, R. P., & Nuechterlein, K. H. (1986). Symptom monitoring in the rehabilitation of schizophrenic patients. *Schizophrenia Bulletin, 12,* 578–593.

Lurie, A. (1982). The social work advocacy role in discharge planning. *Social Work in Health Care, 8*(2), 75–85.

MacPherson, R., Double, D. B., Rowlands, R. P., & Harrison, D. M. (1993). Long-term psychiatric patients' understanding of neuroleptic medication. *Hospital & Community Psychiatry, 44,* 71–73.

Maj, M., Pirozzi, R., & Kemali, D. (1990). Long-term outcome of lithium prophylaxis in bipolar patients. *Archives of General Psychiatry, 47*(7), 665–671.

Mailick, D., & Ashley, A. (1981). Politics of interprofessional collaboration: Challenge to advocacy. *Social Casework, 65,* 131–137.

Mailick, M. D., & Jordan, D. (1977). A multimodel approach to collaborative practice in health care settings. *Social Work in Health Care, 2,* 445–457.

Mancuso, L., & Emrey, B. (Eds.). (1991). Special issue: Serving persons with dual disorders of mental illness and substance abuse. *Psychosocial Rehabilitation Journal, 15.*

Manderscheid, R. W., & Sonnenschein, M. A. (Eds.) (1994). *Mental health, United States, 1994.* Rockville, MD: U.S. Department of Health and Human Services, Center for Mental Health Services.

Manheimer, D., Davidson, S. T., Balter, M. B., Mellinger, G. D., Cisin, I. H., & Parry, H. J. (1973). Popular attitudes and beliefs about tranquilizers. *American Journal of Psychiatry, 130,* 1246–1253.

Marder, S. R. (1998). Facilitating compliance with antipsychotic medication. *Journal of Clinical Psychiatry, 59*(Suppl.3), 21–25.

Marks, I. M. (1987). *Fears, phobias, and rituals: Panic, anxiety, and their disorders.* New York: Oxford University Press.

Mason, S. E., & Pollack, D. (1998). Prozac, families and the law: Implications for social work practice. *Clinical Social Work Journal, 26,* 317–332.

Mason, S. E., Bermanzohn, P. C., & Siris, S. G. (1998). Clinical trials and tribulations: Implementation processes in schizophrenia research outcome. *Psychiatry, 61*(4), 288–301.

Matsuda, K. T., Cho, M. C., Lin, K., Smith, M. W., Youn, A. S., & Adams, J. A. (1996). Clozapine dosage, serum levels, efficacy, and side effect profile: A comparison of Korean-American and Caucasian patients. *Psychopharmacology Bulletin, 32*(2), 253–257.

Mazure, C. M. (Ed.) (1995). *Does stress cause psychiatric illness?* Washington, DC: American Psychiatric Press.

McCandless-Glimcher, L., McKnight, S., Hamera, E., Smith, B. L., Peterson, K. A., & Plumlee, M. N. (1986). Use of symptoms by schizophrenics to monitor and regulate their illness. *Hospital & Community Psychiatry, 37,* 929–933.

McCollum, A., Margolin, C., & Lieb, J. (1978). Consultation on psychoactive medication. *Health & Social Work, 3*(4), 72–98.

McCubbin, M., & Weisstub, D. N. (1998). Toward a pure best interests model of proxy decision making for incompetent psychiatric patients. *International Journal of Law and Psychiatry, 21*(1), 1–30.

McEntee, W. J., & Crook, T. H. (1991). Serotonin, memory, and the aging brain. *Psychopharmacology, 103,* 143–149.

McGill, C., Falloon, I., Boyd, J., & Wood-Siverio, C. (1983). Family educational intervention in the treatment of schizophrenia. *Hospital & Community Psychiatry, 34,* 934–938.

McMiller, T. P., & Weisz, J. R. (1996). Help-seeking preceding mental health clinic intake among African-American, Latino, and Caucasian youths. *Journal of the Academy of Child and Adolescent Psychiatry, 35*(8), 1086–1094.

McPhillips, M., & Sensky, T. (1998). Coercion, adherence or collaboration? Influences on compliance with medication. In T. Wykes, N. Tarrier, & S. Lewis (Eds.) *Outcome and innovation in psychological treatment of schizophrenia* (pp. 161–177). Chichester: Wiley.

Mendoza, R., Smith, M. W., Poland, R. E., Lin, K., & Strickland, T. L. (1991). Ethnic psychopharmacology: The Hispanic and Native American Perspective. *Psychopharmacology Bulletin, 27*(4), 448–458.

Miller, R., Wiedeman, G., & Linn, G. (1980). Prescribing psychotropic drugs: Whose responsibility? *Social Work in Health Care, 6*(1), 51–61.

Mishell, D. R. (1989). Contraception. *New England Journal of Medicine, 320,* 777–787.

Mizrahi, T., & Abramson, J. (1985). Sources of strain between physicians and social workers. Implications for social workers in health care settings. *Social Work in Health Care, 10*(3), 33–51.

Morris, L. S., & Schulz, R. M. (1993). Medication compliance: The patient's perspective. *Clinical Therapeutics, 15*(3), 593–606.

Morris, L. S., & Schulz, R. M. (1992). Patient compliance—An overview. *Journal of Clinical Pharmacy and Therapeutics, 17*(5), 283–295.

Morse, E. V., Simon, P. M., & Balson, P. M. (1993). Using experiential training to enhance health care professionals' awareness of patient compliance issues. *Academic Medicine, 68*(9), 693–697.

Mosher, L. R., & Burti, M. (1992). Relationships in rehabilitation: When technology fails. *Psychosocial Rehabilitation Journal, 15*(4), 11–17.

Moxley, D. P., & Freddolino, P. P. (1990). A model of advocacy for promoting client self-determination in psychosocial rehabilitation. *Psychosocial Rehabilitation Journal, 14*(2), 69–82.

Mueser, K. T., Bellack, A. S., Wade, J. H., Sayers, S. L., & Rosenthal, C. K. (1992). An assessment of the educational needs of chronic psychiatric patients and their relatives. *British Journal of Psychiatry, 160,* 674–680.

Mueser, K. T., & Gingerich, S. (1994). *Coping with schizophrenia: A guide for families.* Oakland, CA: New Harbinger Publications.

Nageotte, C., Sullivan, G., Duan, N., & Camp, P. L. (1997). Medication compliance among the seriously mentally ill in a public mental health system. *Social Psychiatry and Psychiatric Epidemiology, 32*(2), 49–56.

National Association of Social Workers. (1997). *Code of ethics.* Washington, DC: Author.

Neill, J. R. (1989). A social history of psychotropic drug advertisements. *Social Science and Medicine, 28*(4), 333–338.

Nightengale, B. S. Crumley, J. M., Liao, J., Lawrence, B. J., & Jacobs, E. W. (1998). Economic outcomes of antipsychotic agents in a Medicaid population: Traditional agents vs. risperidone. *Psychopharmacology Bulletin, 34*, 373–382.

O'Connell, R. A., Mayo, J. A., Flatow, L., Cuthbertson, B., & O'Brien, B. E. (1991). Outcome of bipolar disorder on long-term treatment with lithium. *British Journal of Psychiatry, 159*(2), 123–129.

Olfson, M., & Klerman, O. (1993). Trends in the prescription of psychotropic medications: The role of the physician specialty. *Medical Care, 31*(6), 559–564.

Olfson, M., & Pincus, H. A. (1994). Use of benzodiazepines in the community. *Archives of Internal Medicine, 154*(11), 1235–1241.

Opdycke, R. A., Ascione, F. J., Shimp, L. A., & Rosen, R. I. (1992). A systematic approach to educating elderly patients about their medications. *Patient Education and Counseling, 19*(1), 43–60.

O'Shea, M., Bicknell, L., & Whatley, D. (1991). Brief multifamily psychoeducation programs for schizophrenia. Strategies for implementation and management. *American Journal of Family Therapy, 19*(1), 33–44.

Parrish, J. (1993). Involuntary use of interventions: Pros & cons. *Innovations and Research, 2*, 15–22.

Peselow, E. D., Fieve, R. R., Difiglia, C., & Sanfilipo, M. P. (1994). Lithium prophylaxis of bipolar illness: The value of combination treatment. *British Journal of Psychiatry, 164*(2), 208–214.

Petr, C. G. (1998). *Social work with children and their families.* New York: Oxford.

Peuskens, J. (1995). Risperidone in the treatment of patients with chronic schizophrenia: A multi-national, multi-centre, double-blind, parallel group study versus haloperidol. *British Journal of Psychiatry, 166*, 712–726.

Piette, J. D., & Mah, C. A. (1997). The feasibility of automated voice messaging as an adjunct to diabetes outpatient care. *Diabetes Care, 20*, 15–21.

Pilette, W. L. (1988). The rise of three-party treatment relationships. *Psychotherapy, 25*, 420–423.

Pirodsky, D. M., & Cohen, J. S. (1992). *Clinical primer of psychopharmacology: A practical guide* (2nd ed.). New York: McGraw-Hill.

Pollio, D. E., North, C. S., & Foster, D. A. (1998). Content and curriculum in psychoeducation groups for families of persons with severe mental illness. *Psychiatric Services, 49*, 816–822.

Pollock, B. G. (1997). Gender differences in psychotropic drug metabolism. *Psychopharmacology Bulletin, 33*(2), 235–241.

Popper, C. W. (1997). Antidepressants in the treatment of attention-deficit/hyperactivity disorder. *Journal of Clinical Psychiatry, 58* (Suppl. 14), 14–29.

Popper, C. W. (1995). Balancing knowledge and judgment. *Child and Adolescent Psychiatry Clinics of North America, 4*, 483–513.

Posner, C. M., Wilson, K. G., Kral, M. J., Lander, S., & McIlwraith, R. D. (1992). Family psychoeducational support groups in schizophrenia. *American Journal of Orthopsychiatry, 62*, 206–218.

Post, R. M., Ketter, T. A., Denicoff, K., Pazzaglia, P. J., Leverich, G. S., Marangell, L. B., Callahan, A. M., George, M. S., & Frye, M A. (1996). The place of anticonvulsant therapy in bipolar illness. *Psychopharmacology, 128*, 115–129.

Potocky, M. (1993). An art therapy group for clients with chronic schizophrenia. *Social Work with Groups, 16*(3), 73–82.

Poulsen, R. L. (1992). Some current factors influencing the prescribing and use of psychotropic drugs. *Public Health Reports, 107*(1), 47–53.

Pray, J. E. (1991). Responding to psychosocial needs: Physician perceptions of their referral practices for hospitalized patients. *Health & Social Work, 16*(3), 184–192.

Preskorn, S. H., Harvey, A. T., & Stanga, C. (1998). Drug interactions and their role in patient care. In A. J. Rush (Ed.), *Mood and anxiety disorders* (pp.

145–164). Philadelphia: Current Science.

Raffoul, P. R., & Haney, C. A. (1989). Interdisciplinary treatment of drug misuse among older people of color: Ethnic considerations for social work practice. *The Journal of Drug Issues, 19*(2), 297–313.

Ramirez, L. F. (1996). Ethnicity and psychopharmacology in Latin America. *Mount Sinai Journal of Medicine, 63*(5–6), 330–331.

Rapp, C. A. (1998). *The strengths model: Case management with people suffering from severe and persistent mental illness.* New York: Oxford University Press.

Rapp, C. A. (1992). The strengths perspective of case management with persons suffering from severe mental illness. In D. Saleebey (Ed.), *The strengths perspective in social work practice* (pp. 45–58). New York: Longman.

Ravid, R., & Menon, S. (1993). Guidelines for disclosure of patient information under the Americans with Disabilities Act. *Hospital & Community Psychiatry, 44*, 280–281.

Reamer, F. G. (1987). Informed consent in social work. *Social Work, 32*, 425–429.

Reid, W. H., Pham, V. A., & Rago, W. (1993). Clozapine use by state programs: Public mental health systems respond to a new medication. *Hospital & Community Psychiatry, 44*, 739–743.

Remler, M., & Cohen, D. (1992). Should the right of mental patients to refuse treatment with psychotropic drugs be severely curtailed? In E. Gambrill & R. Pruger (Eds.), *Controversial issues in social work* (pp. 301–315). Boston: Allyn & Bacon.

Rhodes, L. A. (1984). "This will clear your mind": The use of metaphors for medications in psychiatric settings. *Culture, Medicine and Psychiatry, 8*, 49–70.

Ridgely, M. S., Lambert, D., Goodman, A., Chichester, C. S., & Ralph, R. (1998). Interagency collaboration in services for people with co-occurring mental illness and substance use disorder. *Psychiatric Services, 49*(2), 236–238.

Ries, R. K. (1993). The dually diagnosed patient with psychotic symptoms. *Journal of Addictive Diseases, 12*, 103–122.

Risby, E. D. (1996). Ethnic considerations in the pharmacology of mood disorders. *Pharmacology Bulletin, 32*(2), 231–234.

Robbins, C., & Clayton, R. R. (1989). Gender-related differences in psychoactive drug use among older adults. *The Journal of Drug Issues, 19*(2), 207–219.

Robinson, G., Gilbertson, A., & Litwak, L. (1986). The effects of psychiatric patient education to medication program on post-discharge compliance. *Psychiatric Quarterly, 58*, 113–118.

Rodgers, K. (1996). ADHD medication reformulated: An old drug reenters market. *Drug Topics, 140*(6), 31–32.

Rodin, J., & Ickovics, J. R. (1990). Women's health: Review and research agenda as we approach the 21st century. *American Psychologist, 45*(9), 1018–1034.

Rogers, A., Day, J. C., Williams, B., Randall, F., Wood, P., Healy, D., & Bentall, R. P. (1999). The meaning and management of neuroleptic medication: A study of patients with a diagnosis of schizophrenia. *Social Science & Medicine, 47*, 1313–1323.

Rose, S. M. (1990). Advocacy/empowerment: An approach to clinical practice for social work. *Journal of Sociology and Social Welfare, 17*(2), 41–52.

Rosenson, M., & Kasten, A. M. (1991). Another view of autonomy: Arranging for consent in advance. *Hospital & Community Psychiatry, 17*, 1–7.

Rosenson, M. K. (1993). Social work and the right of psychiatric patients to refuse medication: A family advocate's response. *Social Work, 38*, 107–112.

Roth, L., Meisel, A., & Lidz, C. (1977). Tests of competence to consent to treatment. *American Journal of Psychiatry, 134*, 279–284.

Rothman, J. (1989). Client self-determination: Untangling the knot. *Social Service Review, 63*(4), 598–612.

Runyan, C. L., & Faria, G. (1992). Community support for the long-term mentally ill. *Social Work in Health Care, 16*(4), 37–53.

Saleeby, D. (1985). In clinical social work is the body politic? *Social Service Review, 59*, 578–592.

Saleeby, D. (1992). Introduction: Beginnings of a strength approach to practice. In D. Saleeby (Ed.), *The strengths perspective in social work practice* (pp. 41–44). New York: Longman.

Salzman, C. (1995). Medication compliance in the elderly. *Journal of Clinical Psychiatry, 56*(Suppl.1), 18–22.

Sands, R. (1989). The social worker joins the team: A look at the socialization process. *Social Work in Health Care, 14*(2), 1–14.

Schatzberg, A. F., & Nemeroff, C. B. (Eds.) (1995). *The American Psychiatric Press textbook of psychiatry.* Washington, DC: American Psychiatric Press.

Schardt, D. (1998). Herbs for nerves. *Nutrition Action Newsletter, 25*(8), 8–12.

Schwartz, H., Vingiano, W., & Perez, C. (1988). Autonomy and the right to refuse treatment: Patients' attitudes after involuntary medication. *Hospital & Community Psychiatry, 39*, 1049–1054.

Sclafani, M. (1977). Medication classes for the emotionally ill. *Journal of Psychiatric Nursing, 15*(4), 13–16.

Sclar, D. A. (1991). Improving medication compliance: A review of selected issues. *Clinical Therapeutics, 13*(4), 436–440.

Segal, S. P., Bola, J. R., & Watson, M. A. (1996). Race, quality of care, and antipsychotic prescribing practices in psychiatric emergency rooms. *Psychiatric Services, 47*(3), 282–286.

Segal, S. P., Cohen, D., & Marder, S. R. (1992). Neuroleptic medication and prescription practices with sheltered-care residents: A 12-year perspective. *American Journal of Public Health, 82*, 846–852.

Seltzer, A., Roncari, I., & Garfinkel, P. (1980). Effect of patient education on medical compliance. *Canadian Journal of Psychiatry, 25*, 638–645.

Seltzer, M. M., Litchfield, L., Kapust, L. R., & Mayer, J. B. (1992). Professional and family collaboration in case management: A hospital based replication of a community-based study. *Social Work in Health Care, 17*(1), 1–22.

Sexton, T. L., & Whiston, S. C. (1994). The status of the counseling relationship: An empirical review, theoretical implications, and research directions. *The Counseling Psychologist, 22*(1), 6–78.

Sheline, Y., & Beatti, M. (1992). Effects of the right to refuse medication in an emergency psychiatric service. *Hospital & Community Psychiatry, 43*, 640–642.

Shulman, L. (1992). *The skills of helping individuals, families and groups* (3rd ed.). Itasca, IL: F. E. Peacock Publishers.

Silverstone, T., & Turner, P. (1988). *Drug treatment in psychiatry* (4th ed.). New York: Routledge.

Simon, B. L. (1994). *The empowerment tradition in American social work: A history.* New York: Columbia University Press.

Simpson, G. M., & Angus, J. W. S. (1970). A rating scale for extrapyramidal side effects. *Acta Psychiatirica Scandinavia, 212*, 11–19.

Skolnick, P. (Ed.) (1997). *Antidepressants: New pharmacological strategies.* Totowa, NJ: Humana Press.

Smith, M., Lin, K-M., & Mendoza, R. (1993). "Nonbiological" issues affecting psychopharmacotherapy: Cultural considerations. In K-M Lin, R. E. Poland, & G. Nakasaki (Eds.) *Psychopharmacology and psychobiology of ethnicity* (pp. 37–58). Washington, DC: American Psychiatric Press.

Solomon, P. (1992). The efficacy of case management services for severely mentally disabled clients. *Community Mental Health Journal, 28*(3), 163–180.

Solomon, P., & Marcenko, M. O. (1992). Families of adults with severe mental illness: Their satisfaction with inpatient and outpatient treatment. *Psychosocial Rehabilitation Journal, 16*(1), 121–134.

Sovner, R., & Bailey, K. P. (1993). Nurse clinical specialists as nonphysician prescribers: Reply. *Journal of Clinical Psychiatry, 54*(10), 396.

Southard, E. E., & Jarret, M. C. (1922). *The kingdom of evils*. New York: Macmillan.

Soyer, D. (1963). The right to fail. *Social Work, 8*(3), 72–78.

Spaniol, L., Zipple, A., & FitzGerald, S. (1984). How professionals can share power with families: Practical approaches to working with families of the mentally ill. *Psychosocial Rehabilitation Journal, 8*(2), 77–84.

Spiegel, D., & Wissler, T. (1987). Using family consultation on psychiatric aftercare for schizophrenic patients. *Hospital & Community Psychiatry, 38*, 1096–1099.

Stahl, S. M. (1996). *Essential psychopharmacology: Neuroscientific basis and practical applications*. New York: Cambridge University Press.

Steiner, D., & Marcopulos, B. (1991). Depression in the elderly: Characteristics and clinical management. *Nursing Clinics of North America, 26*(3), 585–596.

Stewart, M. J., Banks, S., Crosson, D., & Poel, D. (1995). Health professionals' perceptions of partnership with self-help groups. *Canadian Journal of Public Health, 86*(5), 340–344.

Stimson, G. V. (1974). Obeying doctor's orders: A view from the other side. *Social Science and Medicine, 8*, 97–104.

Stone, A. (1981). The right to refuse treatment: Why psychiatrists should and can make it work. *Archives of General Psychiatry, 38*, 351–354.

Stone, A. A. (1990). Law, science, and psychiatric malpractice: A response to Klerman's indictment of psychoanalytic psychiatry. *American Journal of Psychiatry, 147*, 419–427.

Strakowski, S. M., Hawkins, J. M., Keck, P. E., McElroy, S. L., West, S. A., Bourne, M. L., Sax, K. W., & Tugrul, K. C. (1997). The effects of race and information variance on disagreement between psychiatric emergency and research diagnoses in first-episode psychosis. *Journal of Clinical Psychiatry, 58*(10), 457–463.

Strakowski, S. M., Shelton, R. C., & Kolbrener, M. L. (1993). The effects of race and comorbidity on clinical diagnosis in patients with psychosis. *Journal of Clinical Psychiatry, 54*(3), 96–102.

Strickland, T. L., Stein, R., Lin, K. M., Risby, E., & Fong, R. (1997). The pharmacologic treatment of anxiety and depression in African Americans: Considerations for the general practitioner. *Archives of Family Medicine, 6*(4), 371–375.

Sturm, R., & Klap, R. (1999). Use of psychiatrists, psychologists and Masters-level therapists in managed behavioral health care carve-out plans. *Psychiatric Services, 50*, 504–508.

Suhail, K., & Cochrane, R. (1998). Seasonal variation in hospital admission for affective disorders by gender and ethnicity. *Social Psychiatry and Psychiatric Epidemiology, 33*(5), 211–217.

Sullivan, G., Wells, K. B., & Leake, B. (1992). Clinical factors associated with better quality of life in a seriously mentally ill population. *Hospital & Community Psychiatry, 43*, 794–798.

Sullivan, W. P. (1992). Reclaiming the community: The strengths perspective and deinstitutionalization. *Social Work, 37*, 204–209.

Sundel, M., & Sundel, S. S. (1998). Psychopharmacological treatment of panic disorder. *Research on Social Work Practice, 8*, 426–451.

Swartz, M. S., Swanson, J. W., Hiday, V. A., Borum, R., Wagner, R., & Burns, B. J. (1998). Taking the wrong drugs: The role of substance abuse and medication noncompliance in violence among severely mentally ill individuals. *Social Psychiatry and Psychiatric Epidemiology, 33*(Suppl. 1), S75–S80.

Swazey, J. P. (1974). *Chlorpromazine in psychiatry: A study of therapeutic innovation.* Cambridge, MA: MIT Press.

Swazey, R. L., & Swazey, A. M. (1976). Educational theory as a basis for patient education. *Journal of Chronic Diseases, 29*, 417–422.

Sylvester, C. (1993). Psychopharmacology of disorders in children. *Psychiatric Clinics of North America, 16*(4), 779–788.

Szasz, T. (1994). *Cruel compassion: Psychiatric control of society's unwanted.* New York: John Wiley.

Szeto, A. Y. J., & Giles, J. A. (1997). Improving oral medication compliance with an electronic aid. *IEEE Engineering in Medicine and Biology, 16*(3), 48–58.

Tarlack, G. M. (1998). Hot herbs: Here are some predictions for the year's popular herbal remedies. *Drug Topics, 142*(4), 60.

Test, M. A., Wallisch, L. S., Allness, D. J., & Ripp, K. (1989). Substance use in young adults with schizophrenic disorders. *Schizophrenia Bulletin, 15*, 465–476.

Thale, T. (1973). Effects of medication on the caseworker-client relationship. *Social Casework, 54*, 27–36.

Thompson, R., & Weisberg, S. (1990). Families as educational consumers: What do they want? What do they receive? *Health & Social Work, 15*, 221–227.

Tobias, M. (1990). Validator: A key role in empowering the chronically mentally ill. *Social Work, 35*, 357–359.

Todman, M., Gordon-Leeds, D., & Taylor, S. (1997). Attitude toward medication and perceived competence among chronically psychotic patients. *Psychological Reports, 80*(pt. 1, 3), 809–810.

Torrey, E. F. (1986). *Witchdoctors and psychiatrists.* Northvale, NJ: J. Aronson.

Toseland, R., Zaneles-Palmer, J., & Chapman, D. (1986). Teamwork in psychiatric settings. *Social Work, 31*, 46–52.

Tracy, A. B. (1994). *Prozac: Panacea or Pandora.* West Jordan, VT: Cassia Publications.

Turk, D., Salovey, P., & Litt, M. (1986). Adherence: A cognitive-behavioral perspective. In K. Gerber & A. Nehemkis (Eds.). *Compliance: The dilemma of the chronically ill* (pp. 44–72). New York: Springer.

Turner, S. E., & Cooley-Quille, M. R. (1996). Socioecological and socio-cultural variables in psychopharmacology research: Methodological considerations. *Psychopharmacology Bulletin, 32*(2), 183–192.

Urrutia, G. (1994). Medication refusal: Clinical picture and outcome after use of administrative review. *Bulletin of the American Academy of Psychiatry and the Law, 22*, 595–603.

Valenstein, E. T. (1998). *Blaming the brain: The truth about drugs and mental health.* New York: The Free Press.

Valenstein, E. T. (1986). *Great and desperate cures: The rise and decline of psychosurgery and other radical treatments for mental illness.* New York: Basic Books.

Valenstein, M., Barry, K. L., Blow, F. C., Copeland, L., & Ullman, E. (1998). Agreement between seriously mentally ill veterans and their clinicians about medication compliance. *Psychiatric Services, 49*, 1043–1048.

Van Putten, T. (1974). Why do schizophrenic patients refuse to take their drugs? *Archives of General Psychiatry, 31*, 67–72.

Varner, R. V., Ruiz, P., & Small, D. R. (1998). Black and white patients' response to antidepressant treatment for major depression. *Psychiatric Quarterly, 69*(2), 117–125.

Veeninga, A. T., Westenberg, H. G. M., & Weusten, J. T. N. (1990). Fluvoxamine in the treatment of menstrually related mood disorders. *Psychopharmacology, 102*, 414–416.

Wadeson, H. (1987). *The dynamic of art psychotherapy*. New York: Wiley.

Walker, S. (1996). *A dose of sanity*. NY: Wiley & Sons.

Walsh, C. B. (1993). This prescription may be hazardous to your health: Who is accountable to the patient? *Journal of Clinical Psychopharmacology, 13*(1), 68–70.

Walsh, J. (2000). *Clinical case management with persons having mental illness: A relationship-based perspective*. Pacific Grove, CA: Brooks/Cole.

Walsh, J. (In press). Anti-anxiety medications: A review for social workers. *Social work in health care.*

Walsh, J. (1998). Psychopharmacological treatment of bipolar disorder. *Research on Social Work Practice, 8*, 406–425.

Walsh, J. (1987). The family education and support group: A psychoeducational aftercare program. *Psychosocial Rehabilitation Journal, 10*, 51–61.

Walsh, J. (1989). Treatment of the bipolar client: Clinical social work contributions. *Clinical Social Work Journal, 17*, 367–381.

Wedding, D., & Boyd, M. A. (1999). *Movies and mental illness: Using film to understand psychopathology*. Boston: McGraw-Hill College.

Weick, A., & Pope, L. (1988). Knowing what's best: A new look at self-determination. *Social Casework, 69*, 10–16.

Weick, A., Rapp, C., Sullivan, W. P., & Kisthardt, W. (1989). A strengths perspective for social work practice. *Social Work, 34*, 350–354.

Weiden, P., Rapkin, B., Mott, T., Zygmut, A., Goldman, D., Horvitz-Lennon, M., & Frances, A. (1994). Rating of medication influences (ROMS) scale in schizophrenia. *Schizophrenia Bulletin, 20*, 297–307.

Weil, M. (1982). Research on issues in collaboration between social workers and lawyers. *Social Service Review, 56*, 393–405.

Weiner, B. (1985). Treatment rights. In S. Brakel, J. Parry, & B. Weiner (Eds.), *The mentally disabled and the law* (pp. 327–367). Chicago: American Bar Association.

Weiss, R. D., Greenfield, S. F., Najavits, L. M., Soto, J. A., Wyner, D., Tohen, M., & Griffin, M. L. (1998). Medication compliance among patients with bipolar disorder and substance use disorder. *Journal of Clinical Psychiatry, 59*(4), 172–174.

Weissman, M. (1972). Casework and pharmacotherapy in the treatment of depression. *Social Casework, 53*, 38–44.

Wesson, V. A., Levitt, A. J., & Joffe, R. T. (1994). Change in folate status with antidepressant medication. *Psychiatry Research, 53*(3), 313–322.

Wettstein, R. M. (1999). The right to refuse psychiatric treatment. *Psychiatric Clinics of North America, 22*, 173–182.

Wettstein, R. M. (1992). Legal aspects of prescribing. In M. S. Keshavan & J. S. Kennedy (Eds.), *Drug-induced dysfunction in psychiatry* (pp. 9-19). New York: Hemisphere Publishing.

Whiteside, S. E., Harris, A., & Whiteside, H. (1983). Patient education: Effectiveness of medication programs for psychiatric clients. *Journal of Psychosocial Nursing and Mental Health Services, 21*(10), 16–21.

Wilk, R. J. (1994). Are the rights of people with mental illness still important? *Social Work, 39*, 167–177.

Willetts, R. (1980). Advocacy and the mentally ill. *Social Work, 25*, 372–377.

Williams, G. C., Rodin, G. C., Ryan, R. M., Grolnick, W. S., & Deci, E. L. (1998). Autonomous regulation and long-term medication adherence in adult outpatients. *Health Psychology, 17*, 269–276.

Wilson, S. R. (1993). Patient and physician behavior models related to asthma care. *Medical Care, 31*(Suppl.), MS49–MS60

Wilson, W. H., & Claussen, A. M. (1993). New antipsychotic medications: Hope for the future. *Innovations & Research, 2*, 3–11.

Wing, Y. K., Chan, E., Chan, K., Lee, S., & Shek, C. C. (1997). Lithium pharmacokinetics in Chinese manic-depressive patients. *Journal of Clinical Psychopharmacology, 17*(3), 179–184.

Winick, B. J. (1997). *The right to refuse mental health treatment.* Washington, DC: American Psychological Association.

Winslade, W. (1981). Ethical issues. In E. A. Serafetinides (Ed.), *Psychiatric research in practice: Biobehavioral terms* (pp. 227–240). New York: Grune & Stratton.

Wise, M. G., & Tierney, J. (1992). Psychopharmacology in the elderly. *Journal of the Louisiana State Medical Society, 144*(10), 471–476.

Wolpe, P. R., Gorton, G., Serota, R., & Sanford, B. (1993). Predicting compliance of dual diagnosis inpatients with aftercare treatment. *Hospital & Community Psychiatry, 44*, 45–53.

Wong, A. H. C., Smith, M., & Boon, H. S. (1998). Herbal remedies in psychiatric practice. *Archives of General Psychiatry, 55*(11), 1033–1044.

Wyatt, R. J., Apud, J. A., & Potkin, S. (1996). New directions in the prevention and treatment of schizophrenia: A biological perspective. *Psychiatry, 58*, 357–370.

Xie, C. X., Piecoro, L. T., & Wermeling, D. P. (1997). Gender-related considerations in clinical pharmacology and drug therapeutics. *Critical Care Nursing Clinics of North America, 9*(4), 459–468.

Yank, G. R., Bentley, K. J., & Hargrove, D. S. (1993). The vulnerability-stress model of schizophrenia: Advances in psychosocial treatment. *American Journal of Orthopsychiatry, 63*(1), 55–69.

Yonkers, K. A., & Ellison, J. M. (1996). Anxiety disorders in women and their pharmacological treatment. In M. F. Jensfold, U. Halbreich, & J. A. Hamilton (Eds.), *Psychopharmacology and women* (pp. 261–285). Washington, DC: American Psychiatric Press.

Yonkers, K. A., Kando, J. C., Cole, J. O. & Blumenthal, S. (1992). Gender differences in pharmacokinetics and pharmacodynamics of psychotropic medication. *The American Journal of Psychiatry, 149*(5), 587–595.

Young, R. C., Biggs, J. T., Ziegler, V. E., & Meyer, D. A. (1978). A rating scale for mania: Reliability, validity, sensitivity. *British Journal of Psychiatry, 133*, 429–435.

Youssef, F. (1984). Adherence to therapy in psychiatric patients: An empirical investigation of the impact of patient education. *International Journal of Nursing Studies, 21*, 51–57.

Ziedonis, D. M., Rayford, B. S., Bryant, K. J., & Rounsaville, B. J. (1994). Psychiatric comorbidity in white and African-American cocaine addicts seeking substance abuse treatment. *Hospital & Community Psychiatry, 45*(1), 43–48.

Zind, R. (1991). Mental health care and illness knowledge among chronic schizophrenics. *Military Medicine, 156*, 159–166.

Zipple, A. M., Langle, S., Spaniol, L., & Fisher, H. (1990). Client confidentiality and the family's need to know: Strategies for resolving the conflict. *Community Mental Health Journal, 26*, 533–545.

Zito, J. M., Safer, D. J., dosReis, S., & Riddle, M. A. (1998). Racial disparity in psychotropic medications prescribed for youths with Medicaid insurance in Maryland. *Journal of the Academy of Child and Adolescent Psychiatry, 37*(2), 179–184.

Zito, J. M., Routt, W. W., Mitchell, J. E., & Roering, J. C. (1985). Clinical characteristics of hospitalized psychotic patients who refuse antipsychotic drug therapy. *American Journal of Psychiatry, 142*, 822–826.

Alphabetical Listing of Currently Available Prescription Medications Described in This Book

Chemical Name (and pronunciation)	Major Trade Name	Primary Use (as discussed in this book)
Acetophenazine (uh-SEE-tah-FEN-uh-zeen)	Tindal	Antipsychotic
Alprazolam (al-PRAH-zoe-lamb)	Xanax	Anti-anxiety
Amantadine (uh-MAN-tah-dean)	Symmetrel	Adverse effects of antipsychotic meds
Amitriptyline (am-uh-TRIP-tuh-lean)	Elavil	Antidepressant
Amoxapine (am-OX-uh-peen)	Asendin	Antidepressant
Amperozide (am-PEAR-owe-zide)	(None in U.S.)	Antipsychotic
Amphetamine (am-FET-uh-mean)	Adderal	Psychostimulant
Atenolol (uh-TEN-uh-lawl)	Tenormin	Anti-anxiety
Benztropine (bends-TROPE-een)	Cogentin	Adverse effects of antipsychotic meds
Biperiden (bye-PEAR-uh-den)	Akineton	Adverse effects of antipsychotic meds
Bupropion (bue-PRO-pee-on)	Wellbutrin	Antidepressant
Buspirone (BUS-pih-roan)	Buspar	Anti-anxiety

Chemical Name (and pronunciation)	Major Trade Name	Primary Use (as discussed in this book)
Carbamazepine (car-bah-MAZ-uh-peen)	Tegretol	Mood stabilizer
Chlordiazepoxide (clore-die-AS-uh-POX-ide)	Librium	Anti-anxiety
Chlorpromazine (clore-PRO-muh-zeen)	Thorazine	Antipsychotic
Chlorprothixene (clore-pro-THICK-seen)	Taractan	Antipsychotic
Citaprolam (sit-AH-pro-lamb)	Celexa	Antidepressant
Clomipramine (clo-MIP-rah-mean)	Anafranil	Antidepressant
Clonazepam (clo-NAZ-uh-pam)	Klonipin	Anti-anxiety; adverse effects of anti-psychotic meds
Clonidine (CLAHN-uh-dean)	Catapres	Attention-deficit hyper-activity disorder
Clorazepate (clore-AS-uh-pate)	Tranxene	Anti-anxiety
Clozapine (CLAUS-uh-peen)	Clozaril	Antipsychotic
Desipramine (des-IP-rah-mean)	Norpramin	Antidepressant
Dextroamphetamine (DECKS-trow-am-FET-uh-mean)	Dexedrine	Psychostimulant
Diazepam (dye-AS-uh-pam)	Valium	Anti-anxiety
Diphenhydramine (DIE-fen-HI-drah-mean)	Benadryl	Anti-anxiety; adverse effects of anti-psychotic meds
Doxepin (DOCKS-uh-pin)	Sinequan	Antidepressant
Ethoprozapine (ETH-owe-PRO-zah-peen)	Parsidol	Adverse effects of antipsychotic meds
Estazolam (es-TAZ-uh-lamb)	ProSom	Anti-anxiety
Fluoxetine (flew-OX-uh-teen)	Prozac	Antidepressant
Fluphenazine (flew-FEN-uh-zeen)	Prolixin	Antipsychotic
Flurazepam (fler-AS-uh-pam)	Dalmane	Anti-anxiety
Halazepam (hal-AS-uh-pam)	Paxipam	Anti-anxiety
Haloperidol (HAL-oh-PEAR-uh-doll)	Haldol	Antipsychotic
Imipramine (im-IP-rah-mean)	Tofranil	Antidepressant
Isocarboxazid (EYE-so-car-BOX-uh-zid)	Marplan	Antidepressant

Chemical Name (and pronunciation)	Major Trade Name	Primary Use (as discussed in this book)
Lithium (LI-thee-um)	Lithium carbonate	Mood stabilizer
Lorazepam (loar-AS-uh-pam)	Ativan	Anti-anxiety; adverse effects of anti-psychotic meds
Loxapine (LOCKS-uh-peen)	Loxitane	Antipsychotic
Maprotilene (map-ROW-ti-lean)	Ludiomil	Antidepressant
Mesoridazine (MESS-or-ID-uh-zeen)	Serentil	Antipsychotic
Methamphetamine (meth-am-FET-uh-mean)	Desoxyn	Psychostimulant
Methylphenidate (METH-ill-FEN-uh-date	Ritalin	Psychostimulant
Metoprolol (met-OH-pro-lol)	Lopressor	Anti-anxiety
Midazolam (mid-AS-oh-lamb)	Versed	Anti-anxiety
Mirtazapine (mir-TAZ-uh-peen)	Remeron	Antidepressant
Moclobemide (MO-cloe-BEM-ide)	(None in U.S.)	Antidepressant
Molindone (MOLL-in-doan)	Moban	Antipsychotic
Nadolol (NAH-da-lol)	Corgard	Anti-anxiety
Nefasodone (neh-FA-so-doan)	Serzone	Antidepressant
Nortriptyline (nor-TRIP-tuh-lean)	Pamelor	Antidepressant
Olanzapine (oh-LANDS-uh-peen)	Zyprexa	Antipsychotic
Orphenadrine (or-FEN-uh-dreen)	Norflex	Adverse effects of antipsychotic meds
Oxazepam (ox-AS-uh-pam)	Serax	Anti-anxiety
Paroxetine (pair-OX-uh-teen)	Paxil	Antidepressant
Pemoline (PEM-oh-line)	Cylert	Psychostimulant
Perphenazine (per-FEN-uh-zeen)	Trilafon	Antipsychotic
Phenylzine (FEN-ill-zeen)	Nardil	Antidepressant
Prazepam (PRAH-zuh-pam)	Centrax	Anti-anxiety
Procyclidine (pro-SICK-luh-dean)	Kemadrin	Adverse effects of antipsychotic meds

Chemical Name (and pronunciation)	Major Trade Name	Primary Use (as discussed in this book)
Propranolol (pro-PRAN-oh-lol)	Inderal	Anti-anxiety; adverse effects of anti-psychotic meds
Protriptyline (pro-TRIP-til-lean)	Vivactil	Antidepressant
Quazepam (KWAS-uh-pam)	Doral	Anti-anxiety
Quetiapene (quit-EYE-uh-peen)	Seroquel	Antidepressant
Risperidone (riss-PEAR-uh-doan)	Risperdal	Antipsychotic
Sertraline (SIR-truh-lean)	Zoloft	Antidepressant
Temazepam (tem-AS-uh-pam)	Restoril	Anti-anxiety
Thioridazine (THIGH-or-ID-uh-zeen)	Mellaril	Antipsychotic
Thiothixene (THIGH-oh-THICK-seen)	Navane	Antipsychotic
Tranylaypromine (tran-luh-PRO-mean)	Parnate	Antidepressant
Trazodone (TRAH-zoe-doan)	Desyrel	Antidepressant
Triazolam (try-AS-oh-lamb)	Halcion	Anti-anxiety
Trifluoperazine (try-FLEW-oh-PEAR-uh-zeen)	Stelazine	Antipsychotic
Triflupromazine (TRY-flew-PRO-muh-zeen)	Vesprin	Antipsychotic
Trihexiphenidyl (try-HEX-uh-FEN-uh-dill)	Artane	Adverse effects of antipsychotic meds
Trimipramine (try-MIP-ram-een)	Surmontil	Antidepressant
Valproic Acid (val-PRO-ick acid)	Depakote	Mood stabilizer
Venlafaxine (VEN-lah-FAX-een)	Effexor	Antidepressant
Ziprasidone (zip-RAZ-uh-doan)	(None in U.S.)	Antipsychotic

Glossary

Absorption The process by which the bloodstream takes in a drug, most commonly through diffusion into the bowel wall. Absorption efficiency is affected by the chemical nature of the drug, its method of delivery, and the time of day, as well as the client's gender and physiology. Intravenous injection provides the most rapid form of drug absorption, followed by intramuscular injection and oral administration.

Acetylcholine (ah-SEAT-till-CO-leen) A type of neurotransmitter released by all neurons; controls the activity of the skeletal muscles, the heartbeat, some glandular functions, mood, sleep, and memory. It is essential to the transmission of brain/spinal-cord messages.

Acute stress disorder A diagnosis based on a person's development of incapacitating symptoms of anxiety within one month of experiencing a traumatic event. The disorder remits within four weeks; if symptoms persist the person is diagnosed with a different anxiety disorder.

Adherence The degree to which the client follows a prescribed course of medication administration. It is used as an alternative term to "compliance," which has overtones of client passivity and "noncompliance," which has overtones of deviance.

Adjustment disorder According to the DSM-IV, an excessive and maladaptive response, lasting 6 months or less, to an identifiable external stressor. Psychosocial functioning of the individual is impaired beyond what would be expected given the known stressors. The disorder may include symptoms of depression and/or anxiety.

Adverse effects The physical, psychological, or social effects of a medication that are unintentional, unrelated to its therapeutic effect, and unpleasant or potentially harmful to the consumer. These are also referred to as side effects.

Advocacy role The role in which the social worker uses knowledge of law, mental illness, and advocacy strategies to help represent the wishes of the client to some decision-making authority, in hopes of achieving changes in practice and/or policy related to access to care or services.

Affect   Feeling, emotion, or mood.

Aftercare   Outdated term commonly used in the 1960s and 1970s that refers to all mental health services provided to people with mental illness after they have been discharged from a psychiatric hospital or other inpatient facility. Services are focused on coping, personal growth, skill building, and community adaptation. Terms more commonly used at present include psychosocial rehabilitation, case management, and community care.

Agitation   A state of tension in which a person's anxiety is manifested in increased psychomotor activity, usually indicating perturbation.

Agoraphobia (ah-GORE-ah-FOE-bee-ah)   According to the DSM-IV, a type of panic disorder that arises when an individual becomes anxious about being alone outside the home to the extent of experiencing an incapacitating fear. The individual suffering from agoraphobia also fears having an unexpected panic attack in a public setting in which withdrawal is difficult or embarrassing.

Agranulocytosis (ay-GRAN-you-low-sigh-TOE-sis)   A dramatic decrease in the number of infection-fighting white blood cells. This is a rare side effect of antipsychotic drugs, most notably of clozapine. Even in the case of clozapine, this disease is said to afflict only 1–2% of users, and its ill effects can be reversed if identified early and the drug is discontinued.

Akathesia (ack-ah-THEE-zsha)   The experience of extreme internal restlessness, accompanied by muscle discomfort. Akathesia is an extrapyramidal side effect of antipsychotic drugs.

Amines (AM-meens)   Organic substances that are the building blocks for amino acids. GABA and glutamate are amino acids.

Amphetamine (am-FET-uh-MEEN)   A chemical substance that is the prototype of the current psychostimulant drugs. It is structurally similar to epinephrine, a natural substance that stimulates the peripheral nervous system.

Anorexia (an-or-EX-ee-ah)   An eating disorder (also known as anorexia nervosa) characterized by a self-imposed and deliberate restriction of food intake, regardless of appetite or nutritional needs, and leading to pronounced and physically harmful weight loss, possibly requiring hospitalization.

Anti-anxiety medications   All prescription medications specifically developed, or having demonstrated effectiveness, for alleviating the symptoms of anxiety disorders and other disorders in which anxiety is a prominent symptom. They include the benzodiazepines and buspirone, among other drugs.

Anticholinergic effects (AN-tie-koh-lin-UR-jick) (ACEs)   Adverse effects that result from the suppressive action of certain antipsychotic and antidepressant medications on the action of acetylcholine in the brain and peripheral nervous system. These effects include dry mouth, blurred vision, constipation, and urinary hesitancy.

Anticonvulsant drugs   Those medications, initially developed to treat persons with seizure disorders, that are also effective in the treatment of bipolar disorder. Carbamazepine and valproate are the best known.

Antidepressant drugs   All prescription medications specifically developed, or having demonstrated effectiveness, for alleviating the symptoms of depressive disorders. The medications include the monoamine oxidase inhibitors, cyclic antidepressants, and the selective serotonin reuptake inhibitors.

Antihistamines   A class of drugs that can impede the effects of naturally occurring chemical compounds in the body called histamines; these drugs can dilate capillaries, produce headaches, and decrease blood pressure. They may be employed for their sedative and hypnotic properties and to treat extrapyramidal symptoms.

Antipsychotic drugs All prescription medications specifically developed, or having demonstrated effectiveness, for alleviating the symptoms of psychosis and agitation in disorders such as schizophrenia, schizoaffective disorder, the manic phase of bipolar disorder, and other disorders in which such symptoms may be prominent.

Anxiety The presence of high levels of physiological and psychological distress unconnected to any immediate threats in the environment. It is distinguished from fear by the fact that the threat is not known and by its serious and negative impact on psychosocial functioning. Anxiety is manifested in feelings of helplessness, self-doubt, self-absorption, and excessive preoccupation with perceived threats in the environment. The disorder may also be expressed as a variety of somatic complaints and symptoms, such as headaches and false "heart attacks," for which no organic cause can be found.

Aplastic anemia (ay-PLAS-tick) A condition in which the body cannot produce a normal amount of red blood cells or cannot correct a deficiency in hemoglobin. It ordinarily occurs when a drug, toxic agent, radiation, or disease acts to inhibit the red blood cell production.

Arrhythmia (ah-RITH-me-ah) Variation in the normal rhythm of the heartbeat, which normally ranges between 60 and 90 beats per minute in adults. The term for the high end (above 100 beats per minute) is tachycardia; the term for the low end (below 60 beats per minute) is bradycardia. Tachycardia or bradycardia may indicate heart disease or a drug adverse effect.

Attention-deficit/hyperactivity disorder (ADHD) A mental disorder characterized by a persistent pattern (six months or more) of inattention and/or hyperactivity and impulsivity in behavior that is more frequent and severe than typically observed in others at a comparable developmental level. ADHD is most often treated medically with the psychostimulant drugs.

Autonomic nervous system (ought-oh-NAW-mick) Regulates the involuntary processes of the internal organs and blood vessels. Many of the functions controlled by the autonomic nervous system are self-regulating or autonomous. It is comprised of two primary subsystems: the *sympathetic* and *parasympathetic*, which sometimes work in cooperation but at other times are antagonistic in their contrasting roles of "arousal" and "rest."

Autoreceptors Receptors on presynaptic neurons that regulate the release of neurotransmitters.

Axon A fiber projection from the neuron that serves to transmit signals to adjacent neurons. Contained within an axon are neurotransmitter substances. The axon terminal (or end) is also the site of the neurotransmitter release.

Balanced perspective Maintaining a balance between competing and sometimes conflicting needs, rights, and aspirations of the individual, family, and society with regard to human behavior. Although the client's perspective should be preeminent, the effective collaboration needed for positive outcomes depends on balancing the perspectives of all stakeholders and participants.

Barbiturates (bar-BIT-sure-its) A class of medications used as sedatives and hypnotics; popular from the late 19th through the mid-20th centuries. These medications are still available but have largely been replaced by the benzodiazepines.

Basal ganglia (BAY-zill GANG-lee-ah) Structures located on both sides of the limbic system, involved in the regulation and initiation of movement and in a variety of neuropsychiatric symptoms, including dementia, major depression, and psychosis. These structures may be inadvertently affected by certain psychotropic drugs, resulting in adverse side effects.

Behavior disturbances Marked changes, typical of psychotic disorders, in a person's behavior patterns. The disturbances may feature withdrawal, apathy, and bizarre actions.

Benzodiazepines (BENS-oh-dye-AZ-uh-peens) A class of drugs used both as anti-anxiety drugs and as sedatives.

Beta-blockers (BAY-ta)   A class of drugs that reduces the physiological analogs of anxiety by blocking beta receptors in the autonomic nervous system. These drugs block receptors that stimulate the heartbeat and those that dilate blood vessels and air channels in the lungs. Although the drugs are not addicting, they are short-acting and do not remain long in the client's system.

Bioavailability   The amount of a drug that reaches the bloodstream without being metabolized, or chemically changed.

Biogenic amines (BYE-oh-JEN-ick AH-meens)   Neurotransmitters synthesized in the nerve terminals (as opposed to the cell body); the neurotransmitters affect nerve functioning through the synapses.

Bipolar disorder (BYE-pole-ur)   A disorder of mood in which, over time, a person experiences one or more manic episodes, usually accompanied by one or more major depressive episodes. There are two types of bipolar disorder. *Bipolar I* disorder is characterized by one or more manic episodes, usually accompanied by a major depressive episode. *Bipolar II* disorder is characterized by one or more major depressive episodes accompanied by at least one hypomanic episode (see also).

Blood-brain barrier   A semi-permeable barrier between the blood vessels and the brain. The medications and other compounds must be fat-soluble to pass through the parts of the barrier where the capillaries are tightly constricted. In areas where capillaries are not so tightly constricted, water-soluble substances may pass through.

Blood level   The measure of a drug's presence in the blood plasma at a given time.

Borderline personality disorder   Personality disorder characterized by emotional instability, narcissism, controlling behavior, identity diffusion, feelings of loneliness and abandonment, and troubled interpersonal relationships.

Bromides (BROH-mides)   Sedative medications introduced into mental health treatments in the second half of the 19th century and used until the mid-20th century. The chief result of such medications seems to have been the quieting of psychiatric wards rather than improvement of clients' mental and emotional conditions.

Bulimia (boo-LEE-me-uh)   An eating disorder that is characterized by periods of uncontrollable binge eating followed by purging of ingested food or by other compensatory behaviors so as to prevent weight gain.

Buspirone (BUS-pih-rohn)   An anti-anxiety drug, classified as an azapirone, that, unlike the benzodiazepine drugs, does not carry the risk of physical addiction.

Calcium channel blockers   Primarily used in the treatment of cardiovascular disorders, this class of medications is under investigation as antimanic drugs. If effective, their relatively mild side-effect profiles, including safety during pregnancy, will make them attractive treatment alternatives.

Case management   An approach to social service delivery that attempts to ensure that clients with multiple, complex problems and disabilities receive the services they need in a timely, appropriate fashion.

Catecholamines (kat-ah-KOH-la-meens)   A group of biogenic amines, belonging to the catechol group, that play an important role in nervous system functioning, particularly regarding sleep, mood states, sexual behavior, and aggression.

Cell body   The central area of the neuron, in which cell metabolism takes place.

Cell membrane   A barrier that separates the contents of the cell from the fluid enveloping it.

Central nervous system   The system of nerves comprising the brain and spinal cord, which serves as the body's major nerve control system. It directs and regulates all parts of the body in receiving stimuli from external and internal environments, interpreting those stimuli, and organizing the body to react.

Cerebellum   Located in the hindbrain, the cerebellum controls bodily functions that operate below the level of consciousness, including posture, balance, and movement through space. It receives information directly from sense organs, muscles, and joints.

Cerebral cortex   The folded, outermost region of the cerebrum, responsible for primary sensory functioning, visual processing, long-term memory, motor and perceptual coordination and integration, language, thinking, and problem-solving. These functions are managed by the four lobes, each with a distinct function: the frontal lobe, the temporal lobe, the parietal lobe, and the occipital lobe.

Cerebrum   The largest and most imposing structure of the brain. Along with the cerebral cortex, it is the locus of higher mental functions such as memory, reasoning, language, judgment, and abstract thought.

Chloral hydrate   (KLO-roll HIDE-rate) A generic sedative popular among hospital psychiatrists during the late 19th century for its expediency, despite grave side effects, in producing more manageable behaviors from clients.

Clearance   The measure of the amount of a drug excreted through pores and bodily secretions (such as saliva), in a given amount of time.

Client system   The person or persons for whom the social worker provides services. The client system may be an individual client, a family, a couple, a group, or any combination. The worker contracts with the client system to provide specified treatment, ideally through a collaborative partnership.

Community care   The range of treatments and support services available to clients outside of institutions; the level of care is usually less intensive or restricted. Medication management is often an important part of community care, inasmuch as it helps the client function more independently in the community.

Consultant role   The role in which the social worker helps to evaluate the client's need for medication, makes physician referrals, and consults with the psychiatrist/physician on treatment issues as needed. In this role, the worker avoids taking either adversarial or advocacy stances with respect to client medication adherence.

Continuity of care   The continuous provision of needed services for clients moving from one setting, or care provider, to another, including client and care provider collaboration in relocation, discharge contacts, and planning and follow-up.

Counselor role   The role in which the social worker helps the client problem-solve and make decisions about practical matters related to actual or possible medication use, rather than about issues related to mental illness. It is a process of providing clients with information and advice, social skills, problem-solving skills, and assistance with goal-setting.

Cyclic antidepressant drugs   (SIGH-click) A group of antidepressant drugs, mostly developed between the late 1950s and mid 1980s, named for the varying number of chemical rings that determine the drugs' structure. These include heterocyclic, tricyclic, dicyclic, and monocyclic drugs.

Cyclothymia   (SIGH-kloh-THIGH-mee-ah) According to the DSM-IV, a mood disorder characterized by the manifestation of several hypomanic episodes and periods of depressed mood, which do not meet the full criteria for mania or major depression. Psychotic symptoms are absent in cyclothymia.

Deinstitutionalization   The mass release of institutionalized persons to the community over the course of three decades (from the 1950s to the 1980s). Specifically, the term refers to the reduced census at state hospitals.

Delusion   A false belief that is maintained even when contradicted by social reality. Delusions may include persecutory (people or forces are attempting to bring one harm), erotomanic (another person is in love with the individual), somatic (pertaining to body functioning), and grandiose beliefs (an exaggerated sense of one's power, knowledge, or identity); thought broadcasting (one's thoughts are overheard by others), thought insertion or withdrawal (others are putting thoughts into or taking thoughts out of one's head), delusions of being controlled (thoughts, feelings, or actions are imposed by an external force), and delusions of reference (neutral events have special significance for the person).

Delusional disorder   A cognitive orientation to the external world characterized by delusions (see above) that persist for at least one month.

Dendrite (DEN-dright)   The short extension of the neuron that is its "receiving end" for signals sent from other cells. The dendrite is located close to the axons of other cells but separated by a short distance from the synaptic cleft.

Depression   A disturbance in mood, characterized by a sadness that is out of the range of normal emotion. It may be primary (autonomous) or secondary to other physical and emotional conditions. "Clinical" depression is characterized by an intensity of mood that seems to permeate all aspects of the person's life.

Distribution   The process by which a drug travels from the bloodstream to its target site by one of two routes: dissolving in blood plasma, which is relatively efficient in getting drugs to the target brain site, or attaching to proteins in the blood plasma, which is problematic because of individual differences in protein-binding rates. Only the unbound portion of the drug can cross into the brain. Most psychotropic drugs have a fairly high protein binding rate.

Dopamine (DOPE-ah-meen)   A type of neurotransmitter thought to be involved in disorders of cognition (such as schizophrenia), motor control systems, and limbic activity (emotional behavior).

Dose response   The measure of therapeutic effect as a function of dosage.

Drug agonist (AG-un-ist)   A drug that acts to facilitate or enhance the effect of another drug.

Drug antagonist   A drug that acts against or hinders the effect of another drug.

Drug half-life   The time it takes for the concentration of a drug within the body to fall to 50% of its previous (peak) level.

Dysthymic disorder (diss-THIGH-mick)   A mood disorder that represents a generally depressed personality style, featuring symptoms that are similar to but less intense than those of major depression. The diagnosis requires two years of a continuously depressed mood (more bad days than good ones). It often has an early age of onset (childhood through early adulthood) and produces impairments in school, vocational, and social functioning.

Dystonias (diss-TONE-ee-ahz)   Uncoordinated, involuntary twisting movements of the jaw, tongue, or entire body, produced by sustained muscle spasms.

Educator role   The social worker's role of helping clients and their families understand the reasons for medication and other treatments, the benefits and risks of such treatments, and the various treatment options available to them.

Efferent (EHF-ur-rent) Nerve impulse conduction from the central nervous system outward to the periphery (muscles and glands).

Electroconvulsive therapy (ECT)   A procedure used in the treatment of severe depression in which an electric current is briefly applied through electrodes to one or both sides of the brain. Temporary side effects may include convulsions, unconsciousness, and temporary memory loss.

Elimination   All bodily processes that lower the concentration of a drug in the body. Metabolism, excretion (e.g., bodily wastes), and secretion (e.g., tears) are processes involved in elimination.

Enzymes (EN-zimes) Proteins in the body that facilitate chemical changes but are not affected by those changes. Enzymes are important catalysts for bodily functions such as metabolism, which in turn can affect drug potency and rates of drug absorption.

Euthymic mood state (you-THIGH-mick)   A generally positive mood state, or state of emotional wellness, marked by the absence of symptoms of mood disorders.

Excitatory (ex-SITE-uh-tore-ee)   Activity or substance that stimulates nerve cell activity.

Excretion (ex-KREE-shun)   The process following metabolism, in which the body eliminates a drug, generally through the bile, feces, urine, sweat, saliva, tears, or milk.

Extrapyramidal pathways (EX-truh-pee-RA-mid-ill)   Long nerve pathways stretching from the cerebral cortex to the spinal cord and used by motor nerves. This diffuse set of neural structures influences movement, coordination, and posture.

Extrapyramidal symptoms (EPS)   Side effects, including akathisia, dystonias, and parkinsonian effects, of antipsychotic drugs and the cyclic antidepressants.

Fat-soluble drugs   Drugs that only dissolve in body tissues that absorb fat (see also water soluble drugs). The concentration of fat-soluble drugs varies in proportion to the ratio of fat-to-water in the body. Individuals with proportionately more fat tissues than water tissues will have lower concentrations of fat-soluble drugs than those persons with proportionately more water tissues than fat tissues. Increased age is associated with higher fat-to-water ratios, and women tend to have greater fat-to-water ratios than men. Virtually all antipsychotic drugs are fat-soluble.

Fine motor movements   Relating to coordinated small-muscle movements, such as those in the hands.

"First pass" metabolism   The initial, rather extensive, breakdown of a drug within the liver before the drug reaches the circulatory system. This substantially reduces the amount of drug available for the target site.

Forebrain   The last of the three parts of the brain to evolve in embryonic development. The forebrain is highly specialized in many areas; it contains the limbic system, which is responsible for emotions and homeostasis of bodily functions and which is a target of many psychotropic medications. In the forebrain is the location of the cerebrum and the cerebral cortex, centers of higher functioning processes, such as reasoning, decision making, and abstract thought.

Frontal lobe   One of four major hemispheres in the cerebrum of the human brain. It is located behind the forehead and controls the functions of speech, thought, and consciousness.

Gama aminobutyric acid (GABA) (GAM-uh am-MEEN-oh-byu-TIE-rick ASS-id)   An amino acid and neurotransmitter found throughout the central nervous system; GABA has a vital dampening effect on the excitability of nerve cells.

Generalized anxiety   According to the DSM-IV, excessive and pervasive worrying that is difficult to control and that leads to restlessness, lack of focus, tachycardia, irritability, motor tension, heightened apprehension, and vigilance.

Glial cells (GLEE-ahl)   A class of cells in the nervous system; these cells support neuron functioning and play an important role in neuronal activity by contributing to blood-brain barrier permeability of compounds entering and leaving the brain and central nervous system.

Glutamate (GLUE-tuh-mate)   An excitatory neurotransmitter in the brain, and also a chemical precursor of GABA; obtained from food and from metabolic processes. Glutmate is stored in and released from nerve terminals, and its four types of receptors are found on the surfaces of virtually all neurons. Glutamate activity has a major influence on cognitive functions via the cortex and hippocampus, motor functions in the pyramidal and extrapyramidal systems, and on many cerebellar and sensory functions. This neurotransmitter may influence the development of a variety of mental disorders, including schizophrenia and Alzheimer's disease.

Gross motor movements   Relating to large-muscle movements, such as those in the thigh.

Hallucinations   Sense perceptions of external objects that are not present. These perceptions may be auditory, visual, gustatory (the perception of taste), tactile (feeling an object), somatic (an unreal experience within the body), and olfactory (a false sense of smell).

Health belief model   Postulates that individuals will choose a course of action based on their motivational investment in the goal of action and the perceived relevance of that goal to a recommended behavior. Medication education or any other change-based intervention will be effective insofar as they tap into a personal goal that the learner is motivated to achieve. For instance, a client may be motivated to take medications enabling him or her to work a steady job, which in turn makes it possible to sustain independent living.

Herbs   Low-growing plants with soft, succulent tissues; often used for medicinal purposes.

Hindbrain   The first part of the brain to evolve in embryonic development, the hindbrain consists of the brain stem, reticular formation, and cerebellum, all of which regulate vital bodily functions (such as breathing rate and heartbeat), posture, balance, kinesthetic motion, and rudimentary memory functions, among others.

Hippocampus (hip-po-CAM-pus) A brain structure that is part of the limbic system and thus concerned with emotion and motivation. The hippocampus appears to be important in learning and long-term memory; the structure also extends efferent neuron pathways (conduits for nerve impulses) to the hypothalamus.

Hypericum (high-PEAR-uh-some)   The active chemical agent in St. John's wort and other herbs that are used to treat mild depression.

Hypertension   High, life-threatening blood pressure, possibly due to hereditary predisposition and/or lifestyle (stress levels), health habits (smoking, overeating, food choices), and emotional habits (expressed and repressed hostility).

Hyperthymia (HIGH-per-THIGH-mee-ah)   An affective state characterized by heightened activity and emotional responses that exceed the norm but fall short of manic proportions.

Hypnotic drugs   Drugs that induce calmness when administered in low doses. Properly administered, hypnotic drugs do not induce sleep.

Hypomanic episode, hypomania (HIGH-po-MANE-ee-uh)   A mild form of mania that may be pleasurable for the person and result in high social and occupational productivity. Its related behaviors are often socially acceptable, and consequently the hypomanic person may receive positive reinforcement from friends and employers. The person has high self-esteem, a decreased need for sleep, a high energy level, an increase in overall productivity, and more intensive involvement in pleasurable activities. Hypomania, however, often leads to a full manic episode.

Hypothalamus (HIGH-poh-THAL-ah-muss)   A peanut-sized structure at the base of the brain; involved in the regulation of temperature, balance, appetite, fundamental emotional states, and sexual arousal.

Iatrogenic effects (eye-AT-tro-JEN-ik)   Harmful effects presumed to be inadvertently caused by the treatment itself.

Impotence (IM-poe-tents)   The inability of a man to perform sexual intercourse, usually because of an inability to achieve erection or experience ejaculation. This condition is a side effect of some medications but can also exist as a psychological problem.

Individual dignity   A fundamental value of the social work profession, arising from the notion that all people are intrinsically equal, regardless of status, income, religion, creed, color, language/dialect, ethnic group, ability, sexual orientation, etc.

Insight   In this context, the awareness of having a mental illness requiring intervention. Insight also means that the client understands that changes or exacerbations in symptoms are indicators that he or she is under stress and is reacting to it. The client is aware that he or she needs to take certain steps to reverse these changes.

Kindling process   Much as the burning of kindling wood and other flammables enables a beginning fire to take hold, this term describes the electrophysiological process of kindling that generates an action potential (electrochemical "fire") in a neuron, following repeated stimulation below the threshold level. Kindling is considered to be a causal process in the onset of a manic episode.

Lag time   The amount of time required for a drug to have its desired effect, depending on factors such as the body's tolerance of the drug; the drug's absorption, protein binding, and metabolizing rate; and individual differences in clients' physiologies.

Lobotomy (lob–OUGHT–uh–me)   A surgical procedure in which certain nerve tracts in the frontal lobe area are severed to produce a reduction in the client's tension and psychotic symptoms. Today, prefrontal lobotomies are seldom performed because of the irreversible apathy, decision-making impairments, and seizures that result from the procedure.

Loose associations   The result of a disturbance in one's ability to control the innumerable threads that guide conscious thinking. The person's thinking consequently becomes illogical, confused, and incoherent.

Mania, manic episode   A physiological and emotional state that persists for at least two weeks and in which a person's predominant mood is elevated, expansive, or irritable to a degree that seriously impairs social functioning. This state may be characterized by unrealistically inflated self-esteem, a decreased need for sleep, pressured speech, racing thoughts, distractibility, an increase in unrealistic goal-directed activity, and involvement in activities that have a potential for painful consequences.

Major depression   A mood disorder of at least two weeks duration in which a person experiences a depressed mood or loss of interest in nearly all common life activities. Symptoms may include depressed mood, diminished interest or pleasure in most activities, significant and unintentional weight loss *or* gain, insomnia *or* hypersomnia, feelings of physical agitation *or* retardation, loss of energy, feelings of worthlessness or excessive guilt, a diminished ability to think or concentrate, and persistent thoughts of death or suicide.

Median effective dose   The dose of a drug that is known to produce a therapeutic effect in 50% of consumers. It is sometimes signified as ED50.

Medication education programs   Mental health service programs that provide clients and their families with information on drug dosages and uses, as well as potential physical, psychological, and social side effects associated with the use of psychotropic medication (see also psychoeducational programs).

Mental hygiene movement   One of several social reform movements in the early 20th century concerned with public education, research, and prevention services. It was begun with the efforts of Clifford Beers, a Yale-educated psychiatric client, who helped found the National Committee on Mental Hygiene in 1909.

Metabolism (met–TAB–oh–liz–um)   The process by which the body breaks down a drug into its chemical derivatives, which can then be eliminated from the body. The metabolic process is usually carried out by enzymes in the liver.

Metabolites (meh–TAB–oh–lights)   The chemical by-products of drug metabolism, substances that can still maintain a therapeutic effect on cognition or affect because they can be psychopharmacologically active, despite having been altered.

Midbrain   The second portion of the brain to evolve in embryonic development, the midbrain integrates and monitors many sensory functions and is the center for visual and auditory stimulation. Certain cells in the midbrain serve as relays for information passing from the sense organs to more sophisticated levels of the brain.

Monitor role The role in which the social worker continues to help determine the outcomes, both positive and negative, of medication on social, psychological, and physical functioning, through ongoing client system contact.

Monoamine oxidase (MAO) inhibitors (MAHN-oh-AM-meen OX-id-aze) A class of drugs that were developed in the 1950s as the first antidepressants. These drugs are not widely used today because of the strict dietary regimes required to preclude adverse physical effects. They have been shown, however, to relieve some depressions that are not responsive to other antidepressants. There are two types of MAO inhibitors, type A, which breaks down norepinephrine and serotonin, and type B, which breaks down dopamine. Medications that selectively impact type A, still in development, may not produce the side effect of tyramine deamination.

Monoamines (MAHN-oh-AM-meens) Neurotransmitters with a single amine (organic compound). This group includes dopamine, norepinephrine, epinephrine, acetylcholine, and serotonin.

Mood disorders While most mental disorders negatively impact both the cognitive and emotional aspects of a person's life, these disorders most dramatically impact one's moods. Examples include major depression and generalized anxiety disorder.

Mood stabilizers All prescription medications that have been specifically developed, or have demonstrated effectiveness, for stabilizing the moods of persons with bipolar disorder. Lithium, carbamazepine, and valproate are the most common mood stabilizers.

Moral treatment (of mental illness) The predominant mental illness treatment model in America for the first half of the 19th century, based upon the notion that active rehabilitation and a structured life would help to steady uncontrolled thoughts and "problematic" emotions. Structured activities commonly included occupational therapy, religious exercises, sports, amusements, and reading. The typical time frame for such treatment was six weeks to three months.

Narcissism (NAHR-siss-is-um) Egocentrism, or self-centeredness, and self-preoccupation of excessive proportions.

Narcissistic injury (NAHR-siss-SISS-tick) Occurs when an individual interprets a situation or event as a personal attack or a condemnation that wounds his or her core being. An individual with a mental illness who interprets the prescription of antipsychotic drugs as proof that "I must be sicker than I thought I was" has suffered a narcissistic injury.

Negative symptoms (of schizophrenia) Those symptoms that represent a diminution of what would be considered normal affective behavior, including flat or blunted affect (the absence of expression), social withdrawal, non-communication, anhedonia (blandness) or passivity, and ambivalence in decision making. (See also Positive symptoms.)

Neonatal withdrawal syndrome (NEE-oh-NATE-al) Drug withdrawal symptoms experienced by a newborn child because of drug exposure and addiction in utero. Symptoms include insomnia, increased respiratory efforts and heart rate, and spontaneous body tremors. Behaviors that mark neonatal drug withdrawal symptoms can be recorded using the Neonatal Abstinence Score Tool.

Nervous system The body's information-processing unit consisting of 100 billion nerve cells, and the "action site" for psychotropic medications. It is comprised of the entire system of neurons and their supporting material. The nervous system is commonly divided into three branches: the central nervous system (brain and spinal cord), the peripheral nervous system (cranial, spinal nerves, and peripheral ganglia), and the autonomic nervous system (internal organs). The autonomic nervous system includes the sympathetic and the parasympathetic subsystems.

Neurohormones (NEW-row-HOAR-moans) Chemical messengers that are released into the bloodstream. They can be chemically indistinguishable from neurotransmitters.

Neuroleptic malignant syndrome (new-row-LEHP-tick) A potentially fatal but rare toxic complication of antipsychotic drug treatment; usually occurs within two weeks of drug initiation. Symptoms include high fever, muscle rigidity, instability of the autonomic nervous system (e.g., rapid heartbeat), and alternating levels of consciousness (from confusion to coma).

Neuron (NEW-rahn) A nerve cell, consisting of a cell body (nucleus and cytoplasm), a single axon, and several branched dendrites.

Neurotransmitter (NEW-row-TRANS-mit-er) A chemical found in nerve cells; acts as a messenger by carrying electrical impulses between cells and along cell pathways. Some principle neurotransmitters in the nervous system include GABA, dopamine, serotonin, norepinephrine, acetylcholine, and glutamate.

Norepinephrine (NOR-epp-in-EH-frin) A type of neurotransmitter secreted by the adrenal glands in response to arousal-provoking events such as stress. It influences affective behavior, alertness, anxiety, and tension.

Obsessive-compulsive disorder An anxiety disorder characterized by uncontrollable recurrent thoughts or compulsive behaviors that are time-consuming and cause significant distress or social impairment.

Occipital lobes (ox-SIP-it-all) An area of the cerebral cortex; serves as the foremost processing center for visual signals.

Organic mental disorders Mental disorders that result from the temporary or permanent dysfunction of brain tissue; attributable to specific organic factors such as aging, drug use, stroke, and metabolic disorders.

Orgasmic dysfunction (oar-GAZ-mick) The inability of a woman to achieve orgasm because of decreased libido or the inability to experience sexual stimulation. This is an adverse effect of some medications but can also exist as a psychological problem.

Orthostatic hypotension (OAR-thow-STAT-ick HI-poe-TEN-shun) An abrupt lowering of blood pressure; can cause fainting, dizziness upon standing, or falling, particularly if the client is elderly. It is most commonly a side effect of some low-potency antipsychotic drugs, usually occurring during the early phase of treatment, before the body has had time to develop a tolerance.

Panic disorder A condition in which panic attacks are experienced, followed by at least one month of persistent concerns about having another attack, concerns about the implications of the attack, or significant behavioral changes related to the attack. A panic attack is characterized by a period of intense fear or physiological discomfort with sudden onset and rapid buildup to a peak (usually within 10 minutes). The attack is often accompanied by a sense of imminent danger or impending doom and an urge to escape the situation.

Paranoia, paranoid ideation A cognitive state that features systematized delusions and includes emotional experience and behavior congruent with those delusions. The ideas and beliefs do not include hallucinations, and the person's intelligence is unaffected. The condition may be related to a mental disorder such as a delusional disorder or schizophrenia or to a personality disorder.

Parasympathetic nervous system (PAIR-ah-SIMP-ah-THEH-tick) That part of the autonomic nervous system that functions to support "at-rest" bodily processes, such as digestion. It is prominent in the body's conservation of energy reserves.

Parietal lobe (purr-EYE-it-ahl) An area of the cerebral cortex responsible for the intellectual processing of sensory information (visual, tactile, auditory) and also for verbal and visual-spatial processing.

Parkinsonian effects (PARK-in-SO-nee-an) Adverse effects resulting from some antipsychotic medications that mirror Parkinson's disease symptoms, such as reduction in motor abilities and coordination, shuffling gait, drooling, muscle rigidity, and tremors. The effect usually occurs within 5 to 90 days of drug initiation.

Partnership model of practice   A model of clinical practice with clients and families in which the social worker forges a nonthreatening alliance with the client/family that validates and respects their perspectives, concerns, strengths, and aspirations and that features a mutual, collaborative, and action-oriented helping process. This model is client-centered in its focus and in its goals, advocating for and representing the client system's needs, wants, and aspirations.

Partial response, responder   The experience of a reduction in some symptoms of a mental disorder with the use of psychotropic medication, but the degree of symptom reduction is less than what was desired or what is typical for other users of the medication who have the same symptom profile.

Peak plasma level   The point at which the maximum amount of a dose of medication is present in the client's bloodstream.

Peptides   Strings of amino acids.

Peripheral nervous system (purr-IF-ur-all)   The system of neurons branching from the central nervous system into the body from the lower brain and spinal cord. These nerves influence such sensations and actions as sight, smell, chewing and swallowing, and muscle movement.

Personality disorder   According to the DSM-IV, a personality is disordered when traits are inflexible, maladaptive, and cause significant distress or functional impairment. The idea of a personality as disordered is controversial among some human service professionals.

Pharmacodynamics (FARM-ah-co-dye-NAM-icks)   The study of the effects of a drug on the body. Factors affecting the effects of the drug include client age, gender, physical characteristics, and any organic pathologies.

Pharmacokinetics (FARM-ah-co-kin-ET-icks)   All issues regarding how the human body handles a drug; in particular, the blood plasma concentration of a drug. Pharmacokinetics refers to the absorption, distribution, metabolism, and excretion of the medication.

Phenothiazine (FEE-no-THIGH-ah-zeen)   A type of antipsychotic drug used in the treatment of schizophrenia and other psychotic disorders.

Phobia (FOE-be-uh)   An irrational fear, manifesting a high level of anxiety, which results in a person's conscious avoidance of the feared object, activity, or situation. Phobias may be specific (of birds, for example) or general (open spaces).

Physician's assistant role   A traditional role that social workers may still play but that was played most often through the 1970s when collaborating with physicians or psychiatrists. The social worker prepares the client for referral to the physician and enforces the directives of the physician with the client.

Placebo (pluh-SEE-bowe)   Any medication or inert substance that, by design or serendipity, relieves a consumer's symptoms not by pharmacologic action but by reinforcing the consumer's favorable expectancies about the intervention.

Polypharmacy (PAH-lee-FARM-ah-see)   The use of more than one drug for treatment of the same ailment.

Positive symptoms (of psychosis)   Those symptoms that represent bizarre exaggerations of normal behavior, including hallucinations, delusions, disorganized thought processes, and tendencies toward agitation.

Postpartum psychosis   A psychotic episode of the mother following childbirth, sometimes called puerperal psychosis. This disorder afflicts mothers within one month of delivery. Its causes are thought to include personality factors, life stressors, and endocrinological factors.

Postsynaptic membrane (post-sin-AP-tick)   The wall of the dendrite cell body, located at the opposite side of the synaptic cleft from the axon, on which receptor sites are located to receive neurotransmitter input and pass an impulse through the rest of the cell.

Posttraumatic stress disorder (PTSD) An emotional disorder in which, following exposure to a traumatic event, a person persistently reexperiences the event through memories, dreams, or intense psychological distress. The person subsequently tends to avoid any stimuli associated with the trauma.

Potency A drug's relative strength in standard units of measure (e.g., milligrams). Low-potency drugs, such as chlorpromazine, are given in high milligram amounts, while high-potency drugs, such as haloperidol, are given in low milligram doses.

Presynaptic terminal (pree-sin-AP-tick) An axon ending that extends to the synapse and contains neurotransmitters to be released into the synaptic cleft during neuron activation.

Problem-solving A systematic approach to helping clients become more effective problems solvers. It includes six steps: (a) defining the problem, (b) generating possible solutions, (c) evaluating the pros and cons of each solution, (d) choosing the "best" solution, (e) planning how to carry out the solution, and (f) reviewing implementation.

Prodromal (pro-DRO-mull) The phase during which a deteriorating state of health is recognized that later culminates in full-blown illness. During this phase there are subtle warning signs of the impending illness, indicators such as withdrawal, bizarre thoughts, or other behaviors recognized as precursors of a psychotic episode.

Progressivism An early 20th-century middle-class movement of social reforms aimed at promoting harmony among social classes and races. Progressivism was a response to social change that threatened the upheaval of middle-class values such as rationality, efficiency, and incremental upward mobility. Social work is, in part, an outgrowth of progressivism, given the profession's roots in "friendly visitors" to the urban poor to promote self-improvement and social harmony.

Prophylaxis (PRO-fill-AX-is) Prevention of the recurrence of symptoms of a mental disorder with the ongoing supervised use of medications, following the stabilization of symptoms. Dosages are generally lower during prophylaxis than during the active phase of an illness.

Protein binding One of the routes of drug transport in the bloodstream, involving the attachment of the drug to plasma proteins in the blood. Drugs bound to the plasma are essentially lost, because only the unbound portion of the drug can pass into the brain. The protein-binding rate of drugs differs and has a corresponding effect on the amount of drug available for action.

Psychiatric social work A term to describe a specialized area of social work practice, first developed in the early 20th century, that focuses on people who have mental illnesses or severe emotional distress.

Psychoeducational programs Time-limited, open or closed groups conducted by mental health professionals for the purposes of educating and providing support to clients, family members, or significant other persons regarding issues related to mental illness, psychotropic medication, and other professional interventions.

Psychological side effects The negative impact of taking medication on a client's self-image as a competent, self-directed individual.

Psychopharmacology The study of drugs that affect thinking, emotion, and behavior.

Psychosocial rehabilitation A global term that refers to all mental health services provided toward the goal of restoring the client to a level of functioning that will permit him or her to resume life in the community. This process operates on the premise that the best way to help clients progress toward greater self-sufficiency is to help them develop skills and competencies on individual, interpersonal, and social levels. Clients participate in structured activities aimed at improving emotional and cognitive resources, often including vocational training and counseling.

Psychostimulant drugs All prescription medications that have been specifically developed, or have demonstrated effectiveness, for controlling the symptoms of attention-deficit/hyperactivity disorder and narcolepsy.

Psychotic disorders A major group of mental disorders characterized in part by delusions, catatonic or grossly disorganized behavior, and hallucinations. Psychotic disorders are identified in the DSM-IV as falling into the two broad categories of schizophrenia and other psychotic disorders. The category of other psychotic disorders includes schizoaffective disorder, schizophreniform disorder, delusional disorder, brief psychotic disorder, shared psychotic disorder, psychotic disorder due to a general medical condition, and substance-induced psychotic disorder.

Psychotropic drugs (SIKE-oh-TROPE-ick) Drugs that alter psychological functioning, mood, and thoughts.

Pyramidal nerve pathways (purr-RA-mid-ahl) Long nerve pathways stretching from the cerebral cortex to the spinal cord. These are one of two pathways taken by motor nerves (the other being extrapyramidal). Pyramidal pathways carry messages to and from the central nervous system to control groups of muscles that contract simultaneously, such as those involved in gripping a pen.

Rapid cycling A characteristic of approximately 10% of persons with bipolar disorder, in which over a twelve-month period they experience four or more manic or depressive cycles.

Receptors Special receiving areas in the dendrite, composed of nerve cell membranes that are partially exposed to the extracellular fluid and that recognize neuromessengers.

Remission A state of cognitive, emotional, and behavioral functioning in which the symptoms of a mental illness have subsided to a significant degree. This state may be temporary or permanent.

Researcher role The role of the social worker in documenting how medications affect the lives of clients and their families and in expanding the existing knowledge base of psychopharmacology. This role also encompasses collaborations with researchers in other disciplines.

Reticular formation (reh-TICK-you-lar) A diffuse network of neurons that traces the midline of the brain stem, sending impulses up the brain stem to the cerebral cortex. This structure can activate the cortex into a state of wakefulness and transmits information about the environment. Some psychiatric motivational and arousal disorders can be attributed to problems in this area.

Reuptake The process by which a neuron reabsorbs a neurotransmitter after it has been released into the synapse.

Schizoaffective disorder (SKIZ-oh-aff-FECK-tiv) Defined by the DSM-IV as a continuous period of illness during which there are some symptoms of schizophrenia, such as delusions, hallucinations, grossly disorganized behavior; these symptoms occur concurrently with either a major depressive episode, a manic episode, or a mixed episode.

Schizophrenia (SKIZ-oh-FREN-ee-ah) A disorder of the brain characterized by abnormal patterns of thought and perception as inferred from language and behavior. Schizophrenia is characterized by at least six months of continuous symptoms, including two or more positive symptoms (delusions, hallucinations, disorganized speech, and disorganized or catatonic behavior) for at least one month. There are five subtypes of schizophrenia: paranoid, disorganized, catatonic, undifferentiated, and residual.

Schizophreniform disorder (SKIZ-oh-FREN-ih-form) A mental disorder that shares the symptomatology of schizophrenia but not the duration, lasting from two weeks to six months.

Sedation A common effect of some psychotropic drugs; the milder form of which leads to reduced excitability and anxiety and the stronger form of which produces hypnotic (sleep-inducing) effects.

Sedative (SAID-uh-tiv) Any medication that produces a state of decreased responsiveness to stimuli. The state may or may not be experienced as drowsiness.

Self-determination A fundamental value of the social work profession, arising from the belief that each individual is best equipped and, except for rare instances, most competent to judge what is best for himself or herself.

Self-monitoring (drug treatment) The role of the client in noting and systematically recording the effects of drug treatment. The client's monitoring enables the client and professional to assess the impact of taking a psychotropic drug. Self-monitoring includes observations of symptoms, medication-taking times, dosage, frequency, and adverse effects.

Serotonin (sair-ah-TONE-in) A type of neurotransmitter that impacts sensory processes, muscular activity, and cognition. It is a factor in states of consciousness, basic bodily functions, complex sensory and motor activities, and mood. Serotonin is thought to be implicated in mood disorders, aggression, and schizophrenia.

Serotonin-reuptake inhibitors, serotonin-specific drugs The newest group of antidepressant medications, which function by suppressing the reuptake or reabsorption of serotonin by the nerve cell. Sometimes called "atypical" because of their chemical distinctiveness from other antidepressants, these drugs cause less pronounced anticholinergic effects. As a result, they are more popular with many physicians and clients than many other antidepressants.

Sexual dysfunction Changes in sexual desire in men and women, in addition to impotence in men and orgasmic dysfunction in women, that may result from the use of some psychotropic medications.

Side effects See adverse effects.

Skills training A systematic approach to helping a client develop greater life skills, including these six steps: (a) discussing the rationale for the skill, (b) identifying the components of the skill, (c) modeling the skill, (d) role playing each skill component with the client, (e) evaluating the role play, and (f) applying the skill in real life.

Smooth muscles Those muscles in the body that function involuntarily.

Social psychiatry A perspective on the practice of psychiatry developed by Adolf Meyer in the early 20th century. In Meyer's opinion, psychiatry needed to attend to prevention, teaching, and research in the service of comprehensive community treatment. He is said to have perceived a critical role for social workers in helping to bring about a suitable aftercare environment for clients.

Social side effects The interpersonal, community, and organizational barriers that clients encounter when they take psychotropic drugs and are thus labeled as having mental illness.

Spinal cord A long column of neural tissue that runs from the brain stem to the base of the spine. This structure is part of the central nervous system.

Stabilization A stage in the process of recovery from an episode of mental illness in which the client's more extreme symptoms subside. Social functioning returns to normal within the limits of a protective, supportive environment, but the client requires ongoing intervention because he or she may still be at risk for relapse.

Steady state The point at which a consistent level of medication is present in the bloodstream, such that the amount ingested is equal to the amount eliminated.

Stress-diathesis model (dye-ATH-uh-sis) A model for understanding mental illness that takes into account the interplay between biological and environmental influences.

The model asserts that while the causes of mental illness seem to be associated with genetic factors as well as abnormalities in brain chemistry and structure, the course of these disorders is in part related to environmental factors such as skills in coping, social competence, and social support.

Sympathetic system   The part of the autonomic nervous system that functions during the expenditure of energy. The sympathetic system has an arousal function for the internal organs.

Sympathomimetic drugs (sim-PATH-oh-mi-MET-ick)   See psychostimulant drugs.

Synapse (SIN-aps)   The bridge between one nerve cell and the next. Neurotransmitters flow across this space. The synapse is not a physical structure, but rather a point of juncture marked by the synaptic cleft (or gap).

Synaptic cleft   The gap between the axon of a sending neuron and the dendrite of a receiving neuron.

Synaptic vesicles   Small areas located on axon terminals; contain the molecules of a neurotransmitter produced in the cell body.

Tachycardia (tack-ah-CARD-ee-ah)   A form of heart arrhythmia; unusually rapid heartbeat (greater than 100 beats per minute) that may result from the side effects of antidepressant drugs acting on the autonomic nervous system.

Tardive dyskinesia (TAR-dive diss-kin-EASE-yah)   A serious and generally irreversible adverse effect of antipsychotic drugs. The symptoms of coordinated but involuntary rhythmic movements are commonly seen in facial movements, such as grimacing and lip tremors, and in finger, hand, and trunk movements. Controversy exists regarding its prevalence. The longer a client takes antipsychotic drugs, the greater the likelihood that he or she may develop tardive dyskinesia.

Temporal lobe (TEM-pore-all)   One of four major hemispheres in the cerebrum of the human brain; located beneath the frontal lobe; it regulates memory, smell functions, and some aspects of speech.

Teratogenic drugs (tare-AT-uh-JEN-ick)   Any drugs that carry a potential to cause damage to the fetus in a pregnant consumer.

Thalamus (THOW-luh-muss)   A sensory relay station (for all but the olfactory senses) and an important integration and processing center for information passing from the lower body to the brain. The structure is essential to the perception of pain and helps to initiate consciousness and organize sensory signals.

Therapeutic index   A measure of the range of blood levels within which a drug's effects on the consumer are relatively safe. Drugs with a low therapeutic index, such as lithium, must be very closely monitored to avoid toxicity.

Thought disorders   While most mental disorders negatively impact both the cognitive and emotional aspects of a person's life, these disorders most dramatically impact one's cognitive functioning. Examples include schizophrenia and delusional disorders.

Three–party treatment relationships   The network of relationships in the treatment context including the client, medication prescriber (physician), and the social worker.

Tolerance   A person's reduced responsiveness to a drug as a function of the reduced sensitivity of significant nerve receptors over time.

Toxicity   A physical state in which the amount of an active drug in the body exceeds the amount required for therapeutic effect, and which puts the consumer at risk for serious adverse effects.

Two–track model of treatment   The treatment of mental illness proceeding along two parallel tracks, including a medical track (biological) and a psychological or psychosocial track.

Vitamins Organic substances (there are 13 in total) that are essential in minute amounts for the body's normal growth and activity, as they help to convert foods into energy and tissues.

Water-soluble drugs Drugs that dissolve in the water content of the body (other drugs dissolve in the body's fatty tissue). The concentration of water-soluble drugs varies in proportion to the ratio of water to fat in the body. Individuals with proportionately more fat than water will have lower concentrations of water-soluble drugs relative to those individuals with proportionately more fat. Increased age is associated with higher fat-to-water ratios, and women tend to have greater fat-to-water ratios than men. Lithium is the best example of a water-soluble psychotropic drug.

Name Index

Subject Index